THE FUTURE OF AMERICAN FOREIGN POLICY

Third Edition

Edited by

Eugene R. Wittkopf
Louisiana State University

AND

Christopher M. Jones
Northern Illinois University

St. Martin's/WORTH

The Future of American Foreign Policy
Third Edition

Copyright © 1999 by Worth Publishers, Inc.
All rights reserved.
Library of Congress Catalog Card Number: 98-85001
Manufactured in the United States of America.
ISBN: 0-312-15397-X
Printing: 1   2   3   4   5   02   01   00   99

Executive Editor: James R. Headley
Project Director: Scott E. Hitchcock
Editorial Assistant: Brian Nobile
Design Director: Jennie R. Nichols
Production Editor: Douglas Bell
Production Manager: Barbara Anne Seixas
Project Coordination: Publisher's Studio
Cartography: GeoSystems Global Corporation
Cover Design: Lucy Krikorian
Cover Art: Copyright © Lula Francis/Stockworks
Cover Printer: Phoenix Color Corporation
Composition: Stratford Publishing Services
Printing and Binding: R.R. Donnelley & Sons, Inc.

Worth Publishers
33 Irving Place
New York, NY 10003

www.worthpublishers.com

Acknowledgments
Acknowledgments and copyrights are continued at the back of the book on pages 357–358, which constitute an extension of the copyright page.

Richard N. Haass, "Beyond Containment: Competing American Foreign Policy Doctrines for the New Era." This essay was written specifically for this book.

Douglas Brinkley, "Democratic Enlargement: The Clinton Doctrine." Reprinted with permission from Foreign Policy, 106 (Spring 1997). Copyright © 1997 by the Carnegie Endowment for International Peace.

ABOUT THE EDITORS

EUGENE R. WITTKOPF received his doctorate from Syracuse University. He is curently R. Downs Poindexter Distinguished Professor of Political Science at Louisiana State University. He has also held appointments at the University of Florida and the University of North Carolina at Chapel Hill. Wittkopf is author of *Faces of Internationalism: Public Opinion and American Foreign Policy* (Duke University Press, 1990), coauthor, with Charles W. Kegley, Jr., of *World Politics: Trend and Transformation* (St. Martin's/Worth, 7th ed., 1999), and *American Foreign Policy: Pattern and Process* (St. Martin's, 5th ed., 1996), and coeditor, with James M. McCormick, of *The Domestic Sources of American Foreign Policy: Insights and Evidence* (Roman & Littlefield, 3rd ed., 1999). He has also published extensively in professional journal literature. In 1997 he received the highest award given by Louisiana State University in recognition of faculty contributions to research and scholarship when he was named the LSU Distinguished Research Master of Arts, Humanities, and Social Sciences.

CHRISTOPHER M. JONES received his doctorate from Syracuse University, where he was also a University Fellow. He is currently assistant professor of political science at Northern Illinois University. He previously held an appointment at Wittier College. Jones has published several book chapters on American foreign and defense policy and is completing a book entitled *King or Captive? The President and Foreign Policymaking in the New Era.*

In Memory of Loved Ones Departed
ERW

To My Parents, Ann and Cliff
CMJ

CONTRIBUTORS

Madeleine Albright is United States secretary of state.

Peter Andreas is Academy Scholar at the Weatherhead Center for International Affairs, Harvard University.

Richard K. Betts is professor of political science at Columbia University and director of national security studies at the Council of Foreign Relations.

Hans Binnendijk is director of the Institute for National Strategic Studies at the National Defense University.

Douglas Brinkley is professor of history and director of the Eisenhower Center at the University of New Orleans.

Robin Broad is professor of international development at the American University School of International Service.

Janet Walsh Brown is visiting Fellow at the World Resources Institute in Washington, D.C.

John Cavanagh is a Fellow at the Institute for Policy Studies and the Transnational Institute in Washington, D.C.

Robert S. Chase is assistant professor of economics at the Johns Hopkins University School of Advanced International Studies in Bologna, Italy.

Richard N. Cooper is Boas Professor of International Economics at Harvard University.

Terry L. Deibel is professor of national strategy at the National War College.

Jeffrey E. Garten is dean of the Yale University School of Management.

Eugene Gholz is Olin Fellow at Harvard University.

Saul Goldstein was a research assistant at the Economic Strategy Institute in Washington, D.C., and is currently working for a U.S. investment firm in Japan.

Andrew J. Goodpaster is a retired U.S. Army general. He has been superintendent of the U.S. Military Academy and president of the Institute for Defense Analyses.

Richard N. Haass is director of the foreign policy studies program at the Brookings Institution in Washington, D.C.

C. Randall Henning is associate professor at the American University and visiting Fellow at the Institute for International Economics in Washington, D.C.

Emily B. Hill is a doctoral candidate in history at Yale University.

Ole R. Holsti is George V. Allen Professor of Political Science at Duke University.

G. John Ikenberry is associate professor of political science and codirector of the Lauder Institute of Management and International Studies at the University of Pennsylvania.

Josef Joffe is editorial page editor and a columnist at *Süddeutsche Zeitung* and an associate at the Olin Institute for Strategic Studies at Harvard University.

Paul Kennedy is professor of history and director of International Security Studies at Yale University.

Paul Krugman is professor of economics at the Massachusetts Institute of Technology.

Robert A. Manning is senior Fellow at the Council on Foreign Relations.

Walter Russell Mead is presidential Fellow at the World Policy Institute at the New School for Social Research

Steven Metz is Henry L. Stimson Professor of Military Affairs at the United States Army War College and a research professor at the college's Strategic Studies Institute.

Peter Morici is professor of international business at the University of Maryland.

Joseph S. Nye, Jr. is dean of the John F. Kennedy School of Government at Harvard University.

Daryl G. Press is a doctoral candidate in political science at the Massachusetts Institute of Technology.

Clyde V. Prestowitz, Jr. is president of the Economic Strategy Institute in Washington D.C.

Richard Rosecrance is professor of political science and director of the Center for International Relations at the University of California, Los Angeles.

James N. Rosenau is University Professor of International Affairs at the George Washington University.

Robert S. Ross is professor of political science at Boston College and research associate at the John King Fairbank Center for East Asian Research at Harvard University.

Harvey M. Sapolsky is professor of public policy and organization and director of the Securities Studies Program at the Massachusetts Institute of Technology.

Russell E. Travers is an analyst with the Defense Intelligence Agency in the U.S. Department of Defense.

Werner Weidenfeld is coordinator for German-American cooperation in the foreign ministry of the Federal Republic of Germany.

Howard J. Wiarda is Leonard J. Horwitz Professor in Latin American Politics and Studies at the University of Massachusetts.

CONTENTS

New Agendas for a New Era

Part II: RELATIONSHIPS   149

The United States and Europe

The United States and Asia

The United States and the Global South

INTRODUCTION: NEW PRIORITIES FOR A NEW ERA? OR AFLOAT IN UNCHARTED WATERS?

In 1941 Henry Luce, the noted editor and publisher of *Time, Life,* and *Fortune* magazines, envisioned his time as the dawn of the "American century." He based his prediction on the conviction that "only America can effectively state the aims of this war [World War II]," which included, under American leadership, "a vital international economy" and "an international moral order."[1] In many ways Luce's prediction proved prophetic, not just as it applied to World War II but also to the decades-long Cold War contest with the Soviet Union that quickly followed it. But even he might be surprised that the twenty-first century looks to be an even more thoroughly American century than the twentieth. The facts at the dawn of the new millennium are simple and irrefutable: compared with all other states, the United States today is in a class by itself. No other can match the health and productivity of its economy, the extent of its scientific and technological resources, its ability to sustain massive levels of defense spending, or the power, sophistication, and global reach of its armed forces.

American power extends beyond these traditional measures as well, encompassing a wealth of less tangible assets broadly conceived as "soft power." Included are the attraction of its culture and political beliefs and the ability of the United States to establish rules and institutions favorable to its own interests. Thus the United States continues to set the agenda in the international organizations it led in establishing in the 1940s; democracy and market economies have spread throughout the world; and American culture—ranging from pop music, blue jeans, and McDonald's, to personal computers, Windows 98, and Internet communications in English—exhibits universal appeal in our rapidly globalizing world. Impressed with the global reach of America's soft power, one German analyst observed that "one has to go back

1

to the Roman Empire for a similar instance of cultural hegemony. . . . We live in an 'American age,' meaning that American values and arrangements are most closely in tune with the new Zeitgeist."[2]

Little more than a decade ago, many analysts viewed America's future more dimly. In what turned out to be the waning days of the Cold War, analysts who came to be known as "declinists" worried about the consequences of what they saw as the mismatch between America's extensive foreign policy commitments and its increasingly limited economic resources. In his widely acclaimed book *The Rise and Fall of the Great Powers*, historian Paul Kennedy argued that "[the United States] cannot avoid confronting the two great tests which challenge the *longevity* of every major power that occupies the 'number one' position in world affairs: whether it can preserve a reasonable balance between the nation's perceived defense requirements and the means it possesses to maintain those commitments; and whether . . . it can preserve the technological and economic bases of its power from relative erosion in the ever shifting patterns of global production."[3] The danger, he warned, is similar to that faced by hegemonic powers in earlier historical periods, notably the Spanish at the turn of the seventeenth century and the British at the turn of the twentieth. "The United States now runs the risk . . . of . . . 'imperial overstretch': that is to say, decision makers in Washington must face the awkward and enduring fact that the sum total of the United States' global interests and obligations is nowadays far larger than the country's power to defend them all simultaneously."[4]

Today the declinists are in retreat, even if their message is not entirely without merit. The end of the Cold War, the victory of the United States in the Persian Gulf War, the revitalization of the American economy, and the persistent economic problems faced by Germany, Japan, Russia, and others in Europe and Asia all reinforce the widespread conviction that the "next American century" is now on the horizon.

Despite the euphoria that surrounds contemporary American foreign policy, its future remains uncertain. The nation's leaders have yet to devise an overarching grand strategy for the new era that links ends and means to a common, politically popular vision. Absent vision and widespread domestic support for global involvement, "ad hocism" and unilateralism have become commonplace, often accompanied by an arrogance offensive to American friends and allies.[5] Meanwhile, the globalization of the world political economy, encouraged by American policies, has undermined the ability of the United States to chart its own future.

In the early years following World War II, the United States gradually developed a grand strategy—captured in the themes of globalism, anti-communism, containment, military might, and interventionism—for combating the communist and Soviet menace.[6] Historians and political analysts will continue for years to debate whether that strategy was the cause of the eventual U.S. Cold War "victory" over the Soviet Union, but the coincidence between early prescriptions and the eventual outcome of the extensive and intensive conflict between the United States and the Soviet Union is remarkable. In 1947,

George Kennan argued in his famous "X" article that "the United States has in its power to increase enormously the strains under which Soviet policy must operate, to force upon the Kremlin a far greater degree of moderation and circumspection than it has had to observe in recent years, and in this way to promote tendencies which must eventually find their outlet in either the breakup or the gradual mellowing of Soviet power."[7] More than forty years later, that breakup and mellowing occurred. Communism in the Soviet Union and Eastern Europe collapsed, the Soviet Union's internal and external empires disintegrated, the Warsaw Pact disbanded, and the division of Germany ended.

Faced with these dramatic new realities, the United States now searched for a new foreign policy paradigm. President George Bush used Iraq's invasion of Kuwait in August 1990 and the subsequent Persian Gulf War to call for the creation of a "new world order," one "where diverse nations are drawn together in common cause to achieve the universal aspirations of mankind—peace and security, freedom, and the rule of law." The vision embraced the tradition of moral idealism—long evident in American foreign policy, but especially since Woodrow Wilson sought early in this century to create a world safe for democracy. It also harkened back to the 1940s when the United States and the Soviet Union stood shoulder to shoulder in opposing Nazi Germany and, later, in seeking to build a structure of peace premised on the continued cooperation of wartime allies. Still, hubris in the belief that the United States alone now had a special responsibility for creating the new world order was only thinly disguised.

Despite its appeal, Bush's conception of a new world order failed to spark broad-based domestic support. The triumphant mood at home that followed the Persian Gulf War and seemed to validate a return to the role of world policeman (in disrepute since the Vietnam War) quickly faded as the U.S. economy slipped into recession. George Bush now became the victim, as Bill Clinton, governor of a small southern state, won the White House by emphasizing domestic priorities with a simple appeal: "The economy, stupid!"

Clinton's single-minded focus on the economy did have an international dimension: to compete abroad, the United States had to clean up its act at home, a theme central to declinists' prescriptions. His administration would also offer the spread of democracy and the enlargement of the community of democratic capitalist states as a core foreign policy goal. As National Security Advisor Anthony Lake explained in 1993, the successor to the foreign policy of containment "must be a strategy of enlargement . . . of the world's free community of market democracies." He later defended the strategy as one "based on a belief that our most fundamental security interest lies in the expansion and consolidation of democratic and market reform." That viewpoint reflected the long-held belief of liberal internationalists that democracies do not fight one another. Hence promotion of democratic capitalism is not only good for business, it is also good for peace.

Despite the appeal of democracy, its centrality as a pillar of American foreign policy proved as ephemeral as Bush's new world order. Almost immediately critics complained that "democratic enlargement" "had no connection to reality and . . . was an aspiration rather than a strategy."[8] Later events seemed to prove them right. Interventions in Haiti and Bosnia designed to promote democracy quickly confronted the realities of grinding poverty and ethnic animosities that had prevented democracy and civil society in the first place. In the Middle East, the United States faced the uncomfortable fact that its security interests were closely linked to authoritarian states, where democratic promotion could in fact promote instability, not peace. Elsewhere the early enthusiasm that accompanied the rapid spread of democracy following the end of the Cold War cooled in the face of setbacks and retrenchment. As one observer wrote in early 1997, "The headlines announcing that country after country was shrugging off dictatorial rule and embarking on a democratic path have given way to an intermittent but rising stream of troubling reports: a coup in Gambia, civil strife in the Central African Republic, flawed elections in Albania, a deposed government in Pakistan, returning authoritarianism in Zambia, the shedding of democratic forms in Kazakstan, sabotaged elections in Armenia, eroding human rights in Cambodia."[9] Not surprisingly, then, by the time Clinton began his second term in office, his administration had largely abandoned its active advocacy of democratic enlargement, as pragmatism, not idealism, now characterized its foreign policy approach.

Pragmatic leaders have often received high marks from students of American foreign policy,[10] but in Clinton's case critics charged that his foreign policy approach had become prisoner of domestic political considerations to an unprecedented degree.[11] Even Clinton's effort to make the world safe for U.S. exports and investments, arguably his greatest foreign policy achievement, fell victim to charges from abroad that the administration's penchant to extend U.S. laws unilaterally to others and to impose sanctions on international sinners (as defined by the United States) smacked of domestic cronyism, not global vision. Early in Clinton's second term the journal *Foreign Policy* asked a panel of international experts, many from other countries, to rate his foreign policy performance. On the issue of strategic creativity ("the development and expression of a coherent post–Cold War vision for the world"), the eight experts queried gave the president a meager 3.7 on a 10-point scale, his lowest rating among seven questions asked.[12] These viewpoints mirror those of American elites. An October 1997 survey of nearly six hundred opinion leaders found that indecision and lack of direction were the principal criticisms of the Clinton administration's foreign policy record.[13]

From the perspective of other states, the lack of direction in American foreign policy, dictated in part by an excessive concern for domestic politics, often manifests itself in what they see as aggressive unilateralism or, less kindly, "bullying." Whether the issue is trade with Cuba, the expansion of the North Atlantic Treaty Organization (NATO), containment of Iraq, banning land mines, or curbing global warming, the positions of the United States, which were (and remain) often at variance with those of its closest, longtime friends and allies, smack of an arrogance of power which they find offensive. As one commentator noted, "The United States is discovering that its behavior has come under sharpest scrutiny from friendly nations that no longer feel prevented by Cold War loyalties from expressing their disagreements with Washington."[14]

Presidents always face constraints when devising foreign policy strategies. Opinion at home and abroad is important, and the reaction of Congress and others in governmental institutions can shape what the government decides to do. The nature of the international system is also an important—and arguably the most potent—explanation of the perception that Clinton, like Bush before him, was unable to define a sustainable foreign policy strategy for the new era, preferring ad hocism and unilateralism in its place.

During the Cold War, fear of communism, fear of the Soviet Union, and a determination to contain both, gave structure and purpose to American foreign policy. Ironically, the U.S. Cold War "victory" removed these guideposts, which had imposed a rough sense of order and discipline not only on American foreign policy, but also on world politics. Today globalization—which may be defined as "the intensification of economic, political, social, and cultural relations across borders"[15]—has radically altered the context of American foreign policy, as the spread of political democracy and market economies has contributed to the homogenization of economic, social, and cultural forces worldwide. In turn, the distinction long drawn between foreign and domestic politics has become increasingly arbitrary and dubious, and the geopolitical distinctions among states based on borders and territory are increasingly suspect.

As borders become permeable, political leaders are learning that their ability to affect the form and flow of transactions shaping the social and economic well-being of their own peoples is severely constrained. The "virtual state"[16] is becoming a political reality—however uncomfortable that reality may be. Even the United States has been buffeted by the force of globalization, as revealed in the turmoil its own financial and capital markets suffered as the "Asian contagion"—the currency crises and financial instabilities suffered by many Asian economies in late 1997 and early 1998—spread beyond Asia to engulf markets throughout the world.

The Clinton administration actively sought to promote the cause of open trade and open markets, which propels globalization. In little more than four years, for example, it negotiated more than two hundred market-opening agreements with other states. In turn it would claim than liberalism abroad contributed measurably to the period of sustained economic growth enjoyed at home during much of the 1990s. But there is a dark side to liberalism (and globalism) that increasingly vies for attention. Although the United States is the most powerful state in a world that is more receptive to democracy, capitalism, and American culture than at any other time in this century, American policymakers must address critical domestic issues that flow from the marginalization of individuals and groups not bettered by globalization. As Richard Gephardt, Democratic leader of the House of Representatives and a key opponent of the Clinton administration's free trade strategy, observed during the roiling Asian economic crisis, "In a new era of globalization, the forces of commerce and technology are weaving the world closer together but . . . pulling our own people further apart." Thus American policymakers can no longer ignore the domestic consequences of globalization—but they must do so in an international context in which globalization has unleashed forces beyond America's singular control. Increasingly, then, foreign policy success may come to be equated with the nation's ability to adapt at home and collaborate abroad.

The purpose of this book is to provoke inquiry into the future of American foreign policy and the forces that will shape it. Its three parts emphasize *objectives, relationships,* and *capabilities.* Part I—Objectives—begins with a discussion of whether the United States should continue its global activism, revert to isolationism, or reorient its world role in other ways. The wisdom of democratic enlargement, the force of soft power, and the nature of contemporary conflict in world politics are among the topics addressed. The tension between realism and idealism as competing world views, and the forces of fragmentation and integration as characterizations of contemporary world politics, are evident in the competing viewpoints of the authors of the five chapters that begin our inquiry into the future of American foreign policy.

Following these provocative discussions, we turn to history, asking what in the American foreign policy experience applies to the new era now unfolding. Other essays in Part I direct attention to the wisdom of marrying the interests of American business to the interests of the nation's foreign policy, the nature and consequences of the "virtual state," the foreign policy attitudes of American opinion leaders, and the challenge to American foreign policy posed by global environmental issues. New agendas for a new era are suggested by all of the viewpoints presented in these chapters. Political pitfalls face those who would choose to pick among the challenges they present.

Part II—Relationships—focuses attention on the impact that the new era will exert on America's relations with its former adversaries and allies in Europe and Asia, as well as with the states in the Global South that were once courted as potential partisans by the Cold War contestants. The selections highlight the critical importance of the United States' securing its interests, largely by preserving the status quo, while not creating a level of resentment that would lead other states to challenge America's preeminent international standing, rather than following its leadership.

Part III—Capabilities—critically examines ideas about the diplomatic resources, military means, and economic tactics appropriate for the realization of America's foreign policy objectives in the new era. At issue are the military and nonmilitary challenges to security that the United States faces now and those it might expect in the future, the means necessary to meet those challenges, and the political feasibility of creating proper instruments of foreign policy in a domestic environment of new priorities and financial constraints. Concern for how the forces of globalization both enhance and challenge American capabilities in the new era underlies the discussion throughout the book.

NOTES

1. Cited in Walter LaFeber, *The American Age: United States Foreign Policy at Home and Abroad since 1750* (New York: Norton, 1989), p. 380.

2. Josef Joffe, "America the Inescapable," *New York Times Magazine,* June 8, 1997, p. 43. Joffe's essay is reprinted in Part I of this book.

3. Paul Kennedy, *The Rise and Fall of the Great Powers: Economic Change and Military Conflict from 1500 to 2000* (New York: Random House, 1987), pp. 514–515.

4. Ibid., p. 515.

5. For a contrary viewpoint, which is based on the premise that "policy is about as coherent and consensual today as it has ever been—or ever gets," see John Mueller, "Policy Principles for Unthreatened Wealth-Seekers," *Foreign Policy* 102 (Summer 1996), pp. 22–33.

6. See Charles W. Kegley, Jr., and Eugene R. Wittkopf, *American Foreign Policy: Pattern and Process,* 5th ed. (New York: St. Martin's Press, 1996).

7. George F. Kennan ["X"], "The Sources of Soviet Conduct," *Foreign Affairs* 25 (July 1947), p. 582.

8. Douglas Brinkley, "Democratic Enlargement: The Clinton Doctrine," *Foreign Policy* 106 (Spring 1997), p. 119. Brinkley's essay is reprinted in Part I of this book. See also Robert J. Lieber, *Eagle Adrift: American Foreign Policy at the End of the Century* (New York: Longman, 1997), p. 14.

9. Thomas Carothers, "Democracy without Illusion," *Foreign Affairs* 76 (January/February 1997), p. 85.

10. See, for example, Cecil V. Crabb, Jr., *Policy-Makers and Critics: Conflicting Theories of American Foreign Policy,* 2nd ed. (New York: Praeger, 1986), and John G. Stoessinger, *Crusaders and Pragmatists: Movers of Modern American Foreign Policy* (New York: Norton, 1985).

11. Representative are the views expressed in the Winter 1997–1998 issue of the prestigious journal *Foreign Policy,* by its contributing editors representing various world regions. See also Larry Berman and Emily O. Goldman, "Clinton's Foreign Policy at Midterm," pp. 290–324 in Colin Campbell and Bert A. Rockman, eds., *The Clinton Presidency: First Appraisals* (Chatham, NJ: Chatham House, 1996).

12. See *Foreign Policy,* Winter 1997–1998, pp. 46ff.

13. Andrew Kohut, *America's Place in the World II* (Washington, D.C.: The Pew Research Center for the People & The Press, 1997), p. 11.

14. William Drozdiak, "Down with Yankee Dominance," *Washington Post National Weekly Report,* November 24, 1997, p. 15. See also Elaine Sciolino, "It Turns Out That All Global Politics Is Local," *New York Times,* December 7, 1997, p. E3.

15. Hans-Henrik Holm and Georg Sørensen, "Introduction: What Has Changed?" in Hans-Henrik Holm and Georg Sørensen, eds., *Whose World Order? Uneven Globalization and the End of the Cold War* (Boulder, CO: Westview, 1995), p. 1.

16. Richard Rosecrance, "The Rise of the Virtual State," *Foreign Affairs* 75 (July/August 1996), pp. 45–61. Rosecrance's essay is reprinted in Part I of this book.

Part I: OBJECTIVES

We live in a one superpower world—a world dominated by the United States politically, militarily, economically, and culturally. The shape of today's world became evident in the immediate aftermath of the Persian Gulf War, which followed the unraveling of the Soviet empire and the end of forty years of intense Cold War competition between what were then regarded as the two superpowers. Syndicated columnist Charles Krauthammer portrayed the time as a "unipolar moment." "The center of world power is the unchallenged superpower, the United States," he wrote. "There is but one first-rate power and no prospect in the immediate future of any power to rival it. . . . American preeminence is based on the fact that it is the only country with the military, diplomatic, political, and economic assets to be a decisive player in any conflict in whatever part of the world it chooses to involve itself." He predicted that other states would turn to the United States for leadership as they did in organizing a response to Iraqi's invasion of Kuwait and, later, in ensuring the distribution of humanitarian assistance in Somalia. "The unipolar moment means that with the close of the century's three great Northern civil wars (World War I, World War II, and the Cold War) an ideologically pacified North seeks security and order by aligning its foreign policy behind that of the United States," Krauthammer argued. "It is the shape of things to come."[1]

Scholars and policy analysts have devised a number of other models or images to portray the shape of the post–Cold War international system. A three-bloc geo-economics model, a reinvigorated multipolar balance of power model, a clash of civilizations model, a zones of peace/zones of turmoil model, and a global village image are among them.[2] Others have suggested that no single idea captures current reality. As Joseph S. Nye, a Harvard political scientist and former Clinton administration official argues:

> No single hierarchy describes adequately a world politics with multiple structures. The distribution of power in world politics has become like a layer cake. The top military layer is largely unipolar, for there is no other military power comparable to the United States. The economic middle layer is tripolar and has been for two decades. The bottom layer of transnational interdependence shows a diffusion of power.[3]

Although analysts may differ about which (if any) image or model adequately captures emergent reality at the dawn of the millennium, each model does focus our attention on particular issues and actors. Thus the questions necessarily arise: "What . . . might be the implications of these competing models for U.S. foreign policy? Can American policy help to determine or shape the emerging system, and if so, what are the pluses and minuses of the alternative systems?"[4]

The unipolar image embraced by Krauthammer (and others) implies a leadership role for the United States. As the world's preeminent power—commonly called a hegemon—the United States could choose to pursue a policy of primacy, which urges that the aspirations of emerging challengers to its power and position be thwarted and recommends that the United States expend whatever treasure may be required to meet the challenge.[5] That policy prescription recognizes that as the preponderant power, the hegemon is able to promote rules for the system as a whole that protect its own interests.

Historically, hegemons have provided benefits which other states also enjoy, including order and predictability, particularly in the international economic system. And they tolerate free riding by others, who realize the benefits hegemons confer but do not share in their costs. Hegemons are willing to tolerate free riders in part because these benefits encourage other states to accept the hegemons' dictates. Thus both gain something.

These simple tenets drawn from hegemonic stability theory,[6] an offshoot of the popular realist tradition in international politics, arguably provide the rationale for an American foreign policy designed to perpetuate the unipolar moment. But the theory also raises some cautions. It notes, for example, that the willingness of a hegemon to tolerate free riders will diminish as the community's shared interests dissipate and the hegemon's own power position, relative to potential competitors, declines. Both have happened in recent years: the end of Soviet-inspired threats to the "free world" has diminished the incentives of America's Cold War allies to follow U.S. dictates, and the costs of American leadership are now much less tolerable in the United States, as others are perceived as having gained disproportionate advantages at U.S. expense during the Cold War era. The latter is a central tenet underlying the declinists' arguments popular in the 1980s, but it also explains much of the Clinton administration's determination to enhance U.S. competitiveness in the world political economy and to encourage, if not compel, others in Europe and Asia to assume a greater share of the "burdens" of the common defense.

The aggressive unilateralism practiced by the Clinton administration across a range of issues smacks of a policy of primacy.[7] The risk, as we noted in the introduction to this book, is that a reputation for "bullying" may cause friends and allies to reject American leadership, not follow it, as Krauthammer predicted. This potential is consistent with neorealism, another popular variant of realist theory. According to this theoretical perspective, states are rational actors who seek to survive in an anarchical world, one devoid of an effective government. Hence there is a natural tendency to balance power with power as a means of achieving order and stability. During the Cold War, the United States and Soviet Union maintained a balance through nuclear deterrence, arms races, and countervailing alliances. Since the disintegration of the Soviet Union, however, no one has balanced the United States, allowing it to "behave as an 'unconstrained' great power with considerable discretion in its statecraft."[8] Yet neorealism posits that such a situation cannot continue indefinitely. Since there is a natural tendency towards systemic equilibrium, the major states of Europe and Asia will gradually move away from the United States, choosing to balance its overwhelming capabilities rather than follow its leadership.[9] From this perspective, complaints of "Yankee dominance"[10] and signs of discord between the United States and its former Cold War allies are both byproducts of unipolarity and precursors of a new balance of power.

For advocates of a policy of primacy, a central challenge for American policymakers in the new era is whether the United States can sustain its preeminent global position. Doing so will tax the nation's capacity to manage its foreign relations skillfully. As political scientist Michael Mastanduno writes, "Through policies of engagement and reassurance, U.S. officials can dissuade or at least delay other states from challenging U.S. hegemony and balancing against the United States." Realizing this goal, Mastanduno continues, will require American leaders to "manage the tension between their international economic and security strategies so that economic conflicts do not erode security relationships, . . . [to] maintain support at home for the preferred policies of engagement and reassurance, . . . [and to avoid] the arrogance of power [with its] . . . strong temptations to go it alone, to dictate rather than consult, to preach . . . virtues, and to impose . . . values."[11]

Of these challenges, gaining and maintaining domestic support for a policy of primacy may be the most difficult. Selective engagement, reliance on cooperative security arrangements with other states, and returning to an isolationist posture are among the alternative postures that have vied for support within elite circles and the general public.[12] Cost considerations figure prominently in the debate. Until recently, large and persistent federal budget deficits constrained policymakers' options, as the soaring costs of domestic entitlement programs and the national debt limited the availability of resources to fund even existing programs. An agreement reached between the Clinton administration and the Republican Congress to balance the budget early in the next century, combined with vigorous economic growth in the 1990s, which stimulated a flood of tax revenues flowing into the federal treasury, eased fiscal constraints. Still, they remain formidable, particularly as the "baby boom" generation (born in the years immediately following World

War II) nears retirement, which will dramatically increase strains on Social Security and government-supported medical programs.

Proponents of primacy recognize that foreign and national security policy resources may be more limited in the future than in the past, but they believe "the problem is not a lack of resources, but a lack of public will."[13] Selective engagers are less sanguine, believing, much as the declinists warned in the 1980s, that an imbalance between means and ends could jeopardize realization of the nation's most pressing foreign policy interests. Still others worry that maintaining preeminence will come at the cost of addressing critical domestic needs. Even Krauthammer, who basked in the unipolar moment's glow, worried that its longevity might fall victim to the nation's "low savings rate, poor educational system, stagnant productivity, declining work habits, rising demand for welfare-state entitlements, and new taste for ecological luxuries."[14]

The costs of leadership are not only material, they are also human. Today, however, it is virtually axiomatic that the American people will not tolerate significant casualties or loss of life in pursuit of foreign policy objectives. Ironically, the swift and nearly costless (in terms of casualties) victory of the United States in the Persian Gulf War contributed to the public's timidity, making it more difficult for political leaders to place American troops in harm's way. Journalist Thomas Friedman, commenting on the suggestion that the Gulf War had removed the constraining influence of the "Vietnam syndrome" on policymakers' latitude, remarked wryly that it had been replaced by the "Gulf War syndrome:" "The United States will engage in military operations abroad only if they take place in a desert with nowhere for the enemy to hide, if the fighting can be guaranteed to last no more than five days, if casualties can be counted on one hand, if both oil and nuclear weapons are at stake, if the enemy is a madman who will not accept any compromise, and if the whole operation will be paid for by Germany and Japan."[15]

Cooperative security as a foreign policy strategy draws on the liberal (idealistic) tradition in American foreign policy. It recognizes that the costs of leadership might be more palatable domestically if they are shared with others, as in the Persian Gulf War. And it searches for an alternative to the anarchy and violence that characterize world politics, through efforts like the promotion of democracy to realize peace and reliance on international law and organizations, rather than military power, to manage and resolve conflict. However, as the fate of George Bush's "new world order" demonstrates, the appeal of idealism often founders on the shoals of self-interest and what critics regard as a lack of pragmatism.

Still, cooperative security and the liberal paradigm generally are not easily dismissed. The transnational layer in Nye's layer cake is animated by issues and actors that increasingly challenge the ability of states to cope by relying on traditional instruments of power and influence. Global climate change and transboundary pollution, for example, are not susceptible to national solutions; nor are international agreements likely to be reached without embracing the viewpoints of the hundreds of interests now organized in transnational coalitions spanning countries and continents.[16] With respect to these issues, the global village is a compelling image of the emergent international system.[17] Nonetheless, even these transnationally organized interests will be buffeted by the forces of globalization sweeping the world: as people are drawn more closely together by political, economic, and cultural forces, their ability to protect their autonomy and separate identities will diminish.

In Part I of *The Future of American Foreign Policy,* we probe in detail the many models, images, and other ideas that animate debate about America's foreign policy strategy for the next century. The chapters also address how the United States can best shape the emerging international system to ensure that it enhances American interests and values.

DEFINING AMERICA'S INTERESTS

We begin our probe with a broad-ranging essay by Richard N. Haass, director of foreign policy studies at the Brookings Institution. In "Beyond Containment: Competing American Foreign Policy Doctrines for the New Era," Haass provides an intellectual road map through the maze of ideas that now compete for the attention of policymakers and the public as the United States searches for a grand strategy appropriate for the next century.

Haass argues that setting priorities and devising a foreign policy approach for the twenty-first century must begin with an evaluation of interests, opportunities, and threats. That assessment is warranted because both the international and domestic contexts in which American interests are promoted and defended have changed. On one hand, Haass sees a global arena marked by "international deregulation"—a less structured state of affairs in which multiple actors have the capacity to shape outcomes but where new rules and norms to govern interaction have yet to emerge. On the other hand, he observes there is typically a disparity between foreign policy goals and resources, or between what a country seeks to accomplish internationally and what it can afford to do economically. This, of course, captures the reality of the current U.S. domestic environment, in which the political imperative to balance the federal budget—in the face of costly current and projected entitlement programs and declining public enthusiasm for foreign affairs spending—constrains policymakers' freedom of action. According to Haass, these environmental changes require choices: "Only by deciding priorities—in effect, by deciding what we are willing to do without—is it possible to allocate resources intelligently. . . . And only by determining priorities do we have a basis for deciding what to do when more than one interest is at stake at one time and something has to give."

What is the range of choices available to foreign policy leaders as they struggle to define America's role and interests in the new era? Haass identifies six alternatives currently competing for dominance—hegemony, isolationism, Wilsonianism, economism, humanitarianism, and realism—and then examines their wellsprings and what he sees as the weaknesses of each. He subscribes to the neorealist argument that continued hegemony is unlikely, as challengers to the unipolar moment are likely to emerge; he recognizes the appeal of isolationism in an environment of diminished external threats and a declining resource base, but he believes it is an unrealistic alternative in a rapidly globalizing world and one that "ignores what [the United States] can usefully do"; he argues that Wilsonianism (the liberal tradition), and democratic promotion in particular, ignores the fact that many current problems "cannot wait until the long-term process of democratization works its uncertain ways"; he worries that a focus on economics, and on bilateral trade promotion in particular, risks either turning into a neomercantilist program that ignores the benefits free trade promises to many Americans or, alternatively, alienating the nation's most important trade partners, thus undermining the benefits of multilateral cooperation in the security arena as well as the economic. Humanitarianism and realism come under similar scrutiny.

Haass' own preference is for a new "doctrine of regulation," a foreign policy approach in which the United States would seek to preserve international order through collective action. At times it might be necessary and feasible for the United States to act alone, Haass argues, but more frequently he sees it engaged internationally as a "multilateral leader" with the capacity to create and direct "posses"—ad hoc coalitions of states willing and able to address sources of global instability. Haass takes care to explain, however, that "relations *between* states should normally take precedence over the conditions *within* states as the former is more likely to directly affect our interests as opposed to our preferences."

Haass' cautious skepticism of democratic promotion, a central tenet of the liberal (idealist) paradigm, contrasts sharply with the enthusiasm with which the Clinton administration first embraced Wilsonianism. As Clinton explained less than six months after his inauguration, "The spread of democracy is one of the best guarantees of regional peace and prosperity and stability that we would ever have. . . . Democracies . . . don't wage war on each other, engage in terrorism, or generate refugees. Democracy makes it possible for allies to continue their close relations despite changes in leadership." As we noted in the introduction, the Clinton administration distanced itself from democratic promotion as a foreign policy strategy as its time in office lengthened. Still, is useful to ask what vision of the future stimulated its early enthusiasm for the liberal paradigm and, perhaps more importantly, what will be its legacy.

In "Democratic Enlargement: The Clinton Doctrine," diplomatic historian Douglas Brinkley provides a glimpse of the Clinton administration's thinking and priorities. As Brinkley explains, in formulating a strategy to replace containment, the Clinton administration purposely adopted an internationalist posture designed to shape domestic as well as international conditions. Specifically, Clinton's "democratic enlargement" emphasis sought to promote American prosperity by encouraging free trade agreements and the spread of market economies worldwide. Expanding the number of open economies was believed in turn to facilitate the rise of democracies. Brinkley explains the logic behind this "trade-as-foreign-policy" approach: "Only countries with free-spending middle classes . . . [can] become democratic and adopt the Western values of embracing ethnic diversity, protecting citizens' rights, and cooperating with the world community to stop terrorism." Thus, beneath the realism of ensuring the nation's economic standing lay the more idealistic goal of remaking the world in America's image. Brinkley applauds the effort, concluding that "democratic enlargement, a concept drawn from geoeconomics, . . . could well be remembered by future historians as the Clinton Doctrine."

Eugene R. Gholz, Daryl G. Press, and Harvey M. Sapolsky are decidedly less enthusiastic supporters of an active and intrusive foreign policy. Instead, they prefer a principled isolationism. As they argue in "Come Home, America: The Strategy of Restraint in the Face of Temptation," "rather than lead a new crusade, America should absorb itself in the somewhat delayed task of addressing imperfections in its own society." Thus the more prudent U.S. course of action is a policy of "restraint," which would lead the United States to end its alliance commitments and withdraw its military forces from overseas bases. Such a posture is necessary, they argue, because a "new strategic setting" has emerged in which U.S. military power is unrivaled and where nuclear weapons alone can deter the few threats that exist. The authors stress, however, this is a "modern form of isolationism." It does not call for a weak military or an end to free trade. Instead, it recognizes that recent changes in the global environment allow the United States to redirect its attention and resources to domestic priorities.

In a lively essay entitled "America the Inescapable," German journalist Josef Joffe agrees with Gholz, Press, and Sapolsky that the United States holds a predominant position globally. He asks us to "think of the United States as a gambler who can play simultaneously at each and every table that matters—and with more chips than anybody else." For Joffe, however, this state of affairs is reason to rejoice, not retreat. It allows the United States to lead an international community that is increasingly a manifestation of itself as its "soft power" assures preeminence in ways neither military nor economic power alone could promise. Globalization has hastened this opportunity. As economic and political relations have intensified across national borders, the appeal of American culture has spread universally, permitting the United States to achieve its goals through less coercive and expensive forms of power.

Unlike Joffe, Joseph S. Nye, Jr. in "Conflicts After the Cold War: Realism, Liberalism, and U.S. Interests" is more concerned with the forces of fragmentation, rather than integration, that now engulf the world. Drawing on realist and liberal international relations theories, the dean of the John F. Kennedy School of Government at Harvard University examines the types of conflicts most likely to disrupt international order in the coming years. Encouragingly, Nye finds the wars most threatening to American interests—those centered around global or regional balances of power—are less likely to occur due to reduced tensions and the U.S. defense posture. But, he argues, the world is not well prepared to address the most prevalent type of conflict of the new era—internal communal conflicts. For this reason, Nye sees American leadership as essential in addressing these and other types of conflict, even when its interests warrant less than direct military involvement.

THE PAST AS PROLOGUE

The United States emerged from World War II as the single most powerful nation in the world. Eventually the Soviet Union would rival the United States militarily, as each developed the capacity to devastate the other with nuclear warheads. The strategic posture of both superpowers thus came to emphasize deterrence rather than compellence, with the result that the concentration of power in two poles and the destructiveness of nuclear weapons produced caution and stability, rather than recklessness and war. To be sure, crises were endemic, interventions in the developing world were frequent and often bloody, and the fear of widespread destruction was always present, but systemwide war among the great powers did not occur. Paradoxically, then, the half century following World War II is appropriately characterized as the *long peace*.[18]

As noted, the United States begins the new era following the long peace as the world's preeminent power. While the decline in great power tension accompanying the end of the Cold War is a welcome development, the United States must now operate in a far less predictable global environment, as Nye and the other authors of the first five chapters make clear. Thus the United States must find new foundations on which to base its foreign policy objectives and international behavior. The two chapters in this section suggest the appropriate guideposts might not require innovation, but rather an examination of past experience.

Terry L. Deibel probes the history of American foreign relations for lessons applicable to the future in "Strategies Before Containment: Patterns for the Future." Deibel's concern is how "strategies designed to serve U.S. interests before the Soviet threat dominated American statecraft may . . . prove suggestive for strategists attempting to further those interests" in the new era. As in the past, he argues the United States will continue to see its national interests in terms of threats to its physical security, economic prosperity, and capacity to project American values abroad. The continuing relevance of practices once used to pursue these interests—including balance of power politics, collective security, hemispheric defense, and isolationism—is considered. Although the past clearly provides insights applicable to the future, Deibel concludes that new thinking is required, not simply to address the demise of the Soviet and communist threats, but also to understand the pertinence of domestic renewal.

Taking a different approach, the next chapter sees the answer for future American foreign policy lying in the period following, rather than preceding, World War II. In "The Myth of Post–Cold War Chaos," G. John Ikenberry argues that the significance of the Cold War's conclusion has been exaggerated, because it merely signals the end of bipolarity, nuclear stalemate, and containment, rather than the demise of an international order. For Ikenberry, the more important and enduring feature of world politics is the Western liberal democratic order founded in the 1940s under U.S. leadership. It embraces the principles of free trade, multilateral management, constitutionalism, and socioeconomic stability, which are reflected in such institutions as the United Nations, the International Monetary Fund, and the World Trade Organization. Thus "America is not adrift in unchartered seas. It is at the center of a world of its own making." Its main challenge today, Ikenberry instructs, is to reclaim "the postwar political order that was largely obscured by the more dramatic struggles between East and West." Realization of this goal is necessary not only to ensure the solidarity of the Western world in the absence of the Cold War security threat, but as a basis for stabilizing and integrating a world drawn ever closer by the forces of globalization.

NEW AGENDAS FOR A NEW ERA

To those persuaded by the logic of realpolitik, the new era requires no fundamental redefinition of American interests and policies—the search for power, prestige, and position should be pursued much as it was in the past. "I know of no change in policy, only circumstances," was the way Secretary of State John Quincy Adams in 1823 extolled the primacy of power as a principle of statecraft.

To others, the new era permits problems other than power and military security to receive greater attention. Many observers, for instance, now see economics at the center of U.S. foreign policy. This is clearly the view espoused by Jeffrey E. Garten in "Business and Foreign Policy: Time for a Strategic Alliance?," in which he comments, "Barring a militarily aggressive Russia or China, odds are that commercial considerations will play an ever greater role in American foreign policy . . . into the next century." This reality has been fostered by the forces of globalization which have intensified interactions across borders and made the health of the U.S. economy more dependent on international trade than at any other time. Ensuring American prosperity in this environment, Garten argues, requires a new partnership between business and government where the realization of each community's goals and the larger objectives of American foreign policy will require collective action. "On one hand, the resources of the American government—money, people with adequate global experience—are shrinking, and the role of American firms as de facto agents of foreign policy is expanding. On the other hand, . . . American business depends on Washington's help to liberalize trade, protect intellectual property, remove regulatory barriers, . . . encourage continued economic reform, [and] win major contracts in many other countries." Garten concludes with a detailed framework for the development of a mutually beneficial relationship between business and government where commerce is considered an end in itself, rather than simply a tool of American foreign policy.

In "The Rise of the Virtual State: Implications for U.S. Policy," Richard Rosecrance shares the view that economics are playing an ever greater role in shaping national priorities in the new era. Yet for Rosecrance, globalization has prompted much more than the need for cooperation between the private and public sectors. It has actually transformed the objectives and functions of developed states within the world political economy. He writes, "As capital has become increasingly mobile, advanced nations have come to recognize that exporting is no longer the only means to economic growth: one can instead produce goods overseas for the foreign market." This development has facilitated "the rise of the virtual state"—a national economy (like that of the United States) that increasingly specializes in high-value-added, technical services such as research and design, financing, marketing, and consulting while relying on foreign workers and facilities to manufacture products. Rosecrance argues this trend in economic relations portends less global conflict as well as a chance for America to "reshape its pattern of comparative advantage." Yet it will also displace domestic workers and businesses, making it essential that they acquire the international knowledge and training to exploit opportunities in other countries.

Insight into the thinking and attitudes of American leaders is particularly important in anticipating the coalitions of support and opposition for the initiatives suggested in the previous two reading selections. More importantly, an understanding of elite opinions may indicate whether an internationalist foreign agenda can be sustained in the absence of a central, compelling security threat. In "Internationalism: Intact or in Trouble?," Ole R. Holsti and James N. Rosenau examine the foreign policy attitudes of Americans based on a 1996 survey of opinion leaders, with particular attention given to historian Arthur Schlesinger's oft-cited "back to the womb" thesis. Schlesinger contends that domestic beliefs concerning America's role in the world are presently undergoing a fundamental shift toward isolationism. He writes:

> It is now surely clear that the upsurge in American internationalism during the Cold War was a reaction to what was seen as the direct and urgent Soviet threat to the security of the United States. It is to Joseph Stalin that Americans owe the forty-year suppression of the isolationist impulse. The collapse of the Soviet threat faces us today with the prospect that haunted Roosevelt half a century ago—the return to the womb in American foreign policy. . . . The isolationist impulse has risen from the grave, and it has taken the new form of unilateralism.[19]

Holsti and Rosenau's analysis points in a different direction, however. They find "a greater degree of continuity than change in the views of American elites," regardless of whether policy issues or attitude structures are taken into consideration. Further, the authors conclude there is little evidence within the available survey data to validate Schlesinger's thesis that post–Cold War attitudes reflect a return to isolationism. "The dominant theme," they assert, "is that most American leaders were no less prepared in 1996 than they were four years earlier—or even during the Cold War—to accept major international responsibilities, and to do so in cooperation with allies and other countries." Holsti and Rosenau do temper these findings by recognizing that their research pertains to a single group that has traditionally been more receptive to global engagement and cooperation than the general public. Thus Schlesinger's thesis, in their view, might be best treated as a warning about the potential, growing divide between elite and mass foreign policy views.

How the traditional internationalist-isolationist divide relates to the many environmental issues that now populate the global agenda is not entirely clear. Public opinion polls routinely show broad support among elites and the general public for such goals as "improving the global environment."[20] Still, when specific proposals for improving the environment are considered, they typically fall victim to what some lament as the increasingly "particularistic" and "interest-based" calculations of Americans and their leaders.[21] Partisan and ideological differences often reinforce these calculations.

Illustrative are the domestic responses to international efforts to negotiate an agreement that would reduce the level of greenhouse gases, believed by many scientists to be responsible for a gradual rise in global temperatures, which may have devastating long-term consequences. Following an agreement at the 1992 Earth Summit in Rio de Janeiro on the principle of stabilizing greenhouse gas emissions, negotiators met in Kyoto, Japan, in 1997 in an effort to reach a binding agreement that would reduce emission levels in the next century to previous levels. The United States, the largest producer of carbon dioxide and other greenhouse gases, was a reluctant partner. However, following prodding by Vice President Al Gore, an ardent environmental proponent, the United States finally agreed to a modest program of targeted reductions in greenhouse gas emissions. Even as the negotiations were taking place, media advertisements in the United States (paid for by the oil industry, among others) declared that the proposed treaty "isn't global, won't work." Meanwhile, the Senate majority leader, Trent Lott, announced, "If they come back and think we're going to go along with what they're doing in Kyoto, they've got another thing coming." Later, when the Kyoto negotiators finally reached an accord, members of Congress pronounced the treaty "dead on arrival."

The final chapter in Part I embraces a "global village" image of the future. The vision is consistent with the foreign policy approach described by Richard Haass as "humanitarian," one that enjoyed support by the Clinton administration (if not always at levels environmentalists and their supporters would prefer). In "Population, Consumption, and the Path to Sustainability: The U.S. Role," Janet Welsh Brown examines a set of related issues—population growth and environmental degradation—which she argues will require American and international action if they are not to become major, new security threats. The problem, according to the author, is that the "American patterns of production and consumption—admired and imitated by most of the world—are not sustainable." If these patterns, which have a devastating impact on the environment, are adopted by developing states with burgeoning populations, the likely result will be the collapse of "some basic physical and biological systems" later in the twenty-first century. Further, an accompanying "downward spiral of population growth, debt, inequality, and loss of soil and agricultural production could lead to economic decline and widespread political cal instability" throughout the Global South. Optimistically, Welsh Brown contends that there is time to avert future disasters if governments act today. For its part, the United States must assume the lead internationally by cutting its staggering rates of resource consumption and pollution. This change will not only benefit the environment tremendously, but it will prompt other states to follow America's example. Collective action is critical because, as Welsh Brown points out, no government is singularly prepared to meet these transnational challenges. Still, the political viability of a foreign policy approach which emphasizes global humanitarian principles is dubious, regardless of how compelling the challenges may be.

NOTES

1. Charles Krauthammer, "The Unipolar Moment," *Foreign Affairs* 70 (No. 1, 1991), pp. 23–25. See also Charles Krauthammer, "Universal Domination: Toward a Unipolar World," *The National Interest* 18 (Winter 1989–1990), pp. 46–49.

2. Robert E. Harkavy, "Images of the Coming International System," *Orbis* 41 (Fall 1997), pp. 569–590.

3. Joseph S. Nye, Jr., "What New World Order?," *Foreign Affairs* 71 (Spring 1992), p. 88. Nye's conceptualization implies that realism and liberalism, competing explanations of states' foreign policy behavior, might both provide insight into the future of American foreign policy, a viewpoint explored in his essay "Conflicts After the Cold War: Realism, Liberalism, and U.S. Interests," *Washington Quarterly* 19 (Winter 1996), pp. 5–24, which is reprinted in Chapter 5 in this book.

4. Harkavy, p. 587.

5. Barry R. Posen and Andrew L. Ross, "Competing U.S. Grand Strategies," in Robert J. Lieber, ed., *Adrift: American Foreign Policy at the End of the Century* (New York: Longman, 1997), pp. 118–124.

6. For elaborations, see Robert Gilpin, *War and Change in World Politics* (Cambridge, England: Cambridge University Press, 1981); Charles P. Kindleberger, *The World in Depression, 1929–1939* (Berkeley: University of California Press, 1973); and Stephen D. Krasner, "State Power and the Structure of International Trade," *World Politics* 28 (April 1976), pp. 317–347.

7. See Michael Mastanduno, "Preserving the Unipolar Moment: Realist Theories and U.S. Grand Strategy After the Cold War," *International Security* 21 (Spring 1997), pp. 49–88; and Barry R. Posen and Andrew L. Ross, "Competing Visions for U.S. Grand Strategy," *International Security* 21 (Winter 1996–1997), pp. 5–48.

8. Mastanduno, p. 56.

9. See Mastanduno, pp. 52–57; Christopher Layne, "The Unipolar Illusion: Why New Great Powers Will Rise," *International Security* 17 (Spring 1993), pp. 5–51; and Kenneth N. Waltz, *International Security* 18 (Fall 1993), pp. 44–79.

10. William Drozdiak, "Down with Yankee Dominance," *Washington Post National Weekly Report*, November 24, 1997, pp. 15–16.

11. Mastanduno, pp. 86–88.

12. Posen and Ross, 1996–1997. See also Richard N. Haass, *The Reluctant Sheriff: The United States After the Cold War* (New York: Council on Foreign Relations, 1997); Janne E. Nolan, ed., *Global Engagement: Cooperation and Security in the Twenty-first Century* (Washington, DC: Brookings Institution, 1994); and Eugene Gholz, Daryl G. Press, and Harvey M. Sapolsky, "Come Home, America: The Strategy of Restraint in the Face of Temptation," *International Security* 21 (Spring 1997), pp. 5–48. An excerpt from the Gholz, Press, and Sapolsky article is reprinted in Chapter 3 in this book.

13. Posen and Ross, 1996–1997, p. 35.

14. Krauthammer, pp. 26–27.

15. Thomas Friedman, "Global Mandate," *New York Times,* March 5, 1995, p. 15.

16. See Thomas Princen and Matthais Finger, *Environmental NGOs in World Politics: Linking the Local with the Global* (London: Routledge, 1994).

17. Harkavy describes the global village image as one "based on the apparent shift of power and sovereignty from nation-states to international or nongovernmental organizations, and the growth of functional global regimes" (p. 570).

18. See, among others, John Lewis Gaddis, *The Long Peace: Inquiries into the History of the Cold War* (New York: Oxford University Press, 1987); and Charles W. Kegley, Jr., ed., *The Long Postwar Peace* (New York: HarperCollins, 1991).

19. Arthur Schlesinger, Jr., "Back to the Womb? Isolationism's Renewed Threat," *Foreign Affairs* 74 (July/August 1995), p. 5.

20. See, for example, Andrew Kohut, *America's Place in the World II* (Washington, D.C.: Pew Research Center for the People and the Press, 1997); and John E. Rielly, ed., *American Public Opinion and U.S. Foreign Policy 1995* (Chicago: Chicago Council on Foreign Relations, 1995).

21. Samuel P. Huntington, "The Erosion of American National Interests," *Foreign Affairs* 76 (September/October 1997), pp. 28–49.

Defining America's Interests

1. BEYOND CONTAINMENT: COMPETING AMERICAN FOREIGN POLICY DOCTRINES FOR THE NEW ERA

Richard N. Haass

*T*he post–Cold War period is proving to be a time of great change, including rising and falling powers, a large number of small conflicts, considerable shifts in wealth, and new technologies that will both enhance and endanger our lives. The concept "international deregulation" captures the new era, as we move from a highly structured world dominated by two actors to one in which many global actors affect world political outcomes. New rules, relationships, and arrangements have yet to evolve which will harness the dynamic political and economic forces now engulfing the world, thus posing challenges to American foreign policy.

What are the most pressing U.S. interests in such a world? An illustrative list (in no particular order) might include: protecting U.S. territory and American citizens from attack; controlling access to U.S. territory against illegal drugs and immigrants as well as disease; preventing the emergence of a hostile superpower; avoiding the domination of Europe, the Asia-Pacific, the Persian Gulf or the Caribbean littoral by a hostile power; reducing existing inventories of weapons of mass destruction and lesser arms; preventing the spread or use of weapons of mass destruction; maintaining an open trading order; discouraging the use of force in international affairs and encouraging the peaceful resolution of conflicts; promoting American exports; safeguarding Israel's security; maintaining a functioning international monetary system; guaranteeing access to needed energy supplies and other raw materials; fostering democracy, human rights, and market economic reforms; safeguarding the global environment against severe degradation; and preventing genocide or mass suffering.

Other interests could no doubt be added while some might deserve to be subtracted. What is most noteworthy, though, is how little U.S. interests have changed since the end of the Cold War and how extensive they remain. Rather, what has changed most are the threats, which are arguably greater in number and smaller in scale.

Formulating and implementing a foreign policy to protect and promote American interests will prove difficult, in part because there is no obvious, much less accepted, answer as to what constitutes American priorities. Determining priorities for policy—designing a foreign policy doctrine—involves a complex, three-way calculation of national interests, likely opportunities, and emerging threats.

First, it is necessary to identify and weigh U.S. interests. All are not equal in value. Some interests are vital, others simply important or modest. All such judgments are unavoidably subjective and controversial, although the importance of an interest must be directly related to its bearing on the country's political freedom, physical safety, and economic prosperity. Contrary to what is often posited, a willingness to use military force is *not* an indication that an interest is vital, any more than a reluctance to use force suggests an interest is minor. Military force is simply one instrument of policy, and its selection reflects its utility relative to other policy tools.

Second, identifying and weighing interests, however necessary and difficult, is not sufficient. Policy must also take into account the potential to promote these interests. Third, it is necessary for policy to assess threats, i.e., the requirement to protect interests. Where there is no threat there is rarely a need to act.

There is a temptation to include a great many interests as vital. This should be avoided. Vital interests are those with the greatest potential to affect what is most basic. Important and minor interests have correspondingly less potential to affect our security, prosperity, and freedom, and, especially in the case of minor or peripheral interests, often reflect preferences as much as anything.

Why is it necessary to calculate interests, opportunity (or feasibility), and threats? Why is such a process necessary? There is an unavoidable gap between what a country seeks and what it can afford. Hiding behind facile formulations of "selective engagement" that provide neither the criteria for selection nor the means of engagement is not enough. Only by deciding priorities—in effect, by deciding what we are willing to do without—is it possible to allocate resources intelligently. Priorities also allow us to size, shape, and deploy our military forces, design and focus our intelligence community, direct our foreign assistance, and train and assign our diplomats. And only by determining priorities do we have a basis for deciding what to do when more than one interest is at stake and something has to give. Proof that this is a task easier said than done is found in the now often contentious debate about which foreign policy doctrine best captures and defines American interests in the new era.

COMPETING DOCTRINES

Six competing foreign policy doctrines now vie to replace the Cold War strategy of containment: hegemony, isolationism, Wilsonianism, economism, humanitarianism, and realism. Together they animate public discourse about how best to promote and defend American interests in an age of deregulation.

Hegemony

A doctrine of hegemony would make the goal of U.S. foreign policy the maintenance of America's relative advantage. It would seek to prolong the unipolar moment and make it an era.

Why would such a goal make sense? It would (by definition) prevent the emergence of new adversaries that could not only threaten U.S. interests, but destroy the United States. "It is in our national interest that no other superpower emerge whose political and social values are profoundly hostile to our own," writes one observer.[1] William Kristol and Robert Kagan suggest that "American hegemony is the only reliable defense against a breakdown of peace and international order. The appropriate goal of American foreign policy, therefore, is to preserve that hegemony as far into the future as possible."[2]

For better or worse, such a goal is beyond our reach. As Kenneth Waltz has pointed out, "For a country to choose not to become a great power is a structural anomaly. . . . Sooner or later, usually sooner, the international status of countries has risen in step with their material resources. Countries with great power economies have become great powers, whether or not reluctantly."[3] There is no way, for example, that the United States can ensure that Russia does not re-create a massive threat or that some future Chinese government will not decide to challenge the United States for regional or even global predominance. The most we can do with any certainty is slow another country's economic and military growth—and then with only the most modest of effects—by denying technology or markets. But all the U.S. denial in the world will count for little given what others (be they governments or firms or criminal groups) will be prepared to provide and what countries can do for themselves. Preventive military strikes are an option only for destroying specific, limited capabilities of an adversary. It is risky even at that, and out of the question when the adversary has a large military capability and a broad capacity to regenerate or retaliate. Quite simply, although it is within the reach of the United States to continue on as a great power and to affect the behavior of other powers, it is beyond our ability to prevent another country from joining the ranks of the great.

A related problem with a doctrine of hegemony is its cost. Kristol and Kagan estimate the annual increase that would be required in defense spending alone to be between $60 and $80 billion. Moreover, the demands of perpetuating primacy will grow at a time when Americans are less inclined to pay the price in both blood and treasure. Indeed, if history is any guide, Americans will consider paying a much larger price for national security only if we reach a juncture when Americans feel themselves and their vital interests clearly threatened.

Isolationism

If hegemony belongs at one end of the spectrum of potential choices, isolationism falls at the other. An isolationist doctrine would produce a minimal foreign policy, one that would be circumscribed in its goals, restrained in its activities, and modest in the resources required.

Contemporary isolationism—or "minimalism"—stems from several wellsprings. First, there are those who believe that the United States *need not* be active in the world, owing to a lack of vital interests or imminent threats. Second, there are those who argue that the United States *should not* be overly ambitious, either because of the intractable nature of many of the world's problems or the belief that U.S. involvement will tend only to exacerbate them. And third, there are those who maintain that the United States *cannot* afford to be active in the world because of pressing domestic priorities and limited resources.

In many important ways, the threats the United States once faced have been significantly reduced. Still, there are potential problems in the world—crises in the Persian Gulf or Northeast Asia, a breakdown of trade, a renewed Russian threat to Europe, a Chinese bid for regional hegemony, the proliferation of weapons of mass destruction, and terrorist attacks—that could directly and dramatically affect Americans' well-being. Economic globalization, the ease with which people can travel, and the growing range of weapons make it difficult for the United States to insulate itself from the world. With such high "connectivity," there is no apparent shortage of interests or potential threats.

There is, however, a related argument that there is little we can do about the state of the world. Ronald Steel, for example, urges that Americans "get over the superpower syndrome" and accept the reality that "there are a good many problems for which there may be no solution at all."[4] Alan Tonelson writes that "foreign policy is not an end in itself but a means to a highly specific end: enhancing the safety and prosperity of the American people. A domestic focus is imperative not in order to rebuild the foundation of American world leadership but to prepare America for a world that cannot be led or stabilized or organized in any meaningful sense of these words."[5]

The problem with this perspective is that it ignores what we can usefully do. The United States' diplomacy alone cannot bring peace to the Middle East, but it can facilitate the process. The United States' arms can deter conflict in the Persian Gulf and the Korean Peninsula and protect American interests and restore stability if deterrence fails. Action by the United States can keep millions of people alive who would otherwise be victims of civil war or hunger brought about by political and economic mismanagement, as was the case in Somalia. Bosnia offers a graphic example of what is likely to happen when the United States stands aloof—as compared to when it not only engages but leads.

The theme most central to the minimalist or neoisolationist perspective, however, is the economic: that the cost of our national security effort—defense, intelligence, assistance, and diplomacy—is one that we can ill afford. Most minimalists see the United States in social and economic decline, in part because of the costs of decades of international activism. With the Cold War won, they favor shifting resources to domestic needs. Such views are intellectually consistent with the writings of Paul Kennedy, the influential historian who attributes the decline of great powers throughout history to "imperial overstretch," his phrase for spending too much on a world role and not enough at home.[6]

To be sure, a minimalist foreign policy would save some resources in the short run. The United States now spends nearly $300 billion a year on national security. It is a considerable sum by any measure. At the same time, it is necessary to place this figure in context. The United States' national security spending represents approximately one-fifth of all federal spending—about the same as what we spend on discretionary civilian programs or Medicare, and less than we spend on Social Security. Spending on national security now comes to under 4 percent of gross national product (GNP), less than half the level during the Kennedy administration and the lowest level at any time since the beginning of the Cold War (see also Chapter 22).

Moreover, it does not figure that spending less on national security will automatically add to prosperity. The United States experienced far higher rates of economic growth during the 1950s and 1960s, decades of far higher rates of spending on defense. Nor is it at all obvious that spending less on defense would ease our domestic problems. Many of them are not the result of lack of resources. It is doubtful that what most ails us at home—crime, illegitimacy, drug use, divorce, racism, etc.—would be fixed by further drawing down resources devoted to our presence abroad and shifting them to domestic purposes.

Worse, over time a minimalist foreign policy could end up being more costly. Neglect will prove to be malign. Conflict on the Korean Peninsula, for example, would disrupt trade and economic life throughout the region. There would be no way the United States could wall itself off from the effects. Successful terrorism against targets in the United States would exact a terrible human and financial toll. A failed Mexico or other collapsed states in the Western Hemisphere would increase immigration pressures on American territory. Hostile control of energy resources in the Persian Gulf could lead to higher prices for oil and gas. Indeed, a posture of minimalism, whatever its near-term savings, could increase the likelihood that critical problems or threats to vital U.S. interests will emerge. The United States' reluctance to act may well encourage others to fill the perceived void. Arms proliferation would likely accelerate; aggression would almost certainly become more commonplace. If and when this occurred, the United States could well have no choice but to act—but in a context far less amenable to relatively inexpensive solutions. The notion that what the United States does overseas comes at the expense of what it could be doing at home is flawed; in a world in which the significance of borders is blurring and that of distance is diminishing, foreign and domestic policy are increasingly two sides of the same coin.

Wilsonianism

This enduring American approach to foreign policy reflects a desire to see other countries adopt a form of democratic governance and civil society that our own experience suggests is best for both the individual and the community. This philosophical preference is buttressed by a practical one—namely, that democracies tend to treat their own citizens with greater tolerance and are far less likely to resort to force in their relations with their fellow democracies. Moreover, established democracies are naturally less brittle and therefore less susceptible to radical and disruptive change. A more democratic world, it is believed, will not only be inherently better, but also more peaceful, stable, and prosperous.

The promotion of democracy constituted the principal attempt of the first Clinton administration to articulate a new foreign policy doctrine. It was National Security Adviser Anthony Lake who, in September 1993, argued that "the successor to a doctrine of containment must be a strategy of enlargement, the enlargement of the world's free community of market democracies."

There are, however, several problems with a doctrine of democracy promotion. Enlarging the community of democracies provides little or no policy-relevant guidance for dealing with a host of pressing problems, many of which cannot wait until the long-term process of democratization works its uncertain way. "Enlargement" was essentially irrelevant in helping the Clinton administration come to grips with Bosnia, Rwanda, North Korea, or Somalia. In addition, the active promotion of democracy is a luxury policy-makers can only sometimes afford. The United States arguably has little choice but to overlook a lack of democracy in friendly states (such as in the Persian Gulf) where other interests (such as energy and security) take precedence.

At the same time, a foreign policy predicated on spreading democracy can be difficult to implement vis-à-vis our foes, either because we lack the means to influence them—it is either difficult to sanction more than we do or, owing to important policy differences, impossible to offer inducements—or because again we have more pressing concerns. Thus, a democratic North Korea would be nice, but in the meantime we had better focus on Pyongyang's nuclear ambitions and the threat it poses to the South. Similarly, we would like to see China demonstrate greater respect for human rights, but for now we need China's help with North Korea while we seek access to China's enormous market and try to discourage Beijing from exporting nuclear weapons technology or using military force against Taiwan.

Moreover, encouraging democracy from the outside is difficult at best—and potentially dangerous. Not every society or culture is ripe for democracy or amenable to intimate American involvement. To "demand" change of one's friends leads the United States down a path of potentially sanctioning those it seeks to bolster; as the Carter administration learned in Iran, this can lead to outcomes that are far worse, from the vantage point of human rights as well as other U.S. interests. In parts of the Arab world, rapid democratization would surely bring to power governments that were not only anti-American but whose commitment to democracy was tactical, a means to gain power rather than share it. What can be particularly destabilizing is pushing for elections before all aspects of a civil society are in place. This is one lesson of Algeria—namely, that elections early in the process of democratization can bring to the fore organized forces willing to exploit, but not live under, greater freedom. Iran is an example of a related phenomenon: that one can have elections without democracy or even rudimentary protection of civil liberties and human rights.

It is also important to note that democracy is no panacea. A more democratic Russia is one in which criminal elements flourish and xenophobic, nationalist elements are increasing. The former Yugoslavia is painful proof that nonliberal democracies can be extremely aggressive in how they treat their own people and their neighbors. Democracy cannot always compete successfully with the lure of nationalism; nor can it ensure responsible behavior on the part of weak leaders looking for a distraction from domestic travails. A more democratic China might actually be more assertive beyond its borders than it is currently, just as Islamic states that have introduced elements of democracy are anything but benign in their behavior. Indeed, while mature democracies tend not to make war on one another, immature or developing democracies seem more prone to being swayed by popular passions and calls for violence.[7]

Economism

This fourth American foreign policy doctrine would be built around the premise that the main purpose of foreign policy is to serve economic ends: principally but not exclusively the promotion of exports. Such a doctrine stems from multiple beliefs, including the view that in the post–Cold War world traditional security concerns are less pressing, that domestic concerns are more salient, and that the United States now needs to jettison its past willingness to look the other way when political and military allies act unfairly in economic matters.

The clearest manifestation of economism is an emphasis on trade issues and the promotion of exports. Such a policy can achieve some modest results, at least for a short period. There are several dangers with such an emphasis, however. Exports per se are not necessarily good if they require subsidies or artificially managed exchange rates to be competitive. Another risk is that a foreign policy based upon export promotion runs the risk of degenerating into a search for specified, quantifiable results—so much market share, this level of trade imbalance—that will only increase the role of domestic political forces (often mercantilist) in economic relationships. Indeed, it is precisely this inherent impatience and demand for specific, near-term bilateral satisfaction from commercial diplomacy that characterizes contemporary results-oriented trade policy and distinguishes it from more comprehensive, long-term, multilateral approaches to expanding world trade through the adoption of common rules and procedures. Failure to meet goals tends to lead to retaliation and protectionist measures that are economically self-destructive and inconsistent with efforts to build an open trading order on either a regional or global basis.

The arguments against protectionism are powerful and, in the end, decisive. Protectionist policies discourage the movement of investment and economic activity to those areas of technological innovation where there is comparative advantage. Protectionism also increases costs. Numerous studies demonstrate how a society pays many times over in higher prices for saving a small number of particular jobs. American protection of its market hurts economic growth in other countries, thereby contributing to instability and migration. Protectionist policies also invite retaliation, thereby reducing export opportunities (and jobs that tend to be higher paying and more productive) for the United States. In addition, the society loses the benefit of imports, including their quality (which gives the consumer greater choice) and competition. Anyone doubting this last consideration needs only to ask what kind of cars Detroit would be producing today without the push from Japan over previous decades.

On one level, the continuing appeal of protectionism is understandable, as individual workers and firms suffer on account of foreign competition and practices, fair and otherwise. But open trade benefits far more Americans than it injures. It has been a boon to American consumers and workers. Exports from the United States have increased rapidly in recent decades; the United States is the largest merchandise exporter in the world. More than 10 percent of what is produced in this country is sold abroad. Several million jobs, many of them high paying, would not exist (although others likely would) were it not for the expansion of U.S. access into overseas markets.

A policy of muscular trade promotion is also of questionable desirability for larger reasons. It is likely to harm the overall bilateral relationship with the country in question. Such spillover or contamination could well set in motion political and military trends that over time would work against the full range of U.S. interests. A Japan or European Union that comes to see its relationship with the United States as being more competitive than cooperative will inevitably reorient its foreign and defense policies away from those desired by the United States. Multilateralizing trade—and using the mechanisms for dispute resolution that form the World Trade Organization (WTO)—promises to make good political as well as economic sense. The goal of American foreign policy ought to be to "de-bilateralize" trade to the extent possible. It is one of the many ironies of the first Clinton administration that it did more to bilateralize and politicize trade at the same time it helped multilateralize and depoliticize it through the passage of both the North American Free Trade Agreement (NAFTA) and the WTO.

The broader critique of economism is that a foreign policy based upon economics can all too easily be overwhelmed. Instability on the Korean peninsula, in the Persian Gulf, or in South Asia can interrupt the emergence of markets and a great deal more. Amidst war or revolution, the primacy of economics will come to a sudden end; "geo-economics" will find itself taking a back seat to geopolitics. Similarly, the desire to sell for economic reasons can easily come into conflict with the need to sanction or isolate a country for political or strategic purposes. The post–Cold War world remains too dangerous for the United States to approach it through an economic lens.

Humanitarianism

The humanitarian approach is embraced by people who tend to see the world less in terms of nation-states than as peoples. They tend to view threats less in terms of aggression than chaos. Foreign policy humanitarians focus on such concerns—the alleviation of poverty, disease, hunger, overpopulation, the environment, and so on—because they are important in their own right and because these problems can lead to more traditional conflicts if their consequences go untended.

The problem with the humanitarian view is not so much its accuracy—over-population, food and water shortages, and environmental degradation are all real problems certain to grow worse over time—as its adequacy. Humanitarianism underestimates other concerns and threats that are more immediate and important and that need to inform any foreign policy. It is at most a supplementary world view, not an independent one. Moreover, many of the problems that animate humanitarianism are extremely difficult to fix. At the same time, these basic social and developmental problems do not normally directly threaten important much less vital interests of the United States. It is thus difficult to rally domestic support for expensive efforts to address humanitarian problems abroad, especially when many of the same socioeconomic problems are to be found in this country. Like Wilsonianism, addressing humanitarian concerns can contribute to a foreign policy doctrine, not define one.

Realism

Realists emphasize balance of power considerations—a basic form of international regulation—when it comes to matters of the national interest. Alliances among like-minded governments are a favored vehicle for promoting these interests. Those of this view are mindful of the continuing threats posed by regional military powers and the potential strategic challenges of Russia or China. Realists are much less concerned with the internal character of foreign societies and with such matters as human rights, democracy, and humanitarian welfare, which they would describe as preferences rather than interests.

The strength of the realist approach is that it highlights the existing and potential threats to major U.S. interests, threats that if they were to materialize could overwhelm all other policy concerns. Realists are also correct in understanding that states continue to be the most powerful units on the global chessboard in most situations, and that dealing with classical forms of inter-state aggression is what U.S. military forces do best. Realism was very much the orientation of both the Nixon and Bush foreign policies.

The principal weakness of realism is that it provides no guidelines (other than to stand aloof) for dealing with important, if less than vital, economic, political, and humanitarian problems within states, arguably the potential source of most post–Cold War instability. Realism offers little help in determining whether and how to deal with such problems as we have seen in Somalia, the former Yugoslavia, Rwanda, Haiti, and post–Cold War Cuba. Such problems can be important even if they do not directly touch the United States. Not all interests need be vital to be worthy of American attention or protection.

Realism suffers as well from its lack of popular appeal. An emphasis on international order and on stability does not impart much in the way of purpose to foreign policy. Indeed, the promotion of order, however important and however necessary, is not enough. It cannot engage the broader American public and Congress who want, and often require, a larger purpose as a prerequisite for supporting foreign policy. The result is that a narrow realism cannot be sustained by a country and a people that are uncomfortable with realpolitik and pride themselves on their morality and their exceptionalism.

TOWARD SYNTHESIS: A DOCTRINE OF REGULATION

What should be done? The ideal doctrine most resembles realism. The principal focus of American foreign policy should be on inter-state relations and the external conduct of states—discouraging classic aggression, acquisition of weapons of mass destruction by rogue states, protectionism, state support for terrorism, and illegal entry. These are the matters that possess the greatest potential to affect the most important U.S. interests most deeply. The focus on inter-state concerns should, however, be dominant rather than exclusive. Considerations of "justice"—democracy, human rights, human welfare— would ordinarily be of a lower priority. So, too, would economic aims. The reasoning is simple. Order is the more basic concern. One can have order without justice but not the other way around. Similarly, one cannot have trade without stability and peace.

The best term for such a policy amalgam is "regulation." Under this doctrine, the United States would act—with others whenever possible but alone when necessary and feasible—to shape the behavior and, in some cases, the capabilities of governments and other actors so that they are less likely or able to act aggressively, either beyond their borders or toward their own citizens, and more likely to conduct trade and other economic relations according to agreed norms and procedures.

A fully regulated world would be one in which democratic governments and other actors comported themselves according to a set of universal norms reflecting the rule of law. Military force would not be used by governments in their relations with one another; no state would harbor or in any way support terrorists. Within states, there would be clear respect for human rights. Trade disputes would be decided under the WTO, while governments would agree to guidelines that would prevent or limit practices that would affect the environment.

Toward this end, relations *between* states should normally take precedence over conditions *within* states as the former is more likely to directly affect our interests as opposed to our preferences. In addition, threats posed to states by states or other externally based or supported actors tend to be more amenable to being fixed, or at least ameliorated, by available policy tools. In those instances where a state's foreign policy is of little consequence, the United States has the luxury of focusing its policy on the country's internal practices. This will lead to charges of inconsistency, but inconsistency is the price of priorities. It is better for the United States to be selective in the priority accorded to promoting democracy, human rights, and market reforms than to make any one of them the priority for foreign policy everywhere, something we cannot afford given our other interests, or nowhere, something that would unnecessarily limit our potential to be a positive force.

REGULATING THE POST–COLD WAR WORLD: TRANSLATING MEANS INTO ENDS

If history is any guide, such a perfect world is not about to emerge—certainly not on its own. Thus it is necessary to connect the means of American foreign policy to its goals or objectives. At least four strategies warrant consideration: alliances, unilateralism, institutionalism, and multilateral leadership.

Alliances

During the Cold War, the principal vehicle for American foreign policy was a network of alliances in which the United States worked closely with selected states who shared a perception of the Soviet Union and communism. The question naturally arises whether alliances in general, and whether these alliances in particular, will and should continue to play so central a role in American foreign policy. And, if not, what should take their place?

Standing alliances require predictability, as regards the source of problems, and clarity, as regards those friends and allies who can be counted upon to act against them. There needs to be time to consider scenarios and to prepare plans and capabilities for addressing them. The North Atlantic Treaty Organization (NATO) was made possible by the potential for a Soviet/Warsaw Pact attack on Western Europe and the collective readiness of the United States, Canada, and NATO's fourteen European members to resist aggression in that place.

What about the future? Could NATO become even more important in the deregulated world, essentially exchanging its mission of deterring Soviet invasion in Europe for one of regional or even global peacemaking and defense?

The short answer is "no." NATO's military capabilities are much reduced and getting smaller as members adjust to the post–Cold War environment, including the demise of the Warsaw Pact and the weakening of Russia. In addition, there is barely enough political will and consensus to deal with the Bosnian contingency, much less the threats posed by Iran and Iraq. Moreover, to get NATO members to devote more resources to defense would probably require the reemergence of a clear Russian threat. But dealing with such a challenge would absorb any new NATO strength, leaving little or nothing left over for the rest of the world or for other contingencies within Europe. The United States would be wiser to tap individually those NATO members able and willing to assist in particular situations, such as France and Great Britain in the Gulf conflict, and draw on organizational assets such as communications and intelligence links, rather than deal with the organization itself.

What about this country's other alliances? The U.S.–South Korean tie is robust, but mostly for a single contingency, to deter and if need be defend against the threat from the North. The relationship would need to be modified significantly if the peninsula comes to be reunified. The U.S.–Japanese alliance is something else again. The end of the Cold War does not alter the reality that this alliance continues to provide a useful umbrella for managing Japan's participation in the world, making it less necessary for it to become self-reliant in the defense realm, something that could set in motion a chain of events in the region that could prove costly and destabilizing. In addition, this alliance remains relevant but still limited in its potential to help deal with a war on the Korean peninsula or if a Chinese or Russian threat emerges.

In the Persian Gulf, the scene of the first major war in the age of deregulation, there is no prospect for an alliance in the traditional sense. The local states that the United States would want to defend from attack would be unwilling (for fear of alienating powerful anti-Western domestic constituencies) to enter into such a bond. Moreover, they would have little to contribute militarily beyond access to their territory and support. Just as important, such states are potentially vulnerable to internal instability, something that a traditional alliance presence cannot manage and may actually exacerbate. Lesser forms of defense collaboration are all that can be anticipated.

Alliances can contribute to but by themselves will not be able to furnish a mechanism for implementing a doctrine of regulation. Groups of countries that once shared a common purpose do so no longer or do so only in increasingly less common circumstances. Alliances require a large degree of predictability, as regards threats, and a large degree of commonality, as regards priorities and what countries are willing to do on their behalf, characteristics that are lacking in the age of deregulation.

Unilateralism

Unilateralism is an approach to U.S. involvement in the world that minimizes, and wherever possible excludes, the participation of other governments and organizations. Unilateralists are uncomfortable with the compromises necessary for the smooth functioning of alliances and opposed to any transfer of substantial authority to international organizations. It is much easier to act without having to gain the consent of others. Unilateralism maximizes speed and freedom of decision making and implementation. It can be the best option for acting when narrow interests are at stake and where the involvement of others is not necessary logistically, or is deemed undesirable lest surprise be sacrificed or a friend embarrassed.

There are, however, considerable problems with a unilateral approach. It potentially reinforces a mode of activism that can easily be emulated and abused by others. In addition, American unilateralism will inevitably produce resistance if not a backlash. An à la carte approach to international commitments risks resulting in the demise of these arrangements, as well as broader fallout to bilateral relationships. If we pay a price for multilateralism we also receive dividends; if we see an advantage for unilateralism we also must be sensitive to its costs.

In most instances unilateralism is neither wise nor sustainable. Most military interventions, for example, require either the indirect or direct support and participation of others, be it to share the military burden, to distribute economic costs, or to assuage domestic political demands that the United States not assume a disproportionate share of the costs of acting in the world when the interests of others are engaged alongside our own. The support of others for an intervention or policy can also help politically in other ways. The endorsement of a course of action by the United Nations (UN) or a relevant regional body can add an aura of legitimacy and, in the eyes of some, legality to an undertaking. This can have several advantages: generating domestic political support, bringing about the military and economic participation of others, and reducing resistance on the part of the target government or its backers.

Thus, despite its undeniable domestic political appeal, unilateralism is rarely a realistic foreign policy orientation for this country. Unilateralism is not a form of leadership—something that presumes the willing participation of others—but an alternative to it. As a result, the real choice facing this country in the foreseeable future is not between unilateralism and multilateralism, but between various forms of the latter.

Institutionalism

This approach actually covers a range of options. What they have in common is a commitment to building international bodies and arrangements with authority to meaningfully affect international relations in all spheres. Where such proposals or charters differ is in degree, that is, in the powers and capabilities that are either sought or accorded such institutions. Organizations can range from the relatively modest, promoting coordination where consensus exists, to the ambitious, acting even when some of its members do not concur.

An ambitious or expansive form of institutionalized multilateralism would go beyond the initial and apparently abandoned "assertive multilateralism" impulse of the Clinton administration. In the security realm, it would involve creating a standing force responsible to the UN Security Council and, in some circumstances, to the UN Secretary General. Such a force could in theory be dispatched quickly to help prevent conflicts or (under Chapter VII of the UN Charter) to enforce Security Council resolutions. An expanded multilateralism of this sort could also seek to establish machinery (a strengthened International Court of Justice, for example) for resolving political disputes between states that in some instances would constitute binding arbitration, not just mediation. Economically, this form of multilateralism would require not simply rules regulating trade, but mandatory dispute settlement mechanisms and strict monetary coordination. In the environmental area, one could imagine a body that would set standards for individual countries and companies to follow.

There are obvious difficulties with multilateralism of this sort. National sovereignty may be much battered but it is still alive and kicking. Few governments (notably our own) would be prepared to cede to some agency (run by international civil servants) the independence they enjoy in the political, economic, or military realms. Moreover, even if there were some desire to do so, it would be an enormous task to create the needed capacities to do the job. Just as important, effective institutionalism requires the existence of widespread agreement among the major powers over what needs to be done in the world. Such agreement—tantamount to a concert—does not exist now and is unlikely to for the foreseeable future. To delegate such power to international institutions in the absence of such a concert is to invite inaction and its consequences.

More realistic and considerably more desirable is a scaled-down version of such multilateralism, one that would still try to develop stronger and more independent international institutions, but with limited powers and for narrow purposes. Robert Keohane makes the case for this more modest form of multilateralism: "Institutions that facilitate cooperation do not mandate what governments can do; rather, they help governments pursue their own interests through cooperation.[8] Such institutionalism tends to be most appealing and practical in relatively "technical" endeavors.

Peacekeeping or purely humanitarian operations come to mind, as do international arrangements in such fields as transportation, communications, and both patent and copyright protection, where we want and benefit from a degree of regulation. It also applies to trade, where expanding the scope and coverage of the dispute-settlement mechanisms of the WTO would lubricate trade and help insulate bilateral relationships from inevitable disagreements. Similarly, environmental arrangements by which states voluntarily agree to abide by certain standards or limits (such as on emissions that cause global warming) have potential to be beneficial. The International Energy Agency provides a mechanism for sharing energy supplies during times of shortage. Yet another area of functioning institutionalism are so-called supplier groups, i.e., those coalitions of states that agree not to provide designated technologies or capabilities to selected states in order to slow their efforts to develop certain military capacities. The result is that institutionalism is a useful component of carrying out a foreign policy of regulation, one that can and should be expanded where necessary political consensus exists and where capabilities can be created or pooled.

Multilateral Leadership

There is another approach to multilateralism, one more informal in nature. It differs from both alliances and institutionalism in its shunning of standing, formal organizations and in its not requiring broad or complete consent. At its core is the idea of selected nation-states coalescing for narrow tasks or purposes—and in some cases disbanding once the specific aim is accomplished. Membership is made available to those able and willing to participate. As a result, this approach is sometimes referred to as "coalitions of the willing." Less formally it can be described as *foreign policy by posse.*

Examples of this approach are multiplying. The most famous case and in some ways the model for the idea were operations *Desert Shield* and *Desert Storm.* Ad hoc coalitions are also popping up in the economic sphere. The Mexican bailout is an interesting case in this regard. Viewing the potential failure of the Mexican economy as a major threat to U.S. and world economic health, and realizing that no existing institution or set of arrangements could provide the Mexican government the backing it required, the Clinton administration lashed together in early 1995 an ad hoc coalition that included (in addition to itself) the International Monetary Fund, the Bank for International Settlements, Canada, a consortium of Latin American governments, and private banks.

Diplomacy increasingly turns to informal coalitions. The management of the Middle East peace process since the October 1991 Madrid Conference is something coordinated by the United States (with Russia as nominal cosponsor) that involves not only the immediate protagonists but also Egypt, the Gulf states, the European Union, and others. Similarly, diplomacy toward Bosnia is informally coordinated by a Contact Group consisting of the United States, Russia, France, Great Britain, and Germany. Yet another informal coalition is the Korean Peninsula Energy Development Corporation, or KEDO. The United States is in charge, with the Republic of Korea and Japan in principal supporting roles. The purpose is to provide light water reactors and alternative energy (in this case, heavy fuel oil) to the North Koreans on terms they can afford in exchange for their foregoing a nuclear weapons option.

What these and similar efforts have in common is that they tend to be U.S.-led groups that come together for a limited set of tasks. They are voluntary as regards membership in general and involvement in particular actions. Their charter is their own. They are often for a limited span of time. They possess little or nothing in the way of headquarters or permanent staff although they often draw on existing alliances and international institutions. They are better understood as an activity than as an organization.

It is not difficult to imagine other applications. Bosnia is one. Some form of ad hoc coalition may well prove useful in the future to help preserve peace (if not justice) in that war-torn country. Taiwan is another possibility. If China threatened or used military force against Taiwan, the United States could not hope to get the UN Security Council to act, given China's veto. Instead, the United States would have to take the lead in fashioning a coalition that would work to convince China not to use force—and to come to Taiwan's assistance if it did.

Obviously, the informal coalition approach is not without significant drawbacks. By definition, such groups do not exist before the problem or crisis emerges. They therefore offer no deterrent effect—although, if formed quickly enough, they can still provide a preventive function. A lack of common equipment, military doctrine, and common experience are likely to limit effectiveness. So, too, will a lack of resources. It is difficult if not impossible to imagine additional bailouts on the scale of Mexico being arranged in an ad hoc fashion. Posses will often lack clear political or legal authority and a means of financing. The United States will more often than not have to act and provide the bulk of the impetus and resources. And, as is the case with any variant of multilateralism, informal coalitions constrain the behavior of their members.

There is also the concern that others will follow suit and that a world of multiple sheriffs and numerous posses will be inherently unstable and conflict-prone. Some analysts suggest that the corollary to such an argument is that the United States should be precluded from acting in this vein in the absence of a Security Council authorization. Otherwise, it is argued, American-led posses will be nothing more than self-appointed vigilantes. But such a requirement would effectively hand the other four members of the Council a veto over U.S. options. What counts most are the inherent purposes of any action and the steps undertaken toward those ends. The approval of the United Nations is not required to make an intervention or any foreign policy legitimate—any more than the lack of approval necessarily makes it illegitimate.

THE RELUCTANT SHERIFF

The United States has the potential capacity to create posses wherever and whenever it chooses. For this capacity to be real, however, the United States needs to ensure that it retains the ability to participate in a significant way. Just as important, the United States needs to continue to invest diplomatically in cultivating potential partners. Formal alliances may not be as central as they once were, but alignments and allies are. There is thus no substitute for regular and intimate consultations with other governments. The core justification for posses or coalitions of the willing—and one that outweighs the drawbacks—is that they constitute an approach to international engagement that reflects the basic personality and characteristics of the post–Cold War world.

This is a time in history when there are multiple great powers involved in relationships that resist clear definition and range from the cooperative to the competitive, as well as a growing number of small and medium-sized sovereign entities, proliferating regional and international bodies as well as nongovernmental organizations, an increasing diffusion of power in all its forms, and new sorts of problems (or old problems on a new scale) for which institutions do not yet exist or which they are not prepared to handle. What is needed as a result is an approach to foreign policy that is inherently flexible, one able to respond to unforeseen situations in unprecedented ways. Coalitions of the willing bring with them some of the advantages that derive from collective effort, without the need for consensus or prearranged authority. They also enjoy some measure of international legitimacy.

None of this is meant to exaggerate the strengths of posses. It is better understood as necessary rather than ideal. The goal of foreign policy ought to be to promote norms and build institutions and other arrangements wherever need, consensus, and capability exist. Fortunately, the posse approach can become more structured and institutionalized if warranted and possible.

Again, though, it is the absence of consensus on major issues—the absence of a concert of the great powers—that places limits on what can be expected from institutionalism and creates the need for posses. For now and for the immediate future, the real question hanging over the promise of posses is not so much their utility as it is the willingness and ability of the United States to saddle up and to lead. A posse without a strong sheriff is more likely to sit on its hands or get into trouble than to act and accomplish something of value. Strength, however, is a direct result of resources and will. The United States can only be an effective leader if it has the tools in hand and is prepared to wield them.

NOTES

1. Irving Kristol, "Defining our National Interest," *National Interest* 21 (Fall 1990), p. 23.

2. William Kristol and Robert Kagan, "Toward a Neo-Reaganite Foreign Policy," *Foreign Affairs* 75 (July/August 1996), p. 23.

3. Kenneth N. Waltz, "The Emerging Structure of International Politics," *International Security* 18 (Fall 1993), p. 66.

4. Ronald Steel, "Beware the Superpower Syndrome," *New York Times,* April 25, 1994, p. A15. See also Steel's *Temptations of a Superpower* (Cambridge, MA: Harvard University Press, 1995).

5. Alan Tonelson, "Clinton's World: The Realities of America's Post–Cold War Foreign Policy," in Eugene R. Wittkopf, ed., *The Future of American Foreign Policy,* 2nd ed. (New York: St. Martin's Press, 1994), p. 49.

6. Paul Kennedy, *The Rise and Fall of the Great Powers: Economic Change and Military Conflict from 1500 to 2000* (New York: Random House, 1987).

7. See Edward D. Mansfield and Jack Snyder, "Democratization and War," *Foreign Affairs* 74 (May/June, 1995), pp. 79–97; William R. Thompson, "Democracy and Peace: Putting the Cart Before the Horse?" *International Organization* 50 (Winter 1996), pp. 141–174; and Samuel P. Huntington, "Democracy for the Long Haul," *Journal of Democracy* 7 (April 1966), pp. 3–13.

8. Robert O. Keohane, *After Hegemony: Cooperation and Discord in the World Political Economy* (Princeton, NJ: Princeton University Press, 1984), p. 246.

2. DEMOCRATIC ENLARGEMENT: THE CLINTON DOCTRINE

Douglas Brinkley

*E*ver since *Foreign Affairs* published George Kennan's seminal article, "The Sources of Soviet Conduct," which outlined what was to become President Harry Truman's strategy of "containment," succeeding administrations have sought to coin a phrase that encapsulates their foreign and defense policies. From the Eisenhower-Dulles "New Look" to Bush-Baker's multinational "new world order," foreign policy monikers have been concocted for the purpose of convincing both America's overseas allies and its domestic electorate that the current administration, far from being caught in the shifting tides of ad hoc diplomacy, had a long-range grand plan. Thus it came as no surprise when on September 27, 1993, in a speech to the United Nations General Assembly, President Bill Clinton tried to elucidate his foreign policy agenda by offering up the concept of "democratic enlargement." . . .

[The president's speech followed on the heels of a speech by his national security adviser, Anthony Lake, in which Lake explained that]. . . the successor to containment "must be a strategy of enlargement . . . of the world's free community of market democracies." The blueprint focused on four points: (1) to "strengthen the community of market democracies"; (2) to "foster and consolidate new democracies and market economies where possible"; (3) to "counter the aggression and support the liberalization of states hostile to democracy"; and (4) to "help democracy and market economies take root in regions of greatest humanitarian concern."

Note: Notes have been deleted.

ENLARGEMENT IN ACTION

Clinton likened enlargement to the old anticommunist "domino theory" in reverse: It posited that where communist command economies collapsed, free markets would eventually arise and flourish. "Now the age of geopolitics has given way to an age of what might be called geo-economics," journalist Martin Walker wrote in the October 7, 1996, *New Yorker.* "The new virility symbols are exports and productivity and growth rates and the great international encounters are the trade pacts of the economic superpowers." Or, as Clinton himself put it in his 1994 budget message to Congress, "We have put our economic competitiveness at the heart of our foreign policy."

As for the emerging democracies, Clinton believed that if they developed consumer-oriented middle classes with the desired appetites for American products, peace and prosperity could become a reality. Relations with countries with bright economic futures such as Mexico and South Korea would thus be placed on the front burner in his administration; poor, blighted nations, particularly in sub-Saharan Africa and Central America, would receive back-burner attention, at best. Only when the international clamor for humanitarian aid rang too loudly to ignore would the administration focus on other nations. By the same token, the United States would no longer concern itself with the bloody, unprofitable civil and religious wars that raged from Angola to the Caucasus to Kashmir. Only when anarchy reigned in a major trade pact region—Bosnia or Northern Ireland, for example—would Clinton play global peacemaker. Likewise, the continuation of the Middle East peace process was considered to be important to the global economy.

Simply put, to the Clinton administration economic policy was the means to global leverage. "Information, ideas, and money now pulse across the planet at light speed," enthused [National Security Adviser Anthony] Lake. "This borderless global economy has generated an entrepreneurial boom and a demand for political openness." There were even trade pact precedents that fit nicely into enlargement's world view: the GATT Uruguay Round and NAFTA—two international economic regimes inherited from the Bush administration that required bipartisan congressional support for passage. These tied domestic growth to a foreign policy that promotes U.S. exports and global free trade. In fact, what Clinton liked best about [the] enlargement policy [his advisers recommended] was the way it was inextricably linked to domestic renewal, with its emphasis on making sure the United States remained the world's largest exporter. The area of greatest export expansion has been services, with the U.S. trade surplus in that sector rising from $5 billion in 1986 to $58 billion in 1992. By the time Clinton began his second term, exports of services exceeded imports by $80 billion. Unlike many of his critics, Clinton was quick to understand that in the post–Cold War era good trade policy was the sine qua non of sound foreign policy, as the presence of market-based democracies plausibly would render the world a safer, richer place. If the Cold War enemy was communism, the post–Cold War villain was protectionism.

Clinton's NSC [National Security Council] staff accepted that enlargement would have to begin with nations that were well on the way to becoming open-market democracies: the countries of Central and Eastern Europe and the Asia-Pacific region. Rogue or terrorist regimes—like Iran or Iraq—would be dealt with firmly if they tried to undermine the new order. The vision of democratic enlargement was econocentric: only countries with free-spending middle classes, it was believed, could become democratic and adopt the Western values of embracing ethnic diversity, protecting citizens' rights, and cooperating with the world community to stop terrorism. . . .

Unfortunately for the administration, "enlargement" proved to be a public relations dud; few liked it or even took a passing interest. . . . While some [critics] allowed that enlargement could make for an interesting white paper, most of the priests of geopolitics complained that this policy had no connection to reality and that it was an aspiration rather than a strategy. That charge was difficult to refute after October 3, 1993, when 18 U.S. Army soldiers were killed in an ill-planned operation in Mogadishu. It was even more difficult to refute after October 12, when anti-American demonstrations broke out in Haiti following the president's decision to recall a U.S. Navy ship carrying American and Canadian military personnel en route to Port-au-Prince in response to the junta there. . . .

What the administration's critics failed to see was that the events in both Somalia and Haiti were holdovers from President Bush's multinational "new world order." The Clinton administration's enlargement strategy suggested that both Somalia and Haiti—because they were incapable of developing middle class consumer markets in the foreseeable future—should be on the periphery of U.S. foreign policy interests. There were to be no more blind humanitarian interventions under the Clinton administration, and the likes of Haiti would be handled not in terms of U.S. national security, economic policy, or humanitarian aid, but mostly in response to domestic pressures. In 1994, for example, it was relentless pressure from the Cuban-American community in Florida and the Congressional Black Caucus that persuaded Clinton to intervene in Haiti, forcing the junta's ouster.

In July 1994, Clinton tried to weave the enlargement theme into the so-called En-En document: the National Security Strategy of Engagement and Enlargement. At the center of that policy paper is the belief that "the line between our domestic and foreign policies has increasingly disappeared—that we must revitalize our economy if we are to sustain our military forces, foreign initiatives, and global influence, and that we must engage actively abroad if we are to open foreign markets and create jobs for our people." When two subsequent En-En policy papers were released by the White House—in February 1995 and February 1996—domestic renewal was portrayed as the linchpin of U.S. foreign policy.

Perhaps the most ardent booster of enlargement within the administration, after Lake, was [Vice President Al] Gore. Convinced that trade pacts like NAFTA and GATT were bridges of economic prosperity into the next millennium, Gore became the poster child for free trade. Imbued with a low-tariff, reciprocal trade outlook long popular in the South, Gore took his internationalist lead from fellow Tennesseean Cordell Hull, who served as Franklin Roosevelt's secretary of state from 1933 to 1944 and engineered the Reciprocal Trade Agreements Act of 1934. As a senator, Gore had not only found federal funds to save the Hull cabin birthplace in Pickett County, Tennessee, but in White House foreign policy meetings the vice president had sometimes invoked the former secretary's "Trade for Peace" belief that global economic instability could be curtailed through trade agreements that check counterproductive nationalistic competition. Like Hull in the 1930s, Gore insisted that it was essential for America's economic well-being that open-market democracies flourish worldwide.

Another important example of how [the] enlargement concept took hold can be seen in then U.S. ambassador to the U.N. Madeleine Albright's abrupt conversion from a multinational moralist worried about genocidal wars to a realpolitik maverick who, with Senator Jesse Helms (R–North Carolina) cheering her on, became an archcritic of the U.N. Most commentators attributed Albright's turnabout to the Republican takeover of Congress in 1994. There, conservatives were all too happy to scapegoat the U.N. for any number of global woes, from Bosnia to Somalia. Instead of challenging the Republicans' anti–U.N. premise, Albright essentially joined their ad hominem chorus, denouncing U.N. Secretary-General Boutros-Boutros Ghali and his slow pace of reform.

But electoral politics played only a partial role in her change of heart. The White House made it clear that the enlargement doctrine was official policy. U.N. peacekeeping, which flourished under Bush, was in disrepute, and under the strategy of enlargement it will continue to be eclipsed, even with Ghana's pro-American Kofi Annan serving as the new secretary-general. "We live in an era without power blocs in which old assumptions must be reexamined, institutions modernized and relationships transformed," Albright, now the secretary of state, noted in December 1996. The new blocs are an enlarged NATO and America's trade alliances, with the United States serving as locomotive for them all. . . .

[The NATO enlargement] priority first emerged at the January 1994 NATO summit in Brussels. . . . Clinton called on the NATO allies to "enlarge" the transatlantic military alliance to include the new free market democracies of Central and Eastern Europe, with most foreign policy experts believing that this meant the Czech Republic, Hungary, and Poland (the Visegrad states). Encouraged by the United States's bold lead, the heads of the NATO countries agreed in principle to a process of enlargement that "would reach to democratic states to our East as part of an evolutionary process, taking into account political and security developments in the whole of Europe." Clinton also led the way in creating the alliance's Partnership for Peace (PFP) in 1994, an agreement among NATO's current members intended to facilitate an orderly process of enlargement that will admit new members while modernizing the organization. "Partnership will serve one of the most important goals in our enlargement strategy . . . building a stable environment in which the new democracies and free markets of Eastern and Central Europe and the former USSR can flourish," Lake said. . . .

FREE TRADE AT THE CORE

A *New York Times*/CBS News opinion poll taken in September 1996 found that Clinton's foreign policy approval rating was a solid 53 percent. The *New York Times'* R. W. Apple, Jr., concluded that Clinton had "escaped any significant damage from crises overseas." Apple also suggested that the polls showed how little foreign policy had to do with Clinton's odds of reelection; again, it was "the economy, stupid." What Apple failed to take into account was that Clinton viewed domestic renewal as partially dependent upon foreign trade policy: From 1993 to 1996, more than 200 new market-opening agreements helped to create 1.6 million American jobs, [Secretary of State Warren] Christopher proudly noted in a farewell address at Harvard University. During Clinton's first administration, the dollar grew stronger largely due to a combination of trade and fiscal policy, and from there it is not hard to understand one major reason why Michigan and Ohio voted for Clinton: Automobile exports increased dramatically during his first term. All over the world the United States was negotiating trade pacts. If John Foster Dulles had been accused of "pactomania" for engineering so many security treaties, Clinton was practicing pactomania for free trade.

With the possible exception of splitting his own party in Congress to push through NAFTA and GATT, nowhere has Clinton executed his enlargement strategy of free trade so boldly as in the Asia-Pacific region. In office only one year, Clinton decided to convene the 15 heads of state of the Pacific region at an APEC conference in Seattle to galvanize the creation of a giant free trade zone. A year later, in Jakarta, at the second APEC conference, its members signed an accord pledging to develop a free-trading Pacific Rim by 2010.

After trade talks between Tokyo and Washington collapsed in February 1994, Clinton decided the time for toughness had come. The administration's subsequent moves were unprecedented in postwar U.S.–Japanese relations. U.S. trade representative Mickey Kantor threatened Tokyo with trade sanctions for violating a 1989 agreement to open its market to American cellular phones. "America for 10 years tried 30 different trade agreements," Clinton announced, "and nothing ever happened. . . . The trade deficit just got bigger and bigger. So we're going to try to pursue a more aggressive policy now which will actually open markets." Over the ensuing years, the threat worked well—as several of Japan's key markets were pried open.

Ignoring trade policy in the recent campaign, Republicans contended that Clinton's foreign policy was weak and visionless. "My biggest criticism is that this administration lacks a conceptual framework to shape the world going into the next century and [to] explain what threatens that vision," Senator John McCain of Arizona, a Dole adviser, complained. "Without that global strategy, we keep getting ourselves involved in peripheral matters such as Northern Ireland and Haiti."

What McCain failed to realize was that both Northern Ireland and Haiti *were* on the periphery of the Clinton administration's foreign policy agenda . . . , despite all the media attention they had attracted. On the Democratic side, pro–U.N. forces berated Clinton for refusing to pay America's bills to the organization and for scapegoating Boutros-Ghali over Somalia and Bosnia. Ignoring enlargement, McCain and other critics dismissed Clinton as an amateur juggler in the realm of foreign policy. They were half right. Clinton, after a rough beginning, slowly overcame his proclivity for procrastination and developed into an able practitioner of Band-Aid diplomacy. By 1995, he demonstrated the flexibility and decisiveness necessary to deal adroitly with such trouble spots as Bosnia, Haiti, North Korea, the Persian Gulf, and the Taiwan Strait. "U.S. foreign policy has been increasingly successful precisely because Bill Clinton has refused to embrace chimerical visions," Jacob Heilbrunn observed in the November 11, 1996, *New Republic.* "As a result, he has skillfully piloted the United States through a sea of new world disorder."

Regardless of how well Clinton maneuvers through crises, free trade remains the heart of enlargement and the core of his foreign policy—not that Clinton was the first postwar American leader to lead the way in the establishment of free trade zones. A number of presidents, from Truman to Richard Nixon—all devoted to the vision of Jean Monnet—pushed for Atlantic community trade agreements that eventually led to the Kennedy Round, where the GATT was jump-started. When Clinton went to Madrid in December 1995 to launch a new transatlantic agenda with EU leaders, he was giving credence to a half-century of noble attempts to integrate North America and Western Europe economically. Nor should it be forgotten that Reagan was chiefly responsible for engineering the free trade pact with Canada and that Bush brought Mexico into the NAFTA framework. But it was Clinton who advanced the view that democracy would prevail in the post–Cold War world through trade pacts as much as ballot boxes.

Put another way, enlargement was about spreading democracy through promoting the gospel of geoeconomics. "The elegance of the Clinton strategy was that the Pacific, the European, and Western Hemisphere blocs should all have one thing in common; Clinton's America was locking itself steadily into the heart of each one," Martin Walker has observed. Some critics prefer a more militarily activist approach, even a new sort of gunboat diplomacy, but Clinton favors enlargement, he is more interested in helping Toys "R" Us and Nike to flourish in Central Europe and Asia than in dispatching Marines to quell unrest in economically inconsequential nations. "With our help, the forces of reform in Europe's newly free nations have laid the foundations of democracy," Clinton boasted at an October 1996 campaign rally in Detroit. "We've helped them to develop successful market economies, and now are moving from aid to trade and investment." The *New York Times*' Thomas Friedman identified one key tenet of Clinton's enlargement strategy in a

December 8, 1996, column titled "Big Mac I": "No two countries that both have a McDonald's have ever fought a war against each other."

But many emerging democracies would have preferred U.S. dollars to "deterrent" hamburgers—Russia in particular. The U.S. budget deficit [prevented] Clinton from devising some sort of grandiose Marshall Plan for Russia, but his administration [came] up with $43 billion in bilateral assistance for Yeltsin's government since 1993. This aid in the name of enlargement . . . helped to facilitate economic reform in Russia by curbing inflation and stabilizing the ruble—with the net result being that more than 60 percent of Russia's gross domestic product is now generated by its private sector. In fact, the Clinton administration's assistance . . . helped Russia to privatize more property in less time than any other foreign-development venture in history. . . .

Meanwhile, again thanks to enlargement, the United States became Russia's largest foreign investor, with the U.S. Export-Import Bank, the Overseas Private Investment Corporation, and the Trade and Development Agency supporting commercial transactions with Moscow valued at more than $4 billion. This expansion of the global free market, coupled with Russia's 1995 parliamentary elections and 1996 presidential contest, indicates that democracy may finally be taking root there. With Russia becoming more stabilized economically and politically—and with U.S.–Russian relations "normalized" for the first time since the First World War—the Clinton administration is eager to push the enlargement of NATO.

Far into the next century, various trade agreements—APEC, the Free Trade Agreement of the Americas, GATT, NAFTA, the Trans Atlantic Free Trade Area, and the World Trade Organization—will advance Washington's global agenda while promoting American domestic renewal. Critics like former Secretary of State Lawrence Eagleburger—who complains about a lack of "hard strategic thinking about how we want to see the world in the first part of the next century"—fail to recognize that Clinton's enlargement policy [has] already [catapulted] America into the next millennium, even if the word "enlargement" itself has been largely ignored. . . . Democratic enlargement, a concept drawn from geoeconomics, . . . could well be remembered by future historians as the Clinton Doctrine.

3. COME HOME, AMERICA: THE STRATEGY OF RESTRAINT IN THE FACE OF TEMPTATION

Eugene Gholz, Daryl G. Press, and
Harvey M. Sapolsky

*T*he Cold War lasted so long and grew to be such a comfortable part of everyday life that it is now very difficult to chart a new foreign policy course for the nation. U.S. national strategy is a confusing mix of grand rhetoric, false starts, and well-advised caution. U.S. troops remain forward deployed, but in smaller numbers than they were during the Cold War. The United States intervenes often in the conflicts of others, but without a consistent rationale, without a clear sense of how to advance U.S. interests, and sometimes with unintended and expensive consequences. It is time to choose a new course. Here we advocate a foreign policy of restraint—the disengagement of America's military forces from the rest of the world. Restraint is a modern form of isolationism: we adopt its military policy of withdrawal, but reject its traditional economic protectionism.

The Cold War was worth fighting and winning. Soviet expansionism threatened vital U.S. interests; it seemed ready to swallow America's allies in Europe and Asia, who were exhausted by World War II and racked by national self-doubt. After victory over the monumental insanity of Nazism and Japanese militarism, the United States sought the prosperity interrupted by depression and a long war. But full enjoyment of its national wealth was postponed by the need to ward off the Soviet Union.

Despite the collapse of the Soviet threat, American interests have not changed. The United States still seeks peace and prosperity. But now this preferred state is best obtained by restraining America's great power, a power unmatched by any rival and unchallenged in any important dimension.

Note: Notes have been deleted.

Rather than lead a new crusade, America should absorb itself in the somewhat delayed task of addressing imperfections in its own society.

The restraint we propose should not be misdescribed as a total withdrawal from the world. On the contrary, we believe in a vigorous trade with other nations and the thriving commerce of ideas. Military restraint need not, and will not, bring economic protectionism.

In fact, restraint does not even require unconditional military isolation. Terrorism should still elicit a strong response, and if America's vital interests are challenged, there should be hell to pay. We advocate a strong military, just not a large or busy one. Isolationism in the 1920s was inappropriate, because conquest on a continental scale was then possible. Now, nuclear weapons assure great power sovereignty—and certainly America's defense.

Americans want to enjoy the freedom and opportunity that their forefathers sought and for which many of them fought and died. They can achieve this, if only they restrain the urge to claim interconnectivity in all human conflict. U.S. power may be massive, but it is still limited. To quote a famous, although premature, expression of the policy we advocate: it is time to come home, America. Now that the Cold War is over, George McGovern is right. . . . The highest priorities of American foreign policy are to protect U.S. national security and to promote America's prosperity. A policy of restraint is the best way to satisfy these objectives. . . . Restraint is not a universally good policy; in fact it has not been an appropriate American strategy until now. It is, however, America's best option today because of the paucity of international threats. . . .

THE CORE ARGUMENT FOR RESTRAINT

To develop the case for a new American foreign policy, we begin with a discussion of America's foreign policy goals. Those national interests are then considered in light of the post–Cold War security environment.

Matching Military Means to Foreign Policy Ends

America has many foreign policy goals and two tools with which to achieve them: economic and military power. Some goals are well suited to military means, but for others, military force will be ineffective, too costly, or even counterproductive. In this chapter we ask, "when should the United States use, or threaten to use, *military* power to secure its national interests?" This analysis finds that America is in an extremely rare historical position. The United States can achieve its most critical goals without sending its children to fight and without spending great amounts of national wealth on defense.

Most Americans share a global vision in which America has many national interests: ensuring U.S. physical security, facilitating American prosperity, protecting human rights, spreading democracy and market-based economic systems, ending the drug trade, safeguarding the environment, etc. Americans assign various priorities to these interests, but two of them stand out—security and prosperity. Advocates of policies to address the other interests on the list, e.g., protecting the environment, routinely couch their appeals in terms of national security to make their concerns seem urgent to a wider audience. Ultimately, however, the environment is important because Americans value the environment. Deforestation in South America may make the world less pleasant for everyone, and policy should address that problem, but deforestation would not undermine America's national security. Once we separate America's goals into distinct categories (e.g., security, prosperity, democracy abroad, environmental management), we can assess the critical issue: which of these national goals should be pursued with military power?

Of America's goals, the highest priority is the physical security of the United States—the protection of territory and the ability to make domestic political decisions as free as possible from foreign coercion. The great news is that America faces almost no discernible security threats. To the north and south are weak, friendly neighbors; to the east and west are fish. Nobody can cross the oceans to threaten America at home.

The United States towers over other nations in terms of its current and potential military power. Its defense budget, measuring more than a quarter of a trillion dollars, accounts for about 35 percent of the world's total annual military expenditures. . . . The United States not only leads the pack but outdistances its closest rival by more than a factor of three. . . .

The result of America's profligate defense spending is that the United States has by far the largest and most capable of the world's air forces and navies; an army that can defeat any other; and a marine corps that has personnel and equipment comparable to the entire armed forces of the United Kingdom, one of America's leading "competitors." The United States can project and sustain military strength further and longer than anyone else.

In the past, the United States feared that a hostile adversary might unite the rest of the world's industrial capacity through conquest, generating enough military and economic power to threaten U.S. security. But unlike the situation during the Cold War, no hostile country now has a chance of conquering Europe or East Asia. Each of the Eurasian great powers (with the exception of Russia) spends about the same amount on its military as the others, which suggests that none could easily overpower the rest. There is a rough balance of power on the continent. Furthermore, France, the United Kingdom, Russia, and China all have nuclear weapons, which provide the ultimate guarantee against conquest. Great power conflict may continue, but Eurasia's industrial resources will stay divided. America's primary national interest, physical security, does not demand much in the way of defense spending or overseas deployment.

The second most fundamental American interest is continued prosperity. Prosperity is both a "means" and an "end." As a means, economic strength is the foundation for long-term security, because wealth can be converted into military power; as an end, prosperity provides a high standard of living. Fortunately, America's prosperity is almost as insulated from hostile foreign actions as its security is. The bulk of America's economic interactions with the world are decentralized, market-based trade and investment decisions that are affected only indirectly by government policy. The exception would be a scenario in which a hostile country in the Persian Gulf gained leverage to hurt America's economy by consolidating the world's major oil reserves. The small populations of the oil-rich Gulf states do not suggest a natural balance of power, and none of the oil-rich states is shielded by nuclear weapons. Consequently, the United States should maintain sufficient military forces in the region to prevent regional conquest.

But the oil scenario aside, other countries have little power over the U.S. economy. Even Japan, America's biggest creditor, would have difficulty exercising leverage against American prosperity. Sophisticated international capital markets adjust rapidly to changes in supply and demand. If Japanese lenders shifted their money to other borrowers, alternate sources would emerge to satisfy American demand, and the equilibrium world interest rate would not be changed much. The American cost of capital, specifically including the rate of interest on the national debt, would not increase, and American prosperity would not be harmed.

The key to America's economic future lies in maintaining a well-educated workforce and addressing its problems at home, not in stationing troops overseas. America's prospects are quite bright. The greatest foreign policy threat to U.S. prosperity is that America will spend too much on the military.

Unlike security and prosperity, however, America's other foreign policy goals are unlikely to be achieved effortlessly. The questions to address are whether military force is the best means to pursue these goals and whether the costs of these operations are justified by the likely results. We conclude that the answer to each question is "no." First, military organizations are not well suited to spreading democracy, protecting human rights, or stemming drug abuse in America. Militaries' hierarchical design and sophisticated command and control capabilities make them extremely capable in response to intense, short-term problems such as those found on the battlefield. But spreading values, monitoring human rights, or reducing drug abuse require different types of skills than militaries supply. . . .

Second, the costs of campaigning for democracy or human rights with military force would be staggering. These missions could require tens of billions of dollars each year just to outfit enough troops, in addition to significant financial costs and casualties every time America deployed. Using the military to spread democratic values would likely be costly and bloody and could endanger America's paramount concerns: the physical security and economic strength of the nation.

For the first time in five decades, America's core national interests are easily within reach. Small wars will likely continue to be frequent, but those wars cannot spread easily to U.S. shores, and their results will not shift the global power balance. Similarly, military threats to America's prosperity are quite low. In fact, the only way the United States could jeopardize its favorable position is to meddle in other nations' affairs, join their wars, and overspend on defense.

Balancing Security and Prosperity

The United States is a very wealthy country and . . . America's high per capita gross domestic product (GDP) allows the United States to spend more on defense than its competitors. The right question to ask, however, is, what are Americans getting for that extra investment? The money spent on defense could be used for education, entitlements, private consumption (through tax reductions), or other opportunities. Even during the Cold War, defense spending was constrained by the high value Americans place on freedom from too onerous a military burden. America's interest in prosperity commands attention to "right-sizing" the defense budget.

The marginal increment of security that the United States gains from high levels of defense spending is vanishingly small. Security, like most investments, is subject to diminishing returns, even for a country that has as much comparative advantage in defense production as the United States. Capitalizing on the learning effects of the Cold War, the advantages of scale economies, America's wonderful natural resource endowments, and important geographic advantages, the United States is far more capable than any of its competitors of squeezing security from a marginal defense dollar. But once Americans are already quite secure, there is a tremendous cost to incremental additions to their safety.

The rate at which cost and security trade off depends on the technologies available to the offense and the defense, on the geographic relationship between a country and its adversaries, on the type of terrain on which battles might be fought, and on the opportunity cost of devoting resources to defense that could otherwise be employed productively in other ways. The absolute level of security that is purchased for each dollar of investment in the defense budget, however, is largely dependent on the harshness of the threat environment: facing many severe threats, a small defense budget will not buy much security; that same expenditure will buy a great deal of security if most other countries are weak or are supporters of the territorial status quo.

Given its geographical advantages and nuclear arsenal, the United States would be very secure even if Japan, China, and Russia matched its defense expenditures. The fact is that, since the collapse of the Soviet Union, no one else comes close. It is not at all clear what, if anything, Americans are getting for their extra defense dollars. The United States can spend much less than it does today and still be much more secure than it was during the Cold War. . . .

Advocates of a larger defense budget often point out that America's defense spending as a share of GDP has dropped to pre–Cold War levels, largely because of the steady growth of the U.S. economy. This statistic indicates a reduction in the defense budget's drain on the economy, but the fact remains that America is buying as much military capability as it bought during typical Cold War years. Unless this military capability is needed, America is wasting valuable resources. . . .

Advocates of continued military activism argue that their policy is a form of insurance. Insurance is intended to mitigate the costs of unlikely events, but military engagement abroad accomplishes the reverse: it magnifies the costs and risks of faraway wars by involving Americans directly in them. Its hefty premiums sap U.S. prosperity.

The Foundations of Restraint

The case for restraint rests on three theoretical foundations. First, the offense-defense balance influences both the likelihood of war and the mechanisms by which wars start. War begins either when status quo powers fail to deter aggressor states (the "deterrence model") or when a status quo state's defense policies undermine the security of one of its status quo neighbors, precipitating an action-reaction cycle (the "spiral model"). Second, when faced with external threats to their security, states tend to balance against the emerging threat, either internally by converting latent military power into deployed forces, or externally by searching for allies. As threats become more intense, governments think more seriously about their security and are more likely to use "realist" analysis in designing their defense policy.

Third, nuclear weapons do not make war obsolete, but they make it impossible to conquer a nuclear-armed adversary. Because nuclear weapons explode with far more destructive force than conventional munitions, a devastating strike can be delivered with a handful of ballistic missiles or other delivery vehicles not subject to interception. Even the loser of a war—a country that has completely lost control of its airspace, sea lanes, and strategic, elevated territory—can now fire off a last-ditch punitive strike, devastating the "winner." No conquest would justify the costs of a large nuclear exchange, so no aggressor can conquer a nuclear-armed great power. Wars may still happen; risk-tolerant leaders might still engage in limited wars against nuclear powers. But because of the risk of nuclear escalation, even conventional battles between nuclear powers should be rare. The bottom line on nuclear weapons is that they make the conquest of great powers unthinkable.

Is Restraint a Break from the Past?

The policy of restraint advocated here means specifically two things: a significant reduction in the number of active-duty forces and a significant reduction in America's overseas military presence. Spending $120 billion a year, the United States would still spend more than the second biggest military power, even if that power's budget were to increase in response to America's retrenchment. A $120 billion budget would buy the capability to deal with one major regional contingency (MRC)—needed to respond to, e.g., a Persian Gulf oil grab.

Proposing to cut the defense budget by 50 percent and to withdraw from long-standing alliances in Europe and Asia may seem radical, but restraint would bring more continuity than change. During the Cold War the United States sought to ensure its security and prosperity by maintaining the division of Eurasia's industrial might, preserving freedom of the seas, and, since at least the 1970s, preventing the consolidation of Persian Gulf oil. These goals should still be the guiding principles of U.S. foreign policy today and into the future, and a strategy of restraint is explicitly designed to achieve them. Advocates of continued American engagement, however, have created new, revolutionary principles to guide U.S. foreign policy. They propose to take on new overseas tasks like ensuring global "stability." Restraint is the best strategy for achieving America's traditional national interests; it is not a "break from the past" but a continuation of classical goals in a new strategic setting.

Other Benefits of Restraint

Military restraint has other benefits. First, and perhaps most important, an American withdrawal would force U.S. allies to accept political responsibility for managing their own affairs. Starting in the early days of the Cold War, the United States discouraged initiative on the part of its allies. The British and French concentrated on their economic recovery; America promised to defend them until they got back on their feet. The vanquished World War II enemies were held back for a different reason: they were on probation. But now, fifty years later, America's allies still depend on the United States to solve problems they could tackle themselves. They lack the incentive to act responsibly.

America's NATO allies are among the most powerful countries in the world. But not only did they fail to stop the war in Yugoslavia, they dithered for four years, not even deciding whether to try. President Bill Clinton sent U.S. troops to Bosnia as the next step in the history of America's twentieth-century leadership, but why do 300 million wealthy West Europeans need the United States to shake them into action? When will they take these responsibilities upon themselves? America's willingness to provide assistance surely dampens any leadership urges among U.S. allies. . . .

It may be that America's allies, left to their own devices, will not choose policies that would have been preferred by an engaged United States. Accepting that reality is the key to the strategy of restraint; the United States need not manage every crisis in the world. America's preferences should not dictate its allies' affairs. As long as no outcome can threaten the core American interests of security and prosperity, the United States can afford to accept the solutions of powers whose interests are directly engaged.

A second subsidiary benefit to restraint comes on the economic front. For fifty years, America encouraged its allies to concentrate on economic development while it carried most of the defense burden. Today, the United States subsidizes Japan's defense, which allows Japanese industry to compete "unfairly": Japanese firms pay lower taxes than they otherwise would. The Cold War did not bankrupt America, but it did have economic and social costs. The allies, now in the same economic league as America, should discover the full cost of their defense while the United States turns to long-avoided problems with its infrastructure, education system, budget deficit, and race relations.

IMPLEMENTING A POLICY OF RESTRAINT

Shifting to a restrained military policy will require major changes to America's alliance commitments, regional crisis planning, and force structure. This section reviews the steps required to withdraw from strategic commitments. . . .

Pulling Out of Europe

Since the collapse of the Berlin Wall, the United States has expanded its security commitments, sending troops into the Balkans and pledging to admit Eastern Europe's newly democratized countries into NATO. NATO has been trying to make it appear that its European members are now less dependent on America, but its reforms have not changed America's role as the heavyweight military backstop to the alliance. Due to America's near monopoly in logistics and mobility resources, the United States will be centrally involved in any future NATO operation.

To implement a policy of restraint, the United States should reverse course on NATO policy. The threat that NATO was created to deter disappeared when the Soviet Union collapsed. Consequently, NATO should be dismantled. In an orderly fashion, America should withdraw the 100,000 soldiers currently stationed in Europe, demobilize most of them, and bring home the equipment currently strewn around Europe; . . . this would be a clear signal that America would not return U.S. forces to the continent at the drop of a hat. It would take time, perhaps a year or two, for the U.S. military to pack up its units and for America's allies to acquire equipment to replace that currently provided by the United States. If the allies decide to purchase new equipment, America should eagerly sell it to them; if they insist on supporting their own domestic defense industries, America should license its designs to get their production capability up to speed. In the interim, the United States should honor its commitments to provide the conventional capabilities that the European powers lack. The key to the transition to a restrained national security policy is quick reduction of the exposure of American forces to overseas conflicts without opening "windows of vulnerability" for current allies.

NATO's European members are wealthy, and they will be able to provide for their own conventional defense without American help. In an extreme scenario, if Russia were to elect a hyper-nationalist leader, he could not magically restore the power of the Warsaw Pact. Germany's economy is nearly twice the size of Russia's. Even if Russia's GDP were to double in the next ten years, Germany *alone* should be able to match Russian military spending. Furthermore, unified Germany's eastern border is far shorter than the Inter-German Border that NATO patrolled during the Cold War. It is hard to believe that prosperous, technologically sophisticated Germany—let alone the combined European force that would likely evolve if there were a serious threat of Russian hegemony—would be unable to stop a resurgent Russian invasion.

Potentially the most complicated transition issue resulting from America's withdrawal from NATO would be the closure of America's nuclear umbrella over Germany. The other major European powers—France, the United Kingdom, and Russia—have their own nuclear arsenals, but Germany would be left exposed by an American withdrawal. For many years Germany has had the capability to build nuclear weapons almost instantly, but has chosen not to, because the United States provided nuclear cover; if America were to withdraw, Germany would be unlikely to deny itself the protection that nuclear weapons afford.

The primary danger associated with German nuclear proliferation is transition instability. Russia or another current nuclear power might have an interest in preventive war or at least in applying nuclear coercion to keep Germany nonnuclear. Facing such a threat, the most dangerous time for Germany to go nuclear would be during a crisis, but that is a danger that the United States can address directly by helping Germany develop a secure nuclear deterrent now, in a time of relatively low tension. If the United States maintains its current nuclear guarantee during the German weaponization program, Germany can develop nuclear weapons without opening a window of vulnerability.

Military Withdrawal from Asia

American foreign policy in Asia, too, has been captured by Cold War alliances, although in this region the formal institutions are less developed than the European NATO structure. The United States has already pulled out of its largest overseas bases, the facilities at Clark Air Force Base and Subic Bay Naval Base in the Philippines, but has reinvigorated the Japan–U.S. Security Treaty and reaffirmed the "tripwire" deployment in Korea. . . . This forward presence in Asia has lost its Cold War security rationale, exposes American soldiers to risk, costs Americans money, and artificially reduces the defense burden on America's leading economic competitors, helping them compete against U.S. companies.

As in Europe, the United States currently has about 100,000 military personnel stationed in Asia, all of whom should be brought home and demobilized. The United States should end its commitments to Japan and South Korea, cease military cooperation with the Association of Southeast Asian Nations (ASEAN), withdraw from the Australia, New Zealand, United States Pact (ANZUS), and terminate the implicit guarantee to Taiwan, giving those nations new incentives to take care of themselves.

No Asian ally of the United States faces an overwhelming conventional threat. It requires astounding assumptions about the relative fighting strength of North and South Korean soldiers to develop a military balance requirement for U.S. troops on the Korean peninsula. South Korea may want to improve its defenses further to replace capabilities that the United States is expected to supply—e.g., build a larger air force—but it is difficult to understand how a country with twice the population and twenty times the economic power of its primary competitor, not to mention a substantial technological lead, cannot find the resources to defend itself.

Current U.S. strategy implicitly assumes that America must remain engaged because of the Asian countries' failure to balance against Chinese strength. But Japan and Taiwan, the two plausible targets for Chinese aggression, are more than capable of defending themselves from conventional attack. Both enjoy the geographic advantage of being islands. The surrounding oceans ensure a defense dominance that could only be overcome with enormous material or technological advantages. . . .

. . . Some Asian powers might feel pressure at the nuclear level from an American withdrawal. Japan and South Korea currently enjoy the security of the American nuclear umbrella, and some of their neighbors, with whom they share a history of conflict, already have nuclear arsenals. It would not be surprising if South Korea and Japan wished to replace the American nuclear commitment with their own deterrent forces. . . . Fortunately, if they do decide to develop nuclear weapons, Japan and South Korea are good candidates for safe proliferation. Both countries have the military power to protect their nuclear forces from conventional attack, mitigating fears of inadvertent escalation, and both possess the technological prowess to develop secure, second-strike arsenals. The only proliferation danger lies in transition. The United States, therefore, should maintain its current nuclear commitments while it pulls out of Asia. During that time America should offer assistance on nuclear technology issues to the South Koreans and Japanese if they decide to pursue their own deterrent forces.

Taiwan is a less likely candidate for nuclear proliferation. America's withdrawal from Asia would not deprive Taiwan of an American nuclear commitment, because Taiwan never had one. Even with the United States engaged in Asia, Taiwan is vulnerable to a nuclear first strike from China; restraint will do nothing to change this. Taiwan seems to have concluded that the risks of a Chinese nuclear strike do not require a nuclear deterrent. Many analysts have long doubted the utility of nuclear weapons in civil wars, and if China really believes it "owns" Taiwan, then a nuclear attack would be like an attack on itself. The bottom line for American defense policy is that, while the issue of Taiwan's nuclear vulnerability is tricky, America's current military posture in Asia does little to relieve any nuclear tension there. With or without American power in the region, Taiwan will do what it has to do to defend itself.

The final issue to be considered regarding America's withdrawal from Asia is the possibility of economic retaliation by U.S. allies. Japan might retaliate for an American withdrawal from the U.S.–Japan Security Treaty by escalating its export competition with American industry or by raising the interest rates at which it is willing to loan money to the United States. Although neither of these alternatives would threaten American security, both could attack the other core American goal: prosperity.

These concerns are unfounded. <u>First, a significant fraction of Japanese politicians favor a transition to a</u> "normal" international role, including expanded attention to self-defense. . . .

<u>Second, the Japanese have few levers to inflict</u> additional economic pain on America. In the trade case, it is hard to imagine how the Japanese could compete more intensively than they already do or how they could more decisively stonewall American market-opening initiatives. In fact, one of the benefits of a policy of restraint might come in the realm of international trade, if the reduction in American resources spent on the military resulted in better American industrial competitiveness, or if the reduction in U.S. defense spending led to a higher domestic savings rate. Restraint could promote a macroeconomic environment better suited to reducing America's trade deficit. . . .

For many years now America's allies in Asia have been getting a cheap ride in the security realm. In the past, facing the Soviet threat, the United States had good reason to provide the public good of Pacific defense; now, however, America's allies are wealthy and its interests are less threatened, so the United States should come home. . . . The U.S. government is not in the business of providing for Japanese security and prosperity; instead, America's core foreign policy interests are its own security and prosperity, which can best be served in the Pacific by a policy of restraint.

A Limited Pullback from the Middle East

The strategic environment in the Middle East is significantly different than in either Asia or Europe. America's allies elsewhere are more than capable of defending themselves, guaranteeing the continued division of global industrial might. But many countries in the Middle East, particularly in the Persian Gulf, are incapable of developing a robust defense capability. Without American military power to defend them, a regional aggressor could consolidate Persian Gulf oil, threatening one of America's core interests, prosperity. The strategic realities of the Middle East, therefore, require a different policy than is appropriate for Asia or Europe. The United States should maintain sufficient forces in the Persian Gulf to prevent any country from monopolizing control over significant amounts of the region's oil.

Several thousand American soldiers are stationed in Saudi Arabia and Kuwait. An additional 3,000 Marines and 1,300 Air Force personnel have been stationed in Jordan on "temporary" duty. Still more troops service American aircraft in Qatar and Bahrain, where the U.S. presence is augmented by the headquarters of the Navy's Fifth Fleet. The Navy's forward deployment is completed by the nearly year-round patrol of an aircraft carrier battle group in Persian Gulf waters, whose aircraft supplement the Air Force's land-based planes in the Southern Watch "no-fly zone" over Iraq. None of these deployments is required by a formal treaty, and in fact the United States goes to great lengths to move its forces around regularly, supposedly reducing the visibility of the American military to the populace of each Middle Eastern country.

Defending American interests in the Gulf requires the United States to balance two conflicting concerns. The United States needs to maintain sufficient forces to prevent cross-border attacks that could conquer significant oil fields. At the same time, the U.S. military presence must be minimized to avoid heightening religious or nationalist pressures that destabilize the regimes of friendly Gulf countries. Balancing the "external" and "internal" threats to U.S. allies should be the principal concern of American military policy in the Gulf.

Specifically, the United States should withdraw its ground forces from the Persian Gulf, leaving behind [pre-positioned military material] serviced by civilian contractors. Maintaining approximately 100 air superiority aircraft and 100 attack aircraft at remote Saudi air bases would ensure a robust ability to protect U.S. allies from external attack. The no-fly zone over Iraq would be terminated, but if Iraq moved ground forces toward the borders of America's allies, the United States should strike first, not allowing Iraq to pull back and repeat the process later.

The reason that the United States needs to prevent the consolidation of Persian Gulf oil has changed since the end of the Cold War, but preventing consolidation is still critical. During the Cold War, the United States feared Soviet conquest of the region, which would have strengthened the Soviet military machine and offered new political leverage against America's European and Asian allies. Now that the Soviet threat is gone, the threat of future changes to the territorial status quo in the Gulf would come from a regional hegemon, who would not add the oil reserves to nearly as formidable a base as the Soviets would have. Even if the GDPs of all of the Gulf oil states were combined, the total would pale in comparison to the GDP of the United States. Consolidation of Gulf oil would no longer create a security threat.

However, allowing a regional hegemon to seize significant quantities of Gulf oil would constitute a threat to America's prosperity. . . . The risk . . . is that a regional hegemon could manipulate supply as a method of economic coercion. In the past, the Saudis have adjusted their production levels to preserve price stability in the face of accelerations and cutbacks by other Gulf states. When Iranian production ceased after the overthrow of the shah, Saudi Arabia made up for most of the production shortfall. When four million barrels per day of Iraqi and Kuwaiti output suddenly disappeared from the world market in August 1990, the Saudis rapidly expanded their production to make up the difference, minimizing the effects of the Gulf War on the world price of oil. But if Saudi production capacity were conquered, damaged, or politically neutralized (in the case of a hostile Saudi Arabia), the global economy would be vulnerable to manipulations in supply. American military policy in the Gulf must be designed to ensure that significant amounts of Saudi, Kuwaiti, Iraqi, and other Middle Eastern oil are not monopolized by a regional hegemon. . . .

All of the usual arguments about adopting an American economic policy to limit the effects of a future surge in the price of oil remain true under a policy of restraint. Use of alternate sources of energy, renewed conservation efforts, and more responsive operation of the Strategic Petroleum Reserve would help insulate the American economy from oil shocks and reduce the need for American engagement in the Persian Gulf. But all of these responses have costs, and at the current price of oil it has not been worthwhile to invest a great deal in reducing short-term dependence on oil. An American military policy of restraint would highlight the defense budget costs of its lone remaining overseas military engagement, help Americans recognize the true costs of "cheap" oil, and spur the United States to find ways to reduce this vulnerability.

In the meantime, America must be prepared to defend its Middle Eastern oil interests. Luckily, this is not a very demanding job. To conquer the majority of territory containing Gulf oil, an aggressor's army would have to cover a vast area. Even modern, mechanized armies do not move very fast, and two hundred American aircraft stationed in Saudi Arabia should take the steam out of a ground advance. The aircraft would harass enemy forces and drop air-deployed minefields along their route of advance. American reinforcements would begin to flow into the theater in less than 48 hours. Within a week, ground units could begin to marry up with [pre-positioned] equipment, blocking the aggressor's advance entirely.

The security environment with respect to America's other Middle Eastern ally is quite different. Israel, like U.S. allies in Europe and Asia, is quite capable of defending itself. No American forces need to be earmarked for its defense. Analysis of the military capabilities of the Arab ring states (Lebanon, Syria, Jordan, and Egypt) suggests that Israel's conventional defenses are in little danger. Israel continues to field the best conventional military in the region. As a last resort, Israel's territorial integrity is guaranteed by a nuclear arsenal.

For decades America has been a close friend of Israel, and a policy of restraint would not change this. The United States is better off when its friends are safe and secure, even if their safety has no effect on American security or prosperity. Surrounded by enemies, Israel has always fought its own battles, never requiring American troops to protect its borders. Israel's determination to defend itself without American troops should embarrass America's allies in Europe and Asia. As long as Americans feel strongly about Israel's well-being, loan guarantees, direct economic aid, and military sales will continue. But Israeli security makes no demands on American force structure and in no way justifies American military engagement.

The Limits of Restraint: Continued Engagement in World Affairs

American military restraint does not imply a total withdrawal from the world. The U.S. economy will remain open, and the United States will participate in international economic, environmental, and humanitarian agreements. America will help allies in need with financial support and will use its great economic might to sanction aggressive countries.

The United States should continue its efforts to prevent and respond to terrorism. Restraint should reduce the incentive of terrorists to attack the United

States, and it will minimize the vulnerability of American forces to overseas bombings, but it will not stop all attacks against U.S. targets. The United States should redouble its intelligence efforts against terrorists, and their sponsors should feel America's wrath. Restraint should not be confused with pacifism; America will no longer meddle in other countries' disputes, but it should respond with force when its citizens are attacked.

Finally, the United States should continue in its traditional role of cooperating with allies to maintain freedom of the seas. Stopping interference with seaborne trade has always been a mission of the world's navies, and continuing that mission would enhance America's wealth. Some of America's allies have sizable navies and will see cooperation with the United States against pirates to be in their interest. . . . [At this point the authors examine counterarguments and rebuttals to their advocacy of a policy of restraint.—Eds.]

WHEN TO REENGAGE

Adopting a foreign policy of restraint should not commit the United States to isolation for all time. Just as it was right for America to defend its allies during the Cold War, it may eventually be right for the United States to seek new overseas alliances. Although the conditions are not likely to be realized any time soon, it is important to consider when the United States should reengage militarily.

Before America's core national interests can be threatened, three stringent conditions must be satisfied. First, an aggressive state must develop the conventional capabilities for rapid conquest of its neighbors. A slow conquest, even if successful, would tend to destroy many of the conquered states' economic assets and impose high costs on the aggressor, ending its hegemonic aspirations. Second, the aggressor state must threaten to bring together enough power after its conquests to either mount an attack across the oceans or threaten U.S. prosperity by denying America access to the global economy. At present, only Western Europe or East Asia united with Russia's resource wealth constitutes a sufficiently dangerous union to satisfy this condition. That these are the same regions that George Kennan identified fifty years ago as the key to global power speaks volumes about the real pace of change in the international threat environment.

Finally, any potential aggressor must solve the "nuclear problem." In order to agglomerate the world's power under one empire, a challenger would have to overcome the nuclear capabilities of other great powers:. Russia would have to neutralize the British and French nuclear arsenals, if not a German arsenal as well; the Western European countries would face the overwhelming Russian nuclear force in addition to each other's second-strike capabilities. If China were to develop power-projection forces, it would drive its powerful neighbors to nuclearize. The regions of the world that boast significant industrial potential are inhabited by nuclear and potentially nuclear regional powers. In the unlikely event that a potential hegemon solved the nuclear problem and returned the world to pre–World War II conditions in which hostile states could accumulate significant power through rapid conquest, the United States should not stand idly by. Then, it would be time to reengage. . . .

To justify America's continued role of global engagement, and argue for a defense budget three times as big as America's closest competitor, [the American foreign policy establishment] will need a new threat or a fresh mission. Americans will have to be sold on some new, ambitious strategy—to prevent war everywhere, to make everyone democratic, or to keep everyone else down. But if Americans simply want to be free, enjoy peace, and concentrate more on the problems closer to home, the choice is clear: it is time to come home, America.

4. AMERICA THE INESCAPABLE

Josef Joffe

Something funny happened on the way down from the cold war.

Not so long ago, young Europeans used to burn the American flag. Now they wear it—like that big brash replica of Old Glory knit into a line of pricey Ralph Lauren sweaters. When hurling rocks at the local American cultural center, these kids used to sport Che Guevara on their chests; today it is "Tommy Hilfiger" and "DKNY."

Unconsciously, they might be making more than just a fashion statement—like the mullah in Teheran who had just completed a two-hour tirade against "Am'rikah" in front of the former United States Embassy on the anniversary of the takeover. Grabbing a Western journalist by the arm, he smiled and said, "We don't really hate you Americans." Drawing close, the crowd that had just been screaming "Death to America" nodded vigorously. And the cleric pulled a pair of Ray-Bans out of his robes, as if to say, "Look, man, I'm cool, too."

Even the European left, which cut its teeth on the anti-Vietnam and anti-nuke rallies of the 1970s and 1980s, has rediscovered America. Consider, for example, Britain's new Prime Minister, Tony Blair, whose minions were all over the 1996 Democratic convention in Chicago to learn how to run a Clinton-style campaign. A less-inspiring, but still-telling example: Neo-Nazi punks are more likely to taunt German burghers with the extended middle finger—strictly an American import—than with the stiff-arm Hitler salute.

On the verge of the 21st century, the United States isn't just the "last remaining superpower." It is a continent-size "demonstration effect," which is a locution sociologists prefer to value-laden terms like "model." Why this comeback, considering that in decades past, the United States was rather a model to abhor? America stood for capitalism at its cruelest, social and racial injustice, economic failure and cultural decadence. And, of course, for ruthless imperialism masked by self-serving, moralizing cant.

One explanation is the demise of the Soviet Union and the end of the cold war. While fighting in the trenches of bipolarity, Big Brother remained an unloved benefactor, like a rich but obnoxious relative you can't afford to cross. Washington was always demanding loathsome proofs of fealty from its allies. Don't finance this Soviet gas pipeline. Don't go to the Moscow Olympics. Punish the "evil empire." Take our nuclear missiles.

Worse, the United States instilled angst. Fearing entrapment in quarrels not their own, Europeans liked to see themselves as hapless victims of American hauteur. If war broke out, Europe would turn into the "shooting gallery of the superpowers." Dependency bred resentment and then aggression—the unconscious desire to discredit or vilify a troublesome patron who disturbed the peace while purporting to protect it. If the United States could be tainted as a cultural inferior and as the home of Cowboy Imperialism, then no loyalty was due—that was the subliminal logic of cold-war anti-Americanism.

Today's conflicts are but a pale copy of the cold-war years: a bit of Helms-Burton, a tit-for-tat on meat imports. Europe, indeed, much of the world, can stand back and take a more relaxed view of Mr. Big. Also, what is the countermodel? As long as the Soviet Union persisted, as long as a flawed dream was still married to great power, socialism served as a realistic utopia to hold up against the perversion of capitalism that was America. Now only North Korea and Cuba clutch the torch—failed societies whose company even the faithful will not cherish.

Of course, America was always No. 1, no matter how rich doomsayers like Paul Kennedy became with books like "The Rise and Fall of the Great Powers" [several] years ago. Kennedy and his epigones spawned a school of thought called Declinism. The British historian from Yale and co-declinists like David Calleo ("Beyond American Hegemony") and Walter Russell Mead ("Mortal Splendor") thought that America was like Hapsburg Spain of the 16th and 17th centuries: arrogant, overreaching, oblivious to the fact that military ambitions were outpacing economic resources.

Apart from ignoring the numbers (Philip II's Spain and Louis XIV's France devoted more than 75 percent of spending to the military, while Washington allocated less than 30 percent), the Declinists fundamentally misunderstood American power. Hapsburg Spain was strong as long as it was rich. A key source of wealth was gold and silver from its Latin American possessions. When that dried up, Hapsburg's muscle shriveled.

America's wealth is different; it comes not from silver mines but from production and, above all, from relentless adaptation and innovation. If steel falters, let's do microchips; if the Japanese grab the camera market, Hollywood will flood the world with movies. Unlike Hapsburg's, America's riches aren't dug from the ground; they roll out of labs, research outfits and universities. And that is an inexhaustible resource.

But there is much more. Hapsburg et al. were like the Big Blue [IBM] of yesterday, when it had a lock on mainframes and not much else. Hapsburg and France had big armies because they were rich and populous. But they were just as vulnerable to the competition as was I.B.M. when the PC age dawned. Britain, though much smaller, could throw many and diverse assets into the balance. It had the better fleets, and it enjoyed the great strategic advantage of insularity. It was backed up by a far-flung trading network, and tapped into the exponential growth unleashed by the Industrial Revolution. Finally, Britain could leverage superb diplomatic skills into alliances that proved the undoing of the Philips.

With respect to the diversity of power, America is Britain cubed. Think of the United States as a gambler who can play simultaneously at each and every table that matters—and with more chips than anybody else. Whichever heap you choose, America sits on top of it. It is the largest economy, the fastest-running job machine and, again, the world's biggest exporter; even the dollar, declining since the mid-80s, has been rising against its former twin-nemeses, the German mark and the Japanese yen.

America's armed forces, though shrinking, are racing into the 21st century while the Russian Army is disintegrating and the Chinese are just beginning to modernize. The Persian Gulf war was a sneak preview, a duel between Saddam's huge but clumsy World War II army and Stormin' Norman's battalions practicing for World War IV. It was cruise missiles against bunkers, laser-guided bombs against dug-in tanks, satellites against spotter planes, radar-fooling bombers against antiaircraft guns, Global Positioning System (G.P.S.) against map and compass.

While Europeans can't find the money for their "Eurofighter," a new combat plane that will be all-but-obsolete when it enters the inventory, the Pentagon has deployed stealth aircraft against which there is presently no defense. It is testing weapons that can knock out a tank at a hundred miles. Planners are playing with robotics and space-based weaponry as well as with spooky, nonlethal stuff that will immobilize enemy soldiers before they ever get to the FEBA (army-speak for "forward edge of battle").

To bring it down from the sci-fi level, look at Bosnia. At the beginning, in 1992, the Europeans told the U.S.: "Hands off, this is our war." It was ended (for now) in 1995, when the U.S., grudgingly accepting the responsibility that comes with being No. 1, dispatched a handful of cruise missiles to Pale, the capital of the Bosnian Serbs. The Tomahawks swooped in silently and invisibly, reminding the Serbs' leader, Radovan Karadzic (and his patron in Belgrade, Slobodan Milosevic), that they were suddenly up against a different kind of opponent than the British and the French.

In global diplomacy, nothing happens unless Washington shakes off its lethargy and grabs the helm. North Korea is above all an East Asian nuisance that should be dealt with by China, Russia, and Japan. But only Washington can defang Pyongyang's nuclear ambitions. In the Middle East, the French never get past meddling; only Bill Clinton can knock heads when Israelis and Palestinians overreach.

Culturally, America's clout is so overwhelming that its oldest ally, France, is once more building Maginot lines—this time not against German panzers but against American movies and even words. You know you're on a roll when other governments threaten their own citizens with hefty fines for calling a *lavage voiture* a "car wash." Chances are that French deejays (sorry, make that *disque tourneurs*) might be fired for playing "Meat Loaf," unless they use the linguistically correct moniker *Faux Filet* on the French *Parade de Frappé*.

The United States as No. 1 and soaring—that was not supposed to happen. And it may not last. The history books say that Mr. Big always invites his own demise. Nos. 2, 3, 4 will gang up on him, form countervailing alliances and plot his downfall. That happened to Napoleon, as it happened to Louis XIV and the mighty Hapsburgs, to Hitler and to Stalin. Power begets superior counterpower; it's the oldest rule of world politics.

For now, that rule does not operate. The French would like to take the Americans down a peg or two, but they have a hard time corralling the Germans, Brits, and Italians. Actually, these were only too happy when Richard Holbrooke and the Navy's cruise missiles bludgeoned the Serbs to the negotiating table. The Russians and Chinese huddled in Moscow in April and came up with a "strategic partnership" against you know who—somebody who wants to "push the world toward a unipolar order." It barely made the last page of the news section. What are they going to do? Will Boris Yeltsin go to Beijing for credits, computers, and know-how? Will China risk its most important export market?

There is something anachronistic about such textbook moves. It's like trying to surf the Web with a typewriter. In the old days, power grew out of the barrel of a gun; the more barrels (and men), the better. A nation became great by grabbing territory. By that measure—population and size—China, Russia, and Canada should rule the roost. But they don't.

There are two ways to crack this paradox. One is a traditional answer: Only the United States is a truly global power, with global interests and the global wherewithals for intervention. This is why everybody looks to Washington when it comes to chastening the Saddams and the Karadzics. But nasty as these fellows are, they do not define the essence, or the bulk, of 21st-century world politics.

And hence the second, and new, answer. Unlike centuries past, when war was the great arbiter, today the most interesting types of power do not grow out of the barrel of a gun. As the Harvard political scientist Joseph S. Nye, Jr., dean of the Kennedy School of Government at Harvard, put it, power has become "less coercive and less tangible." He coined the term "soft power" to contrast it with the traditional currency of clout.

The classic way was to force other nations to do what they did not want to do, ultimately by costly war. Today there is a much bigger payoff in "getting others to want what you want," and that has to do with "cultural attraction" and "ideology," with "agenda setting" and holding out big prizes for cooperation, like the vastness and sophistication of the American market. On that gaming table, China, Russia, and Japan, even the West Europeans, cannot match the pile of chips held by the United States.

Are people risking death on the high seas to get into China? How many are willing to go for an M.B.A. at Moscow U.? Imagine a roomful of 14-year-olds—from Germany, Japan, Israel, Russia, and Argentina. Obviously, they would all be wearing Levi's and baseball caps. But how would they relate to one another? They would communicate in English, though haltingly and with heavy accents. About what? The Fugees, Beavis and Butt-head, Ace Ventura, Michael Jordan. They would debate the merits of Nike versus Converse, of Chameleon versus Netscape. Sure, they would not discuss Herman Melville or George Gershwin, but neither would they compare notes on Dante or Thomas Mann. The point is that they would talk about icons and images "made in the U.S.A."

One has to go back to the Roman Empire for a similar instance of cultural hegemony. Actually, there is no comparison. The cultural sway of Greece and Rome, of France in the age of Louis XIV and Napoleon, of Germany between 1871 and 1933 never reached much beyond the economic and educational elites of the Western world. But America's writ encircles the globe, penetrating all layers of society. Modern mass culture, for better or for worse, is American.

Nor is it just a matter of McDonald's and MTV. Why would Helmut Kohl, Germany's chancellor-in-perpetuity, send his two sons to Harvard and M.I.T.? The answer is sad and simple. Heidelberg and the Humboldt University of Berlin no longer measure up, though German universities served as the model for the rest of the world in the late 19th century. When Europeans today bemoan the decline of their universities, they look across the Atlantic for ideas. European academics who want to demonstrate class have to publish in the standard-setting American journals. European intellectuals would rather place their articles in the New York Review of Books than in Commentaire (France) or Merkur (Germany)—just as the hoi polloi would rather watch American movies.

"The Discovery of America" is the title of a cover article in Capital, the German business monthly. Reporting on a survey of business leaders, the magazine writes: "80 percent say that the future belongs to the American system." The boss of the German Federation of Industry calls the American labor market—with its flexibility and mobility—"a model for Germany." Even beyond German boardrooms, words like "downsizing," "restructuring," and "shareholder value" have become household terms.

The magazine Der Spiegel, a bastion of anti-Americanism in the heady 60s and 70s, writes admiringly about the "Jobwunder in Amerika." The leftist weekly Die Woche grudgingly praises America's work ethic and its willingness to let the markets call the shots. Why? "In 20 years, the U.S. has thus managed the greatest quantum-jump of the industrial age—from manufacturing into the service and communication society." A lead story in the Swiss magazine Weltwoche proclaims: "America, you are better off." In the magazine Focus, the Labor Minister of Chancellor Kohl's home state writes a column titled: "What We Can Learn From America." Der Stern, another former America-basher, asks: "Is It Better to Study in America?" Subtract a few reflexive swipes and the answer is "yes."

Why is it suddenly "America the Beautiful?" And how long will it last? Fashions change, Wall Street can go bust, Europe with its 12 percent unemployment rates will eventually restructure. Sometime in the next century, there will be a Russian resurgence, and China's double-digit growth rates will spawn a great military panoply. But it is far harder to foresee a turnaround in the fundamentals of American "soft power."

China, Russia, and Europe are strong in some areas and potentially mighty in others. But their cultures do not "radiate." They do not offer a universal allure—values and ways of doing things that appeal to the rest of the world. Take Japan. Its consumer electronics have conquered the planet, and its banks are not far behind. O.K., throw in sushi too. But how many people want to dress and live like the Japanese, or send their children to Tokyo University?

Sure, the United States dominates music and movies in part because American companies control the global distribution networks. But in the 1920s the Germans were the cinematographic pacesetters, as were the French and Italians in the 1950s and 1960s. India produces many more films than does Hollywood, but all the distribution channels in the world couldn't turn Indian movies into global blockbusters.

One explanation is obvious. America has the world's most open culture, and therefore the world is most open to it. America keeps drawing the world's best and brightest, allowing them to rise to the top within one generation. That makes for a universalist culture with a universal appeal. But there is more. We live in an "American age," meaning that American values and arrangements are most closely in tune with the new Zeitgeist.

Whether it is the "modes of production" (as Marx called it) or modes of organizing our private lives, traditions are being cracked right and left. The trend is toward individualization, nonhierarchical cooperation, and breathless innovation. Creativity rather than order rules. These values have always defined American culture, but today they are shaping Europe and Asia willynilly because otherwise they could not keep up.

In the information age, you cannot afford telephone monopolies that, if they could, would still sell black rotary phones connected by mechanical relays and copper wires. When the premium is on innovation, traditions are out—and so are production methods that force individuals into the straitjacket of top-down management. Why did Big Mac blanket the world? Not just because culinary abomination is convenient, cheap, and timesaving. It also promises a bit of individual freedom, as certified by an angry Hamburg parent: "My kids don't have to be at the dinner table anymore when they can stay out and wolf down a couple of Quarter Pounders."

Rome and France had to conquer territory before they could conquer minds. America's culture is unique; its power comes from pull, not from push. Even the French will acknowledge that nobody ever used a gun to make people learn English (the American-accented version, of course) or watch Hollywood's latest.

The great British philosopher John Locke, theorizing about the "state of nature," wrote, "In the beginning all the world was America." Today he might muse, "All the world is becoming like America." That is a nightmare for the guardians of traditional culture round the world. But how can they stop McDonald's and Microsoft, Harvard and Hollywood? By adapting, competing, and improving. But isn't that the American way, too?

5. CONFLICTS AFTER THE COLD WAR: REALISM, LIBERALISM, AND U.S. INTERESTS

Joseph S. Nye, Jr.

"War" is a term that covers a myriad of activities. Through much of history, war has been the norm rather than the exception in relations among nations. For example, there have been wars among the great powers for 60 percent of the years since 1500. Nine of these wars were general or "world" wars involving nearly all the great powers. Although not the most prevalent, these are by far the most devastating wars and have the strongest effects on the international system. If we divide today's wars into the three categories of great power, regional, and internal wars, the first is the least likely, but still the most important.

Each of the major great power wars since 1500 was followed by a period of uncertainty in which statesmen attempted to change the international system or adapt it to prevent a recurrence of great power war. We are at present in a new period of uncertainty after the equivalent of a major great power "war"—the Cold War. This is very different from past postwar periods for several reasons. First, in some ways it is the most uncertain transition of all because there has been no single, decisive military confrontation or postwar negotiation. Second, the rise and fall of great powers and technological, economic, and cultural change have all accelerated. Third, future conflicts may have very different sources from those of the recently concluded Cold War, which was partly rooted in ideological tensions that are unlikely to reappear, and these conflicts may be altered or constrained by the presence of weapons of mass destruction.

This [chapter] briefly reviews the likelihood of these three types of conflict after the Cold War. One encouraging conclusion is that the conflicts with the

Note: Some notes have been deleted or renumbered.

greatest potential for devastation—great power conflicts over the global balance of power—are the least likely given the deterrent effects of nuclear weapons and the decreasing importance of territorially defined resources. Still, such conflicts cannot be ruled out entirely because the potential remains for misunderstandings, security dilemmas, and internally unstable great powers.

Regional balance of power conflicts like the Persian Gulf War are more probable than world wars and could have wide and lasting regional or global implications, although they are less likely than in the past to catalyze direct military clashes between the great powers. Their prevalence will depend in large part on the constraining role played by the United States as the largest external power.

Communal conflicts, scattered around the globe and often taking place within states, are likely to be the prevalent form of conflict. Almost all of the approximately 30 significant conflicts since the end of the Cold War have been internal. The most likely locations of these conflicts are the regions of collapsed empires—Africa and the rim of the former Soviet Union. Although most of these conflicts are not immediately damaging beyond their respective borders, they can spread geographically, induce humanitarian intervention, and cumulatively create long-term and global threats to international security. Thus, although great power conflicts are less likely than ever before to arise out of global or regional balance of power considerations, the great powers will continue to face difficult choices on how to prevent communal conflicts from occurring or from escalating in intensity, spreading geographically, and proliferating in number.

American leadership is a key factor in limiting the frequency and destructiveness of all three kinds of conflicts. This does not mean that the United States could or should get involved in every potential or ongoing conflict. Its role must be proportionate to its interests in each conflict, and the nation cannot afford the military, economic, and political costs of being a global policeman. Instead, where it has important interests, the United States must continue to aspire to a role more like the sheriff of the posse, enabling international coalitions to pursue interests that it shares whether or not the United States itself supplies the bulk of the military forces involved.

PREVENTING THE LAST WAR: CONTINUITY AND CHANGE IN THE SOURCES OF CONFLICT

There are two basic schools of thought that purport to explain wars: Realism and Liberalism. Both perspectives are essential to understanding post–cold war conflicts. Realists argue that wars arise from the efforts of states to acquire power and security in an anarchic world, or one in which there is no ultimate arbiter of order other than self-help and the force of arms. In this view, power transitions, disequilibriums in the balance of power, and competition over allies, territory, and other power resources are the root of causes of war. Also, security dilemmas arise when states try to promote their own security through arms buildups, creation of alliances, or efforts to acquire buffer states. This causes other states to feel insecure, leading to arms races, rigidifying alliances, and competition over strategic territory and resources. In the Realist view, strong international institutions can only exist when the balance of power is satisfactory to leading states, so these institutions are effective only when they are not needed, and needed only when they are not effective.

Liberals argue that conflicts and their prevention are determined not only by the balance of power, but by the domestic structures of states, their values, identities, and cultures, and international institutions for conflict resolution. In this view, trade is important, not because it prevents war between states, but because it may lead states to define their interests in ways that make war less likely, encouraging them to seek gain through commerce rather than conquest. Moreover, the domestic structures and values of states greatly affect their propensity for international conflict. In particular, the most striking correlation to emerge from recent studies of war is that liberal democracies have rarely, if ever, fought with other democracies, even though democracies have frequently fought with nondemocratic states. In contrast to Realists, Liberals argue that international institutions can help prevent conflict by stabilizing expectations, creating a sense of continuity and a feeling that current cooperation will be reciprocated in the future, providing information on whether states are abiding by international norms, and establishing mechanisms for conflict resolution.

Neither of these schools of thought is adequate by itself in understanding the causes of conflict after the Cold War. The Realist emphasis on the balance of power is necessary but not sufficient when long-term societal changes are eroding the norms of state sovereignty. The Liberal view that peace has broken out among the major liberal democracies is accurate, but it is not a panacea when many states, including great powers, are not liberal democracies. Yet both schools of thought point to important realities, and it is necessary to address the international, domestic, and institutional dimensions of conflict. Drawing upon each school of thought, then, what are the most likely sources of conflict after the Cold War?

GLOBAL BALANCE OF POWER CONFLICTS

As historians and political observers since Thucydides have noted, rapid power transitions are one of the leading causes of great power conflict. Such power transitions were a deep structural cause of historically recent great power conflicts, including the rise and fall of Napoleonic France, Germany's rise before each World War, and the relative rise and resulting rivalry of the United States and the Soviet Union after World War II. Power transitions can lead to preemptive strikes by declining powers against their rising competitors, or to aggression by rising powers who feel their role in the system is lagging behind their military prowess. In addition, wars can result from security dilemmas between rising powers and counterbalancing coalitions, as in

World War I. Similarly, wars can arise from uncertainties over how fast-changing military balances might play out in battle—wars are less likely when it is clear to all which side would win.

There is a strong consensus that we are in a period of rapid power transitions. There is considerable debate over the direction and magnitude of these transitions, however, and the center of gravity of this debate has shifted in recent years. Such debates are indicative of the unpredictability that makes such transitions a potential source of conflict. In the late 1980s, many commentators, following the lead of Paul Kennedy's best-selling *Rise and Fall of the Great Powers,* argued that the United States was in a period of long-term decline relative to other leading powers. At that time, I argued that the U.S. decline relative to other states was only natural as they recovered from the devastation of World War II, and that by the 1970s America's relative decline had leveled off, with the nation at its prewar share of about 22 to 25 percent of world gross national product (GNP).[1] Moreover, I argued that of all the leading powers, only the United States had a diverse and deep range of power resources across all the key dimensions of power, including military power, economic power, and "soft power," the broad appeal of cultural, ideological, and institutional factors.

The intervening five years have largely reaffirmed these observations. The Soviet Union and Russia have declined farther and faster than almost anyone expected in 1990. China has risen faster than most anticipated, with a long period of double-digit economic growth. Japan and Germany have not become the full-fledged superpowers that many predicted at the 1990 summit . . . of the group of seven industrialized countries (G-7). Unpredictable lurches and lags in growth are likely to continue, but the central reality of the global balance of power is the same as it was in 1990: the United States is the only true superpower, with global assets in all the dimensions of power.

This does not mean that a unipolar world has replaced the bipolar balance of the Cold War. There are many important security, economic, and political goals that the United States cannot achieve by itself. Neither is the world multipolar, as every great power but the United States lacks one or more key power resource. Instead, power is distributed in a complex three-dimensional pattern. Military power is largely unipolar, with the United States the only country with both intercontinental nuclear weapons and large, modern, air, naval, and ground forces capable of deploying around the globe. Economic power is tripolar, with the United States, Europe, and Japan representing two-thirds of world product. China's growth may make economic power quadripolar after the turn of the century. At the level of transnational relations that cross borders outside the control of government, and that include actors as diverse as bankers and terrorists, power is widely dispersed.

Just as important as these changes in the distribution of power are changes in the nature of power and the processes through which it can be exercised. Some Liberals argue that economic power has replaced military power as the central medium of international politics, but this is greatly overstated. Realists rightly argue that economic instruments still cannot compare with military forces in their coercive and deterrent effects. Economic sanctions, for example, did not compel the Iraqis to withdraw from Kuwait. In addition, all it takes is one good security crisis to send stock and commodity markets spinning, set off capital flight, stifle investment, and raise the risk premium on the full range of economic transactions. Economic instruments have grown slightly in importance relative to military ones, but this was already true by the 1970s. The main change has been in the fungibility of military power itself. Nuclear weapons have so greatly raised the potential costs of conflict that the great power states that have them have worked hard to prevent any direct military conflicts among themselves, including conventional conflicts that could escalate to the nuclear level.

Taken together, these changes in the balance and nature of power indicate that the most dangerous kind of conflict—a direct clash among two or more of the five major power centers of the United States, Russia, China, Europe, and Japan over the fundamental shape of the international system—is very unlikely. None of the paths through which power transitions have historically led to conflict is very likely to open up. There is no temptation for the United States to overreact to rising powers because it is not in a steep power decline, as some pessimists suggested a few years ago. Rising powers today have fewer incentives for territorial aggression than they have had throughout most of history because the route to prestige, power, and economic success in the modern era lies in high-technology production and human capital.

Whereas World War II armies could seize territory and factories and convert them from commercial to military production fairly quickly, it is enormously difficult to convert highly specialized modern production lines. Nor do countries aspire to increase their economic production by taking over neighboring software or service industries in the same way that past aggressors coveted agricultural land or raw materials deposits. Indeed, transnational economic ties are such that it is increasingly difficult to tell whether a particular company is "American" if its headquarters are in one country, its production facilities in several others, and its raw material inputs, distribution system, and export markets in still others. Iraq's invasion of Kuwait is one of the increasingly rare cases in which a state seized territory in the hope of gaining resources that could increase its economic and military power. Finally, uncertainty over the balance of power and arms races represent perhaps the most likely dangers, but even these are muted in an era in which nuclear weapons are the ultimate deterrent and satellite intelligence quickly informs a potential counterbalancing coalition of a rising power's military capabilities. All of these factors help explain why there were no large-scale and direct military clashes between American and Soviet troops despite more than 40 years of intense rivalry, and why the hegemonic power transition of the decline and breakup of the Soviet Union took place without even a small risk of great power war of the kind that has accompanied the decline of most empires throughout history.

Perhaps even more important than these Realist considerations, two of the leading power centers—Japan and Europe—consist of democratic states that are allied with the United States and that largely share its view of world order. It is often said that democracies do not fight each other. A more accurate formulation is that *Liberal* democracies do not fight each other. As the political scientist Karl Deutsch argued, a "pluralistic security community," or an island of peace, has emerged among the United States, Europe, and Japan.[2] Shared values, stable expectations, and interlocking institutions have become so powerful among these three power centers that wars among them, including wars among European powers that have fought with one another over several centuries, are unthinkable. Anyone today who warned of impending military conflict among the Scandinavian countries would be considered a lunatic, but in past centuries, wars among these states were commonplace.

The low likelihood of direct great power clashes does not mean that there will be no tensions between them. Disagreements are likely to continue over regional conflicts, like those that [arose] over how to deal with the conflict in the former Yugoslavia. Efforts to stop the spread of weapons of mass destruction and means of their delivery are another source of friction, as is the case over Russian and Chinese nuclear cooperation with Iran, which the United States steadfastly opposes. The sharing of burdens and responsibilities for maintaining international security and protecting the natural environment are a further subject of debate among the great powers. Furthermore, in contrast to the views of classical liberals, increased trade and economic interdependence can increase as well as decrease conflict and competition among trading partners. The main point, however, is that such disagreements are very unlikely to escalate to military conflicts.

UNCERTAIN TRANSITIONS AMONG THE GREAT POWERS: CHINA AND RUSSIA

The key uncertainties in the long-run continuation of this island of peace among the great powers are long-term developments in China and Russia. Of all the great powers, these two states' long-term growth rates and domestic politics, the indices of greatest concern to Realists and Liberals respectively, are hardest to predict. Even so, the general analysis of great power interests outlined above applies to U.S. relations with both China and Russia. Although the three powers have many disagreements, their vital national interests are not at odds. In addition to the post–cold war constraints on great power conflict noted above, these three powers have no direct territorial disagreements of the kind that led to great power wars in the past.

There remains a residual risk for the United States of greater tension with Russia and China in the long term if they misunderstand the realities of the post–cold war world outlined above, or if domestic political instabilities—ideological blinders, internal power struggles, military-industrial-governmental interest groups, or ethno-nationalism—push their foreign policies in extreme directions. Yet to treat China and Russia as adversaries would become a self-fulfilling prophecy. . . . Both powers are preoccupied with their domestic political and economic situations, and they are more concerned about joining the world economy, and having a voice in international political affairs commensurate with their status as great powers, than about throwing their weight around the globe in ways that would only cause their neighbors to band together against them. Still, these two states retain considerable potential for either bolstering or undermining security and stability in their respective regions, where their interests are greatest. Thus, efforts by the democratic great powers to engage them in the international community and to urge them to make their intentions and military forces transparent are the best means of limiting the potential for conflicts. . . . Russia and China . . . remain important players in world politics and . . . the prospects for international security are much brighter with their cooperation. Still, success will depend not only on international mechanisms and the balance of power, but also on domestic political developments in the states with the potential to disrupt the system. Even in the worst-case post–cold war scenario, however—the emergence of an aggressive regime in a great power at the same time that it experiences rapid growth—a strong counterbalancing coalition of democratic great powers, nuclear deterrence, and the limited benefits of territorial conquest would continue to make direct great power conflict unlikely.

REGIONAL BALANCE OF POWER CONFLICTS

A more likely and near-term risk than great power conflicts is that of attempts by rising regional powers to acquire weapons of mass destruction and establish regional hegemony. Wars initiated by these regional powers may draw in the great powers, although the latter will probably see aspiring regional hegemons as shared threats rather than potential allies. This was exemplified when Iraq's seizure of Kuwait posed a threat to world oil markets. In other regions, however, like South Asia, great power interests and constraints are weaker after the Cold War.

Deterring regional powers from aggression requires that the great powers seek to contain aspiring regional hegemons, and that they maintain sufficient forward military forces to do so. In particular, three states have capabilities to upset regional power balances, have shown a willingness to do so in the past, and continue to be governed by insular and autocratic rulers: North Korea, Iraq, and Iran.

North Korea's history of aggression and its isolation from the rest of Asia have made it a source of regional instability. Despite severe economic problems, North Korea continues to devote a large share of its national resources to maintaining and improving one of the world's largest military forces. Given its history of aggression, the development of nuclear weapons by North Korea would threaten the regional balance of power and could spark a regional arms race. In this context, the October 1994 Agreed Framework is an important step in reducing the North Korean nuclear threat. Still, the Framework will take a long time to implement, and North Korean conventional forces continue to pose a potential threat to the South. As explained in the Department of Defense's report *United States Security Strategy for the East Asia-Pacific Region,* to help deter this threat the United States continues to maintain about 37,000 troops in South Korea, and 100,000 troops in Asia as a whole. In addition, the United States has undertaken dialogues with Japan and Korea to reaffirm its alliances for the post–cold war era.

In the Middle East, Iran and Iraq continue to pose the foremost threats to regional stability. Despite losing more than half its forces in the Gulf war, Iraq continues to have the largest military forces in the Gulf region. Iraq's ominous troop movements in October 1994 demonstrated its continuing capacity to threaten the region. Iran also harbors ambitions of hegemony over the Persian Gulf and has pursued its goals using every available means, including terrorism and subversion. Although its conventional forces remain limited, its recent purchases of submarines, attack aircraft, and anti-ship missiles are worrisome. Most dangerous of all are Iran's efforts to develop weapons of mass destruction.

Although U.S. Gulf allies are working to contain the Iraqi and Iranian threats, they cannot do so alone. The United States is thus continuing to strengthen its rapid deployment capabilities in the region. In 1979, when the Rapid Deployment force was created, it would have taken three months to get a division of heavy ground forces into the region. When Iraq invaded Kuwait in 1990, the U.S. military was able to get seven combat brigades, three carriers, and numerous aircraft into the Gulf in three weeks. In October 1994, when Iraqi forces again moved toward Kuwait, the first heavy ground units to the Gulf, in Operation Vigilant Warrior, arrived in three days, and a total of 150,000 troops were poised to deploy quickly if necessary. Whereas the Gulf war demonstrated the ability of the United States to defeat Iraq, Vigilant Warrior showed its ability to deter it. . . .

THE SOURCES OF COMMUNAL CONFLICTS

Communal conflicts over competing identities, territorial claims, and political institutions are, of course, not unique to the modern era. What has changed, however, is the complex interplay of transnational, national, and subnational identities with rapid and far-reaching social, technological, and economic changes. This potent mix can spark latent tensions into sudden conflict because of instantaneous communications.

The rapid rise and fall of great powers, the end of the Soviet empire and the demise of communism, and the technological and communications revolution have led not to the end of history, as some have argued, but to the return of history in the form of clashes over identity among individuals, groups, and nations. Such clashes can happen at three levels—over transnational identities, like Islam; national identities, as in Russia; and subnational identities based on religious, ethnic, or linguistic divisions, as in Africa or the former Yugoslavia. These have challenged conflict management institutions on each level—transnational, national, and subnational.

Technological change has had transnational and contradictory effects. It has made the economy global but made politics more parochial. It has globalized communications, but instead of creating a global village, as Marshall McLuhan predicted, this has created global villages. "Village" connotes community, but it also connotes parochialism. Individuals are now more vulnerable to the vagaries of international labor, currency, and commercial markets. With state sovereignty eroded through global interdependence, the political efficacy and legitimacy of many governments is less assured. Many groups have had their sense of identity and community challenged by economic dislocation and the collapse of communism. They have become susceptible to the parochial political appeals of political entrepreneurs who hope to seize power in states whose governments have been weakened by the collapse of communism or the ebb and flow of the global economy. In this context, it is not surprising to find former Communist apparatchiks suddenly transformed into ethnic demagogues. With modern technology, such demagogues can now communicate their hateful messages more easily to both wide and select groups.

The result has not been a clash between Toynbee's world civilizations, as Samuel P. Huntington has argued.[3] Huntington is correct that communalism and competing identities are a major source of conflict after the Cold War, but he captures only one dimension or level of analysis of clashing identities. There are more clashes among competing identities *within* grand civilizations than between them. The Iran-Iraq War, for example, was between states within the Islamic world. Moreover, Huntington calls Africa a "civilization," yet the largest number of current wars are within Africa.

Closer to the mark are Freud's observations on the "narcissism of small differences"—the tendency to focus on the 10 percent that is different between individuals instead of the 90 percent that is the same. We have seen these small differences exaggerated by combatants in Somalia, Northern Ireland, and elsewhere, including conflict between family or clan groupings. Even in Rwanda, the site of the worst genocide since the Holocaust, the differences between Hutu and Tutsi were far from absolute. Many intermarriages had occurred. But once Rwanda's politics became polarized into a zero-sum "kill or be killed" atmosphere, genocide tore its society apart.

Bosnia, which is often depicted solely as a civilizational clash, includes many other elements: for example, Serbs who define themselves as Bosnians and have stayed in Sarajevo side-by-side with Bosnian Muslims. In many cities of the former Yugoslavia, neighbors paid little attention to their own or others' "ethnic" identity until propaganda created a frenzy of ethnic conflict and a Hobbesian zero-sum politics. As one Bosnian-Croat officer told me during a battle between Muslims and Croats in Mostar, "Before the war I could not tell on sight who was a Muslim, but now the uniforms make it easy." In a sense, the war in the former Yugoslavia represents the victory of the countryside and villages, where identities changed slowly compared to the assimilation that had advanced in the cities.

DOMESTIC POLITICS AND COMMUNAL CONFLICTS

Just as domestic politics and values affect the likelihood of conflict among the great powers, they also have a powerful influence on the likelihood of communal conflicts within or between states, and on the propensity for other regional or great powers to become involved in these conflicts. Communal conflicts often arise in states undergoing a legitimacy crisis because of two related dynamics. First, established mechanisms for mediating such conflicts lose force in delegitimized states, just as the practice of a rotating presidency broke down in Yugoslavia after the collapse of communism. Second, those who aspire to attain power within delegitimized states are tempted to appeal to ethnic or other identities as a means of establishing a new claim to legitimacy.

Again, the case of Yugoslavia is a clear example, as Slobodan Milosevic transformed himself from a Communist apparatchik to a born-again ethnonationalist. It is thus not surprising that many communal conflicts have arisen within the former Soviet empire, where the identity crises are sharpest and have multiple roots in the collapse of Communist governments, the economic dislocation of individuals, and the reemergence of ethnic identities long suppressed or mediated by Communist regimes.

A second category of states susceptible to communal conflicts includes so-called "failed states," which refers in this context to states that either have never had a strong central government, or whose moderately strong central government has been undermined by economic or political developments. Afghanistan fits the former pattern, many states in Africa fit the latter, and some, like Somalia, have elements of both. By definition, in such states power is contested and political and economic problems provide opportunities for ethnic scapegoating. Thus, even though the end of the bipolar contest over the developing world has led to the withdrawal of foreign troops from Afghanistan, Angola, Cambodia, and elsewhere, communal conflicts in these states have taken the place of conflicts between factions backed by the United States and those sponsored by the Soviet Union.

A very different set of domestic pressures affects the democratic great powers that are not themselves at risk of experiencing communal conflicts. The instantaneous and all-intrusive nature of modern communications imparts conflicting impulses to the leading democracies. On the one hand, graphic televised reports of humanitarian abuses by combatants in communal conflicts can galvanize a strong impulse to act. On the other, equally graphic coverage of peacekeepers killed, wounded, or taken hostage can stimulate public pressure to withdraw from conflicts that do not directly threaten the democracies' vital security interests. Even worse, such pressures will inevitably fall unevenly on those states that feel the closest cultural or geographic ties to suffering populations, and those whose troops take casualties, leading to tensions over definitions of missions, rules of engagement, and burden sharing. Moreover, both the victims and perpetrators of humanitarian abuses are well aware of the power of media coverage, and they seek to exploit it to their own ends, with victims publicizing or even exaggerating their plight and aggressors seeking to inflict casualties upon or take hostages from the contributing states that they see as most vulnerable to such blackmail. This underscores the difficulty for the leading democracies of engaging in consistent, coordinated, and long-term approaches to communal conflicts.

LIKELIHOOD AND CONSEQUENCES OF COMMUNAL CONFLICTS

While generally less threatening to U.S. interests than global or regional balance of power conflicts, communal conflicts are the most likely kind of post–cold war conflict and have thus far proved the most frequent. Less than 10 percent of the 170 states in today's world are ethnically homogenous. Only half have one ethnic group that accounts for as much as 75 percent of their population. Africa, in particular, is a continent of a thousand ethnic and linguistic groups squeezed into some 50-odd states, many of them with borders determined by colonial powers in the last century with little regard to traditional ethnic boundaries. The former Yugoslavia was a country with five nationalities, four languages, three religions, and two alphabets. As a result of such disjunctions between borders and peoples, there have been some 30 communal conflicts since the end of the Cold War, many of them still ongoing.

Communal conflicts, particularly those involving wars of secession, are very difficult to manage through the UN and other institutions built to address interstate conflicts. The UN, regional organizations, alliances, and individual states cannot provide a universal answer to the dilemma of self-determination versus the inviolability of established borders, particularly when so many states face potential communal conflicts of their own. In a world of identity crises on many levels of analysis, it is not clear which selves deserve sovereignty: nationalities, ethnic groups, linguistic groups, or religious groups. Similarly, uses of force for deterrence, compellence, and reassurance are much harder to carry out when both those using force and those on the receiving end are disparate coalitions of international organizations, states, and subnational groups.

Moreover, although few communal conflicts by themselves threaten security beyond their regions, some impose risks of "horizontal" escalation, or the spread to other states within their respective regions. This can happen through the involvement of affiliated ethnic groups that spread across borders, the sudden flood of refugees into neighboring states, or the use of neighboring territories to ship weapons to combatants. The use of ethnic propaganda also raises the risk of "vertical" escalation to more intense violence, more sophisticated and destructive weapons, and harsher attacks on civilian populations as well as military personnel. There is also the danger that communal conflicts could become more numerous if the UN and regional security organizations lose the credibility, willingness, and capabilities necessary to deal with such conflicts.

PREVENTING AND ADDRESSING CONFLICTS: THE PIVOTAL U.S. ROLE

Leadership by the United States, as the world's leading economy, its most powerful military force, and a leading democracy, is a key factor in limiting the frequency and destructiveness of great power, regional, and communal conflicts. The paradox of the post–cold war role of the United States is that it is the most powerful state in terms of both "hard" power resources (its economy and military forces) and "soft" ones (the appeal of its political system and culture), yet it is not so powerful that it can achieve all its international goals by acting alone. The United States lacks both the international and domestic prerequisites to resolve every conflict, and in each case its role must be proportionate to its interests at stake and the costs of pursuing them. Yet the United States can continue to enable and mobilize international coalitions to pursue shared security interests, whether or not the United States itself supplies large military forces.

The U.S. role will thus not be that of a lone global policeman; rather, the United States can frequently serve as the sheriff of the posse, leading shifting coalitions of friends and allies to address shared security concerns within the legitimizing framework of international organizations. This requires sustained attention to the infrastructure and institutional mechanisms that make U.S. leadership effective and joint action possible: forward stationing and preventive deployments of U.S. and allied forces, prepositioning of U.S. and allied equipment, advance planning and joint training to ensure interoperability with allied forces, and steady improvement in the conflict resolution abilities of an interlocking set of bilateral alliances, regional security organizations and alliances, and global institutions.

The United States has already had several important successes in leading international security coalitions while at the same time sharing burdens and responsibilities with its allies. U.S. leadership of the Desert Storm coalition, which involved international contributions of more than 240,000 troops and $70 billion, was one such success. More recently, in the fall of 1994 when Iraq again moved troops south toward Kuwait, prepositioning agreements with allies in the region were a key factor in allowing the United States to mobilize 150,000 U.S. troops quickly and deter any Iraqi aggression. In Macedonia, the United States and others . . . engaged in a preventive deployment that . . . deterred the spread of conflict from the former Yugoslavia, and American diplomacy has made progress toward resolving the Greek-Macedonian dispute. In Haiti, the United States provided most of the troops for the initial intervention, yet others also contributed and the operation took place with the backing of the UN Security Council and has subsequently been turned over to a UN force. On the Korean peninsula, the United States has reached an agreement with North Korea to dismantle its nuclear weapons program, and its South Korean and Japanese allies will pay the great majority of the financial costs of implementing this agreement.

[Former] Defense Secretary Perry . . . distinguished vital, important, and humanitarian national interests and identified appropriate U.S. options on each level. When its vital interests are threatened and it cannot protect them by means short of force, the United States is ready to use force, unilaterally if necessary, to defend them. When U.S. interests are important but not vital, the United States has to weigh the costs and risks of using force, and must also consider more carefully whether it can bring together a multinational coalition rather than acting alone. When U.S. interests are primarily humanitarian, the use of U.S. military capabilities in a non-combat mode is appropriate when a humanitarian catastrophe threatens to overwhelm relief agencies, when the response requires capabilities that are unique to the U.S. military, and when the risk to American troops is minimal.

An important consideration in each of these three categories, and especially when U.S. interests are less than vital, is whether U.S. participation can win public and congressional support. Contrary to conventional wisdom, the U.S. public does not become weak-kneed at the risk of high casualties when vital interests are at stake—witness the high level of public support for the Desert Storm operation despite early predictions of thousands of casualties. Unless vital or important U.S. interests are involved, however, it can be counterproductive to send U.S. ground troops, who can become symbolic political targets, when peacekeepers from other states can serve equally well. To incur significant casualties where interests are few could jeopardize public support for the forward presence abroad that is crucial for deterring global or regional balance of power conflicts that could inflict grave damage to U.S. vital interests in the long run. The comparative advantages of the United States in many peacekeeping operations often lie in air and naval forces, logistics, transport, and intelligence assets. Thus, it is a measure of successful sharing of international responsibilities that the vast majority of UN peacekeepers have not been Americans.

Although the United States cannot single-handedly resolve the many communal conflicts that have erupted, it can work to make international institutions better able to deal with these conflicts. The Clinton administration is working to create a web of security cooperation, from bilateral alliances, to regional alliances and security organizations, to global organizations like the UN. At times, this will involve building new alliance structures, as in the enlargement of NATO and the revitalization of the U.S.–Japan alliance, or regional security organizations, as in the reinvigorated OSCE [Organization for Security and Cooperation in Europe] and the ARF [Southeast Asian Nations Regional Forum]. In other cases, it will require creating and leading ad hoc coalitions, like the Desert Storm coalition that defeated Iraq in the Gulf war. Sometimes, as in the Gulf war, the United States may work primarily through the UN to advance its diplomatic interests while at the same time retaining leadership of the military component of the operation as the leading contributor. In other cases where U.S. interests and forces are not as directly engaged, allies who have greater interests will naturally step into the lead. The key is to take the steps necessary to make ad hoc coalitions of the willing effective, such as developing agreed-upon mechanisms for burden-sharing, interoperability of forces, and decision-making mechanisms on missions and rules of engagement. This approach enables some states to act even when not all are willing to contribute, and, for those states most willing to contribute to internationally recognized missions, to lead the military component of the operation.

Those who sing the siren song of unilateralism without being willing to invest in international infrastructure fail to understand what makes U.S. leadership possible. They would unilaterally change the rules for paying for UN peacekeeping operations, for example, in which roughly seven foreign troops have served for every American peacekeeper deployed over the last year. The end result of such unilateralism would be the same as that of neo-isolationism: abandonment of the United States by its allies and friends in the face of cumulating threats.

CONCLUSION

Technological, social, and political change have made the sources of modern conflicts very different from those of the past. A good illustration of this is the changing role of the Balkans in World War I, World War II, and the [recent] conflict in the former Yugoslavia. The great powers clashed over the Balkans in both World Wars, in part out of concern that Balkan conflicts with communal roots could upset a multipolar balance of power that was already complicated and rapidly shifting. In the present Balkan conflict, global balance of power considerations have played little role. . . . The danger that the conflict will spread arises not from balance of power considerations as in the past, but from the possibility of escalating conflicts over identity that drag in neighboring states.

Realists, usually the pessimists when it comes to international politics, have it right that the balance of power, the nature of military technology, and the importance of territorially defined resources are important determinants of the sources, nature, and frequency of conflicts. Ironically, it is on these grounds that there is the most room for optimism. The United States has the deepest and most diverse range of power resources; other democratic leading powers are its close allies; nuclear deterrence inhibits great power conflicts; and territorial aggression is not as tempting as it once was. It is the factors that Liberals focus upon—the domestic structures of states, their values, identities, and cultures, and the international institutions for conflict resolution—that give cause for concern. States unhinged by the collapse of communism or rapid economic change are at risk of internal and external conflicts. Ethnic demagogues have leapt into the breach, using modern communications to incite groups dislocated by rapid economic and political change as a means of gaining power in weakened states.

Most important, international institutions designed around past conflicts have not yet caught up to the changed nature of post–cold war conflicts. The experience of past efforts to prevent conflicts provides ample evidence for the Liberal view that international institutions for conflict management, or their weakness or absence, matter.

In short, the bad news about post–cold war conflicts is that the world is least prepared for the most prevalent type—internal communal conflicts. The good news is that U.S.–led alliance systems and forward-stationed forces are creating a strong structural base for avoiding the most devastating types: regional and great power wars.

NOTES

1. Joseph S. Nye, Jr., *Bound to Lead: The Changing Nature of American Power* (New York: Basic Books, 1990).

2. Karl W. Deutsch, *Political Community and the North Atlantic Area: International Organization in the Light of Experience* (Princeton, NJ: Princeton University Press, 1957).

3. Samuel P. Huntington, "The Clash of Civilizations?" *Foreign Affairs* 72 (Summer 1993).

The Past as Prologue

6. STRATEGIES BEFORE CONTAINMENT: PATTERNS FOR THE FUTURE

Terry L. Deibel

*T*he end of the Cold War and the disintegration of the Soviet Union demand that American foreign policy analysts rethink their most basic assumptions. This [chapter] is intended to contribute to that effort by comparing past strategic patterns with future strategic possibilities. . . . Its purpose is to broaden the range of possibilities under consideration, on the premise that strategies designed to serve U.S. interests before the Soviet threat dominated American statecraft may well prove suggestive for strategists attempting to further those interests after the Soviet threat has disappeared. . . .

THREE CATEGORIES OF THE NATIONAL INTEREST

One way to envision a foreign affairs strategy without a Soviet threat is to look at the contours of American policy before the era of containment. . . . Looking at foreign affairs strategies from a time when the Soviet threat was not the dominating force in American policy can be very suggestive for those accustomed to Cold War patterns of thought.

Despite the revolutionary times in which we live, . . . the United States will continue to concern itself, first, with threats to its *physical security*: with the protection from attack of its territory, people, and their property, and with the preservation against all external threats of its domestic political system and structure of civic values. This was the dominant area of the national interest during the Cold War, the one served by various strategies of contain-

Note: Notes have been deleted.

ment. Its primacy was underlined by unprecedented spending on a wide variety of policy tools, including foreign economic and security assistance, nuclear weaponry, intelligence and covert action, and conventional military forces.

Second, Americans will expect their government to see to their nation's and their own *economic prosperity,* to promote the domestic welfare. During the Cold War period this interest was safeguarded by American hegemony in the world economic system, a position enshrined in the Bretton Woods institutions (the World Bank and International Monetary Fund) and in the role of the dollar as reserve currency and source of global financial liquidity. Economic prosperity required less attention from decisionmakers than did physical security because of the overwhelming preponderance of American economic power after World War II, a state of affairs that was underlined by the country's willingness to sacrifice economic advantage to support its security interests.

Third, Americans will probably continue to insist, as they have since revolutionary times, that their government attune its foreign policies to the values for which they believe their country stands. During the Cold War, the *projection of American values* abroad was accomplished under the negative rubric of anti-communism, a strategy that occasionally assumed the dimensions of a moralistic crusade. As such, anti-communism sometimes overwhelmed the mere containment of Soviet state power, with very different consequences for U.S. strategy.

Today, with no new hegemonic threat on the horizon, . . . and with communism utterly bankrupt as an ideology, it seems obvious that containment, economic hegemony, and anti-communism can no longer serve the nation's interests as they did in the Cold War. But American statesmen have always had to fashion strategies to deal with physical security, economic prosperity, and value projection (see Table 6–1), and many of their earlier approaches relate in interesting ways to the contemporary policy environment. What follows is an effort to review those past strategies in bold strokes, seeking in them some perspective on the future of American statecraft.

Table 6-1. American Strategies in Three Areas of the National Interest

| | Cold War | | Pre–Cold War | |
	Global		Regional	Inward-Looking
Physical Security	Containment	Balance of power Collective security	Hemispheric defense	Isolationism
Value Projection	Anti-communism	Human rights Democratic and market systems		Great Exemplar
Economic Prosperity	Hegemony	Free trade	Trade blocs	Protectionism

PROTECTING THE NATION'S SECURITY

Balance of Power

Perhaps the oldest method by which nation-states have sought to protect their physical security in a hostile world is that of the balance of power. Although condemned in theory by Americans since before Woodrow Wilson's time as immoral and war-prone, balance of power policies have been honored in practice when the nation has felt weak or vulnerable. In the early days of the Republic, when the new United States was a small nation surrounded by the territorial outposts of hostile and much more powerful countries, the founding fathers used balance of power statecraft to protect and expand American independence. Even that supposed moralist Woodrow Wilson, and after him Franklin D. Roosevelt, considered it a vital interest—over which they led the United States into war—to prevent the land mass of Eurasia from being dominated by a single power which would thereby have sufficient industrial capacity to bring war across the oceans to American shores.

After World War II, such thinking was applied beyond Eurasia to the entire world. Indeed, containment was essentially the application of balance of power thinking to the particular configuration of the state system that emerged after 1945. George Kennan's original view was that only three contested areas were of sufficient economic importance that they had to be kept out of Soviet hands: the United Kingdom, the Ruhr Valley in Europe, and Japan. Later, under the influence of the domino theory and other dubious views of how power might shift in the international system, others expanded the idea to argue that if the Soviet Union acquired too many allies anywhere—even poor, unstable Third World allies—it could irrevocably tip the global balance against the United States. But however applied, the concept learned by the earliest American statesmen from their European forebears remained essentially the same: that some combinations of power overseas might be so critical as to pose a military threat to U.S. physical security, and that American statecraft had to be engaged, the sooner the better, to thwart any such eventuality.

The question suggested by balance of power thinking for the post-containment era is whether, with the collapse of Soviet power, any nation is likely in the foreseeable future to pose a similar threat. Among the current great power candidates, Japan seems too anti-military, China too weak, Germany too enveloped by Europe, Europe (at the same time) too disunited, Brazil or India too young, and recovery by any of the larger [former] Soviet republics . . . too far in the future to worry about. Although some degree of nuclear threat will continue in spite of accelerated arms reductions, and occasional terrorist attacks will remain a feature of the international landscape, catastrophic military dangers to American physical security seem hard to imagine for at least the next 15 to 25 years.

Nevertheless, it is difficult to believe that the United States will dismiss balance of power thinking altogether. Certainly the characteristics of equilibrium in the emerging post–Cold War international system will concern the United States, as will balances in various regions. Moreover, the possibilities for applying a flexible balance of power policy will increase in the post–Cold War era for two reasons: first, because the emerging multipolar system offers as potential allies more states of relatively equal power; and second, because ideological differences that constrain realignments have declined in importance. Ultimately, unless states are able to create some other system to manage a new world order, the balance of power will remain the only game in town. Although its relative power may seem less overwhelming than in the early Cold War years, the United States remains—and is welcomed by a surprising array of states across the globe as—the indispensable balancer.

Still, with a vastly reduced threat, the balance of power game will be played for far lower stakes in the future, freeing the system's major actors to experiment with other security strategies. One of these is collective security.

Collective Security

Although not labeled as collective security until the 1930s, the ideas elaborated by Woodrow Wilson stood on a long tradition of American interest in anti-war schemes that can be traced from Thomas Paine and Benjamin Franklin, through the American Peace Society in the 1820s and 1830s, and into the movement for international law and arbitration that culminated in the Hague conferences of 1899 and 1907. Wilson's own contribution was less to jettison or deny the balance of power than to envision its regulation by a community of power, based on mutual, reciprocal norms of conduct and managed through a multilateral organization. The heart of his proposal for a League of Nations was to guarantee the political independence and territorial integrity of all states while, at the same time, providing machinery (including a council of the world's foreign ministers and an international court) that could negotiate changes in the status quo and settle disputes without armed conflict. The genius of the League Covenant was to link these two aspects legally, pledging members to apply sanctions against any state that used force across established international boundaries before it had exhausted the full range of available settlement procedures.

It was the extraordinary bad luck of this first great experiment in collective security, and of the United Nations after it, to be attempted amidst the twentieth century's hegemonic enterprises. However stunning their improvisations in economic and social affairs, decolonization, and peacekeeping, the failure of these organizations' original collective security machinery was so complete that the very term "collective security" was appropriated for defensive alliances, like the North Atlantic Treaty Organization (NATO), the South East Asia Treaty Organization (SEATO), the Central Treaty Organization (CENTO), and other artifacts of containment. But today there is a multiplicity of signs that the broad tradition of collective security, adapted in less formulaic and more flexible forms, may be applicable to the post–Cold War world on a variety of levels.

Regionally, for example, it is almost impossible to envision a Europe comprising the former Soviet republics in various states of association, a united Germany, and a free Eastern Europe without some kind of collective security arrangement. A transformed NATO, an expanded European Community (EC), a revamped Western European Union (WEU), and . . . the Conference on Security and Cooperation in Europe (CSCE) [now the Organization for Security and Cooperation in Europe] could all perform this role or parts of it. . . .

The most dramatic development bearing on the prospects for a working peace system, however, was the Persian Gulf crisis occasioned by Iraq's invasion of Kuwait, in the course of which President Bush explicitly linked U.S. action to a "new world order." Here, in marked contrast to League experience in the 1930s, the great powers acted with virtual unanimity through the Security Council to legitimize collective action; economic sanctions were effectively imposed and enforced; a broad coalition was assembled and held together to carry out UN directives despite the pain of economic dislocation and war; and although political and economic pressures failed to reverse aggression, armed force succeeded in doing so, at costs acceptable to the coalition.

On the other hand, the Gulf experience also included some disquieting signs and unfortunate characteristics from a collective security viewpoint. For all the talk of the new world order, the UN's role was limited to providing global legitimacy for a U.S.–managed crisis; not even the fig leaf of a UN command was allowed by Washington. Moreover, although the Gulf crisis underlined the importance of great power leadership to successful collective action, one is hard pressed to imagine another post–Cold War conflict that would so clearly engage the vital interests, not only of the United States, but of nearly the entire world community. Nor was the world as united as might first appear. Germany and Japan, the economic powerhouses of the post–Cold War world, were less than enthusiastic in their support of the coalition's action. Equally ominous, substantial majorities in most Arab states seemed to feel that the international delict of Iraq's armed attack across an international boundary was somehow neutralized by the sins of the rich sheiks of Kuwait. This, too, suggests the limits of consensus on the central maxims of collective security and raises doubts about whether any such scheme can be broadly enforced. . . .

Hemispheric Defense

While balance of power and collective security are globalist strategies for physical security, a third historical American approach with resonance for the future, hemispheric defense, is decidedly regionalist. It dates back at least to the Monroe Doctrine of 1823 and Henry Clay's "American system," both of which were based on the vague idea that the new world was fundamentally different from the old and therefore destined to have a cohesive future (notwithstanding the great social, cultural, and geographic distances between North and South). Although the enormous power of the United States relative to its southern neighbors (and the uses it has chosen to make of that power) has given the Monroe Doctrine a stormy history, there is an equally impressive tradition of cooperative schemes, including the Pan-American Union, the Organization of American States, the Alliance for Progress, and the Caribbean Basin Initiative.

What distinguishes hemispheric defense from a balance of power or even collective security strategy is the notion that the physical security of the United States still depends materially on protecting the borders of the United States. Whereas both balance of power and collective security assume the indivisibility of the peace on a worldwide basis, hemispheric defense gives much more prominence to geographic contiguity, arguing that—even in the missile age—being close enables a country to pose a greater threat to the United States than if it were far away. This perspective gains additional credibility if one focuses on immediate, concrete dangers like illegal and uncontrolled immigration or narcotics trafficking, rather than on global threats like a massive ballistic missile attack, against which no defense . . . seems feasible anyway.

Of course, being close—and the sense of closeness—may be somewhat different in today's world than they were decades ago. Before and during World War II, the hemisphere's borders in the minds of American strategists were extended ever farther as the technology of air transport brought more distant contiguous areas closer. Today it is neither an exaggeration nor an affront to logic to include the Atlantic community (and thus much of Europe), as well as the so-called Pacific Basin or Pacific Rim countries, within the conceptual hemisphere . . . .

Will hemispheric defense become a more important source of American strategic thought in the post-containment era? Certainly we [saw] more of this kind of thinking by American statesmen in the 1980s than in earlier decades, as illustrated by the Reagan administration's policies on Nicaragua and El Salvador, and its invasion of Grenada. Since those concerns were fueled by anticommunism and containment in a Cold War atmosphere, it is quite possible that they will disappear along with Soviet hostility. But the Bush administration's attention to Mexico, its Enterprise for the Americas initiative, and its 1989 invasion of Panama all attest to the post–Cold War salience of the region. With the more-distant world an increasingly friendly or at worst irrelevant place, and with their attention focused more on nontraditional security threats, perhaps American strategists will decide that nearby interests supersede all others.

Isolationism

One might, however, take such logic a step further. The oldest approach devised by Americans to serve their physical security seems hardly worthy of being called a strategy at all. It is isolationism, a tradition neither global nor regional but profoundly inward-looking. Given the fact that this once-honored tradition in American foreign policy has become a loaded term for the present generation, it is important to be clear at the outset about what isolationism was and was not in American history.

First, isolationism never meant total isolation from the world. Quite willing—even eager—to promote overseas economic relations as long as they did not threaten the nation's security, isolationists urged only political detachment. In contrast to collective security or the alliances demanded by a balance of power strategy, isolationism especially meant a determined noncommitment, a refusal to make advance promises in security matters that might detract from the nation's absolute freedom of action. Noncommitment in turn was reinforced by a strong pacifist element, and by the view that the casualties resulting from foreign wars could accomplish nothing of real value for U.S. interests.

Second, it is important to remember that, in spite of its contemporary notoriety, isolationism was long popular with Americans because it worked. Staying out of other nations' troubles and taking advantage of what George Washington called "our detached and distant situation" was a realistic strategy when risks from overseas threats were slight and foreign affairs costs had to be kept low while the nation invested its growing resources in domestic development. What gave isolationism a bad name was not that it failed to provide security to the country for over a century, but that Americans failed to abandon it when the conditions required for its success disappeared at the beginning of the twentieth century.

Thus, the issue for post–Cold War U.S. policy is whether the future will be more like the nineteenth century, a time in which a kind of isolationism might be a realistic and workable strategy; or more like the early twentieth century, in which various domestic pressures sustained isolationism in spite of conditions which made it a dangerous illusion. Ever since the Vietnam War, a substantial group of Americans has believed that the nation's commitments are far out of line with its power, that resources available for either foreign or domestic concerns are increasingly limited, and that problems at home need priority attention. Many other Americans may always have agreed with them, but felt until recently that the Soviet threat could not be ignored. Today, with international dangers vastly diminished . . . and with critical domestic needs demanding attention, multiple pressures combine toward a policy of self-interest that some label "neoisolationist."

GLOBALIZING AMERICAN VALUES

Great nations are rarely satisfied protecting their own territory, people, and property. They want to stand for something, to believe that they are contributing to a better as well as a safer world. Some statesmen may support strategies of value projection in the belief that a world remade in the nation's image can also help promote physical security and economic prosperity, and that programs to project national values overseas are thus important strategic "software." But ordinary Americans mainly seem uncomfortable with the idea that their nation might throw its weight around in the world simply to protect their own security. They want their country to use its power for good, too.

As a result, statesmen know how difficult it is to sustain public support for any policy—especially one demanding sacrifice—without an element of idealism. Whatever he might believe, no president ever told the American people that he was leading them to war to preserve the balance of power; Americans rather have fought "in the cause of humanity" (1898), to make the world "safe for democracy" (1917), to revenge "an unprovoked and dastardly attack" (1941), "to prevent a third world war" (1950), to defend "the value of an American commitment" (1965), or "to forge . . . a new world order" (1991). And from the time when Harry Truman was told to "scare hell out of" the Congress in order to get aid for Greece and Turkey, anti-communism was closely associated with the physical containment of the Soviet Union in American Cold War strategies.

Projecting national values overseas usually involves direct interference in another nation's internal affairs, and because it springs from moralistic roots it is difficult to limit on grounds of realism or feasibility. Some would argue, for example, that American Cold War policies led to serious trouble precisely when decision-makers forgot that their objective was to contain the expansion of Soviet state power and instead made global anticommunism their primary motive. . . .

President Carter was the first modern president to make value projection his signature in foreign affairs. The Carter human rights policy was highly intrusive, attempting to protect individuals in other nations against the arbitrary exercise of power by their own governments. In effect, Carter demanded that rulers worldwide, whatever their societies' traditions or their own philosophies of government, adopt the protections of free speech and assembly written into the U.S. Bill of Rights as well as its prohibitions against deprivation of life, liberty, or property without due process. And Carter tried to give effect to his policy in spite of its cost to security ties with allies thought important to containment (e.g., South Korea or the Philippines) and regardless of its effect on other major objectives of his administration, as when he chastised Soviet rights violations at the same time as he urged the Kremlin to make major cuts in strategic forces.

Despite good intentions, though, the Carter administration could not maintain the unalloyed emphasis on human rights with which it had begun. U.S. security interests in places from Seoul to Moscow forced compromises, and compromises were hard to defend in a policy based on absolute moral standards. As Soviet adventurism and the "loss" of Iran, Nicaragua, and Afghanistan dominated the headlines, Ronald Reagan was able to argue that a policy promoting individual human rights in foreign countries was a luxury Americans could ill afford.

But today, given the [end of] the Soviet threat to U.S. security interests, the United States has at least as much freedom as in 1977 to make human rights overseas a top priority in its foreign affairs strategy. A Carter-like policy, focusing on individual rights with all other foreign policy considerations in second place, is certainly one option for post–Cold War American statecraft. As in the 1970s, such an objective would pose major questions regarding its implementation, but at least strategists would not have to worry about shunned allies turning to the Soviet Union for support. Public rhetoric and aid flows could thus be tied to rights considerations in ways that might have been unrealistic during the Cold War years.

Another human rights–based approach is, ironically, offered by the same Ronald Reagan who so excoriated the Carter policy. For not only did Reagan come to realize the great popularity of value projection with the American people, but his administration also eventually understood the long-run danger to American security interests of corrupt and authoritarian regimes in allied states. The Reagan team ushered Ferdinand Marcos out of power, for example, not primarily because it wanted individual liberties restored to the Philippine people; it did so because it was persuaded that the Marcos government had become so riddled with cronyism and so detached from popular sentiment that it was ineffectual in protecting either its own or American interests.

But in embracing human rights, Reagan also transformed them, changing the focus of value projection from protecting individuals against arbitrary state power to promoting American-style systems of economics and government. This too was a highly pragmatic development, beginning as early as the [1981] Cancun conference, when the president told Third World nations that their only hope of sustained development lay in moving to market-based economic systems. Although the Reagan administration remained quite willing to work with authoritarian dictators around the world from Chun Doo Hwan to Augusto Pinochet, it was also increasingly willing to put pressure on them to move toward democratizing their countries, again on the theory that repression and resulting societal instability were as bad for U.S. security as they were for individual liberties. By the middle of his second term, Reagan had abandoned his preference for dictatorships of the right as bulwarks against communism and had declared U.S. opposition to all forms of tyranny, whether of the left or right. . . . Following the wave of conversions to democracy and capitalism in the late 1980s, a Reaganesque approach to value projection has become perhaps the most often suggested strategy for post–Cold War American foreign policy. . . . Another much less aggressive manner of projecting American values overseas might also appeal to Americans in the post–Cold War era. It is certainly the oldest form of national value projection, captured first in the eighteenth-century evocation by John Winthrop of the United States as a "City upon a Hill." In this approach, rather than engaging in a strident effort to promote American values overseas or applying American power to affect the government of those who have no voice in or control over it, the United States would merely endeavor to be the Great Exemplar of political and economic freedom in the world, showing by example the way others might follow in accordance with their own abilities, will, and traditions. . . . This approach assumes that the United States is—or can become—a society so attractive that it need not impose its principles on others. The force of its example would be the only persuasion it must or should apply. As John Quincy Adams put it in 1821: America is "the well-wisher to the freedom and independence of all. She is the champion and vindicator only of her own."

A strategy of leadership-by-example might well appeal to internationalists who harbor doubts regarding the applicability of democratic forms of government and market economic systems in foreign societies, or who question the skill of Americans confronted by exotic cultures in attempting such delicate transplants. . . . Such an inward-looking strategy might avoid the excesses of another moralistic crusade in U.S. foreign policy and the disillusionment that seems so often to follow. Its distinction from a more active promotional effort would be not only in the relative paucity of policy instruments employed but also in the indeterminacy of its goals. Let others decide what is of value in our culture, politics, and economic life, it would argue; we will concentrate on making them worthy of emulation and on helping others adopt what they wish.

PROMOTING THE GENERAL WELFARE

The recent emphasis on value projection as a central organizing principle for American foreign policy may be seen as part of a much larger shift, cutting across all areas of the national interest, from a threat-based to an interest-based strategy. . . . American policymakers during the Cold War years were often so frightened by the Soviet Union that they fell into the posture of assuming that whatever the Soviets or their clients threatened—from South Vietnam to Angola to Chad—was automatically "of interest" to the United States. Such an approach . . . yielded the initiative to the Soviet Union and dramatically escalated the costs of security policy. Future policymakers, lacking such a threat and with costs an ever more critical factor, may find it easier to focus on promoting interests rather than on defending against threats. The result may well be that no strategy centered on politico-military concern will appeal to Americans in the post–Cold War era. . . .

In the [economic welfare] area of the national interest, U.S. hegemony has been in relative decline for at least two decades. . . . International economists worry, and with good reason, whether any economic system can operate successfully without a single national hegemon to set the rules authoritatively and make the sacrifice-for-privilege trades it requires. A post-hegemonic system would require unprecedented levels of cooperation between the major industrialized countries; whether the United States will be willing and able to lead or even to cooperate with such a grouping will depend on the kind of strategy for economic prosperity it adopts.

To be sure, the practical end of American hegemony does not necessarily mean the end of its underlying philosophy, the belief in free trade and equality of economic opportunity for all nations, large and small. Historically, that philosophy is deeply rooted in the American psyche. It stretches right back to the revolution, when in the Treaty Plan of 1776 the United States offered access to its market and products in the naive hope that Europe would rush to join it in the war against England. Once the United States was independent, an end to the restrictive trade arrangements of the British Navigation Acts and the Spanish colonial monopoly in the West Indies became major policy goals of the new nation, a small power shut out of large states' mercantilist schemes with no hope of creating similar arrangements to benefit itself.

Similarly, throughout the nineteenth century the whole of American policy toward the Far East was shaped by the concept of the Open Door, the idea of free access to markets in the region for all comers on conditions of complete equality. It was a sensible approach for a country without military power in Asia and faced by active European efforts to divide China into exclusive spheres of influence. Using it, the United States opened Japan in the 1850s by suggesting that an American-led free trade regime would help forestall China-like depredations by the Europeans and would allow Japan to become a great trading nation. . . . Free trade ultimately became orthodoxy across all American economic policy in the late 1930s under the reciprocal tariff policy of Cordell Hull, cementing itself firmly into the global economic system after World War II as progressive rounds of multilateral trade negotiations under the General Agreement on Tariffs and Trade (GATT) extended its beneficial effects worldwide.

The principle of equality of economic opportunity has exerted a powerful influence on American security policies as well. Although at the deepest strategic level the causes of the United States' involvement in European wars had to do with preserving the balance of power, the immediate circumstances of the U.S. decisions for war in 1812 and 1917 involved protecting the country's right as a neutral to trade with all belligerents in any conflict. Until the isolationist neutrality legislation of the 1930s, in fact, Americans insisted on commercial equality of opportunity in war as well as in peace, and they proved themselves quite willing to fight for it.

American presidents still talk the language of free trade. But whether trade liberalization will continue . . . will depend first on whether the United States continues its half-century adherence to a free trade strategy in reality as well as in rhetoric, then on whether it has the willingness and skill to shift from a solo hegemonic role to a cooperative leadership stance. . . . As Americans become increasingly convinced that free trade policies will not work with countries like Japan, sustaining vetoes of protectionist legislation will be more and more difficult. At some point, if the political pressure becomes too great, the executive branch may join the Congress in espousing a different strategy for economic prosperity.

One candidate will be regional trading blocs, the idea captured by Margaret Thatcher at the 1990 Economic Summit in Houston when she spoke of "three great groups" of nations, "one based on the dollar, one based on the yen, and one based on the deutschmark." . . .

Some authorities argue that the emergence of trade blocs should be seen as a benign development, since they can push the frontier of liberalization beyond what is possible in a global context and thereby act as pathbreakers for later worldwide trade agreements. But whether reasonable liberality could be maintained between blocs while preferential areas are nurtured within them seems problematic, given that no inward preference is possible without a concomitant outward discrimination. Such a system seems fragile at best, likely to slide under the cover of so-called "fair trade" toward increasingly managed and illiberal forms. . . .

Those who believe that . . . protectionist policies were forever discredited by the Great Depression should take note of how successfully the practice of protectionism has spread under the rhetoric of free trade. The Reagan administration presided over a 23 percent increase in non-tariff barriers, one of the worst performances among nations in the Organization of Economic Cooperation and Development (OECD). Forty percent of Japanese exports to the United States currently enter under some form of protection; over $6 billion worth of Japanese cars are shut out each year. Moreover, the 1988 Trade Act established adjustment machinery that is at best strongly biased in retaliatory directions, enshrining in legislation the debatable premise that protectionist measures are likely to lead to a freer system. And all of this, it should be pointed out, happened in an era of sustained domestic prosperity.

Protectionism may not make economic sense, but its history indicates that it is a highly appealing strategy. It will be all the harder to resist in the future since it will either be invoked as a means to the goal of free or fair trade in an imperfect world, or applied gradually and unannounced by those purporting to believe in the most liberal policies.

STRATEGIC COHERENCE AFTER CONTAINMENT

None of these strategies, to be sure, will simply reappear in their earlier forms to replace containment, anti-communism, and economic hegemony. But it is a fair guess that whatever does emerge will draw on many of the traditions outlined above, combining their features in new ways that respond to new conditions. At present it seems clear only that, with the threat of Soviet expansion gone, strategies other than containment will have to be devised to serve the American interest in physical security. And as physical security itself seems less at risk, economic prosperity and value projection will probably become bigger parts of future foreign affairs strategies. . . .

Until a new hegemonic threat appears, . . . the nation can well afford to worry less about its physical security. In this area, a kind of layered strategy can be envisioned, one that could be conducted with a much lower level of resources than the nation spent during the Cold War. While maintaining a capacity for intervention in isolated incidents that threaten its vital interests, the United States would progressively work to fashion collective mechanisms for dealing with routine instability that poses a threat to American lives and economic activity . . . .

Strategists are realists when necessary, idealists when possible. The relative lack of post–Cold War concern for physical security would seem to free the nation to indulge its idealistic instincts; yet, ironically, it comes at a time when resource constraints would seem to demand idealism on the cheap. This consideration alone will be a formidable restraint on crusades for democracy or human rights abroad. . . . Economic prosperity is, ironically, the one area of the national interest in which an inward focus might be extraordinarily destructive. . . . The internationalization of the domestic economy would certainly make a return to protectionist or mercantilist policies very damaging over the long run, and the financial and commercial elites of the U.S. economy may now be so interdependent with the outside world as to make such a policy turn unlikely. What is needed is rather an inward-looking economic strategy that is simultaneously regionalist if not globalist in nature, a strategy that undertakes domestic renewal while maintaining and strengthening overseas connections. Such a strategy would require both an adroit and committed national leadership and a shift in the popular mood from consumption to investment, from self-gratification to sacrifice. Neither, at present, seems much in evidence.

So today's ultimate strategic question returns to the question of power, to whether in these difficult times the American body politic can summon the will and hence the means to capitalize on the end, not only of the Cold War, but of this century's hegemonic wars. . . . If Americans can disenthrall themselves from Cold War thinking, understand the character of the revolutionary changes they face, and create purposeful strategies to deal with them, we may be poised on the edge of the most hopeful season in international affairs since the Congress of Vienna initiated a century of hegemonic peace.

7. THE MYTH OF POST–COLD WAR CHAOS

G. John Ikenberry

THE 1945 ORDER LIVES ON

A great deal of ink has been shed in recent years describing various versions of the post–Cold War order. These attempts have all failed, because there is no such creature. The world order created in the 1940s is still with us, and in many ways stronger than ever. The challenge for American foreign policy is not to imagine and build a new world order but to reclaim and renew an old one—an innovative and durable order that has been hugely successful and largely unheralded.

The end of the Cold War, the common wisdom holds, was a historical watershed. The collapse of communism brought the collapse of the order that took shape after World War II. While foreign policy theorists and officials scramble to design new grand strategies, the United States is rudderless on uncharted seas.

The common wisdom is wrong. What ended with the Cold War was bipolarity, the nuclear stalemate, and decades of containment of the Soviet Union—seemingly the most dramatic and consequential features of the postwar era. But the world order created in the middle to late 1940s endures, more extensive and in some respects more robust than during its Cold War years. Its basic principles, which deal with organization and relations among the Western liberal democracies, are alive and well.

These less celebrated, less heroic, but more fundamental principles and policies—the real international order—include the commitment to an open world economy and its multilateral management, and the stabilization of

Note: Notes have been deleted.

96

socioeconomic welfare. And the political vision behind the order was as important as the anticipated economic gains. The major industrial democracies took it upon themselves to "domesticate" their dealings through a dense web of multilateral institutions, intergovernmental relations, and joint management of the Western and world political economies. Security and stability in the West were seen as intrinsically tied to an array of institutions—the United Nations and its agencies and the General Agreement on Tariffs and Trade (GATT) only some among many—that bound the democracies together, constrained conflict, and facilitated political community. Embracing common liberal democratic norms and operating within interlocking multilateral institutions, the United States, Western Europe, and, later, Japan built an enduring postwar order.

The end of the Cold War has been so disorienting because it ended the containment order—40 years of policies and bureaucratic missions and an entire intellectual orientation. But the watershed of postwar order predated hostilities with the Soviet Union. The turning point was not a Cold War milestone such as the announcement of the Truman Doctrine in 1947 or the creation of the Atlantic alliance in 1948–1949. It might have come as early as 1941, when Roosevelt and Churchill issued the Atlantic Charter declaring the liberal principles that were to guide the postwar settlement. The process became irreversible in 1944, when representatives at the Bretton Woods conference laid down the core principles and mechanisms of the postwar Western economic order and those at Dumbarton Oaks gave the political aspect of the vision concrete form in their proposals for a United Nations. The Cold War may have reinforced the liberal democratic order, by hastening the reintegration of Germany and Japan and bringing the United States much more directly into the management of the system. But it did not call it forth.

In world historical terms, the end of the Cold War is an overrated event. Former Secretary of State James A. Baker III observes in his 1995 memoir, *The Politics of Diplomacy,* "In three and a half years [from the late 1980s to the early 1990s] . . . the very nature of the international system as we know it was transformed." To be sure, large parts of the non-Western world are undergoing a tremendous and difficult transformation. A great human drama is playing itself out in the former communist states, and the future there hangs in the balance. But the system the United States led the way in creating after World War II has not collapsed; on the contrary, it remains the core of world order. The task today is not to discover or define some mythic new order but to reclaim the policies, commitments, and strategies of the old.

A TALE OF TWO DOCTRINES

World War II produced two postwar settlements. One, a reaction to deteriorating relations with the Soviet Union, led to the containment order, which was based on the balance of power, nuclear deterrence, and political and ideological competition. The other, a reaction to the economic rivalry and political turmoil of the 1930s and the resulting world war, can be called the liberal democratic order. It culminated in a wide range of new institutions and relations among the Western industrial democracies, built around economic openness, political reciprocity, and multilateral management of an American-led liberal political system.

Distinct political visions and intellectual rationales animated the two settlements, and at key moments the American president gave voice to each. On March 12, 1947, President Truman delivered his celebrated speech before Congress announcing aid to Greece and Turkey, wrapping it in an American commitment to support the cause of freedom worldwide. The declaration of the Truman Doctrine was a founding moment of the containment order, rallying Americans to a new great struggle, this one against what was thought to be Soviet communism's quest for world domination. A "fateful hour" had struck, Truman said, and the people of the world "must choose between two alternate ways of life." If the United States failed to exercise leadership, he warned, "we may endanger the peace of the world."

It is often forgotten that six days before, Truman had delivered an equally sweeping speech at Baylor University. On this occasion he spoke of the lessons the world must learn from the disasters of the 1930s. "As each battle of the economic war of the Thirties was fought, the inevitable tragic result became more and more apparent," said Truman. "From the tariff policy of Hawley and Smoot, the world went on to Ottawa and the system of imperial preferences, from Ottawa to the kind of elaborate and detailed restrictions adopted by Nazi Germany." Truman reaffirmed America's commitment to "economic peace," which would involve tariff reductions and rules and institutions of trade and investment. When economic differences arose, he said, "the interests of all will be considered, and a fair and just solution will be found." Conflicts would be captured and tamed in a cage of multilateral rules, standards, safeguards, and procedures for dispute resolution. According to Truman, "This is the way of a civilized community."

But it was the containment order that impressed itself on the popular imagination. In celebrated American accounts of the early years after World War II, intrepid officials struggled to make sense of Soviet military power and geopolitical intentions. A few "wise men" fashioned a reasoned and coherent response to the global challenge of Soviet communism, and their containment strategy gave clarity and purpose to several decades of American foreign policy. Over those decades, sprawling bureaucratic and military organizations were built around containment. The bipolar division of the world, nuclear weapons of growing size and sophistication, the ongoing clash of two expansive ideologies—all these gave life to and reinforced the centrality of the containment order.

By comparison, the thinking behind the liberal democratic order was more diffuse. The liberal democratic agenda was less obviously a grand strategy designed to advance American security interests, and it was inevitably viewed during the Cold War as secondary, a preoccupation of economists and businessmen. The policies and institutions that supported free trade among the advanced industrial societies seemed the stuff of low politics. But the liberal democratic agenda was actually built on a robust yet sophisticated set of ideas about American security interests, the causes of war and depression, and a desirable postwar political order. Although containment overshadowed it, the postwar liberal democratic order was more deeply rooted in the American experience and an understanding of history, economics, and the sources of political stability.

The proper foundations of political order have preoccupied American thinkers from the nation's founding onward, and innovative institutions and practices were developed in response to independence, continental expansion, civil war, economic depression, and world war. The liberal ideal was held high: open and decentralized political institutions could limit and diffuse conflict while integrating diverse peoples and interests. Moreover, a stable and legitimate political order was assured by its grounding in the Constitution, which specified rights, guarantees, and an institutionalized political process. When American officials began to contemplate postwar order, they were drawing on a wellspring of ideas, experiments, and historical lessons and sifting these with an abiding liberal belief in the possibility of peaceful and mutually beneficial international relations.

The most basic conviction underlying the postwar liberal agenda was that the closed autarkic regions that had contributed to the worldwide depression and split the globe into competing blocs before the war must be broken up and replaced by an open, nondiscriminatory economic system. Peace and security, proponents had decided, were impossible in the face of exclusive economic regions. The challengers of liberal multilateralism, however, occupied almost every corner of the advanced industrial world. Germany and Japan were the most overtly hostile; both had pursued a dangerous path that combined authoritarian capitalism with military dictatorship and coercive regional autarky. But the British Commonwealth and its imperial preference system also challenged liberal multilateral order.

The hastily drafted Atlantic Charter was an American effort to ensure that Britain signed on to its liberal democratic war aims. The joint statement of principles affirmed free trade, equal access to natural resources for all interested buyers, and international economic collaboration to advance labor standards, employment security, and social welfare. Roosevelt and Churchill declared before the world that they had learned the lessons of the interwar years—and those lessons were fundamentally about the proper organization of the Western political economy. America's enemies, its friends, and even America itself had to be reformed and integrated into the postwar economic system.

THE LIBERAL MANIFESTO

The postwar liberal democratic order was designed to solve the internal problems of Western industrial capitalism. It was not intended to fight Soviet communism, nor was it simply a plan to get American business back on its feet after the war by opening up the world to trade and investment. It was a strategy to build Western solidarity through economic openness and joint political governance. Four principles pursued in the 1940s gave shape to this order.

The most obvious principle was economic openness, which would ideally take the form of a system of nondiscriminatory trade and investment. As American strategic thinkers of the 1930s watched the world economy collapse and the German and Japanese blocs emerge, they pondered whether the United States could remain a great industrial power within the confines of the western hemisphere. What were the minimum geographical requirements for the country's economic and military viability? For all practical purposes they had their answer by the time the United States entered the war. An American hemispheric bloc would not be sufficient; the United States needed secure markets and supplies of raw materials in Asia and Europe. . . .

American thinking was that economic openness was an essential element of a stable and peaceful world political order. "Prosperous neighbors are the best neighbors," remarked Roosevelt administration Treasury official Harry Dexter White. But officials were convinced that American economic and security interests demanded it as well. Great liberal visionaries and hard-nosed geopolitical strategists could agree on the notion of open markets; it united American postwar planners and was the seminal idea informing the work of the Bretton Woods conference on postwar economic cooperation. In his farewell remarks to the conference, Secretary of the Treasury Henry Morgenthau asserted that the agreements creating the International Monetary Fund and the World Bank marked the end of economic nationalism, by which he meant not that countries would give up pursuit of their national interest but that trade blocs and economic spheres of influence would no longer be their vehicles.

The second principle was joint management of the Western political-economic order. The leading industrial democratic states must not only lower barriers to trade and the movement of capital but must govern the system. This also was a lesson from the 1930s: institutions, rules, and active mutual management by governments were necessary to avoid unproductively competitive and conflictual economic practices. Americans believed such cooperation necessary in a world where national economies were increasingly at the mercy of developments abroad. The unwise or untoward policies of one country threatened contagion, undermining the stability of all. As Roosevelt said at the opening of Bretton Woods, "The economic health of every country is a proper matter of concern to all its neighbors, near and far."

The belief in cooperative economic management also drew inspiration from the government activism of Roosevelt's New Deal. The postwar Western system was organized at a high tide of optimism about the capability of experts, economic and technical knowledge, and government intervention. The rise of Keynesian economics in Europe in the 1930s had begun to encourage an activist role for the state in the economy and society. International economic governance was a natural and inevitable extension of the policies being tried in individual Western industrial societies.

A third principle of liberal democratic order held that the rules and institutions of the Western world economy must be organized to support domestic economic stability and social security. This new commitment was foreshadowed in the Atlantic Charter's call for postwar international collaboration to ensure employment stability and social welfare. It was a sign of the times that Churchill, a conservative Tory, could promise a historic expansion of the government's responsibility for the people's well-being. In their schemes for postwar economic order, both Britain and the United States sought a system that would aid and protect their nascent social and economic commitments. They wanted an open world economy, but one congenial to the emerging welfare state as well as business.

The discovery of a middle way between old political alternatives was a major innovation of the postwar Western economic order. British and American planners began their discussion in 1942 deadlocked, Britain's desire for full employment and economic stabilization after the war running up against the American desire for free trade. The breakthrough came in 1944 with the Bretton Woods agreements on monetary order, which secured a more or less open system of trade and payments while providing safeguards for domestic economic stability through the International Monetary Fund. The settlement was a synthesis that could attract a new coalition of conservative free traders and the liberal prophets of economic planning.

A final element of the liberal democratic system might be termed "constitutionalism"—meaning simply that the Western nations would make systematic efforts to anchor their joint commitments in principled and binding institutional mechanisms. In fact, this may be the order's most basic aspect, encompassing the other principles and policies and giving the whole its distinctive domestic character. Governments might ordinarily seek to keep their options open, cooperating with other states but retaining the possibility of disengagement. The United States and the other Western nations after the war did exactly the opposite. They built long-term economic, political, and security commitments that were difficult to retract, and locked in the relationships, to the extent that sovereign states can. Insofar as the participating governments attempted to construct a political order based on commonly embraced norms and principles along with institutional mechanisms for resolving conflicts and reaching specific agreements, they practiced constitutionalism.

Democracies are particularly capable of making constitutional commitments to each other. For self-regarding states to agree to pursue their interests within binding institutions, they must perceive in their partners a credible sense of commitment—an assurance that they will not exit at the least sign of disagreement. Because policymaking in democracies tends to be decentralized and open, the character of commitments can be more clearly determined and there are opportunities to lobby policymakers in the other democracies. Democracies do not just sign agreements; they create political processes that reduce uncertainty and build confidence in mutual commitments.

A CONSTITUTION FOR THE WEST

The constitutional political order was constructed in the West around economic, political, and security institutions. In the economic realm, the Bretton Woods accords were the first permanent international arrangements for cooperation between states. Rules and institutions were proposed to ensure a stable and expansionary world economy and an orderly exchange rate system. Many of the original agreements for a rule-based monetary order gave way to ad hoc arrangements based more on the American dollar, but the vision of jointly managed, multilateral order remained. The organization of postwar trade relations also had an uncertain start, but ultimately an elaborate system of rules and obligations was developed, with quasi judicial procedures for adjudicating disputes. In effect, the Western governments created an array of transnational political arenas organized by function. The postwar years were filled with economic disputes, but they were largely contained within these arenas.

The constitutional vision informed the creation of the United Nations, which combined political, economic, and security aspirations. To be sure, the U.N. system preserved the sovereign rights of member states. Intent on avoiding the failures of the League of Nations, the architects of the new international body drafted a charter under which the great powers would retain their freedom of action. But despite its weak rules and obligations, the United Nations reflected American and European desires to insure against a relapse of American isolation, to establish principles and mechanisms of conflict resolution, and to mute conflicts between states within a semi-institutionalized political process.

Cold War security structures provided additional constitutional architecture. Lord Ismay's observation that NATO was created to keep the Russians out, the Germans down, and the Americans in encapsulates the alliance's importance in locking in long-term commitments and expectations. The American-Japanese security pact had a similar dual-containment character. These institutions not only served as alliances in the ordinary sense of organized efforts to balance external threats, but offered mechanisms and venues for building relations, conducting business, and regulating conflict. The recent French decision to rejoin NATO can be understood only in this light. If NATO were simply a balancing alliance, the organization would be in an advanced stage of decay. It is NATO's broader political function—binding the democracies together and reinforcing political community—that explains its remarkable durability.

The democratic character of the United States and its partners facilitated construction of these dense interstate connections. The decentralized and open character of domestic institutions encouraged political give-and-take across the advanced industrial world. Thus the Western liberal democratic order was not only defined by a set of institutions and agreements, but made for a particular kind of politics—transnational, pluralistic, reciprocal, legitimate. . . .

WHAT ENDURES

For those who thought cooperation among the advanced industrial democracies was driven primarily by Cold War threats, the last few years must appear puzzling. Relations between the major Western countries have not broken down. Germany has not rearmed, nor has Japan. What the Cold War focus misses is an appreciation of the other, less heralded, postwar American project—the building of a liberal order in the West. Archaeologists remove one stratum only to discover an older one beneath; the end of the Cold War allows us to see a deeper and more enduring layer of the postwar political order that was largely obscured by the more dramatic struggles between East and West.

Fifty years after its founding, the Western liberal democratic world is robust, and its principles and policies remain the core of world order. The challenges to liberal multilateralism both from within and from outside the West have mainly disappeared. Although regional experiments abound, they are fundamentally different from the autarkic blocs of the 1930s. The forces of business and financial integration are moving the globe inexorably toward a more tightly interconnected system that ignores regional as well as national borders. Recent proposals for an Atlantic free trade agreement and a Transatlantic Treaty, whatever their economic merits, reflect the trend toward increased integration across regions. The successful conclusion of the Uruguay Round of international trade talks in 1994 and the launching of the World Trade Organization on January 1, 1995, testify to the vigor of liberal multilateral principles. . . .

The problems the liberal democratic order confronts are mostly problems of success, foremost among them the need to integrate the newly developing and post-communist countries. Here one sees most clearly that the post–Cold War order is really a continuation and extension of the Western order forged during and after World War II. The difference is its increasingly global reach. The world has seen an explosion in the desire of countries and peoples to move toward democracy and capitalism. When the history of the late twentieth century is written, it will be the struggle for more open and democratic polities throughout the world that will mark the era, rather than the failure of communism.

Other challenges to the system are boiling up in its leading states. In its early years, rapid and widely shared economic growth buoyed the system, as working- and middle-class citizens across the advanced industrial world rode the crest of the boom. Today economic globalization is producing much greater inequality between the winners and the losers, the wealthy and the poor. How the subsequent dislocations, dashed expectations, and political grievances are dealt with—whether the benefits are shared and the system as a whole is seen as socially just—will affect the stability of the liberal world order more than regional conflict, however tragic, in places like the Balkans.

To be sure, the Cold War reinforced solidarity and a sense of common identity among the liberal democracies, so it would be a mistake to take these binding forces for granted now. Trade disputes, controversies over burden-sharing, and regional conflict will test the durability of the liberal order. Without a Cold War threat to unite their countries, leaders in the advanced democracies will have to work harder to manage the inevitable conflicts and fissures. An agenda of reform and renewal would be an intelligent move to protect 50 years of investment in stable and thriving relations. Policies, institutions, and political symbols can all be directed at reinforcing liberal order, just as they are in individual liberal polities. At the very least, Western leaders could spend much more time acknowledging and celebrating the political space they share.

It is fashionable to say that the United States after the Cold War faces its third try at forging a durable world order, at reinventing the basic rules of world politics, just as after both world wars. But this view is more rhetorically compelling than historically valid. The end of the Cold War was less the end of a world order than the collapse of the communist world into an expanding Western order. If that order is to be defended and strengthened, its historical roots and accomplishments must be reclaimed. The United States built and then managed the containment order for 40 years, but it also built and continues to enjoy the rewards of an older liberal democratic order. America is not adrift in uncharted seas. It is at the center of a world of its own making.

New Agendas for a New Era

8. BUSINESS AND FOREIGN POLICY: TIME FOR A STRATEGIC ALLIANCE?

Jeffrey E. Garten

DESTINATION UNKNOWN

Throughout most of American history, commercial interests have played a central role in foreign policy, and vice versa. During the next few decades the interaction between them will become more intense, more important, more difficult to manage, and more complicated for the American public to understand. . . . [But today] it is not clear where either Washington or the American business community is headed.

There is a critical need for [policymakers] and business leaders to get their collective act together. Their objective should be a new partnership based on two realities of the changing global marketplace. The first is that the federal government's ability to conduct foreign policy in a world preoccupied with economic stability and progress is dwindling, and Washington has neither the people nor the money to exert the influence it once could. The second is that even though business has the money, technology, and management that make today's world spin, it needs Uncle Sam's help more than ever, particularly in a world where governments are awarding big contracts abroad and companies are becoming ensnared in issues such as human rights, labor practices, environmental protection, and corruption. . . .

FOREIGN POLICY, INC.

For most of America's history, foreign policy has reflected an obsession with open markets for American business. The United States has sought outlets for surplus wheat, new markets for autos and airplanes, and access to raw materials like oil or copper. Business expansion abroad was often seen as an extension of the American frontier, part of the nation's manifest destiny. History even records numerous instances when foreign policy seems to have been made or executed by individual companies; protecting the interests of United Fruit, for example, was once synonymous with Washington's policy toward Latin America. More recently, the Big Three auto companies pushed the first Clinton administration to the brink of a trade war with Japan.

Business was able to drive a good deal of foreign policy because of unique features of American society. Corporate leaders, lawyers, and investment bankers were able to move in and out of the highest levels of government. The names are familiar: Elihu Root, Thomas Lamont, Dean Acheson, Robert McNamara, Donald Regan, and Robert Rubin, among others. In addition, the Constitution gave Congress control over trade policy, thereby providing continuous and unlimited opportunities for business lobbying. America was not a traditional colonial power; to the extent that it acted imperialistically, its agents of influence and control were generally American banks and companies, not the military.

Moreover, the nation's motives were never entirely commercial. The United States has not taken mercantilism as far as France or Japan. Americans have associated commerce with open markets, open markets with political freedom, political freedom with democracy, and democracy with peace. During the Cold War, the nation saw an open trading system that included Europe and Japan as helping those societies resist communism and the Soviet Union.

The United States' fundamental drivers of business and foreign policy will remain constant, since they are deeply rooted in America's history and philosophy. What is rapidly changing now is the context in which the nation's interests are acted out. The new landscape is characterized by globalization of American business, the political and economic fragility of many up-and-coming trading partners, and growing tension between values widely held in America and other countries' economic and political goals.

To begin with, the health of the American economy is more closely linked to foreign markets than ever before. The country can no longer generate enough growth, jobs, profits, and savings from domestic sources. More than one-third of America's economic growth now derives from exports. By the turn of the century, more than 16 million jobs will be supported by overseas sales. From Coca-Cola to Caterpillar, many U.S. companies are taking in more than 50 percent of their revenues abroad. From a foreign policy standpoint, moreover, America's links to most countries, and its potential influence on them, depend increasingly on commercial relationships. Trade, finance, and business investment have become the sine qua non of links with Russia, China, Japan, Southeast Asia, the European Union, and the nations of the western hemisphere.

The most crucial markets are those where not only the opportunities but also the commercial and political risks are the greatest. These big emerging markets include those the Clinton administration . . . identified as America's most promising for trade and investment: Mexico, Brazil, Argentina, South Africa, Poland, Turkey, India, members of the Association of Southeast Asian Nations, the China–Hong Kong–Taiwan region, and South Korea. These countries are growing two to three times faster than the industrialized countries of the Organization for Economic Cooperation and Development; the value of U.S. exports to them already exceeds that to the EU and Japan combined. Over the next decade planners in these markets anticipate spending more than $1.5 trillion on airports and telecommunications and energy systems. [These projections were made prior to the spiral of currency devaluations in Asia and declines in capital markets worldwide in the fall of 1997.—Eds.]

Most of the big emerging markets are undergoing tumultuous political and economic change. From Mexico to South Africa to Indonesia, the simultaneous opening of their economies and political systems is unleashing unprecedented demands and raising profound questions about their ability to sustain high growth, open markets, and political stability. It is in these markets that other American interests—human rights, labor practices, environmental protection, and a reduction of corruption, censorship, and nuclear proliferation—loom large and difficult decisions must be made in Washington regarding an overall approach to foreign policy.

NECESSARY PARTNERS

The globalization of the world economy has vastly complicated the links between Washington and American business. On one hand, the resources of the American government—money, people with adequate global experience—are shrinking, and the role of American firms as de facto agents of foreign policy is expanding. The spread of business across borders may be the most powerful force operating in the world today. On the other hand, the influence of American business, by any measure substantial, does not lack great competition. If Boeing does not play by China's rules, Airbus will. If AT&T does not meet Brazilian requirements, Alcatel would be happy to help.

Globalization, and all the strategic alliances and cross-border mergers it has spawned, raises another question—the definition of an "American" firm and the criteria by which Washington should decide which firms to help. For example, does Northern Telecom, a Canadian firm with substantial manufacturing operations throughout the United States, deserve the same support for overseas contracts from the American government as, say, Bell Atlantic?

Despite shifting international sands, the government and the business community need each other to achieve their goals. The hallmark of involvement with big emerging markets is that American business depends on Washington's help to liberalize trade, protect intellectual property, remove regulatory barriers, and encourage continued economic reform. It needs the government's help to win major contracts in the many countries whose governments award the deals and where French, German, or Japanese firms are getting help from their governments. Small and medium-sized firms are also major consumers of information on foreign markets from the Commerce Department's global network and from U.S. embassies around the world.

And Washington needs business more than ever to reinforce its goals. The executive branch depends almost entirely on business for technical information regarding trade negotiations, all the more so as the Washington bureaucracy is downsized even as it negotiates an ever broader range of issues. In all emerging markets, America's political and economic goals depend largely on the direct investments in factories or other hard assets that only business can deliver. It can make an enormous difference, too, if American business executives reinforce Washington's human rights efforts with private diplomacy as well as public actions to improve working conditions.

Moreover, there are areas of great strategic significance where U.S. diplomacy and business could not succeed without each other. Take, for example, the Caspian Sea region, home to the world's largest underdeveloped oil and gas reserves in the newest and most fragile independent states of the former Soviet Union. Vulnerable to pressure from Russia, Iran, and, potentially, China, the countries of this region require heavy Western investment and visible political support. As the role of business in America's foreign policy grows, so will the public scrutiny. The frenzy of media attention [following the 1996 presidential campaign] on the possible connection between campaign contributions and policy favors may cause escalating concern about the overlapping circles of public and private interests. This is all the more reason to devise a framework that measures up to America's requirements and the highest standards.

A WORKING FRAMEWORK

Barring a militarily aggressive Russia or China, odds are that commercial considerations will play an ever greater role in American foreign policy . . . into the next century. Much of our foreign policy could look more like it did during the nineteenth century and up until Pearl Harbor, when, for the most part, commercial goals were paramount. Government and business should consider the following framework to help them work together for their mutual benefit.

First, [policymakers need] to reach a renewed consensus about the centrality of commercial interests in foreign policy. Many in the [executive branch], Congress, and the broader foreign policy community still believe that commercial policy is a tool of foreign policy, when it should more often be the other way around—the United States should use all its foreign policy levers to achieve commercial goals. An aggressive commercial strategy would reignite the fervor for trade liberalization during the [Clinton] administration's first two years, when NAFTA and the Uruguay Round were concluded and the Asia-Pacific Economic Cooperation forum was energized. . . .

Second, the [executive branch], together with business leaders, needs to build a stronger constituency for open global markets in the business community and in Congress. Although the Clinton [administration] was successful in gaining passage of NAFTA and the Uruguay Round, the first vote required a huge political push, difficult to repeat time and again, and the General Agreement on Tariffs and Trade treaty received lukewarm support from the business community. Subsequently the administration . . . had a difficult time getting congressional authority to effectively negotiate an expansion of NAFTA, let alone a sequel to the Uruguay Round. Members of Congress are not elected these days because of their global outlook; local hot-button issues predominate. . . . Business leaders, for their part, are asleep at the switch. They take for granted that the administration—any administration—will always be around to help, without much effort on their part. . . . In short, the globalization of the American economy is weakening the political consensus for free trade.

In building support for an aggressive policy for more open trade, [the executive branch] and the business community must forge a consensus on the growing necessity of multilateral approaches and educate Congress on why they have become so important. In a globalized economy, the value of bilateral pressure is diminishing for both opening markets and enforcing agreements. There are too many alternative suppliers to U.S. companies, and too many ways to enter the American market by using foreign subsidiaries or rerouting products through third markets. If we want China to respect global trading rules, pressure not just from Washington but also from Europe, Japan, and even Southeast Asia will be needed. The same argument can be made for everything from intellectual property rights in Argentina to better access for foreign investors in the Indian insurance sector. Congress and large segments of the American public remain skeptical of the World Trade Organization (WTO) on the grounds that we are surrendering sovereignty. But global free trade, which the United States has promoted for a century, requires acceptance of international rules and procedures, and that must be explained cogently.

Third, the [executive branch] and business both need a better understanding of the interaction of business interests and human rights. The [executive branch] ought to pledge not to legally link trade and human rights except under a multilateral umbrella, such as the former embargo against South Africa's apartheid government. The reason is simple: that is the only way it can work. Unilateral sanctions only put U. S. firms at a major disadvantage vis-à-vis their rivals. At the same time, Washington should keep up every other conceivable means of political pressure, public and private. These include pressure in U.N. organizations and support for nongovernmental human rights organizations that are uncovering and publicizing abhorrent conditions around the world. In return, the business community ought to apply pressure behind the scenes and make efforts to improve the lives of its employees and the foreign communities in which they operate. Expanding

health benefits for local employees, ensuring workplace safety, giving technical assistance to local governments—none of this is new to U.S. firms, but the
level of activity could certainly be higher.

Human rights encompasses fair labor practices. Companies and the
administration can work together to fight exploitation of child labor and
other violations of core standards embraced by the International Labor Organization. . . . Washington should work to extend these standards by pressing
other governments, the World Bank agencies, and other international institutions to work toward the same goals. . . .

America's economic interest in improving the lives of people in emerging
markets goes well beyond enhancing their incomes so that they can purchase
more products and services—important as that may be. The issue is the rule
of law. If foreign governments do not seek to protect basic human rights, they
are more likely to ignore or circumvent other basic laws of great commercial
relevance, such as those that protect intellectual property rights, combat corruption, and mandate the disclosure of critical financial information. The
arrogance of governments that oppress their people transfers easily to other
areas.

American businesses historically have not been on the progressive end of
change abroad, preferring stability to the unknown. But there will be no stability in the big emerging markets in the years ahead. Change will be constant
and sometimes explosive. The American government and business need to
ride this tiger together, not by opposing change, but by trying to move with it,
even helping lead it.

*Fourth, Washington and the business community need to make peace
regarding the use of unilateral export controls for foreign policy purposes.*
The first Clinton administration made great progress in reducing the number
of products subject to controls, particularly in the area of telecommunications and computers, and more can be done. At the same time, [in recent]
years there has been a dramatic increase in laws and executive actions autho-
rizing unilateral economic sanctions for foreign policy purposes. Such controls, sanctions, and embargoes are ill-advised in a world where American
firms no longer have monopolies on capital or technology. Early on, for
example, the Clinton administration imposed unilateral sanctions on the sale
of satellites to China. U.S. companies were hurt, but there was no impact on
Beijing's behavior. Today the United States imposes unilateral sanctions on
Cuba. The Overseas Private Investment Corporation (OPIC) and the Trade
Development Agency, which provides financing for project feasibility studies,
are banned from operating in China. There is a good chance that sanctions
fever will get out of control without a more sensible reaction from Washington. Individual states like Massachusetts and New York are already flirting
with penalties for companies doing business with Burma and Indonesia. The
following principle should govern Washington's commercial strategy: Every
effort should be made to negotiate multilateral sanctions when necessary, and
there should be no unilateral sanctions unless national security is at stake. . . .

Fifth, the [executive branch] and business need to work together to deal with congressional and broader public concerns about commercial diplomacy, including charges of undue foreign influence and corporate welfare. Illegal campaign contributions from Indonesians, Thais, and other foreign nationals are a scandal and need to be eliminated by much tougher campaign contribution laws. There are several other ways to ensure that commercial diplomacy is conducted according to the highest standards of integrity. But the response to any current inadequacies must be measured: we do not eliminate our police forces or our labor unions when there is a need for internal cleanup. By all means, let's upgrade our commercial diplomacy, but not destroy it. . . .

Sixth, it is necessary to change the organization of business-diplomatic interaction in the United States. To help American firms compete, the administration should consolidate trade financing agencies like the Export-Import Bank and OPIC into one streamlined but powerful government-supported trade and investment bank. This should be combined with the Commerce Department's Advocacy Center, the economic "war room" that helps American firms win foreign projects. In addition, there needs to be a quantum leap in the number of Foreign Service officers who understand commercial matters. Not long ago, the U.S. embassy in Brazil had six commercial officers and 42 dealing with political and military issues. A similar pattern could be found in many big emerging markets. Here is an area where business and government could cooperate to educate a new generation of qualified men and women to represent critical American commercial interests abroad.

Seventh, the [executive branch] and business should assist in the design and implementation of political and economic reforms in the big emerging markets. If the global experiment in democratic capitalism goes awry, the international landscape will be ominous for the United States. Washington and American firms should reinforce one another's advice to foreign governments, pooling their efforts in areas like regulatory policy and upgrading education and training. The [executive branch] and American firms need a much deeper dialogue on what it will take for businesses to build a presence in the emerging markets, weather the inevitable storms, and deal with the commercial intelligence gathered from public and private sources.

Finally, the [executive branch] needs to be clear about where the country's interests may diverge from the traditional interests of the business community. All foreign policy does not have commercial ends; the interests of General Motors in the world economy are not always the interests of most Americans.

Washington must be discriminating, for example, when deciding which American firms to support abroad. In an age of companies that manufacture in many countries or have multiple strategic alliances with firms of other nationalities, it is often difficult to decide what is an American firm for purposes of U.S. government support. A set of working criteria is required. In order of priority, the [United States] should help: firms whose incremental overseas activities would add jobs in the United States; firms whose profitability would contribute to the U.S. economy; firms whose incremental activity would add to high-quality technological research in the United States; and firms that are incorporated in the United States. . . .

As the United States experiments with new relationships between government and the private sector at home, it is also time to rethink the connections between foreign policy and business and build a more deliberate and far-reaching partnership. The first Clinton administration made a good start, and it would be a shame not to build on it. What is required is more than a sound bite, more than trade agreements that can be cited in a press release, more than the occasional victory for an American firm. The right mindset requires unrelenting and cooperative leadership from the highest levels of government and business. The success of America's foreign policy and economy depends on it.

9. THE RISE OF THE VIRTUAL STATE: IMPLICATIONS FOR U.S. POLICY

Richard Rosecrance

TERRITORY BECOMES PASSÉ

Amid the supposed clamor of contending cultures and civilizations, a new reality is emerging. The nation-state is becoming a tighter, more vigorous unit capable of sustaining the pressures of worldwide competition. Developed states are putting aside military, political, and territorial ambitions as they struggle not for cultural dominance but for a greater share of world output. Countries are not uniting as civilizations and girding for conflict with one another. Instead, they are downsizing—in function if not in geographic form. Today and for the foreseeable future, the only international civilization worthy of the name is the governing economic culture of the world market. Despite the view of some contemporary observers, the forces of globalization have successfully resisted partition into cultural camps.

Yet the world's attention continues to be mistakenly focused on military and political struggles for territory. In beleaguered Bosnia, Serbian leaders sought to create an independent province with an allegiance to Belgrade. A few years ago Iraqi leader Saddam Hussein aimed to corner the world oil market through military aggression against Kuwait and, in all probability, Saudi Arabia; oil, a product of land, represented the supreme embodiment of his ambitions. In Kashmir, India and Pakistan are vying for territorial dominance over a population that neither may be fully able to control. Similar rivalries beset Rwanda and Burundi and the factions in Liberia.

These examples, however, look to the past. Less developed countries, still producing goods that are derived from land, continue to covet territory. In

Note: Some notes have been deleted.

economies where capital, labor, and information are mobile and have risen to predominance, no land fetish remains. Developed countries would rather plumb the world market than acquire territory. The virtual state—a state that has downsized its territorially based production capability—is the logical consequence of this emancipation from the land.

In recent years the rise of the economic analog of the virtual state—the virtual corporation—has been widely discussed. Firms have discovered the advantages of locating their production facilities wherever it is most profitable. Increasingly, this is not in the same location as corporate headquarters. Parts of a corporation are dispersed globally according to their specialties. But the more important development is the political one, the rise of the virtual state, the political counterpart of the virtual corporation.

The ascent of the trading state preceded that of the virtual state. After World War II, led by Japan and Germany, the most advanced nations shifted their efforts from controlling territory to augmenting their share of world trade. In that period, goods were more mobile than capital or labor, and selling abroad became the name of the game. As capital has become increasingly mobile, advanced nations have come to recognize that exporting is no longer the only means to economic growth; one can instead produce goods overseas for the foreign market.

As more production by domestic industries takes place abroad and land becomes less valuable than technology, knowledge, and direct investment, the function of the state is being further redefined. The state no longer commands resources as it did in mercantilist yesteryear; it negotiates with foreign and domestic capital and labor to lure them into its own economic sphere and stimulate its growth. A nation's economic strategy is now at least as important as its military strategy; its ambassadors have become foreign trade and investment representatives. Major foreign trade and investment deals command executive attention as political and military issues did two decades ago. The frantic two weeks in December 1994 when the White House outmaneuvered the French to secure for Raytheon Company a deal worth over $1 billion for the management of rainforests and air traffic in Brazil exemplifies the new international crisis.

Timeworn methods of augmenting national power and wealth are no longer effective. Like the headquarters of a virtual corporation, the virtual state determines overall strategy and invests in its people rather than amassing expensive production capacity. It contracts out other functions to states that specialize in or need them. Imperial Great Britain may have been the model for the nineteenth century, but Hong Kong will be the model for the twenty-first.

The virtual state is a country whose economy is reliant on mobile factors of production. Of course it houses virtual corporations and presides over foreign direct investment by its enterprises. But more than this, it encourages, stimulates, and to a degree even coordinates such activities. In formulating economic strategy, the virtual state recognizes that its own production does not have to take place at home; equally, it may play host to the capital and labor of other nations. Unlike imperial Germany, czarist Russia, and the United States of the Gilded Age—which aimed at nineteenth-century omnicompetence—it does not seek to combine or excel in all economic functions, from mining and agriculture to production and distribution. The virtual state specializes in modern technical and research services and derives its income not just from high-value manufacturing, but from product design, marketing, and financing. The rationale for its economy is efficiency attained through productive downsizing. Size no longer determines economic potential. Virtual nations hold the competitive key to greater wealth in the twenty-first century. They will likely supersede the continent-sized and self-sufficient units that prevailed in the past. . . .

THE TRADING STATE

In the past, states were obsessed with land. The international system with its intermittent wars was founded on the assumption that land was the major factor in both production and power. States could improve their position by building empires or invading other nations to seize territory. To acquire land was a boon: a conquered province contained peasants and grain supplies, and its inhabitants rendered tribute to the new sovereign. Before the age of nationalism, a captured principality willingly obeyed its new ruler. Hence the Hapsburg monarchy, Spain, France, and Russia could become major powers through territorial expansion in Europe between the sixteenth and nineteenth centuries.

With the Industrial Revolution, however, capital and labor assumed new importance. Unlike land, they were mobile ingredients of productive strength. Great Britain innovated in discovering sophisticated uses for the new factors. Natural resources—especially coal, iron, and, later, oil—were still economically vital. Agricultural and mineral resources were critical to the development of the United States and other fledgling industrial nations like Australia, Canada, South Africa, and New Zealand in the nineteenth century. Not until late in the twentieth century did mobile factors of production become paramount.

By that time, land had declined in relative value and become harder for nations to hold. Colonial revolutions in the Third World since World War II have shown that nationalist mobilization of the population in developing societies impedes an imperialist or invader trying to extract resources. A nation may expend the effort to occupy new territory without gaining proportionate economic benefits.

In time, nationalist resistance and the shift in the basis of production should have an impact on the frequency of war. Land, which is fixed, can be physically captured, but labor, capital, and information are mobile and cannot be definitively seized; after an attack, these resources can slip away like quicksilver. Saddam Hussein ransacked the computers in downtown Kuwait City in August 1990 only to find that the cash in bank accounts had already been electronically transferred. Even though it had abandoned its territory, the Kuwaiti government could continue to spend billions of dollars to resist Hussein's conquest.

Today, for the wealthiest industrial countries such as Germany, the United States, and Japan, investment in land no longer pays the same dividends. Since mid-century, commodity prices have fallen nearly 40 percent relative to prices of manufactured goods. The returns from the manufacturing trade greatly exceed those from agricultural exports. As a result, the terms of trade for many developing nations have been deteriorating, and in recent years the rise in prices of international services has outpaced that for manufactured products. Land prices have been steeply discounted.

Amid this decline, the 1970s and 1980s brought a new political prototype: the trading state. Rather than territorial expansion, the trading state held trade to be its fundamental purpose. This shift in national strategy was driven by the declining value of fixed productive assets. Smaller states—those for which, initially at any rate, a military-territorial strategy was not feasible— also adopted trade-oriented strategies. Along with small European and East Asian states, Japan and West Germany moved strongly in a trading direction after World War II.

Countries tend to imitate those that are most powerful. Many states followed in the wake of Great Britain in the nineteenth century; in recent decades, numerous states seeking to improve their lot in the world have emulated Japan. Under Mikhail Gorbachev in the 1980s, even the Soviet Union sought to move away from its emphasis on military spending and territorial expansion.

In recent years. however, a further stimulus has hastened this change. Faced with enhanced international competition in the late 1980s and early 1990s, corporations have opted for pervasive downsizing. They have trimmed the ratio of production workers to output, saving on costs. In some cases productivity increases resulted from pruning of the workforce; in others output increased. These improvements have been highly effective. . . . The most efficient corporations are those that can maintain or increase output with a steady or declining amount of labor. Such corporations grew on a worldwide basis.

Meanwhile, corporations in Silicon Valley recognized that cost-cutting, productivity, and competitiveness could be enhanced still further by using the production lines of another company. The typical American plant at the time, such as Ford Motor Company's Willow Run factory in Michigan, was fully integrated, with headquarters, design offices, production workers, and factories located on substantial tracts of land. This comprehensive structure was expensive to maintain and operate, hence a firm that could employ someone else's production line could cut costs dramatically. Land and machines did not have to be bought, labor did not have to be hired, medical benefits did not have to be provided. These advantages could result from what are called economies of scope, with a firm turning out different products on the same production line or quality circle. Or they might be the result of small, specialized firms' ability to perform exacting operations such as the surface mounting of miniaturized components directly on circuit boards without the need for soldering or conventional wiring. In either case, the original equipment manufacturer would contract out its production to other firms. . . .

Thus was born the virtual corporation, an entity with research, development, design, marketing, financing, legal, and other headquarters functions, but few or no manufacturing facilities: a company with a head but no body. It represents the ultimate achievement of corporate downsizing, and the model is spreading rapidly from firm to firm. It is not surprising that the virtual corporation should catch on. "Concept" or "head" corporations can design new products for a range of different production facilities. Strategic alliances between firms, which increase specialization, are also very profitable. According to the October 2, 1995, *Financial Times,* firms that actively pursue strategic alliances are 50 percent more profitable than those that do not.

TOWARD THE VIRTUAL STATE

In a setting where the economic functions of the trading state have displaced the territorial functions of the expansionist nation, the newly pruned corporation has led to the emerging phenomenon of the virtual state. Downsizing has become an index of corporate efficiency and productivity gains. Now the national economy is also being downsized. Among the most efficient economies are those that possess limited production capacity. The archetype is Hong Kong, whose production facilities are now largely situated in southern China. This arrangement may change . . . with Hong Kong's reversion to the mainland, but it may not. It is just as probable that Hong Kong will continue to govern parts of the mainland economically as it is that Beijing will dictate to Hong Kong politically. The one country–two systems formula will likely prevail. In this context, it is important to remember that Britain governed Hong Kong politically and legally for 50 years, but it did not dictate its economics. Nor did this arrangement prevent Hong Kong Chinese from extending economic and quasi-political controls to areas outside their country.

The model of the virtual state suggests that political as well as economic strategy push toward a downsizing and relocation of production capabilities. The trend can be observed in Singapore as well. The successors of Lee Kuan Yew keep the country on a tight political rein but still depend economically on the inflow of foreign factors of production. Singapore's investment in China, Malaysia, and elsewhere is within others' jurisdictions. The virtual state is in this sense a negotiating entity. It depends as much or more on economic access abroad as it does on economic control at home. Despite its past reliance on domestic production, Korea no longer manufactures everything at home, and Japanese production . . . is now increasingly lodged abroad. In Europe, Switzerland is the leading virtual nation; as much as 98 percent of Nestlé's production capacity, for instance, is located abroad. Holland now produces most of its goods outside its borders. England is also moving in tandem with the worldwide trend; according to the Belgian economic historian Paul Bairoch in 1994, Britain's foreign direct investment abroad was almost as large as America's. A remarkable 20 percent of the production of U.S. corporations now takes place outside the United States.

A reflection of how far these tendencies have gone is the growing portion of GDP consisting of high-value-added services, such as concept, design, consulting, and financial services. Services already constitute 70 percent of American GDP. Of the total, 63 percent are in the high-value category. Of course manufacturing matters, but it matters much less than it once did. As a proportion of foreign direct investment, service exports have grown strikingly in most highly industrialized economies. According to a 1994 World Bank report, *Liberalizing International Transactions in Services,* "The reorientation of [foreign direct investment] towards the services sector has occurred in almost all developed market economies, the principal exporters of services capital: in the most important among them, the share of the services sector is around 40 percent of the stock of outward foreign direct investment (FDI), and that share is rising."

Manufacturing, for these nations, will continue to decline in importance. If services productivity increases as much as it has in recent years, it will greatly strengthen U.S. competitiveness abroad. But it can no longer be assumed that services face no international competition. Efficient high-value services will be as important to a nation as the manufacturing of automobiles and electrical equipment once were. Since 1959, services prices have increased more than three times as rapidly as industrial prices. This means that many nations will be able to prosper without major manufacturing capabilities.

Australia is an interesting example. Still reliant on the production of sheep and raw materials (both related to land), Australia has little or no industrial sector. Its largest export to the United States is meat for hamburgers. On the other hand, its service industries of media, finance, and telecommunications—represented most notably by the media magnate Rupert Murdoch—are the envy of the world. Canada represents a similar amalgam of raw materials and powerful service industries in newspapers, broadcast media, and telecommunications.

As a result of these trends, the world may increasingly become divided into "head" and "body" nations, or nations representing some combination of those two functions. While Australia and Canada stress the headquarters or head functions, China will be the twenty-first-century model of a body nation. Although China does not innately or immediately know what to produce for the world market, it has found success in joint ventures with foreign corporations. China will be an attractive place to produce manufactured goods, but only because sophisticated enterprises from other countries design, market, and finance the products China makes. At present China cannot chart its own industrial future.

Neither can Russia. Focusing on the products of land, the Russians are still prisoners of territorial fetishism. Their commercial laws do not yet permit the delicate and sophisticated arrangements that ensure that "body" manufacturers deliver quality goods for their foreign "head." Russia's transportation network is also primitive. These, however, are temporary obstacles. In time Russia, with China and India, will serve as an important locus of the world's production plant.

THE VESTIGES OF SERFDOM

The world is embarked on a progressive emancipation from land as a determinant of production and power. For the Third World, the past unchangeable strictures of comparative advantage can be overcome through the acquisition of a highly trained labor force. Africa and Latin America may not have to rely on the exporting of raw materials or agricultural products; through education, they can capitalize on an educated labor force, as India has in Bangalore and Ireland in Dublin. Investing in human capital can substitute for trying to foresee the vagaries of the commodities markets and avoid the constant threat of overproduction. Meanwhile, land continues to decline in value. Recent studies of 180 countries show that as population density rises, per capita GDP falls. In a new study, economist Deepak Lal notes that investment as well as growth is inversely related to land holdings.[1]

These findings are a dramatic reversal of past theories of power in international politics. In the 1930s the standard international relations textbook would have ranked the great powers in terms of key natural resources: oil, iron ore, coal, bauxite, copper, tungsten, and manganese. Analysts presumed that the state with the largest stock of raw materials and goods derived from land would prevail. CIA estimates during the Cold War were based on such conclusions. It turns out, however, that the most prosperous countries often have a negligible endowment of natural resources. For instance, Japan has shut down its coal industry and has no iron ore, bauxite, or oil. Except for most of its rice, it imports much of its food. Japan is richly endowed with human capital, however, and that makes all the difference.

The implications for the United States are equally striking. As capital, labor, and knowledge become more important than land in charting economic success, America can influence and possibly even reshape its pattern of comparative advantage. The "new trade theory," articulated clearly by the economist Paul Krugman, focuses on path dependence, the so-called QWERTY effect of past choices. The QWERTY keyboard was not the arrangement of letter-coded keys that produced the fastest typing, except perhaps for left-handers. But . . . the QWERTY keyboard became the standard for the typewriter (and computer) industry, and everyone else had to adapt to it. Nations that invested from the start in production facilities for the 16-kilobyte computer memory chip also had great advantages down the line in 4- and 16-megabyte chips. Intervention at an early point in the chain of development can influence results later on, which suggests that the United States and other nations can and should deliberately alter their pattern of comparative advantage and choose their economic activity.

American college and graduate education, for example, has supported the decisive U.S. role in the international services industry in research and development, consulting, design, packaging, financing, and the marketing of new products. Mergers and acquisitions are American subspecialties that draw on the skills of financial analysts and attorneys. The American failure, rather, has been in the first 12 years of education. Unlike that of Germany and Japan (or even Taiwan, Korea, and Singapore), American elementary and secondary education falls well below the world standard.

Economics teaches that products should be valued according to their economic importance. For a long period, education was undervalued, socially and economically speaking, despite productivity studies . . . that showed its long-term importance to U.S. growth and innovation. Recent studies have underscored this importance. According to the World Bank, 64 percent of the world's wealth consists of human capital. But the social and economic valuation of kindergarten through 12th-grade education has still not appreciably increased. Educators, psychologists, and school boards debate how education should be structured, but Americans do not invest more money in it. Corporations have sought to upgrade the standards of teaching and learning in their regions, but localities and states have lagged behind, as has the federal government. Elementary and high school teachers should be rewarded as patient creators of high-value capital in the United States and elsewhere. In Switzerland, elementary school teachers are paid around $70,000 per year, about the salary of a starting lawyer at a New York firm. In international economic competition, human capital has turned out to be at least as important as other varieties of capital. In spite of their reduced functions, states liberated from the confines of their geography have been able, with appropriate education, to transform their industrial and economic futures.

THE REDUCED DANGER OF CONFLICT

As nations turn to the cultivation of human capital, what will a world of virtual states be like? Production for one company or country can now take place in many parts of the world. In the process of downsizing, corporations and nation-states will have to get used to reliance on others. Virtual corporations need other corporations' production facilities. Virtual nations need other states' production capabilities. As a result, economic relations between states will come to resemble nerves connecting heads in one place to bodies somewhere else. Naturally, producer nations will be working quickly to become the brains behind emerging industries elsewhere. But in time, few nations will have within their borders all the components of a technically advanced economic existence.

To sever the connections between states would undermine the organic unit. States joined in this way are therefore less likely to engage in conflict. In the past, international norms underlying the balance of power, the Concert of Europe, or even rule by the British Raj helped specify appropriate courses of action for parties in dispute. The international economy also rested partially on normative agreement. Free trade, open domestic economies, and, more recently, freedom of movement for capital were normative notions. In addition to specifying conditions for borrowing, the International Monetary Fund is a norm-setting agency that inculcates market economics in nations not fully ready to accept their international obligations.

Like national commercial strategies, these norms have been largely abstracted from the practices of successful nations. In the nineteenth century many countries emulated Great Britain and its precepts. In the British pantheon of virtues, free trade was a norm that could be extended to other nations without self-defeat. Success for one nation did not undermine the prospects for others. But the acquisition of empire did cause congestion for other nations on the paths to industrialization and growth. Once imperial Britain had taken the lion's share, there was little left for others. The inability of all nations to live up to the norms Britain established fomented conflict between them.

In a similar vein, Japan's current trading strategy could be emulated by many other countries. Its pacific principles and dependence on world markets and raw materials supplies have engendered greater economic cooperation among other countries. At the same time, Japan's insistence on maintaining a quasi-closed domestic economy and a foreign trade surplus cannot be successfully imitated by everyone; if some achieve the desired result, others necessarily will not. In this respect, Japan's recent practices and norms stand athwart progress and emulation by other nations.

President Clinton rightly [argued] that the newly capitalist developmental states, such as Korea and Taiwan, have simply modeled themselves on restrictionist Japan. If this precedent were extended to China, the results would endanger the long-term stability of the world economic and financial system. Accordingly, new norms calling for greater openness in trade, finance, and the movement of factors of production will be necessary to stabilize the international system. Appropriate norms reinforce economic incentives to reduce conflict between differentiated international units. . . .

Diminishing their command of real estate and productive assets, nations are downsizing, in functional if not in geographic terms. Small nations have attained peak efficiency and competitiveness, and even large nations have begun to think small. If durable access to assets elsewhere can be assured, the need to physically possess them diminishes. Norms are potent reinforcements of such arrangements. Free movement of capital and goods, substantial international and domestic investment, and high levels of technical education have been the recipe for success in the industrial world of the late twentieth century. Those who depended on others did better than those who depended only on themselves. Can the result be different in the future? Virtual states, corporate alliances, and essential trading relationships augur peaceful times. They may not solve domestic problems, but the economic bonds that link virtual and other nations will help ease security concerns.

THE CIVIC CRISIS

Though peaceful in its international implications, the rise of the virtual state portends a crisis for democratic politics. Western democracies have traditionally believed that political reform, extension of suffrage, and economic restructuring could solve their problems. In the twenty-first century none of these measures can fully succeed. Domestic political change does not suffice because it has insufficient jurisdiction to deal with global problems. The people in a particular state cannot determine international outcomes by holding an election. Economic restructuring in one state does not necessarily affect others. And the political state is growing smaller, not larger.

If ethnic movements are victorious in Canada, Mexico, and elsewhere, they will divide the state into smaller entities. Even the powers of existing states are becoming circumscribed. In the United States, if Congress has its way, the federal government will lose authority. In response to such changes, the market fills the vacuum, gaining power.

As states downsize, malaise among working people is bound to spread. . . . The economy may temporarily be prosperous, but there is no guarantee that favorable conditions will last. The flow of international factors of production—technology, capital, and labor—will swamp the stock of economic power at home. The state will become just one of many players in the international marketplace and will have to negotiate directly with foreign factors of production to solve domestic economic problems. Countries must induce foreign capital to enter their domain. To keep such investment, national economic authorities will need to maintain low inflation, rising productivity, a strong currency, and a flexible and trained labor force. These demands will sometimes conflict with domestic interests that want more government spending, larger budget deficits, and more benefits. That conflict will result in continued domestic insecurity over jobs, welfare, and medical care. Unlike the remedies applied in the insulated and partly closed economies of the past, purely domestic policies can no longer solve these problems.

THE NECESSITY OF INTERNATIONALIZATION

The state can compensate for its deficient jurisdiction by seeking to influence economic factors abroad. The domestic state therefore must not only become a negotiating state but must also be internationalized. This is a lesson already learned in Europe, and well on the way to codification in East Asia. Among the world's major economies and polities, only the United States remains, despite its potent economic sector, essentially introverted politically and culturally. Compared with their counterparts in other nations, citizens born in the United States know fewer foreign languages, understand less about foreign cultures, and live abroad reluctantly, if at all. In recent years, many English industrial workers who could not find jobs migrated to Germany, learning the language to work there. They had few American imitators.

The virtual state is an agile entity operating in twin jurisdictions: abroad and at home. It is as prepared to mine gains overseas as in the domestic economy. But in large countries, internationalization operates differentially. Political and economic decision-makers have begun to recast their horizons, but middle managers and workers lag behind. They expect too much and give and learn too little. That is why the dawn of the virtual state must also be the sunrise of international education and training. The virtual state cannot satisfy all its citizens. The possibility of commanding economic power in the sense of effective state control has greatly declined. Displaced workers and businesspeople must be willing to look abroad for opportunities. In the United States, they can do this only if American education prepares the way.

NOTE

1. Daniel Garstka, "Land and Economic Prowess" (unpublished mimeograph), UCLA, 1995; Deepak Lal, "Factor Endowments, Culture and Politics: On Economic Performance in the Long Run" (unpublished mimeograph), UCLA, 1996.

10. INTERNATIONLISM: INTACT OR IN TROUBLE?

Ole R. Holsti and James N. Rosenau

*H*istorian and former presidential adviser Arthur Schlesinger, once a vocal critic of American intervention in the Vietnam war, recently wrote that the age of American internationalism is coming to an end.[1] Looking back on the commitment to collective security during the Cold War, he described as "an illusion" the hope that "Americans had made the great turning and would forever after accept collective responsibilities."

> It is now surely clear that the upsurge in American internationalism during the Cold War was a reaction to what was seen as the direct and urgent Soviet threat to the security of the United States. It is to Joseph Stalin that Americans owe the forty-year suppression of the isolationist impulse. The collapse of the Soviet threat faces us today with the prospect that haunted Roosevelt half a century ago—the return to the womb in American foreign policy.... The isolationist impulse has risen from the grave, and it has taken the new form of unilateralism.[2]

Schlesinger's essay went on to describe declining support for internationalism across the entire spectrum of American society, from the "housewife in Xenia, Ohio," to members of the Council on Foreign Relations, to many officials in Washington.

For almost six decades since Pearl Harbor there has been a widespread belief among American leaders that vital national interests require the United States to play an active leadership role in world affairs; disagreements among elites have tended to focus not on the desirability of assuming the burdens—and enjoying the benefit—of international leadership but, rather, on the goals, strategies, and tactics that should be employed in implementing that role. For example, even the sharp differences between incumbent Jimmy

Carter and challenger Ronald Reagan that surfaced during the 1980 presidential campaign were not about whether the United States should take an active position in world affairs, but rather about the goals, values, and strategies that should inform and guide it in its international undertakings. Reagan emphasized the need to restore a military status that he charged had been compromised by the misguided pursuit of détente and arms control by the Nixon, Ford, and Carter administrations, and to confront more forcefully an evil and expansionist Soviet empire. In contrast, Carter was no more inclined than Reagan to reduce America's internationalist stance, but he sought to use that leadership position in the service of rather different goals and values. His definition of a "foreign policy that the American people can be proud of" included an emphasis on arms control rather than arms racing and promoting such values as human rights. Thus, if Schlesinger's diagnosis of contemporary American foreign policy has correctly unearthed a surge toward isolationism and unilateralism, it would be a watershed in thinking about foreign affairs comparable to that triggered by the attack on Pearl Harbor more than half a century ago.

There is, of course, a contradiction implicit in Schlesinger's argument. Unilateralism can readily be viewed as a form of internationalism rather than as a rejection of it, a perspective which holds that it is appropriate to be deeply involved in the world, but that the involvement should be on America's terms and not ratified by multilateral approval. In other words, to "go it alone" is hardly a posture that argues for avoiding foreign entanglements. At the same time, it might be said that Schlesinger may recognize this subtlety and that his emphasis is essentially on the idea of a vast transformation in American foreign policy, whether it be in an isolationist or unilateralist direction.

How compelling is the thesis that we are undergoing such a fundamental change in beliefs about the country's appropriate role in the world? With the advent of a new millennium and the end of the first decade of the post–Cold War era, are we indeed witnessing a fundamental redefinition of the U.S. world role along the lines described in Schlesinger's obituary for "a magnificent dream"? What evidence suggests that Schlesinger may in fact have discerned an important transformation in American thinking about foreign affairs? While a case can be made for Schlesinger's thesis, we see it as resting on weak premises and thus are inclined to reject it. Neither our newly generated data offered later in this chapter nor Schlesinger's own line of reasoning provides a convincing argument for viewing the American public, its leaders and its citizens, as undergoing a shift in foreign policy attitudes and beliefs that can legitimately be described as movement toward either an isolationist or a unilateralist posture.

Let us consider first the reasoning that leads Schlesinger (and others) to such a conclusion. A major tenet of their logic is that the United States has lost the guiding beacon of the Cold War—opposition to the expansion of Soviet influence—with the result that American policymakers have been deprived of a prime basis for mobilizing the public behind their goals and the means used to pursue them. Hence it is difficult to establish links between core American interests and such post–Cold War conflicts as those in Haiti, Somalia, and Bosnia, not to mention the many important issues that receive little attention in the print and electronic media. Indeed, in the absence of an overriding threat such as the Soviet Union posed, it is not easy to agree on the indicators of success or failure of military intervention in even those conflicts that are widely covered by the media.

A second, and related, tenet of the Schlesinger argument involves the negative reaction of the American people to troop casualties in Vietnam, Lebanon, and Somalia—and the threat of casualties in Haiti and Bosnia—which is interpreted as evidence that a new isolationism is evolving in the form of a reluctance to support any policies that risk the loss of American lives in combat—a reluctance commonly called the "Vietnam syndrome." The ultimate sacrifice was seen as plausible in the contest with the Soviet Union, but in the absence of such a viable threat, the idea of committing American forces to battle, or even to battle stations, has become increasingly problematic. The decision to send troops into battle against Saddam Hussein in the Persian Gulf, for example, was upheld by only five votes in the U.S. Senate in January of 1991, while forty-seven senators preferred economic sanctions to military actions. Indeed, it can be argued that the United States did not pull out of the Gulf operation (as it had earlier in Lebanon and Somalia) precisely because there were so few casualties—a line of reasoning that suggests it is erroneous to interpret, as many observers have, that the Gulf operation signified an end to the Vietnam syndrome. In short, it is hardly surprising that one of the major themes in Schlesinger's essay is that Americans have allegedly lost a willingness to risk casualties in undertakings that may be vital to the security of allies and the preservation of a decent world order.

Domestic politics offers a third strand of the reasoning that transformations are at work in the American approach to foreign affairs. The 1994 midterm elections provided the Republicans with majorities in both the Senate and House for the first time in forty years. The Republican "contract with America" included provisions with isolationist and unilateralist overtones. Moreover, the 1992 and 1996 presidential candidacies of Patrick Buchanan and Ross Perot, while ultimately failing to gain either the Republican nomination or the White House, represented nontrivial alternative conceptions of the general U.S. role in international affairs, as well as of preferences on such specific issues as trade and protectionism, alliance commitments, immigration policy, and the like. Hence it is by no means certain that results of the 1992 and 1996 elections are the final acts in isolationist or unilateralist challenges within either political party.

Finally, although generational theses have rarely provided wholly persuasive explanations of continuity and change in foreign policy, the 1990s have in fact witnessed a major change at the leadership level that might plausibly be linked to new ways of thinking about international affairs. The defeats of George Bush and Bob Dole in the 1992 and 1996 elections, respectively, represent the "last hurrah" of a generation that came to adulthood during World

War II, a conflict in which both Bush and Dole served with valor. Indeed, until Bill Clinton's inauguration, all post–World War presidents save Ronald Reagan had had combat experience. In contrast, their successors as leaders in the White House, House of Representatives (Newt Gingrich), and Senate (Trent Lott) share an important common experience—extraordinary efforts to escape military service.

Accurate as these lines of reasoning may be, however, we regard them as far from compelling. There are several reasons to suspect that continuity has not fully given way to change in recent years. In the first place, surveys of the general public reveal that a substantial majority of Americans continue to support an "active role in world affairs,"[3] a point acknowledged by Schlesinger but dismissed as little more than lip service to "euphonious generalities in support of internationalism" because of declining public enthusiasm for some more specific international goals. Nor have opinion leaders, the most internationalist stratum of American society for many decades, shown much inclination to abandon their views in this respect.

That public enthusiasm for specific international goals may be declining even as support for internationalism remains unchanged can be readily discerned from the evidence in an October 1997 survey, which suggests that "most Americans fundamentally doubt the relevance of international events to their own lives," a finding which represents "a new and dramatic opinion gap with America's Opinion Leaders." Such findings, however, do not seemed to be linked to growing isolationist sentiments. On the contrary, "the percentage of people holding isolationist views did not increase (as it had in previous surveys in this series)."[4] Put differently, skepticism of the relevance of international issues does not necessarily mean a preference for disengagement from world affairs. It can just as easily reflect an awareness that the absence of a threatening enemy enables people to focus on domestic concerns, a respite from the challenges of foreign issues rather than a turning away from them. Quiescence, in other words, is probably a more logical response to the absence of an overriding challenge from abroad than is isolationism.

More detailed studies, drawing on evidence from the late 1980s and early 1990s, have generally found that even the startling events marking the end of the Cold War, culminating in disintegration of the Soviet Union, did not give rise to equally dramatic changes in public opinion. Appraisals of quite specific aspects of foreign affairs (such as the perceived level of threat from the Soviet Union) may have changed to reflect international events, but the basic structures of attitudes toward foreign affairs proved quite resistant to change.[5] If the spectacular developments of 1988–1992 did not yield substantial changes in foreign policy orientations, are there compelling reasons to believe that subsequent years have done so? Three perceptive observers of the American political arena noted in the early 1980s that the formulation of American foreign policy had become increasingly marked by strident partisan and ideological bickering.[6] There is little evidence that the end of the Cold War or events of the post–Cold War period have softened, much less bridged, these partisan and ideological cleavages. More specifically, it is far from clear that recent years have witnessed the emergence of a bipartisan post–Cold War consensus favoring isolationism and unilateralism.

Furthermore, in the post–Cold War era of globalization that has witnessed a major shift of the global agenda from security concerns to the salience of economic issues, it may well be fallacious to use attitudes toward military commitments as a measure of resurgent isolationism. The "Vietnam syndrome" may be alive and well even as Americans also appreciate the necessity of the United States' participating fully in the global flow of goods, services, ideas, and people. The large degree to which domestic prosperity has become linked to the well-being of foreign economies is surely a major obstacle to what Schlesinger sees as a possible "return to the womb in American foreign policy."

Finally, and perhaps most important, it seems reasonable to presume that most citizens are capable of learning and adapting to new circumstances. If this is so, if the American people are aware that their country has in the past five decades contributed substantially to a more peaceful world that is increasingly democratic, then it is hard to conceive of sizable segments of the public and its leaders retreating to updated forms of isolationism and unilateralism.

In sum, Schlesinger's lament that the United States is undergoing a fundamental shift in the direction of either a more isolationist or unilateralist stance toward world affairs is not persuasive. Although it cannot be summarily dismissed either, we will show that it does not fit well with our newly generated data on orientations toward world affairs among one important constituency—opinion leaders. The following analysis examines trends on some important questions that have been posed over an extended period of time—spanning the Cold War, the end of that conflict, and the initial years of the post–Cold War period. Data are presented on attitudes on such important issues as the proper U.S. role in the world, appropriate foreign policy goals, and the circumstances that might warrant the use of American military power. The analysis also assesses change and continuity in attitude *structures* on foreign policy issues by examining the consistency of linkages among discrete opinions during and after the Cold War. Our goal is not to disprove Schlesinger's reasoning, but rather to demonstrate that continuity in thought about America's role in world affairs is more prevalent than change.

TRENDS IN ATTITUDES

The Foreign Policy Leadership Project (FPLP) surveys, initiated in 1976 and replicated every four years since, provide the primary sources of evidence for our analyses. Each of the six surveys was conducted by means of a long questionnaire that was mailed to samples of approximately four thousand opinion leaders whose names had been drawn from such general sources as *Who's Who in America,* and *Who's Who of American Women,* as well as more specialized directories listing leaders in occupations that are underrepresented in *Who's Who,* including media leaders, politicians, military officers, labor leaders, State Department and Foreign Service Officers, foreign policy experts outside government, and the like.[7]

Twelve of the questions in the 1992 and 1996 surveys address aspects of the proper U.S. role in the world; some had also been included in the preceding four studies. The results, summarized in Table 10-1, provide little evidence of a stampede among American leaders toward withdrawal from world affairs during recent years. Indeed, the most apparent change occurred in 1992, and that was in the direction of assuming *more* rather than fewer international obligations. Whereas in the surveys conducted during the Cold War (1976–1988) only about one-third of the opinion leaders agreed that the United States "should take all steps including the use of force to prevent the spread of communism," the post–Cold War surveys in 1992 and 1996 reveal that solid majorities agreed that the United States should be prepared to use force to "prevent aggression by any expansionist power" (Table 1, item C). Although we must be careful not to read too much into the responses to only one question, these data call into question the charge that Americans have only cared about stopping aggression by communist countries and that, with the disappearance of the Soviet threat, they have lost an interest in maintaining a stable world order.

Responses to several other items would also challenge the validity of Schlesinger's fears of a rush toward isolationism or unilateralism. There has been a rather sharp decline since 1992 in support for the propositions that the United States should let its allies shoulder their own defense burdens (item E), and that "America's conception of its leadership role in the world must be scaled down" (item F). Moreover, only a quarter of American leaders agree with a restrictive view of the country's vital interests which sees them as "largely confined to Western Europe, Japan and the Americas" (item I).

The 1996 survey did, however, find some evidence of reduced support for internationalism and multilateralism. Compared to 1992, Patrick Buchanan's call for a foreign policy that puts the United States first, second, and third (item G) gained some support, as did the proposition that the nation should limit its international role to preserving peace and stability (item J). Additionally, a declining proportion (only one in ten respondents) registered a willingness to intervene in the domestic affairs of other countries in the name of peace and democracy (item L). The lack of enthusiasm for the latter proposition may reflect increased support for isolationism. Alternatively, it may indicate that, after sobering experiences in Vietnam, Nicaragua, El Salvador, Somalia, and elsewhere, Americans have become skeptical about the consequences of such interventions, no matter how well intended. The latter interpretation is consistent with Jentleson's finding that a "pretty prudent public" supports the use of force to restrain aggressor states but not to impose internal changes within another country.[8]

On balance, then, the evidence in Table 10-1 provides meager support for the thesis of a post–Cold War American retreat into isolationism or

Table 10-1. The U.S. Role in the World: American Leaders Respond, 1976–1996 (percentages)

Please indicate how strongly you agree or disagree with each statement.	Respondents Who Agree Strongly or Agree Somewhat					
	1976	1980	1984	1988	1992	1996
A. The United States should be as ready to form economic and diplomatic coalitions to cope with the world's problems of hunger and poverty as it is to leading military coalitions against aggressors.	—	—	—	—	92	87
B. The United States is the dominant power of the post–Cold War era and is capable of channeling the course of change toward a new world order.	—	—	—	—	64	62
C. The United States should take all steps including the use of force to prevent aggression by any expansionist power (1976–1988 wording: "To prevent the spread of communism").	33	36	34	36	70	59
D. The best way to encourage democratic development in the "Third World" is for the United States to solve its own problems.	65	67	51	52	56	54
E. Our allies are perfectly capable of defending themselves and they can afford it, thus allowing the United States to focus on internal rather than external threats to its well-being.	—	—	—	—	59	46
F. America's conception of its leadership role in the world must be scaled down.	56	49	59	59	57	42
G. What we need is a new foreign policy that puts America first, and second and third as well.	—	—	—	—	23	30
H. We shouldn't think so much in international terms but concentrate more on our own national problems.	37	36	28	27	35	29
I. Vital interests of the United States are largely confined to Western Europe, Japan and the Americas.	39	25	33	31	29	26
J. The United States should only be involved in world affairs to the extent that its military power is needed to maintain international peace and stability.	—	—	—	—	15	25
K. Third World conflicts cannot jeopardize vital American interests.	—	9	12	11	14	19
L. The United States should not hesitate to intrude upon the domestic affairs of other countries in order to establish and preserve a more democratic world order.	—	—	—	—	19	10

unilateralism. Although support for some items with isolationist or unilateralist implications (items G, J, K, and L) increased during the four-year interval ending in 1996, it is also worth noting that none of them gained the approval of as many as one respondent in three.

Further insight into trends on American thinking about international affairs may be gleaned from a cluster of questions about the importance of various foreign policy goals. Many of the items have appeared in each of the six FPLP surveys, as well as in six studies of mass public opinion conducted between 1974 and 1994 by the Chicago Council on Foreign Relations. The evidence in Table 10-2 provides considerable support for the thesis of declining importance attached to foreign affairs, especially when the 1996 results are compared with those of the survey four years earlier. However, a longer-term perspective indicates that in several cases the 1992 results may be an anomaly. For example, the importance attributed to strengthening the United Nations (UN) (item C) reached an exceptionally high level in 1992, no doubt in part because the successful Gulf War of 1991 was conducted under the formal authorization of several Security Council resolutions. Support for the goal of strengthening the UN declined quite sharply in 1996, but to a level that was quite typical of each of the other surveys. A similar pattern emerged on several other questions, including the importance of protecting weaker nations, a goal that probably received higher than normal support in 1992 as a result of the successful liberation of Kuwait a year earlier (item D).

That said, the evidence in Table 10-2 points toward a declining sense of urgency about many foreign policy goals, especially those clustered under the heading of "world order economic issues." The end of the Cold War has coincided with an especially sharp decline in importance attributed to combating hunger (item G) and improving the standard of living in less-developed countries (item H). Moreover, the 1996 results on these questions are not merely a drop from abnormally high levels in 1992; they are part of a longer-term trend that has sometimes been labeled "compassion fatigue." Still, whatever the varied reasons for the consistent pattern of declines in 1996 presented in Table 10-2, there is no inherent reason why a diminished sense of urgency about foreign policy issues reflects a surge in isolationist or unilateral orientations. The declines could just as easily be interpreted as expressive of a greater preoccupation with domestic issues in the absence of external military threats.

As for the "Vietnam syndrome," the FPLP surveys provide little support for its continued viability. The 1996 survey did ask respondents to indicate whether they favor or oppose the use of American military forces in a dozen hypothetical situations which span a broad range of issues and geographical areas. As indicated in Table 10-3, support for the deployment of U.S. forces varies widely, from a high of 88 percent who would support such action if Russia were to invade Western Europe, to a low of only 3 percent who would do so if a civil war were to break out in South Africa. Several generalizations emerge from the evidence in Table 10-3. First, support for assisting traditional allies and friendly nations is quite high. By margins of well over two-to-one, American leaders still favor using U.S. troops if Western Europe, Saudi

Table 10-2. American Leaders Assess the Importance of Possible U.S. Foreign Policy Goals, 1976–1996 (percentages)

Please indicate how much importance should be attached to each goal.	Those Responding "Very Important"					
	1976	1980	1984	1988	1992	1996
World Order Security Issues						
A. Preventing the spread of nuclear weapons	—	55	—	—	87	83
B. Worldwide arms control	66	55	70	68	73	60
C. Strengthening the United Nations	25	32	27	27	44	26
D. Protecting weaker nations against foreign aggression	18	23	—	—	28	18
World Order Economic Issues						
E. Fostering international cooperation to solve common problems, such as food, inflation, and energy	70	73	66	70	71	56
F. Protecting the global environment	—	47	53	69	66	47
G. Combatting world hunger	51	51	56	57	55	36
H. Helping to improve the standard of living in less developed countries	38	44	59	51	43	28
U.S. Economic Interests						
I. Securing adequate supplies of energy	72	78	84	75	68	52
J. Protecting the jobs of American workers	31	30	—	36	32	29
K. Protecting the interests of American business abroad	14	19	22	—	24	19
U.S. Values and Institutions Issues						
L. Stopping the flow of illegal drugs into the United States	—	—	—	—	—	58
M. Controlling and reducing illegal immigration	—	—	—	—	—	33
N. Promoting and defending human rights in other countries	—	27	33	39	38	24
O. Helping to bring a democratic form of government to other nations	7	10	18	25	23	15
Cold War/Security Issues						
P. Maintaining superior military power worldwide	—	—	—	—	—	40
Q. Defending our allies' security	37	44	47	51	34	36
R. Containing communism	39	41	38	37	13	15
S. Matching Soviet military power*	—	—	40	33	18	—

*"Russian" instead of "Soviet" in 1992.

Arabia, South Korea, or Israel were to come under attack, and a majority also supports coming to the assistance of Poland should that former Warsaw Pact member be attacked by Russia. On the other hand, there is clearly limited enthusiasm for American military intervention in civil wars, irrespective of geography; overwhelming majorities of opinion leaders would stay out of such conflicts, whether in the Western hemisphere—Mexico, Cuba, and Haiti—or in such distant countries as Rwanda and South Africa.

Because prior FPLP surveys did not include comparable questions, it is not possible to determine whether the results in Table 10-3 represent a significant change from views that may have been espoused earlier. It does seem clear, however, that substantial numbers of respondents favor military undertakings in support of security commitments that originated during the Cold War. It is at least a debatable point whether the manifest reluctance to undertake comparable actions in civil conflicts in less-developed countries constitutes compelling evidence of a retreat to isolationism or merely a prudent recognition that such interventions are likely to entail higher risks and costs than rewards.

Indeed, while the deployment of American troops to Bosnia has probably been the most controversial post–Cold War American military intervention, the available data reveal solid if not overwhelming support for the deployment in that troubled country. Given some of the circumstances surrounding the situation in Bosnia—including the absence of a traditional American security commitment to the area, the difficult terrain that reduces the effectiveness

Table 10-3. American Leaders' Attitudes toward the Use of U.S. Troops Abroad, 1996 (percentages)

Here is another question on the use of American military forces abroad. For each of the situations listed below, please indicate whether you favor or oppose the use of U.S. military forces.

	Favor Use of U.S. Troops	Oppose Use of U.S. Troops	Not Sure
If Russia invaded Western Europe	88	5	7
If Iraq invaded Saudi Arabia	78	12	10
If North Korea invaded South Korea	63	22	15
If Arab forces invaded Israel	61	24	15
If Russia invaded Poland	51	26	23
If drug cartels gained control of the government in Panama	45	38	17
If China invaded Taiwan	40	35	25
If civil war broke out in Mexico	18	59	24
If renewed conflict in Rwanda threatened further acts of genocide	18	60	22
If the Cuban people attempted to overthrow the Castro regime	15	69	16
If civil war broke out in Haiti	14	67	19
If civil war broke out in South Africa	3	84	13

of high-technology military hardware, the long history of ethnic rivalries in the area, and the manifest reluctance of top-ranking military leaders to commit American forces to the conflict—the level of support for the military intervention revealed in the 1996 FPLP survey (nearly 60 percent) suggests that most American leaders are quite willing to become involved even in difficult peacekeeping operations. Whether that support would have survived substantial American casualties is, of course, far from certain. A 1995 Gallup survey indicated that, among the general public, the strong support for involvement in Bosnia would decay in direct proportion to projected casualty levels in a series of hypothetical scenarios.[9] Thus, while the FPLP data would appear to challenge part of Schlesinger's argument, Bosnia does not (fortunately) provide a full test of his thesis that Americans are no longer willing to support military undertakings should they result in casualties.

ATTITUDE STRUCTURES

Much of the research during and immediately after World War II measured public opinion on a single isolationist-to-internationalist scale, but most recent studies show that attitudes on foreign affairs are better described in multidimensional terms. A series of studies of public opinion by Wittkopf has demonstrated that there are two "faces of internationalism." Attitudes toward two dimensions—support for or opposition to *militant internationalism* (MI) and *cooperative internationalism* (CI)—are necessary for describing the belief structures of both elites and the general public.[10] Dichotomizing and crossing these two dimensions yields four types, with quadrants labeled as *hard-liners* (support MI, oppose CI), *accommodationists* (oppose MI, support CI), *internationalists* (support both MI and CI), and *isolationists* (oppose both MI and CI). Analyses of the five FPLP surveys conducted between 1976 and 1992, although using somewhat different methods and questions than those employed by Wittkopf, revealed that the MI/CI scheme is an effective way of classifying opinion leaders' foreign policy beliefs; knowing how respondents are classified provides powerful predictors of their attitudes on a broad array of international issues.[11] And that continues to be the case with the 1996 survey data.

As shown in Table 10-4, when respondents are classified according to the MI/CI scheme, *accommodationists* and *internationalists,* the two groups defined as supporting cooperative internationalism, account for about three-fourths of the entire leadership group in each of the six FPLP surveys.[12] As can also be seen in Table 10-4, the opponents of CI—the *hard-liners* and *isolationists*—recorded slight gains at the expense of the *internationalists* and *accommodationists* when the 1996 results are compared to those four years earlier.

Although the MI/CI scheme continues to provide insight into how American leaders respond to the world around them, some analysts worry that a weakness of this classification scheme is that it fails to adequately address an

Table 10-4. The Foreign Policy Beliefs of American Leaders: Hard-Liners,
Internationalists, Isolationists, and Accommodationists, 1976–1996 (percentages)

			COOPERATIVE INTERNATIONALISM			
			Oppose		Support	
			HARD-LINERS		INTERNATIONALISTS	
I			1976	20	1976	30
N		Support	1980	20	1980	33
T			1984	17	1984	25
E			1988	16	1988	25
M R			1992	9	1992	33
I N			1996	13	1996	29
L A						
I T						
T I						
A O			ISOLATIONISTS		ACCOMMODATIONISTS	
N N			1976	8	1976	42
T A		Oppose	1980	7	1980	41
L			1984	7	1984	51
I			1988	8	1988	52
S			1992	5	1992	53
M			1996	10	1996	48

important distinction between those who would seek to gain international goals through multilateral efforts in conjunction with allies and through international institutions, and others who prefer that the United States pursue its interests unilaterally, unfettered by the need to coordinate policies and compromise with other countries. To address this issue, the 1996 FPLP survey included several questions that addressed aspects of unilateralism and multilateralism, including specific questions about whether the United States should contribute to multilateral peacekeeping forces and what respondents thought about acceptable command structures for such deployments. Table 10-5 summarizes the results.

Although only a small minority of respondents believes that the United Nations is a "very effective" instrument for peace, the results summarized in Table 10-5 indicate that substantial proportions of opinion leaders support multilateral undertakings in general and, more specifically, those conducted under auspices of NATO and the United Nations. In light of the hammering that the United Nations has taken from both the Clinton administration and its Republican critics, it may seem somewhat surprising that most leaders (54 percent) expressed a willingness to have American troops serve under a UN-appointed commander in peacekeeping undertakings. Indeed, responses to

Table 10-5. Multilateralism or Unilateralism? American Leaders Respond, 1996 (percentages)

	Respondents Who Agree with the Statement
Increasingly countries will have to act together to deter and resist aggression.	90
U.S. armed forces should be used in response to requests from NATO for peacekeeping forces.	85
If interests compel the United States to intervene militarily it should be undertaken as part of a multilateral operation.	80
U.S. armed forces should be used in response to requests from the United Nations for peacekeeping forces.	75
The United States should accept a commander appointed by NATO when U.S. troops take part.	68
The United States should accept a commander appointed by the United Nations when U.S. troops take part.	54
The United States should unilaterally reduce its share of contributions to the UN budget.	39
The time is ripe for the United States and other countries to cede some of their sovereignty to strengthen the power of the UN and other international organizations.	34
What we need is a new foreign policy that puts America first, second, and third as well.	30
As an approach to peace, the United Nations and other international organizations should be strengthened.	20

the questions measuring multilateral/unilateral sentiments suggest that a large majority of American leaders prefer multilateral responses to global issues and problems.

Less easy to determine is whether these responses reflect change or continuity. Since comparable unilateral-multilateral questions were not included in prior FPLP surveys, we cannot determine whether changes in attitudes have paralleled those hypothesized by Schlesinger. On balance, however, the available data provide scant support for the view that American leaders prefer either isolationism or unilateralism over multilateral approaches to the issues and problems the global community faces in the post–Cold War era.

CONCLUSION

The focus of this chapter has been on continuity and change in the foreign policy attitudes of American opinion leaders. The evidence reveals two important conclusions. First, it shows a greater degree of continuity than change in the views of American elites during the four-year period ending in 1996. Whether attention is directed at responses to specific issues or attitude structures, similarities between the 1996 survey and those that preceded it are more numerous and striking than evidence suggesting a transformation of elite thinking. There are some exceptions, to be sure. There is a declining sense of urgency about aspects of cooperative internationalism that focus upon poor nations, for example. Nevertheless, the evidence of continuity across a broad range of issues is far stronger.

Second, the evidence on the more specific charge by Arthur Schlesinger that the United States is abandoning a long heritage of responsible internationalism in favor of isolationism or unilateralism receives only modest support. Although the evidence is mixed in some respects, the dominant theme is that most American leaders were no less prepared in 1996 than they were four years earlier—or even during the Cold War—to accept major international responsibilities, and to do so in cooperation with allies and other countries.

Still, these findings are not sufficient to dismiss Schlesinger's warnings out of hand, if only because we have focused only on a single group, American opinion leaders. A multitude of studies have shown that, compared to the general public, leaders are more favorably inclined toward internationalism and multilateral cooperation; indeed, this may be the closest thing we have to an iron law of American public opinion. If it is the case that "a new and dramatic opinion gap between the opinion leaders and the general public is in fact evolving," as one recent study suggests,[13] then the policy implications depend on the direction of influence between leaders and the general public, as well as on whether the gap represents a respite from foreign affairs rather than a turning away from them. If one posits that the dominant pattern of influence in the long run is from the general public to the opinion leaders, and if the gap is more a turning away than a respite, then Schlesinger's essay may well serve as an early warning of a major turning point.

We must also acknowledge that there are some indications of growing unilateralism at policymaking levels. The misguided and probably illegal Helms-Burton Act, which seeks to impose American domestic law upon the trade policies of other nations while abandoning Washington's long-standing and principled objection to secondary boycotts, is a notorious example. Another illustration is the failure of Fast Track legislation authorization for trade negotiations in the fall of 1997. Thus, although the bulk of the evidence reviewed here provides little support for fears such as those expressed by Schlesinger, neither can they be dismissed as unworthy of concern.

NOTES

1. We thank the National Science Foundation for grants that have supported the research described here, including most recently our 1996 survey of American opinion leaders; the Trent Foundation and the George Washington University for their support of the 1996 survey; Dan Harkins, our expert computer programmer; and Rita Dowling, who provided a wide range of secretarial assistance with skill, dedication, and fine humor; and Peter Feaver, who made many useful comments.

2. Arthur Schlesinger, Jr., "Back to the Womb: Isolationism's Renewed Threat," *Foreign Affairs* 74 (July/August 1995), p. 5.

3. John E. Rielly, ed., *American Public Opinion and U.S. Foreign Policy, 1975.* Chicago: Chicago Council on Foreign Relations, 1975. Also similarly titled monographs edited by Rielly in 1979, 1983, 1987, 1991, and 1995.

4. Pew Research Center for the People and the Press, *America's Place in the World, Part II* (Washington, DC, 1997), p. 1. However, compare these findings to those in Steven Kull, I. M. Destler, and Clay Ramsay, *The Foreign Policy Gap: How Policymakers Misread the Public* (College Park: The Center for International and Security Studies, University of Maryland, October 1997).

5. Shoon Murray, *Anchors against Change: American Opinion Leaders' Beliefs After the Cold War* (Ann Arbor: University of Michigan Press, 1996); Eugene R. Wittkopf, "What American Really Thinks About the Cold War," *Washington Quarterly* 19 (1996), pp. 91–106; and Ole R. Holsti, *Public Opinion and American Foreign Policy* (Ann Arbor: University of Michigan Press, 1996), chap. 4.

6. I. M. Destler, Leslie H. Gelb, and Anthony Lake, *Our Own Worst Enemy* (New York: Simon and Schuster, 1984).

7. In two cases—chief editorial writers of high circulation newspapers and students at the National War College—the entire population of the groups (rather than samples) was included in the survey. Forty-four of the items on the 1996 questionnaire have been included in each of the six surveys, providing an opportunity to track trends on responses to them across a twenty-year period. Return rates for the FPLP surveys have ranged between 53 and 63 percent. In 1996, 2,141 opinion leaders filled out and returned the questionnaire for a return rate of 54 percent. As in the previous five surveys, return rates varied widely across occupational groups. Whereas only one-third of the labor leaders returned their questionnaires, well over 55 percent of foreign policy experts, military officers, and those whose names were drawn from *Who's Who in America* and *Who's Who of American Women* did so. The relatively low return rate from labor leaders is one of the constant features in the six surveys.

8. Bruce W. Jentleson, "The Pretty Prudent Public: Post Post-Vietnam American Opinion on the Use of Military Force," *International Studies Quarterly* 36 (1992), pp. 49–73.

9. Survey #105362, October 19–22, 1995, in George Gallup, Jr., *The Gallup Poll: Public Opinion in 1995* (Wilmington, DE: Scholarly Resources, 1996), p. 158.

10. Wittkopf, *Faces of Internationalism.*

11. Ole R. Holsti and James N. Rosenau, "The Structure of Foreign Policy Beliefs Among American Opinion Leaders—After the Cold War," *Millennium* 22 (1993), pp. 235–278; and Holsti, *Public Opinion and American Foreign Policy,* chap. 4. The items that constitute the militant internationalism and cooperative internationalism scales, as well as responses to them in the six FPLP surveys, are presented in Ole R. Holsti, "Continuity and Change in the Domestic and Foreign Policy Beliefs of American Opinion Leaders," a paper presented at the Annual Meeting of the American

Political Science Association (Washington, DC: August 28–31, 1997). Also see Ole R. Holsti and James N. Rosenau, "The Political Foundations of Elites' Domestic and Foreign Policy Beliefs," in Eugene R. Wittkopf and James M. McCormick, eds., *The Domestic Sources of American Foreign Policy: Insights and Evidence,* 3rd ed. (Lanham, MD: Roman & Littlefield, 1999, forthcoming).

12. Each respondent was scored on both the MI and CI scales, with zero serving as the cutting point between supporters (greater than zero) and opponents (less than zero).

13. See Pew Research Center for the People and the Press, *America's Place in the World, Part II.*

11. POPULATION, CONSUMPTION, AND THE PATH TO SUSTAINABILITY: THE U.S. ROLE

Janet Welsh Brown

*I*s world population growth a problem? Most Americans would answer yes, though they do not think of the United States as being part of the problem. The technological optimists among us claim that, theoretically at least, the planet can feed, clothe, and house 10 billion people. But rapid population growth multiplies poverty and environmental degradation, and a laissez-faire attitude about a world population that will double in the next 50 years will assure that for the poor the world over, life will remain harsh.

Does this mean that rapid population growth is a security problem? Not if one equates security with the traditional struggle of major military powers over scarce resources. But if the world pursues the American model of development, with its high levels of consumption, air and water pollution, and damage to the natural resource base, and extrapolates these effects and population growth to 2025 and 2050, some basic physical and biological systems could be at risk of collapse. Less apocalyptic but just as loaded with the potential for human misery is the possibility that in many countries on the upswing, such as Mexico, Egypt, Kenya, or the Philippines, a downward spiral of population growth, debt, inequality, and loss of soil and agricultural production could lead to economic decline and widespread political instability.

There is time—but not a lot—to control pollution and prevent degradation of the natural resource base. Collectively, countries know better ways of assuring development, and a population stabilizing at 10 billion or 11 billion should be able to live humanely on the planet's resources if governments take the difficult steps required to curb excessive consumption and manage resources sustainably—and if the United States takes the lead.

Note: Some notes have been deleted.

140

POPULATION GROWTH NORTH AND SOUTH . . .

Between the Second World War and the 1990s, the world's population increased from 2.5 billion to 5 billion, and the global economy grew fourfold. Most of the population growth occurred in the developing countries, where 80 percent of the worlds people live today. Economic activity exploded commensurately, but with the most impressive advances seen in the highly industrialized states of the Organization for Economic Cooperation and Development (OECD). On a tide of postwar, postindependence economic growth and great reductions in mortality, the quality of life of most people everywhere improved—a fact easily forgotten as headlines of wars and natural disasters repeat themselves.

Using a medium-growth scenario, United Nations population projections promise a world of 8.5 billion people in 2025 and around 10 billion in 2050. Ninety-five percent of the growth will be in developing countries, most of it in the very poorest. The populations of some countries, such as Somalia, Pakistan, Nicaragua, and Honduras, will double in as little as 22 or 23 years. Others—Mexico and Egypt, for instance—will double in 30 years. Even China, which has achieved a remarkable decline in fertility and reached replacement-only levels in the early 1990s, will see 17 million people added to its population each year, assuring growth from its current 1.2 billion to 1.5 billion by 2025. India, the second-largest country with 905 million people in 1994, will surpass China in population soon after 2025 because its population is still increasing at 1.9 percent per year. Bangladesh and the Philippines are growing at more than 2 percent annually. (In the next century, half the world's people will live in Asia.) Growth is also rapid in sub-Saharan Africa and the Arab countries. Most population increases in developing countries will take place in cities, and the ranks of the young will swell throughout these countries. Already 45 percent of all Africans are under the age of 15.

What demands does such growth in the developing world put on economies and ecosystems? Food production must more than double in the next 50 years, and the demand for wood, the main fuel in the poorest communities, will also double. (Even now, some cities in African countries are ringed with deforested areas, and in India demand for fuelwood is six times the sustainable yield of India's forests.) Governments must build twice as many schools and clinics, train twice as many teachers and health-care workers, and scramble desperately to keep from slipping backward in the provision of drinking water and sanitation. Twice as many jobs will be needed, just to stay even with population growth. Pressure on land, air, and water everywhere will double, and waste and pollution levels will soar.

No government is adequately prepared for these tasks—especially in the poorer developing countries of Asia, Africa, and Latin America, where rapidly grossing populations, poverty, and environmental degradation feed on one another. The poor, who are both victims and agents of environmental deterioration, press upon fragile lands, contributing to a cycle of deforestation, soil erosion, periodic flooding, loss of productivity, and further poverty. With few or no educational and health services, poor sanitation, and low status and meager opportunities for women, the populations of poor countries swell. Despite high infant and maternal mortality, the numbers of the poor will increase and feed migration to the cities, where life is only marginally better and where people face a new set of environmental problems—water and air pollution of debilitating intensity. Some developing countries have broken the cycle. South Korea and China represent two different models for development: they have produced stunning economic growth and reduced poverty and fertility rates, but both are paying dearly in pollution and resource degradation.

The population of the former communist countries is likely to increase only slightly by 2025. In the same period the highly industrialized countries will increase from 1.2 billion to 1.4 billion, and most of that growth will be in the United States. Without immigration, the United States is growing at the rate of 0.7 percent annually, compared with 0.2 percent for Europe and 0.38 percent for Japan. Each year the United States adds 2 million people in births over deaths, plus another million through immigration. This is the equivalent of adding another California every 10 years. And alone among all the highly industrialized countries, the United States has seen its fertility rate rise in the 1990s to two children per woman, after hovering between 1.7 and 1.8 for 17 years.

In the United States, a 1 percent population growth rate means adding almost 3 million people to the population each year. It means further suburban sprawl, longer commutes to work, more pollution, and fewer open spaces. Even though these are real problems, few Americans perceive population growth as a domestic issue. Indeed, only when the differing rates at which societies consume materials and energy are taken into account, and when the relative impacts on the environment of different levels of development, wealth, and technology are calculated, does the seriousness of population growth become clear.

. . . AND CONSUMPTION NORTH AND SOUTH

Relative rates of resource consumption have become an issue internationally only since the North-South negotiations that led to the United Nations Conference on Environment and Development (UNCED) in Rio de Janeiro in 1992 at the "Earth Summit." The 180 nations represented at the conference signed a declaration and work plan that acknowledged the links between economic growth and environmental protection and the need for sustainable development. The OECD countries insisted that population growth be addressed, while developing countries charged that the North's extraordinary per capita consumption of energy and natural resources—including many from the South—drives global environmental problems. As a result, both population and consumption concerns found their way into Agenda 21, the conference's blueprint for a sustainable world.

After UNCED, consumption was examined in relation to resource depletion, environmental degradation, and such global environmental problems as atmospheric warming, destruction of the ozone layer, fisheries depletion, and biodiversity loss. The postconference studies have made it clear that the environmental effects of population growth and increasing consumption rates can be tempered by technological improvements that make production, distribution, and disposal more efficient, by incentives to invest and trade, and by taxes and regulations. Examples include reduction of subsidies to resource-hungry industries and tax revisions that make polluters pay and provide incentives for more efficient resource use. Tools such as these are gaining acceptance as countries begin fulfilling their UNCED commitments, though not as rapidly as population is growing or certain resources deteriorating.

Current income and consumption disparities stem from a long history of economic domination of Africa, Asia, and Latin America by Europe, the United States, and Japan. Today there is a great divide, based on purchasing-power parity, between the average per capita GDP of the OECD countries ($18,988 in 1991) and that of the developing countries ($2,377).[1] These averages, of course, mask even wider disparities when the rich countries are compared with the poorest ones and declining commodity prices are taken into account. Hope of quickly closing the gap is dim, since the new technologies promising greater efficiency and substitutes for scarce materials are owned mostly by Northern enterprises.

The rich and the poor take their toll on the environment in different ways: the rich through their high per capita consumption and production of wastes, and the poor through their pressure on fragile lands. In most poor countries a growing upper class consumes on a level comparable to that of citizens of the OECD countries. While the OECD countries have had the greater impact—contributing mightily to global warming and destruction of the ozone layer with their heavy use of fossil fuels and chemicals—the developing countries' production of food and fiber, mining and processing, and disposal of wastes have had mostly local impacts on soils, forests, biodiversity, and water.

Thirty years ago, environmentalists such as the authors of *Limits to Growth,* were mainly worried about the depletion of nonrenewable resources (fossil fuels, metals, and other minerals). Technology has since decreased dependence on natural resources by providing new materials and making the use of resources more efficient. Today it is clear that it is the so-called renewable resources—soil, forests, fisheries, biological diversity, air, and water—that human society is despoiling and using at unsustainable rates. In the worst cases, the depletion of the resource base may exceed its ability to regenerate, perhaps leading to ecosystem collapse.

Consumption, according to the President's Council on Sustainable Development (PCSD), which was organized in 1993, includes the "end-products, their ingredients and by-products, and all wastes generated throughout the life of a product, from raw materials extraction through disposal. It also means resource use by all kinds of consumers—industries, commercial firms, governments, nongovernmental organizations and individuals." Not surprisingly, consumption rates differ starkly between the industrialized and developing countries.

The 20 percent of the world's population that lives in the highly industrialized countries consumes an inordinate share of the world's resources: 80 percent of its paper, iron, and steel; 75 percent of its timber and energy; 60 percent of its meat, fertilizer, and cement; and half of its fish and grain. Per capita consumption comparisons are even more dramatic: in the OECD nations, each person uses 20 times as much aluminum and 17 times as much copper as a person in the developing countries. As for fossil fuels, so central to development and key to global warming, the industrialized countries use almost 50 percent of the total, which is nine times the average per capita consumption in the developing countries. Historically, the highly industrialized countries are responsible for as much as 75 percent of total world consumption, but the developing countries' share of consumption of most materials and energy is slowly rising and will continue to do so.

The United States, with the world's largest economy, is also the largest consumer of natural resources and the largest producer of wastes. In the last 20 years, personal consumption of goods and services in the United States has risen 45 percent. The country is an especially heavy user of plastics and petroleum feedstocks, synthetic fabrics, aluminum and copper, potash, and gravel and cement. With a few exceptions, most notably oil, 70 percent of the minerals the United States uses are produced domestically, so the primary environmental consequences of production, transportation, and use are also felt there. The United States, with barely 5 percent of the world's population, is the leading contributor of greenhouse gases (about 19 percent) and probably the largest producer of toxic wastes. Although per capita consumption in the United States of most materials is decreasing slightly (the exceptions are paper and plastics), overall consumption continues to rise as population grows. For example, per capita energy consumption declined between 1980 and 1993, but total consumption rose 10 percent with the addition of 32 million to the population.

IMPLEMENTING SUSTAINABILITY

Although it is not politically popular to admit it, American patterns of production and consumption—admired and imitated by most of the world—are not sustainable. The environmental effects of high natural resources consumption will be multiplied as the developing countries' economic development requires an increasing share of the earth's largesse. And larger populations in both the industrialized and developing worlds constitute another formidable multiplier. The world faces a dilemma—poor countries need to "grow" out of poverty, just as the United States and Europe and Japan seek to "grow" their economies to provide jobs and services expected by the citizenry.

But growth on the American model, or even on that of the more materials-efficient European and Japanese economies, cannot alone forestall an environmental day of reckoning. Remaining tropical forests and all the diversity they house are disappearing at an annual rate of 0.9 percent—equivalent to the loss of a territory the size of the state of Washington annually. According to the UN Food and Agriculture Organization, all 17 major ocean fisheries have reached or exceeded their limits, mainly from overfishing, and 9 are in serious decline. Stabilizing atmospheric concentrations of greenhouse gases will require as much as a 60 percent reduction in emissions worldwide. Current emission levels, even without the growth required in energy use in developing countries, will result in a doubling and eventually a quadrupling of green-house gases—bringing long-term global warming, changes in precipitation, and sea-level rise.

If a new kind of security threat is to be avoided and these trends diverted, then a more sustainable model of development is clearly required. As was noted earlier, in 1992 at UNCED, nations from around the world produced Agenda 21, their blueprint for sustainable development. Although loaded with political compromises, the 294-page document is instructive in its detail and comprehensiveness. It includes chapters on energy and marine management, as well as on the status of women and the role of nongovernmental organizations in development. By 1996 the President's Council on Sustainable Development had made international and intergenerational equity part of America's definition of sustainable activity—an activity "that can be continued indefinitely without harming the environmental, economic, or social basis on which it depends and without diminishing the opportunities of future generations to enjoy the resources and a quality of life at least equal to our own."

Sustainable development, by definition, means that each nation has to work out its own plan for economically and environmentally sensible development. Among the highly industrialized nations, the Netherlands has moved with greatest determination, ordering a radical reduction of toxic agricultural chemicals and negotiating long-term agreements between major industries and government that set ambitious goals for improving energy efficiency. By setting an example at home, and promoting sustainable development in its bilateral aid program, the Dutch have exerted leadership both in the European Union and in worldwide environmental negotiations that is extraordinary for so small a country.

Not all countries waited for UNCED before tackling their unsustainable development practices. Brazil, in the late 1980s, reversed the policies that had encouraged cattle ranching over tropical forest protection. And the Philippines halted logging subsidies that had encouraged transforming steep uplands from forest to farmland, with all the attendant problems. The transition to sustainable development is as difficult in developing countries as anywhere else, as entrenched political elites defend the old models of development that have benefited them. Further changes in the developing countries will depend largely on the policies and practices of the international financial institutions—the World Bank and the IMF [International Monetary Fund]—which so far have been reluctant partners in the push for sustainable development.

Equally important is the example set by the highly industrialized countries, which must demonstrate that the transition to sustainable development is technically feasible, affordable, and politically possible. The United States, as the largest economic power, consumer, and polluter, is the key country that skeptics are watching. At present the United States is at a difficult point of transition. The nation has taken many steps to control pollution and degradation over the last 25 years, but few politicians are willing seriously to challenge such sacred cows as America's national addiction to the automobile, its extensive subsidies of water and energy, and its unsustainable harvest of public forests and catch from the seas.

The United States does, however, have many tools and experience in using them. In the early 1980s, state and federal legislation stemmed the loss of coastal wetlands, in part by cutting off construction and insurance subsidies for more than 150 undeveloped barrier islands. States like Florida, faced with a huge influx of retirees and tourists in the 1970s and 1980s, enacted land-use management to control development. Along with the federal government and private conservation organizations, states have also purchased sensitive and wilderness areas to protect them from development. The Clean Air Act provided the incentives for rapidly developing such pollution-control technologies as scrubbers, cleaner coal, and fluidized-bed combustion—advances that the energy industry had claimed would be difficult and costly when the legislation was first proposed.

Prices can also trigger technological improvement. The 1970s oil crisis, precipitated by price hikes by the Organization of Petroleum Exporting Countries [or OPEC], led to major savings in fuel costs when airlines invested in more efficient engines. Banning harmful materials—phosphates from detergents, asbestos, chlorofluorocarbons (CFCs)—has also been achieved at both the national and international levels, despite strong opposition from affected industries.

Unlike in some European countries, fiscal measures have not been effectively used in the United States to restrain the use of private automobiles and subsidize public transport. The only serious gasoline tax proposals ever made in the United States were quickly shot down in 1993, although modest measures such as taxes on petroleum and mineral extraction, recycling incentives, and user fees for waste disposal have been employed at state and local levels for conservation purposes.

POLICIES FOR CHANGE

It is clear that the poorer developing countries need steady international assistance and incentives to reduce population growth and to shift to more sustainable models of development. Exhorting these countries to pursue such difficult changes will have little effect until they perceive that the OECD nations are practicing what they preach. The United States in particular must provide such an example.

The task force on population and consumption of the Presidents Council on Sustainable Development has proposed a mix of tools for curbing population growth and consumption in the United States. To reduce population growth, the task force recommends focusing on family planning (specifically on avoiding unintended pregnancies and reducing teen pregnancy) and on immigration. Based on experience in both the United States and other countries that shows reproductive services work best in combination with an attack on related socioeconomic conditions, the task force recommended policies that would reduce poverty and discrimination and improve economic opportunities, especially for poor women. Similarly, the council's recommendations on immigration emphasize not just law enforcement, but also the need to help address, through foreign assistance and trade policies, the conditions in poor countries that give rise to emigration.

A second cluster of PCSD recommendations would help individuals exercise consumer choice—through environmental education and the certification and labeling of products—and also support the reduction of wastes. Public policies to reduce, reuse, and recycle are necessary, as are volume-based garbage fees that produce incentives and practical arrangements for the disposal of household toxic materials. In each case, the role of federal, state, and local governments in procuring and disposing of their own wastes is pivotal. The leverage that governments collectively wield as consumers of goods and services could provide the necessary momentum for fundamental changes in how the whole nation consumes and disposes of goods.

A third set of PCSD recommendations goes right to the heart of economic development interests in the United States. They are the most important to sustainable development and the most difficult to achieve. These prescriptions would affect resource use by eliminating government subsidies to a wide variety of industries and sectors that have come to expect them, and by shifting taxes from labor and investments to consumption—especially consumption of natural resources, virgin materials, and goods and services that harm the environment. Taxpayers are understandably nervous about how such fundamental shifts would personally affect them. Proposals therefore include provisions for "tax neutrality," with new consumption taxes offset by reductions in payroll taxes. . . .

In the past, policymakers in the United States have often been jolted into action by catastrophes. Severe drought-driven crop failure in the Southeast in 1988 riveted Congress's attention for the first time on the dangers of global warming, even though the drought could not be directly attributed to it. Hurricanes and the 1993 flooding of the Missouri and Mississippi Rivers revived the national debate on limits on federal disaster insurance. The United States can count on more such crises—a major crop failure, disease, or destruction associated with the weather, or an unmanageable threat to petroleum supplies from abroad—that will crank up the legislative and policy machinery and provide the impetus for a national shift to sustainable development. But American political leaders could also act before avoidable tragedy strikes again and could govern with the ecological and environmental security of future generations in mind.

NOTE

1. Purchasing power parity is a GDP estimate based on the purchasing power of currencies rather than current exchange rates.

Part II: RELATIONSHIPS

During the height of the Cold War American policymakers had little difficulty distinguishing friends from foes. The world consisted of three groups, they thought: (1) allies who shared U.S. fears of communism and the Soviet Union; (2) the Soviet Union, sometimes China, and others who aligned themselves with America's enemies in the so-called international communist movement; and (3) neutral and nonaligned states that sought refuge from the contest between the superpowers but who often became the objects of their competitive search for clients.

These distinctions have now largely vanished. To be sure, the United States still enjoys the support of some more than others, and it remains rightfully concerned about developments in Russia and the other republics of the former Soviet Union, as well as in China, North Korea, Cuba, and in areas of the Global South that affect its interests. But today the relationships between the United States and others are no longer defined by the bipolar, Cold War conflict. Still, it is clear that all states are not of equal interest or concern to the United States. Thus it might be useful to ask: Are there alternative models of contemporary international politics that usefully distinguish among them?

"Zones of peace/zones of turmoil," one of several images to which we briefly alluded in the introduction to Part I, provides one demarcation. It draws attention to the multiple differences between the rich states of the North and the sometimes developing, sometimes impoverished states in the South. In contrast with the Global North, where "peace, wealth, and democracy" are widespread, most of the world's people live in "zones of turmoil, war, and development," where "poverty, war, tyranny, and anarchy will continue to devastate lives."[1] The characterization may be too stark, but it does direct attention to the often profound differences between the democratic states in the developed (post-industrial) world, within which the democratic peace proposition points toward nonviolent modes of conflict resolution, and much of the rest of the world, where communal conflict and other forms of bitter and often bloody conflict remain prevalent and where the proliferation of weapons of mass destruction is a growing U.S. concern. Indeed, despite the global spread of democracy since the Cold War's demise, many states throughout the world continue to be mired in what journalist Robert Kaplan has described as a state of anarchy.[2] From the point of view of American foreign policy, then, traditional national security concerns are quite different depending on which "zone" we are examining.

Economic interests are also varied. Canada, Japan, and Western Europe have long been the most important U.S. trade partners. Recently Mexico, China, and the fast-growing economies of Asia (particularly South Korea, Taiwan, Hong Kong, Singapore, and Thailand) have joined their ranks. Many of these fall into the "zone of turmoil." Although that image as originally conceived applied more to security than economic concerns, several of these countries have dominated headlines in recent years as their failed economic practices have caused turmoil in international financial and capital markets. Thus, with backing from the United States, the International Monetary Fund (IMF) launched major economic support programs in Mexico in 1994–1995 and in Indonesia, South Korea, and Thailand in 1997–1998, the latter in an effort to contain the "Asian contagion." In the five years ending in 1997, the IMF had intervened more than 130 times in countries throughout the world, including such vastly disparate places as Russia, Mozambique, Argentina, Kyrgyzstan, and Papua New Guinea.[3] The domestic austerity the IMF imposes in return for its support is often unpalatable politically, but it has become a commonplace occurrence in our rapidly globalizing world.

The domestic upheaval in Asia in 1997–1998 occurred in states that had not only exhibited dramatic economic growth rates for many years but which also had comparatively sustained records of political stability. But, as the Asian markets roiled, American policymakers worried that economic instability might precipitate political instability. Thus Secretary of Defense William Cohen, in an unprecedented appearance before the House Banking and Financial Services Committee in January 1998, testified that U.S. security interests in Asia would be jeopardized if the United States refused to provide financial assistance to the countries in need. Noting that 100,000 Americans had lost their lives in three Asian wars in this century, he added, "If we don't lead on economic issues, we won't be able to lead on other issues."

Economic and security concerns have also crossed paths in the U.S.–Japanese relationship. For years Japan has enjoyed a multibillion-dollar trade surplus with the United States, leading to frequently vituperative exchanges between the long-time allies about Japan's neomercantile economic practices, which limit American companies' access to the Japanese market. During the 1980s, a time now referred to as the "bubble economy," Japan's high-flying economic successes also led many analysts to conclude that Japan was the likely successor to the United States as the world's hegemonic power. Fortunes have since turned dramatically. Between 1991 and 1997, the U.S. stock market increased threefold while the Japanese equity market declined by 60 percent.[4] Rising productivity and rapid economic growth in the United States, compared with stagnation in Japan, underlie these sharply different numbers.

Still, Japan remains the mainstay of the U.S. security posture in the Far East. But the security partnership has been as unequal in recent years as the economic partnership—only in the other direction: the United States is the patron, Japan the client. True, the United States provides a nuclear umbrella for Japan and stations large numbers of troops in Japan (increasingly resented by the Japanese), which would be used to parry a North Korean attack on South Korea or a Chinese assault elsewhere (Taiwan?); but Japan in turn provides comparatively little in the way of assurances that it would support U. S. efforts should war erupt. Thus "the United States–Japan security alliance is at risk. In the words of Japanese diplomat Okamoto Yukio, 'We have a security alliance that works fine in peace but which will fail the most likely tests of war.'"[5] Recognizing this imbalance, former assistant secretary of defense for security affairs, Joseph S. Nye (author of "Conflicts After the Cold War," which appears in Part I of this book), launched what is now commonly called the "Nye Initiative." Its purpose is to translate the United States–Japan patron-client relationship into a more traditional alliance among equal partners. Whether it will succeed is the subject of much discussion on both sides of Pacific.

The Atlantic alliance has also figured prominently in policy analysts' discussions since the end the of the Cold War. NATO, the North Atlantic Treaty Organization which served as the mainstay of the America's European defense posture throughout the Cold War, was conceived as a collective defense organization. Its purpose was to defend member states against aggression by a known enemy, the Soviet Union and its Warsaw Pact allies. With the demise of the enemy, what is NATO's purpose now? Beginning with the Bush administration and continuing into Clinton's, an effort has been made through the Partnership for Peace program to bring former Warsaw Pact members into the Atlantic alliance. In the process, the alliance seems to be transforming itself from a collective defense organization into a collective security arrangement (in which members guarantee the defense of each against an aggression by one of their own, not an external enemy). Clinton accelerated the process with the promise to bring Hungary, Poland, and the Czech Republic into the alliance as full members and to later extend full membership to other states that meet the requirements of admission, with democracy at the top of the list.

Notably absent from the list of initial inductees into the expanding NATO is Russia. Many analysts—inside Russia as well as the United States—interpreted the Clinton administration's move to expand NATO to the very borders of the Soviet Union as an affront to the security interests of Russia, a move that smacked of the "capitalist encirclement" Joseph Stalin and other Soviet ideologues long feared. Others viewed the move as a natural progression in the uniting of a Europe which had been artificially divided by two generations of

Cold War conflict. For them, eventually bringing Russia itself into NATO is a logical extension of the current process. To others, that move would be anathema to the very purpose of the Atlantic alliance: the security of the free world.

We begin our exploration of U.S. relationships with a focus on the NATO controversy as it relates to Russia and the other former Soviet republics. As we move from Europe to Asia and then the Global South, we will find that the traditional distinction between "security" and "economics" is sometimes strained. We will also find that "peace" and "turmoil" do not always capture the "zones" that characterize U.S. relations with others in a rapidly globalizing world.

THE UNITED STATES AND EUROPE

For more than forty years the Soviet Union was the focus of American foreign policy. With its demise, the United States has been stimulated to redefine its relationship with its former adversary across a range of political, economic, and security arenas. The redefinition is in flux. The United States first extended Russia foreign aid to assist its transition to democratic capitalism, but has since turned more routinely to international financial institutions for that purpose. The United States enjoyed Russia's support in putting together a coalition to repel Saddam Hussein's aggression against Kuwait in 1990, but has since found Russia a reluctant partner in enforcing the sanctions designed to assure that Iraq lives up to the terms of the Gulf War cease-fire. The United States supported Russia's entry into the elite "Group of Seven," the leading market economies in the world, whose decisions on global financial issues affect everyone, but it has been dismayed by the halting progress Russia has made in meeting the requirements necessary to become a full partner in the management of the world political economy. And in the security sphere, the United States experienced disappointment when the Russian parliament refused to ratify the Strategic Arms Reduction Treaty (START II), thus stalling efforts to move the U.S.–Russian disarmament process forward. In each case, the growing tentativeness of the U.S.–Russian relationship contrasts sharply with the early post–Cold War years, when a sense of euphoria characterized the new environment. Just as the United States had assisted Germany and Japan in their transition to democracy after World War II, cementing their eventual security partnership with the United States, Russia would now join the fold. Has something gone wrong?

Walter Russell Mead addresses that question in the first chapter in Part II, "No Cold War Two: The United States and the Russian Federation." NATO's expansion is Mead's launching pad, as we suggested in the introduction, but this takes him in the direction of a broader survey which ranges beyond Russia to other republics in the former Soviet Union. As he surveys the landscape of U.S. interests with the former Soviet republics, he reminds us of the enormous complexity of the vast former Soviet empire and the equally complex problems its successor states face as they transition from communism and socialism to new forms of governance and economics.

The central question in Mead's essay asks how the United States should approach its former adversary in the new era. As the title of his chapter suggests, Mead is not an advocate of neocontainment and isolation. While conceding Russia is a revisionist state with a capacity to threaten its neighbors' independence, he concludes that "to extend NATO up to, or even past, the former boundaries of the Soviet Union and transform it into an openly anti-Russian alliance" would be a serious mistake. On one hand, "Russia . . . is a weak state more likely to implode into anarchy than to explode beyond its frontiers in an orgy of conquest and aggression." On the other hand, Mead argues neocontainment will not enhance U.S. security. Instead, it will stir Russia's fears, embolden the country's hard-liners, and increase the probability of a needless confrontation between the two states. More important, such a posture would undercut the ability of the United States and Russia to build a constructive partnership based on their many common interests. "Whether as a balancing power in Europe or Asia, as a voice for growth and an advocate for developing countries in global forums, or as a 'bridge' country spanning the gap between the European and non-European branches of human civilization, Russia's global role complements that of the United States." Thus Mead believes that cooperating with Russia would be wiser than "raising up a new coalition to contain it."

Madeleine Albright, the U.S. Secretary of State, takes issue with Mead's conclusions, pointing out in the next chapter that observers who either champion or criticize NATO as an anti-Russian coalition misunderstand the organization's mission in the new era. In "Enlarging NATO: Why Bigger Is Better," she denies that the purpose of NATO's continued existence is to counter a resurgent Russia. Instead, she declares that "NATO does not need an enemy. It has enduring purposes." From facilitating continued American engagement in Europe, to building a cooperative relationship with Russia, to promoting European integration, NATO's goals now embrace a far more ambitious set of objectives. Even the institution's chief function—maintaining security—has changed with the absence of a clearly defined threat and the plan to admit East European states formerly under communist rule. Hence Albright's message is that Americans should welcome NATO's expansion, because "a goal that would have seemed like Utopian delusion just years ago lies within our grasp: a peaceful and undivided Europe working in partnership with the United States, that welcomes every one of the continent's democracies into our transatlantic community."

Werner Weidenfeld disagrees with Albright's assessment that the transatlantic community forged during the Cold War is remaking itself through a redefinition of NATO. In "America and Europe: Is the Break Inevitable?," he argues that "the old structures left over from the era of the East-West conflict . . . cannot meet new challenges." Even though the United States and Europe share similar values and remain congenial, the objectives that once united them in a common outlook and purpose have been eroded by the Soviet Union's demise and newfound attention to domestic priorities. Consequently "new guiding principles for common action are needed to change the old backdrops and to form a consensus on how to tackle the tasks of the future." Weidenfeld proposes that the transatlantic community be rebuilt through new forums for political cooperation, a common market, and the establishment of a "learning community" that would foster consultation and collaboration on domestic as well as foreign issues. If the United States and Europe do not devote energy to renewing their relationship in innovative ways, Weidenfeld warns, "they will inevitably grow apart" as international crises, trade rivalries, and conflicting interests rend their once close partnership.

THE UNITED STATES AND ASIA

We posited in the introduction to this book that the twenty-first century will be an American century. Many others believe it belongs to Asia. An official in Singapore's Foreign Ministry recently expressed a view widely shared by others:

> Since the nineteenth century, the world economy's center of gravity has shifted steadily westward from Europe to North America and now to the Asia-Pacific. As the economic center shifts, the new locus becomes the main theater of global action. From the two world wars to the Cold War, the course of the twentieth century was determined primarily in Europe. In the twenty-first century, the Asia-Pacific will become this hinge of history.[6]

As a Pacific power itself, the United States is already heavily involved in Asia's future. Its trade with Asia is more than twice as large as its trade with Europe; and as its involvement in the world political economy continues to grow, more and more jobs will be dependent on export markets, with Asia an increasingly important one. The United States also remains heavily involved in the region militarily. The 1997 Quadrennial Defense Review anticipates that 100,000 American troops will continue to be deployed there. The report explains that "maintaining this level of capability underscores our commitment to remain engaged as a stabilizing influence in the region, alleviates the potential for destabilizing arms races in the region, underwrites deterrence on the Korean peninsula and elsewhere, and strengthens our voice in international forums dealing not only with Asian security matters but also political and economic matters."

Some critics charge that the continuing heavy military involvement of the United States in Asia reflects the persistence of Cold War thinking in the face of new realities. Beyond North Korea, they ask, who poses a threat to U.S. security interests in the region? Others respond: China is the threat looming on the horizon. For them, revitalizing the U.S.–Japanese alliance takes on added urgency.

In "Futureshock or Renewed Partnership? The U.S.–Japan Alliance Facing the Millennium," Robert A. Manning agrees that both countries are correct to recognize the continuing significance of their security relationship in the new era. The U.S. military presence in Japan not only solidifies America's standing as a Pacific power, but it enhances regional stability by constraining an independent Japanese military posture. Where the United States and Japan have erred, Manning contends, is in their failure to reexamine the underlying assumptions of their relationship. He believes "the starting point to revalidating the security alliance is to recognize the enormously changed context, not just in terms of geopolitical sea change, but in economics and domestic politics on both sides as well." In particular, the "centrifugal economic and political forces in both countries" compel each government to convince its people that the alliance has evolved into a more equal partnership that remains mutually beneficial. Creating such a perception will require new forms of military cooperation and Japan's willingness to accept a greater degree of international responsibility. This task will be difficult, Manning notes, due to the "discernible deficit of political imagination and political leadership in Japan and the United States." But without continued and enhanced cooperation between the two countries, he believes "it is difficult to envision a viable, durable international system."

Redefining and strengthening America's partnership with Japan is an important priority if China in fact wishes to challenge the Far Eastern status quo. Disputes with its neighbors over the Spratly Islands, concern about the balance of power on the Korean peninsula, and a refusal to accept Taiwan's existence as a sovereign entity are flashpoints. Beyond this, China, with more than 1.2 billion people, is rapidly becoming a formidable economic power. Current projections show that China will surpass the United States as the largest economy in the world early in the next century. "When that happens," Singapore's Kishore Mahbubani writes, "the world's established power structure will have to adjust to China's arrival; Washington may no longer be the modern Rome."[7]

Two analysts who subscribe to the malevolent view of China's intentions, described in their widely discussed book *The Coming Conflict with China,* observe:

> During the past decade or so [China] has set goals for itself that are directly contrary to American interests, the most important of those goals being to replace the United States as the preeminent power in Asia, to reduce American influence, to prevent Japan and the United States from creating a kind of "contain China" front, and to extend its power into the South China and East China Seas so that it controls the region's essential sea-lanes. China aims at achieving a kind of hegemony. Its goal is to ensure that no country in its region . . . will act without first taking China's interests into prime consideration.[8]

These geopolitical designs, backed by its rapidly growing economy and an ambitious military modernization program, will supposedly transform China into a twenty-first century world power. This prospect, coupled with Chinese transgressions related to trade and human rights abuses, prompted calls for the Clinton administration to abandon its policy of engagement in favor of a more confrontational stance. Such an approach would seek to "contain" China, implying the imposition of trade sanctions, political isolation, and a larger U.S. military presence in the region.

In "China: Why Our Hard-Liners Are Wrong," Robert S. Ross believes those who criticize the U.S. policy of engagement overstate their case, distorting China's capabilities and its negative effects on American interests. Ross notes that regardless of whether the issue is naval power, weapons development, defense expenditures, or alliance commitments, China is unable to rival the U.S. military. Also China has a far better record on arms sales and weapons proliferation policy than is often recognized. On economic matters, Ross argues a similar pattern emerges. He acknowledges that China's piracy of U.S. intellectual property and its growing trade surplus with the United States are problems, but he argues that the financial impact each issue has on the American economy is exaggerated. Furthermore, although "China's human rights violations are numerous and grave," the United States gives far greater attention to Chinese practices than it does to violations elsewhere in the world. This is not to deny there are serious problems with China's domestic and international behavior. Still, Ross declares "China is not a 'rogue state,' and [the] U.S. policy [of engagement] has made important gains in affecting Chinese behavior over a wide range of issues bearing on important American interests."

THE UNITED STATES AND THE GLOBAL SOUTH

As in Europe and Asia, the dawn of a new era in world politics has profoundly changed America's relationship with the Global South, which incorporates much of the former Third World plus some of the former Soviet republics. Most notably, the end of the Cold War largely removes the incentives for the United States to compete for favors among developing states. Relatedly, many members of the Global South are already painfully aware that their geopolitical importance to the United States has diminished considerably in recent years. The demise of the Soviet Union affords the United States the opportunity to redirect its attention and resources (namely foreign aid) from the Global South to other priorities, whether it be promoting democratization in Eastern Europe or addressing a variety of domestic needs. These altered preferences invite the question of whether the United States should remain engaged in the Global South at all.

Some analysts argue that the United States has a historic opportunity to forge new partnerships and relationships throughout the Global South that are free from the constraints of bipolar conflict. The challenge, however, lies in the fact that the Global South can no longer be viewed or approached as a cohesive unit with common characteristics. Not only are there tremendous differences within the South in terms of political ideology (including differences about the meaning and practice of democracy) and levels of economic development, but, as the readings that follow demonstrate, the nature and intensity of U.S. interests varies considerably.

We begin our examination of U.S. relations with the Global South with a focus on the Middle East, a region where the combination of U.S. political, economic, and security interests have long been strong. In "The Gulf Bottleneck: Middle East Stability and World Oil Supply," Richard N. Cooper considers how secure and reliable the flow of Persian Gulf oil will be in the new era. The issue merits attention since global economic prosperity continues to depend on oil, a relatively cheap source of energy with large reserve deposits in the Middle East. Noteworthy in this respect is that U.S. dependence on imported oil has skyrocketed in recent years, fueled in part by the widely popular but gas-guzzling vans and sport utility vehicles that now jam the nation's streets and highways.[9]

Cooper surveys the Middle Eastern political landscape and concludes that even though sources of instability remain, due to hostility toward Israel, unsettled border disputes, and problems of political succession, Persian Gulf oil producers "have little [economic] incentive to disrupt production and will likely try to limit any interruption of oil flows." Still, regional "production facilities, pipelines, and shipping channels are quite vulnerable both to non-state actors and to regional powers, should they choose to interfere." Thus Cooper believes it is essential the United States and other oil importers help protect these "bottlenecks" as well as develop alternative sources of energy.

The challenges the United States faces closer to home are the focus of the next chapter by Peter Andreas, entitled "U.S.–Mexico: Open Markets, Closed Border." As the title suggests, there is an inherent tension between the policy objectives the United States pursues throughout Latin America and especially with its southern neighbor, Mexico. Specifically, the "promotion of border-less economies based on free market principles in many ways contradicts and undermines . . . efforts to keep borders closed to the clandestine movement of drugs and migrant labor." This dilemma, according to Andreas, has placed public pressure on U.S. policymakers to stem the negative consequences of economic liberalization by treating the drug trade and illegal immigration as national security issues and making good relations with Latin American states contingent upon their assistance with these problems. "Just as politicians in earlier years did not want to appear soft on communism, in today's political climate they do not want to appear soft on drugs or soft on illegal immigrants." But because the trend is toward greater economic integration with Mexico and Latin America, Andreas believes it would be counterproductive (and largely futile) for the U.S. government to establish "a fully militarized border." Instead, U.S. energy would be better devoted to reevaluating present policy directions, largely by treating the drug problem as a public health issue and stringently enforcing existing labor laws.

Howard J. Wiarda broadens the discussion of U.S.–Latin American relations in "Back to Basics: Reassessing U.S. Policy in Latin America." He is concerned with the assumptions underlying the "Washington Consensus" about the goals of U.S. policy in Latin America. Wiarda stresses there is nothing wrong with democracy, open markets, free trade, and counter-narcotics serving as key objectives: "It is hard to conceive the United States could stand for anything other than these principles." The problem lies in "the absence of nuance; the lack of any sense of how to get from here to there; the 'true believer,' missionary, and tunnel vision that accompany these orthodoxies; and the ethnocentrism involved." Wiarda points out, for instance, that U.S. policymakers lack an appreciation for how differently Latin Americans define democracy and human rights and, therefore, how unlikely they are to embrace U.S.–style political systems. Relatedly, Latin Americans are more apt to view open markets as detrimental to democracy and social stability than as paths to prosperity. Similar misconceptions extend to U.S. convictions about the desirability of hemispheric free trade and the proper strategies for waging the drug war. Thus Wiarda urges the United States to go "back to basics" by rethinking the assumptions of its Latin American policy and learning "to understand other cultures and countries on their own terms rather than through its own rose-colored glasses."

To this point, the selections have discussed two regions of the Global South, the Middle East and Latin America, where the United States has established foreign policy interests and a long history of involvement. Unless there is a fundamental reordering of U.S. priorities away from global activism, the expectation is that the United States will remain engaged in these regions. Less clear is whether and how it should approach others in the Global South, particularly states in areas peripheral to its vital interests. The final two readings in Part II outline markedly different prescriptions in answering this question.

In "Pivotal States and U.S. Strategy," Robert S. Chase, Emily B. Hill, and Paul Kennedy advocate a conservative approach, arguing that "the United States needs a policy toward the developing world that does not spread American energies, attention, and resources too thinly across the globe, but rejects isolationist calls to write it off." Their prescription is a policy that seeks to preserve the status quo by concentrating on a select number of pivotal states or "hot spot[s] that could not only determine the fate of their region[s] but also affect international stability." Ideally such states should be large, populous countries with economic potential and important geographic locations. Although the authors identify several states that they believe meet these criteria today, they stress their list is subject to change. The important point, they argue, is the pivotal-state concept offers policymakers a logical and intuitively appealing strategy to maintain domestic political support for global engagement in the new era. Furthermore, this "better wise than wide" approach provides a clear framework for making difficult decisions about the "appropriate focusing of [U.S.] development assistance, . . . trade and investment, . . . intelligence capabilities, and foreign service expertise" throughout the Global South.

In a narrower sense, the Clinton administration has embraced such an approach by designing a U.S. trade strategy that focuses on the ten big emerging markets of the Global South. It is this policy in particular, and selective engagement in general, that the authors of the next chapter sharply criticize. In "Don't Neglect the Impoverished South," Robin Broad and John Cavanagh contend that the Clinton policy is not only too narrowly drawn, but that its underlying assumptions are "deeply flawed." The end result is that any economic prosperity arising in the markets targeted by the United States is not spreading to neighboring states as believed. Instead, "the inescapable conclusion is that the North-South economic gap is narrowing for about a dozen countries but continues to widen for well over one hundred others." Indeed, the United Nations Development Programme has reported recently that even as globalization has contributed to a rapid rise in incomes for as many as 1.5 billion people around the world since 1980, economic decline or stagnation has caused the incomes of an even larger number of people to decline.[10] Increased polarization between the world's rich and poor states and people is the result.

Broad and Cavanagh warn that unless the United States adopts "an overarching policy framework that addresses the deep and changing problems of the [entire Global] South," the world of the twenty-first century will be one of economic apartheid." To avoid this prospect, they advocate a "two-tiered set of policies"—one tier designed to alleviate suffering in the Global South's poorest countries, and the other designed to combat the negative effects of globalization—income inequalities, job losses, environmental degradation—that both the Global North and the more advanced economies of the Global South confront. "The question is simply whether the United States will take the lead in resolving these problems or will instead wait and be led."

NOTES

1. Max Singer and Aaron Wildavsky, *The Real World Order: Zones of Peace/Zones of Turmoil* (Chatham, NJ: Chatham House, 1993), pp. 1, 6.

2. Robert Kaplan, "The Coming Anarchy," *Atlantic Monthly* 273 (February 1994), pp. 44–76; and Robert Kaplan, *The Ends of the Earth: A Journey at the Dawn of the Twenty-First Century* (New York: Random House, 1996).

3. "Second Guessing the Economic Doctor," *New York Times,* February 1, 1998, p. 8.

4. "Making the Case for Asset Allocation," *In the Vanguard,* Winter 1998, p. 1.

5. James Shinn, "Testing the United States–Japan Security Alliance, *Current History* 96 (December 1997), p. 425.

6. Kishore Mahbubani, "An Asia-Pacific Consensus," *Foreign Affairs* 76 (September/October 1997), p. 149.

7. Ibid., p. 150.

8. Richard Bernstein and Ross H. Munro, *The Coming Conflict with China* (New York: Alfred A. Knopf, 1997), p. 11.

9. "Fuel Efficiency Falls, Just as More Is Needed," *New York Times,* October 26, 1997, p. WK3.

10. *Human Development Report 1996* (New York: Oxford University Press, 1996), p. 1.

The United States and Europe

12. NO COLD WAR TWO: THE UNITED STATES AND THE RUSSIAN FEDERATION

Walter Russell Mead

... *R*ecently in the United States we have heard a chorus of voices—Henry Kissinger, Zbigniew Brzezinski, and Dick Cheney to name only three—calling for the nations "to form a solid wall before the speeding apparition" and so to save ourselves, enlightenment, and civilization. The particular solid wall they have in mind is the North Atlantic Treaty (NATO) alliance, and the theorists of "neocontainment" want to extend NATO up to, or even past, the former boundaries of the Soviet Union and transform it into an openly anti-Russian alliance. . . .

Neocontainment and the isolation of Russia will not serve any important American interests. On the contrary, they will create new and unnecessary obstacles to overall American foreign policy interests in the 1990s and beyond. Neocontainment will weaken NATO, increase the prospects of war in Europe, increase American defense spending without enhancing American security, sharpen the nuclear threat to American security posed by Russia's still formidable nuclear arsenal, and create serious problems in regional diplomacy for the United States in both Europe and Asia. Against these negatives, there is not one single advantage that neocontainment would bring the United States. Not one.

... Without cherishing any fond illusions regarding the likely evolution of Russian politics, the United States will be better placed to achieve its central foreign policy goals by cooperating with Russia rather than by raising up a new coalition to contain it.

Note: Notes have been deleted.

THE WRECKAGE OF OUR HOPES

The American debate over Russia today begins in the wreckage of our hopes. In the wave of ill-considered euphoria that swept much of the foreign policy community at the end of the Cold War, it was widely assumed that free markets and democratic politics would quickly set Russia on the road to becoming something very like the industrial democracies of western Europe and North America. Russia would, in this view, become a trusty "little brother" of the United States, loyally seconding American opinions and policies around the world. Like Germany and Japan after the Second World War, it would see the error of its ways and align itself morally as well as politically with the triumphant, and triumphantly right, United States. . . .

. . . The American strategy toward Russia—based on the confident assumption that Boris Yeltsin, Jeffrey Sachs, the IMF [International Monetary Fund] and a few billion dollars could turn Russia into a member of the Western community of nations within a very few years—has been shown to be false. Those who believed in it, and acted on it, are guilty of a gross failure in judgment, and critics are right to demand a change. . . .

American opinion is now facing unpleasant facts. Russia, it is now clear, may be turning into a capitalist country, but it is not turning rapidly—possibly not even at all—into an advanced industrial democracy on the Euro-American model. Furthermore, we face an indeterminate period of time during which Russia will not be a prosperous or stable country. There is a real risk of a drift toward increasingly radical and aggressive nationalism directed toward the other post-Soviet republics; Russia is in any case already beginning to resume a great-power role in eastern Europe. . . .

From an unrealistically optimistic assessment of Russia's prospects, the pendulum of American opinion has now swung to the opposite—and equally inappropriate—extreme. Essentially, the American foreign policy community first assumed that Russia had virtually no interests distinguishable from American plans for a "new world order," and when this assumption proved unfounded, American opinion jumped to the equally improbable assumption that Russian interests would lead inexorably to a clash with American interests in Europe. Throughout the whole sorry debate there has been little or no attention paid to the nature of Russia's interests and prospects, the real state of the Russian nation, and the relationship between American and Russian strategic interests in the contemporary world.

. . . Russian and American interests, although they are not identical, are substantially similar and form the basis for an enduring relationship. Despite the alarms being sounded by the neocontainment alliance . . . , Russia, even an authoritarian and aggressively nationalist Russia, poses no threat to the balance of power in Europe. Russia today is a weak state more likely to implode into anarchy than to explode beyond its frontiers in an orgy of conquest and aggression, but if and when it recovers its footing domestically, it will still be unable to challenge America's security interests in Europe. . . .

RUSSIAN COLLAPSE

The extent of the moral, political, military, and economic collapse in contemporary Russia is one of the most remarkable phenomena of our times. Even the casual traveler in Russia . . . is likely to be approached by military conscripts and officers asking for Western help in getting out of the service or eager to present complaints about low pay or pay in arrears. Draft evasion is widespread and accepted as normal and even commendable by the population at large. Every item in the Soviet arsenal is available on a black market so extensive that it cannot be run without the connivance of a significant portion of the military leadership. Such essential items as fuel and food are diverted wholesale into black-market channels; there are reliable reports of Russian sailors starving for lack of food and of maneuvers canceled for lack of fuel. Accounts from a variety of sources confirm that Russian units are under strength; that pilots are unable to get their required hours in the air, that essential weapons and parts are unavailable; and that the system of supply and military transport has been wrecked. For the foreseeable future, the Russian military will not be the force that smashed its way into France under Alexander I or into Berlin under Stalin; it will be the force that lost the Crimean War, was humiliated by Japan, and was crushed by Germany in the First World War. . . .

The crisis of the Russian military is part of a broader and deeper crisis of the Russian state. The central government has for some years lacked the ability to enforce its decrees or to coordinate the actions of government functionaries across its vast territory. "Privatization" in practice means a scramble for state assets. Intense political struggles in all of Russia's regions and towns are taking place over control of this privatization process. Decrees from Moscow are not enforced, taxes are not collected, and laws are not observed. . . .

As its air and rail transportation networks continue to decay, as its university system and network of scientific research facilities crumbles, and as its health care system moves toward collapse and such facilities as water purification plants fall into desuetude, the basic infrastructure of a modern European state is disappearing across much of Russia. It will be some time before the Russian government—any Russian government—is in full control of its own territory. This weak state will lack the capacity to mount major military actions for some time to come—except in the near abroad, where Russia's neighbors face difficulties in many cases greater than those dogging the Kremlin.

It also seems abundantly clear that the Russian state—democratic or not—must first earn legitimacy by delivering economic relief to the population before it can enlist the Russian people in support of a dangerous and expensive policy of foreign expansion. Election returns from . . . the December 1993 parliamentary elections, as well as opinion polls, show that the elements of the population liable to the appeal of the ultra-nationalists and the ex-Communists [were] predominantly the older, poorer, less well-educated, and less urbanized social groups. But any Russian regime wishing to improve the economy will have to rely on the better educated, younger, and more urbanized people—and these are the least chauvinistic and most skeptical people in the country. They tend to be deeply cynical about government calls for further sacrifices for any cause whatever. To the extent that the Russian government supports the interests of the reactionary masses, it compromises its ability to restore the economy. To the extent that Russia acts to rejuvenate its economy, it must accommodate its foreign policy to a stratum of opinion that, while nationalistic, is opposed to adventures and, above all, to war.

Furthermore, Russia's economic recovery will continue to depend on an open trading relationship with the West; this, too, militates against a foreign policy of confrontation. It should also be noted that it was the burden of sustaining its military might that helped bring down the Soviet edifice. The Russian economy today is incomparably weaker than the Soviet economy ever was, and the Russian military has lost ground to the West in the intervening years. It is extremely improbable that the Russian economy could support a renewed arms race with the West under these conditions.

Russia's position in Asia is even weaker than its position in Europe. The small and widely scattered Russian population in the Far East lacks both the economic and demographic elements required to challenge the balance of power in Asia. With Chinese military capacity rapidly growing, Japan moving toward the status of a major military power, and American interest in the region rekindled both by its growing economic importance and the new crisis on the Korean peninsula, there is quite simply no prospect of Russian domination of this region. For the foreseeable future, the question in Asia is whether Russia can maintain its position rather than whether it can expand its influence.

Those who fear a new threat to the Eurasian balance of power from Russia are making one of the oldest and most dangerous miscalculations in international politics: they are guarding against a danger that has ceased to exist. Like Napoleon III, laboring industriously to weaken Austria while Prussian power grew, like the British government worrying about French designs on the Low Countries as the Prussian artillery gathered on the hills above Sedan, the advocates of neocontainment are missing the signs of the times. Although Russia's interests and its desperate position make it a discontented and revisionist power, and although it is clearly a threat to the independence of its newly independent neighbors, it lacks the means to constitute a threat to the wider European order.

THE NEAR ABROAD

Those who call for a new policy of containment point to Russia's ambitions and policies primarily in the near abroad, the Russian term for the other former Soviet republics. They argue that Russia's actions in the near abroad constitute a threat to the international order and that if Russian nationalism is not stopped there, it will gather strength and pose a new challenge to the security order in Europe.

Admittedly, the Russian republic does not accept the independence of its former fellow republics of the Soviet Union; even when it grudgingly concedes their independence, it does not necessarily accept their boundaries and claims a special right of intervention and oversight with respect to their treatment of their Russian minorities. But here as elsewhere in American-Russian relations, American opinion is a prisoner of its earlier excessive optimism. With the exception of the Baltic states, none of the republics of the near abroad have a modern tradition of self-government. All have economies that were consciously oriented toward the Soviet Union as a whole: the Communists believed economic integration was the surest way to weld their vast empire into a unitary state and so deliberately shaped economic development in ways that increased each republic's dependence on the center.

Furthermore, every one of these republics was the object of Moscow's nationality policy. This included a deliberate program of colonizing the republics with Russian-speakers and of ensuring that ethnic Russians were well represented in strategic technical and political posts. It also included divide-and-rule policies, setting one ethnic group against another—even deliberately creating territorial grievances, such as the Armenian-Azerbaijani feud over the Karabakh enclave There was also the forced relocation of entire ethnic groups, such as the Crimean Tatars and the Volga Germans, who now pose acute political problems as they seek to reclaim their lost homes.

Finally, each of these republics has inherited the moral and economic crisis of the Soviet state—in most cases, in a conspicuously worse form, thanks to their dependence on Russian energy supplies at subsidized prices. Their managers lack experience, their courts lack legitimacy, and their political leaders are profoundly out of touch with the realities of the noncommunist world.

The near-universal belief in American foreign policy circles that republics so situated could speedily achieve stable and secure independence never had any relationship to the actual prospects of the former Soviet republics. Their own weakness and susceptibility to anarchy invite—almost require—Russian intervention. Only those who fail to grasp the situation in these republics can be surprised and shocked by Russia's reviving interest and influence there. . . .

APPROACHING THE REGIONS

The near abroad, of course, is not one place, but four: the five Central Asian republics, the Transcaucasus (Georgia, Armenia, and Azerbaijan), the Baltic republics, and the western republics of Belarus, Moldova, and Ukraine. The United States and Russia have different approaches to each of these regions, and any attempt to make sense of their bilateral relations must be based on the local conditions in each of the regions.

The Central Asian republics are the least likely to cause a conflict between the United States and Russia. Washington is sufficiently concerned about the upsurge of militant Islam in Central Asia that it is reluctant to limit Russia's freedom of action there. Furthermore, if there is one region in the world that the United States is prepared to acknowledge as peripheral to its vital interests, Central Asia is probably it. Russia, on the other hand, still chastened by the Soviet experience in Afghanistan, seems reluctant to pursue its Central Asian objectives through methods that involve Russian troops. This ensures that Russian policy in the region will tend to remain within the letter if not the spirit of international law. Russia appears committed to attempt to exert its hegemony in Central Asia through local rulers and political movements, limiting itself to questions involving external security and protection of ethnic Russians; the United States would be extremely unwise to involve itself in a confrontation over this approach. Even if Russia's presence becomes more heavy-handed, the United States has little ability to influence events in this part of the world and little reason to want to do so. Russian withdrawal from the Central Asian republics could easily lead to the kind of chaos now gripping Afghanistan; one could hardly interpret that as a triumph for democratic principles or world order.

In the Transcaucasus, the United States and Russia also appear to have reason to reach a modus vivendi based on Russian hegemony. Georgia's manifest inability to govern itself without Russian assistance and the dependence of both Armenia and Azerbaijan on a Russian umpire for their wretched conflicts make a major Russian role in this region inevitable and, from a humanitarian point of view, desirable. Endless war in the Transcaucasus, ultimately inviting Iranian involvement, seems to be the alternative to a strong Russian presence in the region.

It is deeply regrettable that the advocates of neocontainment use Russian policy in Georgia as evidence of Russia's subversive and expansionist intentions. Russia certainly exploited the ethnic hostilities in Georgia to force Eduard Shevardnadze to bring his country back into the Commonwealth of Independent States, but it did not create those hostilities or the political blindness of either the Gamsakhurdia government or the Georgian political class as a whole that made widespread conflict inevitable. Russia was not immune to the effects of Georgia's conflicts in any case; its own political difficulties in the Caucasus with the Chechens and other ethnic groups are severe enough that Russia simply could not tolerate the chaotic situation that Gamsakhurdia's chauvinism created. . . .

The Baltic republics are, from an American point of view, the most genuinely and legitimately independent of the newly independent states. The United States never recognized their illegal annexation by the Soviet Union, and even the Soviet authorities ultimately conceded the illegitimacy of their occupation. The Baltic states' historic ties with western Europe, which date back to Hanseatic times, are also an important factor in the situation.

From the Russian point of view, the situation is somewhat more complex. The large Russian minorities in these republics have legitimate interests and rights that have not always been scrupulously observed by the Baltic authorities. Furthermore, the Russians have important security concerns. The approaches to St. Petersburg are controlled by the Baltic states, and the Russian enclave in the former East Prussia is separated from Russia proper by Lithuania.

Here the policy of neocontainment is likely to worsen what is already a bad situation. Any sign that the United States is moving to isolate or contain Russia encourages those elements in the Baltic states who oppose reaching a reasonable accommodation with their neighbor. If the Russians believe that American diplomacy aims to isolate Russia, power within the Russian government will move toward those who advocate a policy of confrontation—and trigger Russian fears that NATO will seek to build bases in the Baltic states or otherwise choke off St. Petersburg's access to the sea. American guarantees to the Baltic republics are more likely to destabilize than to stabilize the situation in this volatile corner of the world.

A good model for the relationship between the Baltic republics and Russia would be the relationship between Finland and the Soviets after the Second World War. Finland, like the Baltic states, was a province of the Russian empire that won its independence in the turmoil surrounding the Russian Revolution. After fighting the Soviet Union in the Second World War, Finland kept its independence but followed a scrupulous policy of friendly neutrality toward the Soviet Union. No one unacceptable to the Soviet Union held high office in the Finnish government, and the Finnish economy was consciously oriented toward serving the needs of its neighbor.

Finlandization was a happy fate for Finland and would be a good one for the Baltic republics. This can only be achieved, however, if the Baltic states adhere to the principles of friendly neutrality toward Russia. NATO membership is obviously incompatible with such a policy. The Russian minorities, including retired members of the Russian armed forces and security organs, must be granted the full citizenship, economic, and cultural rights international law prescribes. The West, and especially the United States, must leave the Baltic republics with no doubts whatever on this score. The Balts must know that if they provoke the bear, they will shoulder the consequences alone. . . .

GREATER DIFFICULTIES

The western republics of Belarus, Moldova, and Ukraine pose greater difficulties still, although even here one must distinguish between the situations of the different states. Belarus appears to be the least sincerely independent of the former Soviet republics, and it will probably ultimately be peacefully reabsorbed in a Greater Russia. In Moldova, the situation is somewhat more complex. The majority population in the republic is Romanian, and left to its own devices would be likely to drift toward union with Bucharest over time. The "Trans-Dniester" enclave of the republic, however, is largely Slavic in population and is unlikely to join Romania unless forced to do so . . . Whether the status of Moldova is ultimately settled by partition and plebescite, or whether the republic as a whole is incorporated into a revived CIS [Commonwealth of Independent States], the West's chief interest is that the ethnic conflict in Moldova not contribute to the overall instability in southeastern Europe.

The Ukrainian situation presents several levels of difficulties and is the issue over which the United States and its Western allies are most likely to come into some sort of conflict with Russia. The Ukrainian nationalist movement is extremely strong and dedicated. Centered in the western part of the country, Ukrainian nationalism is as historically legitimate and strongly felt as any nationalism in eastern Europe. Even Alexander Solzhenitsyn has acknowledged that Ukraine has a legitimate separate national identity that Russia is morally bound to respect. The western Ukraine could not be reabsorbed into a centralized state based in Moscow without a war that would far eclipse the Yugoslav war for brutality and bloodshed.

On the other hand, Ukraine is not—yet—a viable state. Unlike the Baltic republics, it remains absolutely dependent on subsidized Russian fuel. Once the breadbasket of Europe, it remains the most important food-producing region of the former Soviet Union; yet it lacks the resources to produce or pay for the fertilizer and fuel that it needs to plant its crops and bring in its harvest. There is also the bungling incompetence of the Ukrainian government. Its inability to manage and maintain its nuclear power plants makes it a permanent threat to the well-being of its neighbors. With its economic fecklessness, it is destabilizing itself and, therefore, the European order.

It is also and regrettably true that Ukraine's boundaries bear no relationship to ethnic or historic realities. Crimea and the east bank of the Dnieper are largely, although not exclusively, Russian in population. Ukraine's current boundaries—west as well as east—are not defensible, rational, or just; in this they resemble the irrational boundaries of postcolonial Africa. . . .

It is not clear that Ukraine would be an economically viable state if its frontiers were redrawn to take account of ethnic realities. Most of its coal reserves are in the Russian-dominated portions of the country; both its agriculture and its industry would be helpless without subsidized Russian inputs and guaranteed markets in Russia. From a political and economic point of view, Ukraine is a catastrophe waiting to happen. Russia cannot remain indifferent to the crumbling away of central authority and order in this neighboring state, nor can it remain permanently deaf to the concerns of the ethnic Russians trapped on this sinking ship.

Unfortunately, among all the former Soviet republics, the fate of Ukraine raises the most serious balance-of-power issues. . . . With a population of 52 million and a land area larger than Germany and the United Kingdom combined, Ukraine is by far the most strategically significant of the newly independent states. A Russia that absorbs Ukraine is a great power in the heart of Europe; without Ukraine, Russia is a remote if still formidable presence on the European fringe. From the perspective of Russian history there is yet another important consideration: access to the warm waters of the Black Sea, the destination of most of the principal rivers in European Russia and a vital outlet to the world, depends on control of the Crimean littoral and the Black

Sea Fleet. To the extent that Ukraine sets itself against Russian control of the fleet, it directly challenges an interest Russia has regarded as vital since the eighteenth century.

A NEW DOMINO THEORY

The political friction between the Russian majority in Crimea and Ukraine's central authorities has focused the world's attention on this potentially explosive situation. For advocates of neocontainment, it is in Ukraine where the line in the sand must be drawn. The neocontainment theorists have a new domino theory. First the smaller and more marginal ex-Soviet republics—Tajikistan, Azerbaijan, Georgia—will fall. Then Belarus and Ukraine. Next? Presumably, with the Soviet Union restored in fact if not in name, the Visegrad countries would be next on the list. Or the Balkans. Or, the age-old goal of Russian diplomacy: Constantinople and the Straits.

This geopolitical concept is both unrealistic and dangerous. Unrealistic, because even assuming that Russia is able to achieve and maintain a stable position of hegemony in most of the former Soviet Union, it would still pose no real threat to the European order. NATO . . . successfully contained the Soviet Union and the Warsaw Pact for 40 years; there is simply no prospect that a resurgent Russia could overturn the European order as long as NATO holds together. And a resurgent Russia would rejuvenate NATO in short order. The dominoes, in short, won't fall. The concept is also dangerous because it risks a war that the United States doesn't want to fight and would almost certainly lose, and it is self-defeating because it does not present a workable framework for diplomatic action.

The United States needs to work out its Ukrainian policy from a rigorously honest examination of conscience. Are the American people willing to fight a war with Russia to defend the current boundaries of Ukraine? The answer, certainly, is no. The United States is no more prepared to defend Ukraine against Russia than Germany was ready to defend Croatia against Serbia. Moreover, there are no compelling national interests that can or should change this opinion. . . .

THE AMERICAN PROJECT

American policy should recognize that the former Soviet republics need a closer partnership with one another and that this partnership must inevitably embody a leading role for the Russian Federation. A looser rather than a tighter partnership is clearly preferable. The United States should exercise its limited influence to encourage the development of a limited and flexible partnership based on the free consent of all parties as the most attractive course for all the states in the region, including Russia. Funding a clearinghouse for inter-republic trade, working with the European Union to shift the approach from bilateral trade negotiations with the former Soviet republics to discussions with the CIS as a whole, and channeling aid through multilateral East-East organizations might all be ways of ensuring that the emerging structures in the former Soviet Union reflect the desires of all of its republics in a realistic way. In the meantime, the West should not go beyond the levels of cooperation currently envisioned in the Partnership for Peace. NATO's security and the peace of Europe are more likely to be compromised than protected by the admission of any of the former Soviet republics to the organization. . . .

Those Americans who advocate an eastward extension of NATO seem to believe that an expansion of NATO's role and of the American role within it are *ipso facto* good for American interests. Fearful that a post–Soviet Europe might seek a genuinely independent military posture that would eliminate American leverage, they look for ways to insert NATO ever more deeply into the European security structure and feel that the price—American security guarantees to new countries and the costs of supporting these guarantees with logistical support and perhaps troop deployment—is minimal compared to the political payoffs. One even senses a disposition to make concessions to the Europeans in order to win their "permission" for an expanded U.S. military role in their affairs.

This approach is based both on an underestimation of the difficulties and costs involved in an expansion of NATO and on a failure to grasp the essential nature of the American project in Europe. Extending NATO to the east involves much more than faxing membership cards to the foreign ministers of the Visegrad countries. NATO is an alliance, nor a club. Admitting a country to NATO involves the United States in a legal and moral guarantee of its frontiers. Such a guarantee cannot be given without making preparations to enforce it. The French and British guarantees to Poland in 1939 were blunders the United States cannot allow itself to repeat.

At a minimum, extending NATO would involve a new strategic doctrine. How, exactly, would NATO propose to carry out the defense of the Visegrad countries? A new military plan would have to be developed, and the new allies would have the right to participate in its design. Presumably, they would want NATO's defense doctrine to be forward defense once again; they could not welcome a war plan that assumed that any new battles would be fought deep in their territory—or that NATO forces would wait in Germany before launching a liberation offensive after Russian armies had overrun the new allies.

All the old NATO questions would recur in a new and more complex form. Both from the standpoint of deterring attacks and from the standpoint of reassuring the new allies, we would have to find ways of avoiding decoupling American from western European security. In the new circumstances, this would mean a pattern of nuclear and conventional deployment that also avoided decoupling the defense of the old NATO powers from that of the new, more exposed eastern partners.

One can expect that these controversies would raise enormous difficulties among the old members of NATO. Western Europeans believe that the risk of attack from the Russian Federation is extremely low under present conditions. The chancellories of the European Union lean to the view that the security that the Visegrad countries require is psychological rather than military in nature and that this psychological need can be met by a paper security guarantee. The predominant view is that including the Visegrad countries in NATO will not require any significant military expenditures or strategic rethinking by the West.

This position is not acceptable to military authorities in the United States, and for good reason. A "psychological guarantee" for the Visegrad countries that is obviously not backed up by military force has little psychological power. If the "psychological guarantee" rests—as it would have to—on a military doctrine of delayed response in which NATO conserved its forces in Germany for a counteroffensive after Russian forces had occupied the Visegrad countries, the guarantee would be worthless on its face. This would not be a problem for the Visegrad countries alone. Any such policy that gave NATO security responsibilities nor matched by its military capabilities would weaken the credibility and the coherence of the alliance as a whole, something the United States has correctly sought to prevent for 40 years.

On the other hand, any effort to equip NATO to take on these new responsibilities in a meaningful way would cost a great deal of money. The new NATO states would need an infrastructure capable of supporting NATO military operations. Airfields, supply lines, command-and-control facilities, and depots would have to be built. Harbors would have to be configured to support NATO deployments; the new allies would have to build military forces that no longer depended on Russia for spare parts. Clearly, these expenditures are beyond the capacity of any of the Visegrad countries.

It will be difficult, if not impossible, to persuade west Europeans to make significant financial commitments for military expenditures in the Visegrad countries. Every NATO ally in Europe today combines a sense of diminished military danger with pressing domestic economic problems. U.S. efforts to mandate another round of heavy defense expenditures would set off an extremely damaging controversy within NATO at a time when the alliance's future is already uncertain.

UNPALATABLE CHOICES

. . . The assumption that military dominance is the goal of the American presence in Europe is a gross miscalculation. America's military interest in Europe remains what it has been throughout the twentieth century: to provide enough security so that no European state is in a position to overturn the European order and plunge the continent into a general war. During the Cold War, the strength of the Soviet Union and its Warsaw Pact allies was so great compared to the military potential of Western Europe that the United States was forced to maintain large forces in Europe. But this was a cost and a burden that was reluctantly undertaken and regretfully borne.

The disintegration of the Warsaw Pact and the collapse of the Soviet Union mean that a much lighter touch from the American finger can keep the scales of military power in Europe balanced. This is good news, not bad, and it is a profound perversion of strategic thinking to look for excuses to increase a military presence beyond the real requirements of our security interests.

Additionally, the American project in Europe goes far beyond the presentation of a stable security order. That security order is a means; the prosperity and peace of Europe are the ends. Our best interests in Europe are served by helping Russia and its neighbors become richer, not by holding them in quarantine. Rather than engage in a round of pointless negotiations over new security doctrines in NATO, we need to work with our European partners to find new approaches to aiding the Russian economy.

An imploding, anarchic, wretched Russia is a much more powerful threat to the security of Europe and to the prosperity of both Europe and America—than a rich Russia. . . .

. . . The United States actually needs Russia to be stronger than it is today. Russian weakness is a far greater problem for the United States than its strength could ever be. From a purely realistic point of view, the soundest American policy would be to welcome the reemergence of Russia as a great power in Europe, to assist it in upholding its position in Asia, and to explore the not inconsiderable areas of common political interests the two nations share. Ultimately, the case against neocontainment is not just that it creates a pointless confrontation between the United States and Russia but that, even worse, it inhibits our ability to pursue important national interests through an unsentimental but practical relationship based on the genuine needs of both countries.

THE BASIS FOR RUSSIAN-AMERICAN PARTNERSHIP

Americans are used to thinking of our relationship with Russia only in terms of points of conflict. . . . There are three main areas of common interest that can shape the relationship in the coming years: one emerging from Russia's role as a European power, one from its role in Asia, and one from its role as a participant in the global political and economic communities. In all of these spheres the two nations share a community of interests deep and wide enough to serve as the basis for a durable relationship—regardless of whether the "white hats" or the "black hats" win out in Moscow's power struggles.

Contrary to a widely expressed point of view, the return of Russia to great-power status in Europe would be an extremely positive development for the United States in particular and for the West in general. To begin with, there is simply no prospect for stability in eastern Europe and the Balkans without Russian involvement. Real progress toward peace in Bosnia only became possible when Russia appeared as an interlocutor trusted by the Serbs and also potentially capable of imposing limits on Serbian demands. Russian peacekeepers in ex-Yugoslavia are an indispensible component of achieving peace there. . . .

Beyond this, Russia has an important role to play in the broader European scene. Even though Europe has moved past the era of traditional power politics, the existence of a political if not a military balance remains the precondition for Europe's continued evolution toward lasting peace. The Russian role in Europe, like the American role, provides a quiet insurance against the possibility that Germany might become uncomfortably powerful. This is not a resurrection of the Triple Entente against Germany; rather, the existence of a balancing Russian power facilitates cooperation in Europe because it removes a cause for fear. It is one thing for Germany's partners to rely on its frequently expressed—and sincerely felt—good intentions; it is another for them to know that whatever its intentions, Germany's dominance is potentially held in check, in part, by Russia.

The reemergence of Russia as a factor in European politics has wider implications as well. From the American point of view, the greatest danger to our long-term interests in Europe is the remote but not negligible possibility that a Franco-German axis would abandon Europe's free-trade and Atlanticist orientation to build a closed Continental System that would discriminate against American and Asian goods and services. . . .

. . . A strong Russia reminds western Europe of its need to keep its Atlantic connection alive. While a resurgent Russia poses no conceivable threat to a united NATO, it is far more questionable whether the Europeans could handle Russia alone. For the foreseeable future they will not want to try. A Europe conscious of its need for the Atlantic Alliance is a Europe that will not close itself to world trade at the expense of the United States.

On a more positive note, a strong Russia will exert a political pull in Europe in ways that redound to the benefit both of the Europeans and of the United States. Specifically, to the degree that Russia is in a position to have its economic interests respected, the European Union is likely to pursue a more expansionary economic strategy than it would otherwise be inclined to do. The European Union is largely a group of rich, demographically stable or even declining countries. It does not need large investments in new infrastructure; its most powerful economic interests tend to be lenders rather than borrowers. It has a much higher tolerance for high unemployment and low growth than either the United States or Russia. The United States has for many years attempted to cajole the Bundesbank and other European authorities into pursuing more expansionary policies, and it has had little success. Adding a powerful and respected Russian voice to these calls would increase the chance of persuading the Europeans in general and the Germans in particular that expansionary economic policies serve important national interests.

CONVERGENCE IN ASIA

In Asia, the parallel interests of the two countries are, if anything, stronger. The possibility of a power vacuum in the Russian Far East affects the vital interests of the United States far more directly than any of the conflicts over

Russia's boundaries in Europe. The Russian Far East is rich in natural resources but thinly populated and difficult to defend. Much of the most economically valuable portion of this territory was annexed by Russia from China by the "unequal treaties" European powers forced on China in the nineteenth century, and popular opinion in China regards these treaties as no more legitimate than those that gave Britain its claim to Hong Kong.

The prospect of prolonged Russian weakness in Asia is extremely destabilizing in an area that needs no more crisis spots than it already has. One can all too easily imagine a Sino-Japanese struggle for influence in the Russian Far East in which neither country could accept the dominance of the other. A united Korea would also have influence and claims in the region, and it is difficult to envision a stable North Asian order against the background of a weak and conditional Russian presence. The strengthening of the Russian position in the Far East is therefore in the interest of the United States. American investment in the region can act as a counter to help forstall the possibility that any one country could develop a position that the others would view as a threat. Military cooperation between Russia and the United States, preferably as part of a multilateral security system of some kind, would also be advantageous. To some degree, such cooperation is under way already with the U.S. Navy now visiting Vladivostok on a regular basis. The question of war and peace in the North Pacific may in the long run depend on the ability of the United States and Russia to develop a cordial and cooperative understanding in this part of the world.

In the shorter term, there can be no doubt that the collapse of Russian power in the Far East has already complicated America's Pacific diplomacy. China's assertiveness in bilateral relations, in the South China Sea, and in other regional matters reflects new realities in the Asian balance of power. For all practical purposes, China is no longer concerned with Russian strength along its northern frontier. Its need to maintain good relations with the United States and other countries is therefore correspondingly less than in previous years. This amounts to a revolution in Asian politics, one whose repercussions are only beginning to be felt. American interests would therefore also be served by the revival of Russia's position as a great power in Asia.

MARRIED FOR LIFE?

Finally, there is the question of Russia's voice and power in the global community of nations. This voice, Americans must understand, will always be an independent one. The fantasy of converting postcommunist Russia into a sidekick of the United States was unworthy of a serious country. Like France, Russia is a country that will always insist upon its prerogatives and its great-power status. The Russian nation will strive to maintain its independent and sovereign standing in the community of nations at all costs. At times, there will be friction between the United States and Russia in world forums like the United Nations. . . . But given this, it is fortunate for all concerned that on a number of major issues confronting the world the United States and Russia are inclined to see eye to eye.

The first point on which they are likely to agree has to do with the nature of the global community. The United States and Russia are the only two countries that are inextricably intertwined with both Europe and Asia. Both benefit from the existence of a single open global trading system, and Russia is potentially a powerful ally of the United States in the perennial struggle to keep smaller, more regionally oriented powers committed to a global and rule-driven trading system.

Russia and the United States share a number of other important economic interests. Both countries are mixed economies; they produce as well as consume large quantities of raw materials and agricultural commodities in addition to industrial commodities. This separates them from countries like Japan and Germany, which—broadly speaking—import raw materials and export finished goods only. For this reason, and because they are both debtor nations, the United States and Russia are likely to approach a number of global economic policy issues from complementary perspectives. Compared to western Europe and Japan, Russia and the United States are more willing to run the risks of inflation and less willing to beat the costs of stagnation. In this sense, both Russia and the United States are closer to the economic and political outlook of many developing countries, and a positive relationship between the two former Cold War adversaries is likely to benefit the cause of compromise between the interests of rich and poor, North and South, in the global economic forum.

Thus, on the two big economic issues, globalism and growth, the United States and Russia are likely to share common perspectives. This suggests that it would serve strategic American national interests to include Russia sooner rather than later in organizations like the G-7, the OECD, and the . . . World Trade Organization and to seek as much voting power as possible for Russia on the boards of the International Monetary Fund and the World Bank.

At the same time, both countries have a number of common security concerns. Both are substantial weapons exporters, and while this suggests areas of commercial and political conflict, it also suggests that both countries have an interest in the regulation of global arms trade. Both the United States and Russia are concerned about the possibilities of confrontation between Islam and what used to be called Christendom. And both countries favor the territorial status quo in Northern Asia.

This should not blind us to the substantial areas of divergence in the interests of the two countries, and it should not surprise or shock Americans when the Russians pursue a line of policy that does not harmonize with our own. Russia's economic interests will in some ways make it an ally of developing rather than developed countries. Its attitudes toward intellectual property rights, for example, are more likely to parallel those of China and India than to fall in line with [the United States]. Its votes on the Security Council are in the long run likely to favor the cause of revisionist rather than conservative powers, and of poor countries rather than rich ones.

These differences will remain and at times they will be acrimonious. But the Russian Federation has an important role to play in the realization of the deepest and most lasting foreign policy goal of the United States: the creation of the durable and just world order that every president from Woodrow Wilson to Bill Clinton has sought to build. Whether as a balancing power in Europe or Asia, as a voice for growth and an advocate for developing countries in global forums, or as a "bridge" country spanning the gap between the European and non-European branches of human civilization, Russia's global role complements that of the United States. . . . Both the United States and Russia would benefit from a solid relationship based on their similar economic and security interests. Neither will gain from a new cold war.

13. ENLARGING NATO: WHY BIGGER IS BETTER

Madeleine Albright

*I*t is an old diplomatic tradition that American secretaries of state begin their terms by visiting our closest allies and partners. . . . The dominant questions of the day in virtually all these countries, as in my own, involve matters close to home—educating children, building businesses, cutting deficits, fighting unemployment. At a time when much of the world enjoys relative peace, we run the risk of forgetting the decades-long work of diplomacy and institution-building that has made it possible for the great majority of people to worry about domestic improvements rather than national survival.

. . . We have work to do—and quickly—if this space of tranquillity is to endure and spread, rather than be written off by history as a pleasant time of tragically wasted opportunities. That message applies with special force to Europe. Today, the continent is no longer sliced in two, but dangers remain: from Bosnia to Chechnya, more Europeans died violently in the last five years [1992–1997] than in the previous 45. From Serbia to Belarus, reminders are appearing that Europe's democratic revolution is not complete.

Even so, a goal that would have seemed like Utopian delusion just years ago lies within our grasp: a peaceful and undivided Europe working in partnership with the United States, that welcomes every one of the continent's new democracies into our transatlantic community.

An ambitious goal, to be sure. Yet progress toward its realization has been remarkable. Western Europe is moving toward economic and monetary union. Most of Europe's fastest-growing economies lie east of the Elbe. Russia has made a choice for democracy and markets and defied the most dire predictions about its evolution. An independent and robustly democratic

Ukraine is casting its lot with Europe. American and European resolve has stopped the fighting in Bosnia. The military coalition there contains so many former adversaries that no sober student of history would have predicted it: France and Germany, Poland and Lithuania, Turkey and Greece, Russia and America.

Many institutions are playing their part in this effort, and all face critical tests. The European Union (EU) has promised to expand again. . . . The Organization for Economic Cooperation and Development (OECD) has taken in Poland, Hungary, and the Czech Republic; it is now looking to other market democracies, including Russia. The Organization for Security and Cooperation in Europe (OSCE) is promoting the democratic standards that will enable Europe to come together. . . .

But it is NATO, the linchpin of European security and the principal mechanism for American involvement in Europe, that is playing the leading role in bringing Europe together. It is changing its internal structure to create a stronger role for Europe. Its Partnership for Peace, under which other countries can train, plan, exercise, and cooperate with NATO, has brought together old adversaries and longtime neutrals. In the wake of such changes, France and Spain are participating more fully in the alliance. NATO is now more attractive to more nations because it is addressing new challenges in Europe and beyond. . . .

NATO'S OPPORTUNITY

. . . Too often, the debate about NATO's future reduces the alliance's past to a one-dimensional caricature that discounts its relevance to today's European challenges. Certainly, NATO's cold-war task was to contain the Soviet threat. But that is not all it did. It provided the confidence and security shattered economies needed to rebuild themselves. It helped France and Germany become reconciled, making European integration possible. With other institutions, it brought Italy, then Germany and eventually Spain back into the family of European democracies. It denationalized allied defence policies. It has stabilized relations between Greece and Turkey. All without firing a shot.

Now the new NATO can do for Europe's east what the old NATO did for Europe's west: vanquish old hatreds, promote integration, create a secure environment for prosperity, and deter violence in the region where two world wars and the cold war began.

Just the prospect of NATO enlargement has given Central and Eastern Europe greater stability than it has seen in this century. Hungary has settled its border and minority questions with Slovakia and Romania. Poland has reached across an old divide to create joint peacekeeping battalions with Ukraine and Lithuania. Throughout the region, support for NATO membership has rallied political parties of every ideology in favor of joining the West. Country after country has made sure that soldiers take orders from civilians, not the other way around.

To align themselves with NATO, these states are resolving problems that could have led to future Bosnias. This is the productive paradox at NATO's heart: by extending solemn security guarantees, we actually reduce the chance that our troops will again be called to fight in Europe. At the same time, we will gain new allies who are eager and increasingly able to contribute to our common agenda for security, from fighting terrorism and weapons proliferation to ensuring stability in trouble spots like the former Yugoslavia.

NATO enlargement will involve real costs, to the United States, its allies and its partners. But the costs are reasonable and many would arise whether NATO expands or not. Countries aspiring to membership will have to modernize their armed forces whether they are in or out of NATO—if anything, military spending would be higher in an insecure, unattached central Europe. A decision not to enlarge would also carry costs: it would constitute a declaration that NATO will neither address the challenges nor accept the geography of a new Europe. NATO would be stuck in the past, risking irrelevance and even dissolution. Those are costs we cannot afford.

ADDRESSING THE CRITICS

. . . Now that democracy's frontier has moved to Europe's farthest reaches, what logic would dictate that we freeze NATO's eastern edges where they presently lie, along the line where the Red Army stopped in the spring of 1945? President

Clinton said it in Prague [in 1995]: "Freedom's boundaries now should be defined by new behavior, not old history." Or for that matter by old thinking. To define them otherwise would not only create a permanent injustice, mocking the sacrifices made in this century on both sides of the Iron Curtain. It would create a permanent source of tension and insecurity in the heart of Europe.

Some critics point out that none of NATO's prospective members faces an immediate military threat True enough. But then, neither does Italy. Or Denmark. Or Britain. Or Iceland. Or the United States. If NATO were open only to countries menaced by aggressive neighbors, virtually no current ally would qualify.

Those who ask "where is the threat?" mistake NATO's real value. The alliance is not a wild-west posse that we trot out only when danger appears. It is a permanent presence, designed to promote common endeavors and to prevent a threat from ever arising. That is why current allies still need it and why others wish to join. NATO does not need an enemy. It has enduring purposes.

Other critics say that if we want to reunite Europe, the EU can do the job. Besides, they argue, what Central Europe needs is stocks and bonds, not stockpiles and bombs. They are certainly right that EU expansion is vital. Though the United States has no vote in the process, we do have an interest in seeing it happen as rapidly and expansively as possible.

But the security NATO provides has always been essential to the prosperity the EU promises. What is more, EU enlargement requires current and new members to make vast and complex adjustments in subsidy schemes and regulatory regimes. If NATO enlargement can proceed more quickly, why wait until, say, tomato farmers in Central Europe start using the right kinds of pesticides? And because NATO, unlike the EU, is a transatlantic institution, it can ensure that a united Europe maintains its strongest link to North America. The question is not which institution strong democracies should join, but when and how they are prepared to join each.

Critics also say that NATO enlargement will somehow redivide post–cold war Europe. On the contrary. NATO has taken a range of steps to ensure that the erasure of old lines of division does not leave new ones on the map. NATO is strengthening its Partnership for Peace, reaching out to Ukraine and Russia, and giving every new democracy—whether it joins the alliance sooner, later, or not at all—a say in its future through the Atlantic Partnership Council. . . .

Of course, the enlargement of NATO must begin with the strongest candidates; otherwise, it would not begin at all. But when we say that the first new members will not be the last, we mean it. And we expect the new members to export stability eastward, rather than viewing enlargement as a race to escape westward at the expense of their neighbors.

The core of that challenge—and one of the most important tasks for NATO—is to build a close and constructive partnership with Russia. This will take vision and political will. It requires abandoning cold war stereotypes and no longer looking at European security as a zero-sum game.

NATO enlargement is not taking place in response to a new Russian threat. It is motivated by the imperative of creating an integrated Europe—one that includes, not excludes, Russia. The purpose of enlargement is to give Central and Eastern Europe a region whose future stability is key to the future of Europe as a whole, the same kind of security that has become commonplace in Western Europe. Russia, no less than the rest of us, needs stability and prosperity in the center of Europe.

. . . Many Russian leaders express opposition to NATO enlargement. Yet the NATO Russia claims to oppose bears little resemblance to the alliance we are actually building. NATO's conventional and nuclear forces have been dramatically reduced. We have no plan, no need, and no intention to station nuclear weapons on the territory of new members. NATO's actions [since 1991] reveal an alliance focused on building cooperation, not confrontation: an alliance working shoulder-to-shoulder with Russia—as it is in Bosnia—not trying to isolate it.

We recognize that Europe cannot finally be whole and free until a democratic Russia is fully part of Europe. . . . After all, if Russia wishes to be part of an undivided Europe, then it cannot look at countries like Poland or Estonia or Ukraine as a buffer zone that *separates* Russia from Europe. . . . Russia's future as a free and prosperous nation will depend upon the ability of its leaders and citizens to build an open society, to defeat crime and corruption, to spark economic growth and spread its benefits. The Russian people know that their future will be written in Moscow, in Perm, in Irkutsk—and certainly not in Brussels. Poll after poll has shown that few ordinary Russians express concern about an alliance that many of their leaders concede poses no actual military threat to the country. . . .

[TOWARD THE FUTURE]

For half a century now, Europeans and Americans have worked together to shape events, instead of being shaped by them. Today's Europe stands in such stark contrast to the Europe I knew as a child after the second world war. For those who were not there, it must be hard to imagine the days of Franco, Tito, and Stalin, the refugees, the hunger, the constant fear that peace was just an interlude, the Europe Winston Churchill described as "a rubble heap, a charnel house, a breeding ground for pestilence and hate." Thank heaven leaders like Marshall, Monnet, Bevin, and Adenauer had the fortitude to make the hard and controversial decisions needed to build the institutions that gave us 50 years of peace and prosperity. Now it's our turn.

President Clinton observed in his [1997] State of the Union address that a child born today will have almost no memory of the 20th century. Just the same, the children of the transatlantic community who are born today have the chance to grow up knowing a very different Europe. In that new Europe, they will know Checkpoint Charlie only as a museum, Yalta as just a provincial city in a sovereign Ukraine, Sarajevo as a peaceful mountain resort in the heart of Europe. The children of the next century will come of age knowing a very different NATO—one that masses its energies on behalf of integration, rather than massing its forces on the borders of division.

All this is possible if . . . we act now to strengthen the arrangements that have served half of Europe so well for so long and to extend them to new partners and allies. Then, having come together, we will be able to concentrate on what we must do together. That is a goal worth every measure of our common effort.

14. AMERICA AND EUROPE: IS THE BREAK INEVITABLE?

Werner Weidenfeld

Apart from a few contentious trade issues, a cursory look at U.S.–European relations today reveals a general picture of harmony. In particular, an almost perfect symbiosis has prevailed in U.S.–German relations ever since the United States lent unparalleled support for German reunification. President Bill Clinton spoke of a "unique partnership" during his visit to Berlin in 1994. The often wearisome discussions during the 1980s on the deployment of medium- and short-range missiles, the heated dispute between the United States and Europe on the Soviet gas pipeline deal, and the anti-American demonstrations of the 1970s and 80s in front of U.S. embassies and consulates in Europe, so hurtful to the United States, are now forgotten.

Yet, despite U.S.–European congeniality, the way each side views its partner and the expectations placed on cooperation are currently undergoing radical change. Europe's significance in U.S. politics has diminished drastically since the end of the Soviet threat. Western Europe is no longer considered to be threatened militarily from the outside. As a result, less and less attention is being paid to internal developments on the old continent. The United States used to be keen to promote a positive image of itself to the European public to preserve the cohesion of the Western defense community. This required Americans to devote a great deal of effort to assessing the mood in Europe. Today, interest in Europe has been reduced to certain spheres: as an ally in resolving international crises and perhaps as a trading partner—that is, as a market for U.S. goods. . . .

The transatlantic community as it was during the days of the East-West conflict no longer exists. Certainly, the alliance remains, but without the mentality of a defense organization designed to protect against a major attack. Certainly, the political links are still in place, but without the challenge of an

antagonistic system of values. The partnership still exists but it lacks a definition of what specific contribution it has to make in responding to issues
arising in international politics. The old loyalties will not be enough to provide the necessary political and analytical parameters for the next phase in
U.S.–European cooperation. Sooner or later, Europe and the United States
will find themselves redefining their interests.

It would be desirable if this were a process that resulted in positive gains
for both sides. But it is entirely possible that the opposite will happen—in
terms of foreign policy, a drifting apart of the partners under the influence of
the centrifugal forces of international crisis; in terms of economic policy, an
escalation of transatlantic trade rivalries; and in social and cultural terms, a
refocusing of interests away from the transatlantic partner.

This negative scenario would mean more than just a difficult restructuring
of foreign policy priorities for Europe and the United States. In fact, it would
shake the very foundations of the European and U.S. self-image. Historically
speaking, each partner has always formed part of the other's identity. The
commitment of the United States to the reconstruction of Europe after World
War II is a central element in their collective consciousness. For the United
States too, the contribution made by Europeans toward the development of
politics and society has become a basic element of the U.S. psyche—beyond
demographical and ethnic shifts. Thus, for both sides, the loss of their
transatlantic partner would do more than just inflict damage in foreign policy
terms—it would lead to a cultural split with disastrous consequences. So, if
the redefinition of the transatlantic relationship is to succeed, it has to offer
both partners not only a common agenda in practical terms, but also a redefinition of their own identity that incorporates the partner on the other side of
the Atlantic. . . .

THE UNITED STATES IN A NEW ERA

The end of the Cold War allowed both Europe and the United States to turn
to internal problems that had been neglected or concealed for decades. In
Europe, the fall of the Iron Curtain made dramatically clear the wretched
state of the economies of the formerly socialist half of the continent, with all
the consequences that the economic demise of Eastern Europe poses for the
nations of Western Europe. In the United States, the full attention of politicians and the public turned for the first time in decades to the country's
domestic economic and social difficulties. Paradoxically, the election of President Clinton in 1992 and the Republican landslide victory at the 1994 congressional elections sent the same message: U.S. society is less interested in the
"new world order" proclaimed by former president George Bush than in
solving domestic problems that have grown dramatically.

The United States is now engaged in a debate unprecedented in its sheer
breadth—a dialogue that, albeit superficially, contrasts strangely with the
carefully celebrated restoration of U.S. self-confidence vis-à-vis the outside

world, a restoration that had taken place only a few years earlier under presidents Ronald Reagan and George Bush. At the center of the debate lies concern about the serious structural problems of the U.S. economy that, in the view of many Americans, will be an increasing burden on current and future generations. For instance, the total federal debt [grew] from $3 trillion in 1991 to more than $5 trillion [by the mid-1990s]. Each year, approximately $300 billion—or approximately 20 percent of the federal budget—goes toward paying interest on this debt.

The problem of the budget deficit is made worse by the extremely low level of savings in the United States. On average only 5 percent of disposable income is saved, whereas the figures for Germany and Japan are 12 percent and 15 percent respectively. Thus, the deficit in the United States has to be financed from foreign sources to a much greater degree than in Europe. This has led to a situation whereby, in the space of a few years, the United States has moved from being the world's biggest creditor country to being the biggest debtor country. Internationally, it is some $650 billion in the red. At the same time, the effects of economic globalization are now making their full impact felt on the United States. Cheap suppliers from East Asia have surpassed many U.S. producers in their own market: color televisions, for example, are no longer manufactured in the United States. This and similar developments are reflected in the already chronic U.S. trade deficit. . . . The United States's technological lead, which in the eyes of Americans is the crucial factor underlying the country's leading role in the world, has disappeared completely in many areas and has been noticeably reduced in others. Growth in productivity and investment are currently not high enough in the United States to turn the situation around in the short term—that is, in 2 to 3 years. Americans have, quite simply, been consuming too much for too many decades and neglecting the modernization of the country's infrastructure and production sites in the process.

The concrete results of this for most Americans are stagnant or sinking real wages. For example, the income of employees without a college degree has dropped by 18 percent during the last 15 years. Although greater wage flexibility means that the United States does not have the European problem of mass unemployment, the fact is that, in the United States, a job does not guarantee a secure income: More than 3 million Americans living below the poverty line have full-time jobs. The phenomenon of the "working poor" has become a stock-in-trade of the U.S. social debate.

Furthermore, the increasingly visible shortcomings in social integration are closely connected to the state of the economy. An ever greater number of Americans is missing out on the American dream. Today, nearly 15 percent of the population—37 million U.S. citizens—is officially classified as poor. Likewise, about 37 million Americans have no health insurance whatsoever. The increasingly evident shortcomings in the education system pose a particularly severe problem, in that they contribute to the growing marginalization of large sections of the population. At its best, the U.S. education system leads the world. But a concentration on excellence at the top end has led to an increasing neglect of education and training for the masses.

In view of these facts it is not surprising that many Americans demanded a fundamental change in policy and saw the dissolution of the Cold War system as an opportunity to question aspects of domestic and foreign policy that until then had been taken for granted. . . . The main target of all reform attempts during [recent] years—both those of the Republican majority in Congress and those of the Clinton administration—has . . . been the federal deficit, which both sides hope to master through an endless succession of budget cuts in the areas of domestic, social, and foreign policy. . . .

U.S. policies to reduce "big government" in domestic affairs cannot automatically be applied to the field of U.S. foreign policy. It is precisely because the United States must concentrate increasingly on its own economic and social problems that it must also renew its foreign policy efforts: to ensure that the burden of U.S. international involvement, which is as necessary as ever, can be shared more efficiently with its allies and partners.

EUROPE IN TRANSITION

Like the United States, Europe is undergoing far-reaching changes in its self-perception and experiencing internal upheavals of an unpredictable nature. Processes of integration are occurring concurrently with processes of disintegration, and both are affecting the European Union. Supranational political interweaving is running parallel to new splits along social and ethnic lines. The old borders between Catholic and Orthodox Europe, between the Ottoman and Habsburg empires, have reemerged. It is less clear than ever before where Europe begins and ends. The acceleration in the process of developing the EU is being met with a growing degree of skepticism at the national level. The importance of national and regional concerns is increasing.

At the same time, the internationalization of economics and politics is intensifying, and creating several problems. But the development of appropriate decision-making structures at the European level continues to lag and cannot yet offer an adequate response to pressures that are already too great for individual nation-states. Europe is trapped: on the one hand, the magnet of integration is attracting more and more politicians and states—specifically, Eastern European ones—keen to accede to the EU; on the other, the structures that would enable the Union to take political action at the supranational level are not being developed quickly enough. The continent is in danger of becoming a victim of its own success.

In a transitional era like the present one, the foreign policy of many states has reverted to a familiar pattern in the European context—the maintenance of a "balance of power." . . . In Western Europe, integration has become an instrument for such an approach. The shift in the internal balance caused by German unification has prompted France to offer to deepen the European

Union. Britain has countered the prospect of greater integration with the prospect of widening, in the expectation that this will lead to a looser type of integration.

Yet, under present conditions, this process should not be seen as a return to the European tradition of grand diplomacy by nation-states. One of the peculiarities of the present-day policy of maintaining a balance of power is that it combines classic diplomacy with modern levels of integration. Even within the European Union, it is possible to pursue a policy of national interest. European politicians now face the task of giving form to this complex, transitional constellation. National ambitions need to be brought into harmony with the challenges resulting from the situation.

This simultaneity of contrasting developments is what makes Europe such a special case. And it is from this complex Europe that the United States will demand a clear definition of interests. It will expect Europe to have at its disposal the instruments necessary to pursue clearly defined policies. Thus, any realignment of the transatlantic partnership is going to require that Europeans do some very basic homework. . . . Current political problems demand that European politicians devise strategic policies to meet four specific goals: to change the institutions responsible for integration, including their capacity to act; to develop the EU further along the path toward a true political, economic, and monetary union; to stabilize and integrate Central and Eastern Europe; and to preserve peace and security on the continent. . . .

At first glance it appears paradoxical: Of all the times to start raising the issue of the continent's leading role, the United States has to do so in a period of deep-seated insecurity in Europe about the Union's future shape. Yet, given its increasing problems at home and its lonely position as the sole global superpower following the collapse of the Soviet Union, the United States is understandably applying increasing pressure on Europeans to play a greater role in solving global problems. It is thus in the U.S. interest that Europe learn, as soon as possible, to speak with one voice politically, militarily, and economically—or at least to channel the chorus of voices more effectively. The United States, as Europe's main partner, has the important role of constantly reminding the Europeans not to get tied up in seemingly trivial internal quarrels relating to European integration and not to lose sight of wider global challenges.

Europe has to bear responsibility worldwide simply because of its economic might; together with the United States, Europe is one of the main sources of hope in the developing world in terms of support for democracy and economic liberalization. In the future, the United States will increasingly remind Europe of its duty to take on political responsibilities commensurate with its position as a world economic power.

Today, Europe has the full potential to take on this new role of equal partner to the United States. One condition for the full exploitation of this potential is that Europe be politically aware of the new international challenges that have emerged in the wake of the end of the Cold War. If it fails to react to these challenges, or if it reacts inadequately, it risks permanent erosion of the transatlantic community: The United States, in searching for partners prepared to share its burdens, will increasingly begin looking outside Europe if it does not believe the Union is up to the task.

THE RISE AND FALL OF THE TRANSATLANTIC COMMUNITY

Internal social and political changes taking place on both sides of the Atlantic will have several consequences on the transatlantic relationship. Both parties find themselves in a relatively serious identity crisis and lack a firm sense of direction. It is becoming increasingly difficult for Europe and the United States to calculate one another's actions—especially given the shifting political importance of economy, security, and culture. Under circumstances such as these, conflicts could be triggered very easily.

Crises beyond the domain of the North Atlantic Treaty Organization (NATO), trade conflicts both within and outside the Western community, and global challenges such as environmental pollution or nuclear terrorism have moved to the fore as topics demanding high-level political decision-making, yet the transatlantic partners have no commonly accepted guidelines for dealing with them. Differences on individual issues that have always existed are now becoming clearly visible and are being allowed to develop unchecked. . . .

To establish transatlantic consensus, the West continues to use the old structures left over from the era of East-West conflict. But these structures cannot meet new challenges. New guiding principles for common action are needed to change the old backdrops and to form a consensus on how to tackle the tasks of the future. The ability of the Western partners to develop a new outline for a common direction in transatlantic relations will ultimately decide their fate.

If the West does not step up to this challenge, U.S.–European relations seem headed for a cultural split, one whose effects would radically question the structure of 50 years of transatlantic links. This split in the culture of political and social contact would not come about in the form of abrupt cuts or spectacular arguments. Rather, it would lead decisionmakers on both sides of the Atlantic in the medium term to drift apart in terms of their attitudes and subjective political and social designs. . . .

This process would not only lead to a far-reaching drift of political and social orientations, but also, in the worst case, to a direct political division between Europe and the United States—in other words, to a complete abandonment of the concept of the fundamental community of interests. The danger of such a split can be surmounted only if a future-oriented concept for deepening the transatlantic relationship can be developed that takes both partners' topical interests into consideration. Without a renewal of the U.S.–European community along such strategic lines, the very existence and success of the transatlantic relationship will be in jeopardy.

CREATING A NEW TRANSATLANTIC COMMUNITY

Players on both sides of the Atlantic have felt the increasingly painful unraveling of the network of transatlantic relations, the lack of a common new direction, and the ensuing dangers of substantial erosion of the U.S.–European partnership. . . . To reshape cooperation to bring it in line with the times—a move that is absolutely imperative—the partners must develop a structure that is binding for all involved.

The task of finding a new direction can certainly be compared to that facing the transatlantic partners after World War II, one that demanded a radical paradigmatic shift on both sides of the Atlantic. The founders of the postwar order were aware that this change of direction and the quality of the U.S.–European ties they hoped to achieve would not be possible if relations within the Western community were governed only by loose arrangements. The degree of organization within the Western community had to be improved and this improvement found expression in the form of NATO, complemented by its economic counterpart, the Marshall Plan.

Today's new challenges, too, call upon the U.S.–European partnership to take a great step forward in terms of commitment. The first step must be the renaissance of the transatlantic community uniting the United States and the European Union. This task involves defining a clear vision of a continued transatlantic success story, in the face of different external conditions, that is obvious to both domestic and external observers and that will give all partners involved a highly exigent, common goal toward which to work. Furthermore, the new community has to create an organizational framework that enables the diverse and far-reaching common traits of the transatlantic partners to be developed into a coordinated and well-defined strategy for political action.

New Structures for Political Cooperation

Unlike during the period of East-West confrontation, when all partners could rely on a common security policy, no all-encompassing *raison d'être* exists today as a basis for reestablishing the transatlantic community. The creation of new binding structures must therefore revolve around issues in which the partners have an obvious interest in joint action as a matter of paramount importance.

If one considers the focus of European or U.S. political action, the need for binding structures is evident particularly in the coordination of strategy in response to global challenges and/or international crises. Today, Europe and the United States remain the only reliable makers or guarantors of stability in the world. The variety of burning issues in international politics calls for action by the transatlantic partners almost daily, often in regions where the existing institutions of the Atlantic Alliance have no jurisdiction. Thus far, no permanent mechanism exists to coordinate European and U.S. policy to deal with these issues. Moreover, both the United States and members of the European Union have fallen prone to navel-gazing because of problems and challenges at home. Yet, now that the traditional security partnership has been somewhat watered down, there is an increasing danger that the fallout from these conflicts may affect the transatlantic community, too.

Therefore, it is vital to establish a binding structure for transatlantic political consultation and cooperation that would give the transatlantic partners a reliable mandate to coordinate all issues relevant to the transatlantic agenda. The structure of this consultation and cooperation could be similar to that of the European Political Cooperation (EPC) forum, introduced in 1970 as the first permanent forum for coordinating the common policy of the members of the European Economic Community, as the EU was then known. It is now time for the transatlantic partners to institute a similar mechanism, to set up some form of Euro-American Political Cooperation (EAPC), which could deal with all the issues that the international community directs at the transatlantic partners but for which no organizational form has yet been found.

Creating a Transatlantic Common Market

Nowhere is the level of existing transatlantic interdependency more visible than in economic relations. This policy area constitutes one of the central vehicles of previous—and future—progress in transatlantic integration. Great care must therefore be taken to shape the political framework for this tightly woven network of relations so it can become the catalyst driving integration forward, rather than—as has often been the case—the brakes holding it back. The high degree of transatlantic economic interdependency somehow seems to evade the collective consciousness of the European and U.S. populations. What they never fail to notice, however, are the recurring clashes over trivial matters such as bananas, feta cheese, or spaghetti, although the respective trade volumes in these goods account for a mere fraction of their governments' economic interests. . . . Transatlantic settlement mechanisms lag far behind the supranational vitality of trade between Europe and the United States and seriously hamper the further development of trade relations.

Removing existing barriers to trade can succeed only if Europe and the United States manage to make their removal part of a strategic vision and manage to win over their populations by means of proactive arguments. Europe and the United States must categorically declare their faith in a revival of their trade relations; the founding of a Transatlantic Common Market, anchored in an agreement between the European Union and the United States, would be an optimal way of achieving this aim. . . .

Founding a Transatlantic Learning Community

The internal challenges facing the members of the transatlantic partnership increasingly require consultation between Europe and the United States, too. Concerning problems such as international crime, drug trafficking, and immigration, a need for joint action is clear. But other issues, such as reform of social security systems, appear merely to have a national character. Yet, strategies aimed at solving domestic problems can draw on models from other countries within the transatlantic community.

By way of example, President Clinton's health care reforms were clearly inspired by European models. By the same token, U.S. limits on automobile emission levels were crucial for European policymakers in this field. Countless other examples illustrate how the transatlantic partners can learn from each other's experiences. This has created the ideal conditions for founding a transatlantic learning community that would give some structure to the contacts and cross-referencing that have, until now, been somewhat ad hoc.

For the strategic planning of such a learning community, one must realize that the future of international relations will no longer be governed by the *raison d'être* of the security partnership—that is, by a so-called superior motive. In the future, such exchanges will have to serve a specific aim or make a practical contribution to the future lives of citizens on both sides of the Atlantic. . . .

USING THE OPPORTUNITIES OF A NEW BEGINNING

The tenacity of the institutions of the postwar order has, until now, stalled the tendency for Europe and the United States to drift further apart. For example, no one seriously calls into question the existence of NATO, although the reason for its inception—the threat from Eastern Europe—has been reduced considerably. The aftereffects of Western cohesion during the East-West confrontation will be available to the transatlantic partners as spiritual armor for some time yet. The . . . celebrations commemorating the fiftieth anniversary of the Marshall Plan, the Berlin airlift, and the founding of NATO . . . certainly [contributed] to this.

Furthermore, the potential for differences of opinion between the Western partners has decreased considerably since the end of the Cold War. Constant points of friction over the appropriate reaction to the Soviet threat have disappeared. Compared to the controversies of the 1980s, the present state of transatlantic relations exudes considerable harmony. Yet, the current risk is that of increasing transatlantic indifference on a scale to match the disputes of old. Potential sources of friction concerning security policy coordination have ceased to exist, dealing with one's partners seems less and less necessary, and, given the more promising topics of everyday politics, cooperation is now frequently seen as a tiresome obligation.

Any analysis of transatlantic circumstances and options brings us to this central dilemma. On the one hand, as indicated above, no two other regions in the world enjoy such close ties, characterized by friendship and shared common values as well as by political and economic efficiency, as do Europe and the United States. On the other hand, the historical development of this alliance over the last 50 years makes it clear that, without a revitalization of these ties that is both forward-looking and geared toward the changing geopolitical situation, the two partners will inevitably grow apart. . . .

It is only by opening up the transatlantic community to the challenges of the future that we can ensure its continued existence and success. Merely preserving the status quo based on a transfigured romantic view of the past would be the surest way to guarantee the erosion of this partnership. Europe and the United States must seize this historic opportunity to found the transatlantic community anew before the emerging tendency to ignore solidarity means it slips through our fingers for good.

The United States and Asia

15. FUTURESHOCK OR RENEWED PARTNERSHIP? THE U.S.–JAPAN ALLIANCE FACING THE MILLENNIUM

Robert A. Manning

. . . *A*lthough the Cold War is now a matter for historians to debate, a new international system is emerging at only a glacial pace, defined case-by-case in crisis-response fashion. Curiously, however, cold war alliance structures remain in place while governments grope for new organizing principles to replace the global containment strategy. There is broad consensus that an ill-defined uncertainty and unpredictability are the paramount threats to stability. But how many divisions does uncertainty have, and why are current alliances essential to counter it?

. . . Neither the United States nor Japan appears to have made a zero-based assessment of the rationale, value, and durability of the security alliance between them and of the totality of their relationship in post–cold war circumstances. Are there sufficient common threats and/or interests to warrant the alliance's perpetuation? Can the world's largest debtor continue to guarantee the security of the world's largest creditor? Is collective security or cooperative security a substitute? Instead of reexamining core assumptions, both governments tend to merely assert the continuing importance of the alliance with soothing, if time-worn, rhetoric or repeat long-standing arguments while ignoring trends that may undermine it. . . .

. . . Although the 1960 "Treaty of Mutual Cooperation and Security" still has surprising salience, it was a one-way street: the United States defends Japan; not only is Japan not obligated to defend the United States, but article 9 of its U.S.–drafted constitution renders ambiguous its support role in regional contingencies. Certainly, burden sharing, "roles and missions" commitments, and even defense technology cooperation have evolved substantially over the

Note: Notes have been deleted.

192

life of the treaty. But if a U.S.–Japan alliance is indeed to be viable into the twenty-first century, its purpose—and the commitment of both governments—must be clear and it must yield ample benefits demonstrable to both the U.S. and Japanese publics.

Moreover, in both perception and reality, it must be a more equal alliance based on shared responsibility and shared decision making. It must move from *gaiatsu* (external pressure) to *naiatsu* (internal pressure) in a Japan that has become, to borrow a popular term, a more normal nation, that is to say, a Japan able to bring a sense of stewardship not only to the bilateral relationship but, still more important, to the global trade, financial, and political systems. At present, Japan is a considerable distance from being a mature actor of this kind.

This [chapter] argues that, starting from a zero-based assessment of the entire relationship, there is a strong case for building a global partnership in a redefined, mature, and more equal U.S.–Japan relationship. But the rationale for such a partnership in a new era has yet to be articulated adequately and, rhetoric notwithstanding, the dominant feature of U.S.–Japan relations has been palpable mutual distrust and tension arising from omnipresent trade disputes, eroding support on both sides of the Pacific. Nor does it appear that Japan is currently in a position to make the political decisions necessary to adequately update the alliance without great difficulty.

To be renewed, the security link, like the entire relationship, must be redefined. The *tatamae* (surface appearance) of its raison d'être is gone, but what is the *honne* (underlying reality) today? The alliance now is not between a powerful victor and a weak, defeated enemy, both facing a Soviet threat. A half century later, the alliance is between the two largest and most technologically advanced economies in the world, both with substantial regional and global interests and with large areas of convergence in a grey, multipolar world. Yet the legacy of the past to Japan—a psychology of "Let Uncle Sam take care of it" and of being in the world but not of the world—and Japan's failure to come to terms with its actual behavior in the 1930s and 1940s impede Tokyo's quest for a political/security role commensurate with its economic status.

At the same time, there are centrifugal economic and political forces in both countries that could easily lead Washington and Tokyo to gradually drift apart. Both nations give evidence of rising techno-nationalism, inward-looking domestic political trends, and a growth in single-issue politics pursued by interest groups amid weak leadership. Mixed together and ignited, such forces could be a potent brew. In Japan, the entire political system is in a dysfunctional state of flux and, absent an action-forcing crisis . . . , it may be several years before a new, stable political system emerges from the fragmenting of the Liberal Democratic Party (LDP) after 38 years in power.

On foreign policy, the United States is once again enmeshed in an engagement versus isolation debate and in Japan the traditional "Are we part of Asia or the West?" debate has resurfaced—both debates tinged with a heavy dose of nationalism. Sentiment—an emotional mood, not a considered strategy—is growing in Japanese business and intellectual circles (and in some ministries) that Japan should turn to Asia, in part to insulate itself from U.S. pressure.

This occurs as pulls on both the United States and Japan in directions other than that of the alliance grow. For the United States, the pulls are economic and come from the Western Hemisphere; for Japan it is a deepening economic integration in East Asia as its trade with the region has surpassed its trade with the United States. Finally, both countries are infatuated with "multilateralism," seen as a kind of soporific counter to post-Soviet doubt and confusion rather than a hard-edged appreciation of multilateral mechanisms and/or institutions as tools appropriate to the degree they help ameliorate concrete problems. The centrifugal forces mentioned above, combined with burgeoning distrust growing from high-profile trade conflicts, hold the potential to destroy the alliance.

THE NEW CHALLENGE

The starting point to revalidating the security alliance is to recognize its enormously changed context, not just in terms of the geopolitical sea change, but in economics and domestic politics on both sides as well. During the Cold War, the security link carried a disproportionate weight in the U.S.–Japan relationship. Beginning at least by the late 1980s, however, the economic dimension moved center stage. This was certainly evident by the 1990 Bush-Kaifu summit, where the articulated theme was: "We can have an important global partnership, but only if we can redress economic imbalances." For all the reinventing the wheel the Clinton administration has done, it was the Bush administration that held Tokyo's feet to the fire on semiconductors and auto parts, reaching accords that helped expand the U.S. share of Japan's market in those sectors.

The Clinton administration rightly recognized this critical political linkage and accentuated the focus on trade and economics. Where it erred was in allowing tactics to substitute for strategy, and in its belief that the security and political pillars of the relationship would remain static on the back burner while it focused like a laser beam on the economy. With a political calculus almost entirely based on domestic constituencies, and flawed assumptions heavily influenced by revisionist views on Japan, its "results oriented" policy fell prey to the law of unintended consequences.

After two years, the result was an increased trade deficit—a record $66 billion for 1994; a trade policy reduced essentially to sectoral talks; an overvalued yen; and dangerously widespread popular mistrust and resentment on both sides of the Pacific. . . .

In point of fact, . . . there are three key aspects to the economic relationship—macroeconomic, structural, and sectoral—that must be addressed. Although $66 billion annual deficits are not *politically* sustainable, as the president's own Council of Economic Advisers said in its January 1994 report, if Japan responded to all U.S. demands, the trade deficit is likely to be reduced only by some $9 billion to $18 billion. The economic problem must not be defined simply as bilateral merchandise trade figures, which are almost certainly going to show a significant deficit regardless of U.S. trade policy. Rather, the problem is long term, structural, and requires major deregulation, tax reform, and enhanced market access in Japan, and more savings, less consumption, more investment, and a larger commitment to compete in the Japanese market on the U.S. side.

With 20/20 hindsight, the cold war–driven pattern of U.S.–Japan economic relations established in the 1950s—granting Japan generous access to U.S. markets to facilitate its reconstruction as a strategic bulwark—was allowed to continue far too long. By the mid-1970s this had allowed subtle and complex socioeconomic patterns of protectionism to deepen without serious U.S. pressure for reciprocity. By then Japan was clearly a buoyant, reconstructed industrial nation. A full discussion of the economic relationship is beyond the scope of this [chapter], but it defies basic common sense to think that the rich U.S.–Japan security agenda can be addressed, or that the alliance can be sustained, in a political vacuum. Even if "security first" is repeated as a mantra, the security relationship cannot be cordoned off from the ubiquitous economic disputes, nor can the political fallout from them be avoided.

Beyond finding some balance in the economic relationship, determining whether there is sufficient common ground for a security alliance requires a strategic view of the entire U.S.–Japan relationship. That means asking fundamental questions about how both sides see their interests and how the three pillars of the relationship can be integrated into a coherent whole.

The two nations are deeply intertwined through a largely private sector network of trade, investment, and technology linkages; both are market-oriented democracies and global powers whose well-being requires a stable, functional world system. Together they produce almost 40 percent of the world's gross national product (GNP). To the extent, therefore, that they coordinate their respective national security and international economic policies, they can shape the still opaque international system in this formative transition period.

COMMON STRATEGIES?

Although it may seem counterintuitive, the U.S.–Japan security treaty, as the Prime Minister's Advisory Commission [on Defense Issues, August 1994] pointed out, "will assume a greater significance than ever before"; it also continues to be the linchpin of the U.S. forward-deployed presence in the Pacific. This is a reflection of the direct and immediate dangers to Japan and indirect but longer-term dangers to U.S. interests in a potentially treacherous Northeast Asian security environment. China's emergence as an economic and military power, along with uncertainty about its future at a moment of political transition, and possible instability and conflict on the Korean Peninsula (even if there is a "soft landing" and a peaceful reunification process) make for a dangerous neighborhood. Moreover, Russia's transition to a market-oriented democracy is problematic at best, and regardless of the political coloration of Boris Yeltsin's successor, Russian nationalism will be a factor for the foreseeable future.

If China is the most important regional issue about which some real collective soul-searching is necessary, the Korea question is the most urgent. Managing the nuclear problem is only part of the larger issues of reconciliation and reunification, all of which pose real-time security challenges. Indeed, the determinant question informing North Korea's decision making must be: Is regime and state survival better assured by a strategy of controlled economic opening and economic and political engagement to modernize the economy or by pursuing a missile and nuclear weapons program and accepting whatever isolation such strategic independence entails? Such a bargain is the underlying logic of the "Agreed Framework" of October 21, 1994. There is at present little evidence that North Korea is prepared to do more than experiment at the margins with special economic zones in remote regions: fears of destabilizing political consequences from Chinese-type reforms have led Pyongyang to proceed so cautiously that it has attracted few foreign investors. Yet even if an economic opening was successful, the experience of other Communist regimes suggest that the raised expectations from a partial opening may pose a serious danger to the Pyongyang regime rather than ensuring the much-desired soft landing.

The scenarios for North Korea run the spectrum from implosion to explosion. The protracted dispute over the details and implementation of the Light-Water Reactor (LWR) project that is a key part of the bargain in the Agreed Framework suggests how volatile the entire issue is: if North Korea restarts its nuclear program—frozen in return for the LWR package—a confrontational course leading to a call for sanctions by the United Nations (UN) may well ensue. But the United States is unlikely to obtain UN sanctions if North Korea reloads its reactor or even if it reprocesses fuel—if Pyongyang leaves its facilities open to monitoring by the International Atomic Energy Agency (IAEA). In the event, the United States is likely to propose sanctions outside the UN, which could turn the North Korea problem into an issue for the U.S.–Japan alliance.

Managing the Korea question is a matter of vital Japanese interest and key to the U.S.–Japan alliance. But Tokyo would have a difficult time imposing sanctions outside a UN framework. The United States and Japan need to coordinate policies toward Pyongyang aimed both at a soft landing and at a clear understanding of what Japan's role will be if the soft landing does not occur. Will Japan be willing and/or able to halt the flow of hard currency from the Chosen Soren Korean residents of Japan to North Korea? What will Japan's role be in the event of a conflict? The need for contingency planning and clear understanding of what military cooperation would be available could pose a major test for the alliance.

Looking ahead, it is at best highly problematic whether U.S. troops will be based in Korea after reunification. Given the possibility of precipitous change in Korea, the United States and Japan should now be thinking through such issues as what impact a U.S. withdrawal from Korea would have on the

U.S.–Japan alliance and how force structures might be adjusted. To date there has been no reassessment of the U.S. force presence in Japan since the demise of the Soviet Union. If U.S. forces left a unified Korea, Japan would then be the only nation in Asia hosting foreign bases on its soil. Given Japan's security imperatives, that might not foster major political problems, but it would be a new situation that should be carefully thought through.

The largest single challenge to the U.S.–Japan relationship—and to the entire international community—is China's emergence as a major regional and global economic and military power. China has pursued a strategy of calculated ambiguity on a broad range of issues from trade and nuclear proliferation to regional security. The goal of both the United States and Japan is the same: helping China to integrate itself into the international economic and political system. Clearly there are, and will continue to be, tactical differences, for example in approaches to human rights or to security dialogue and military transparency.

But to date, Japan has largely engaged in "checkbook diplomacy" with regard to China, in the hope that China's economic modernization will yield other changes. The United States has done the heavy lifting in regard to pushing China to adopt international norms in areas of trade such as intellectual property rights, in nonproliferation, and in human rights. There is ample political space for tactical differences—perhaps some degree of "good cop, bad cop" is a useful approach—but if the security alliance is to be viable, it requires accord on which issues must be viewed as benchmarks of Chinese behavior.

The fundamental issue is whether China moves toward international norms or seeks to create its own. Beijing's cooperation in regard to the proliferation of weapons of mass destruction is one such issue. Tokyo's moves in May 1995—halting some $90 million in grant aid to Beijing in response to a Chinese nuclear test and protesting China's test launch of a new mobile intercontinental ballistic missile—reflect emerging concern in Japan about China's military modernization. Beijing's unilateral behavior in regard to territorial disputes in the South China Sea is another issue on which to judge the intentions behind its current and planned military posture.

Beyond the South China Sea, another issue that could lead to conflict is the Taiwan problem. A Taiwanese declaration of independence is likely to result in a naval blockade if not an attack by Beijing. The United States might respond militarily, putting Japan in a position when it must take sides, which, depending on the outcome, could have a major impact on the security alliance. U.S. responses to contingencies in Korea, the South China Sea, and Taiwan will also have an impact on Japanese perceptions of the credibility of U.S. extended deterrence—the bottom line of the alliance.

MULTILATERALISM

As Japan embarks upon a more assertive role both in the region and globally, it appears to be according a larger role to multilateral mechanisms—both regional and global—in its security planning. In the view of some Japanese analysts and officials, such an approach carries as much weight as the alliance. As the Advisory Commission report stated, "The mechanism of resolving security problems through international cooperation is still imperfect, but it is showing signs of developing little by little, both at the level of the United Nations and at the regional level." In summing up its call for a more activist Japan, the report says:

> It is necessary to build a coherent and comprehensive security policy . . . which consists of promotion of multilateral security cooperation on a global and regional scale, enhancement of the functions of the U.S.–Japan security relationship, and possession of a highly reliable and efficient defense capability.

This appears in part a hedge against possible U.S. withdrawal, and in part simply a recognition of reality in an emerging multipolar world. It is also in some measure a means to encase Japan's activism in a larger framework both regionally and globally. Further, it dovetails with Japan's acquisition of an increasingly independent defense industrial base to offer hope of, if not an independent posture, then more political distance from the United States. . . .

Regionally, it appears increasingly evident that forums such as the Regional Forum of the Association of Southeast Asian Nations (ASEAN), or a separate security dialogue in Northeast Asia, will not be a substitute for the U.S.–Japan alliance, but rather a supplement to it. It is conceivable, however, that events such as a crisis in Korea could result in a kind of ad hoc multilateral mechanism brought about by the response of South Korea and the four major powers. Nor does it appear that the UN as it is currently constituted will play the role of a collective security mechanism to manage post–cold war conflict to the degree many anticipated at the end of the Cold War.

The Advisory Commission reflects much of the confusion in the ongoing debate about the future of Asian security Experiments in diplomacy such as the official and quasi-official "security dialogues" occurring in the region are frequently mistaken for "new security arrangements." Although they may evolve into a new security architecture eventually, for the foreseeable future they are little more than talk shops. To see such dialogues as more than preliminary efforts at preventive diplomacy is a dangerous illusion. . . .

As Japan becomes a more independent actor it will be increasingly important to improve the U.S.–Japan consultation process so that there is a clear sense of where differences and convergences lie, what belongs in the bilateral relationship, what is part of regional or global mechanisms—and in particular where differences lie that could erode the alliance.

THE BILATERAL SECURITY AGENDA

The bilateral security agenda itself raises a number of key issues, many of which grow out of the respective challenges discussed above. The Prime Minister's Advisory Commission has recommended a course of action that clearly underscores the essentiality of the U.S.–Japan security treaty in the defense of Japan and redefines it in post–cold war terms. In essence, the report lays the basis for a new *taiko* (the national defense program outline, last revised more than two decades ago), which would serve as the foundation for defining roles and missions. In many ways, the Advisory Commission breaks taboos and expands the boundaries of Japan's defense role. It calls for broadening cooperation in several key areas including improved joint military planning and joint training for a number of scenarios; improved logistics support, particularly reaching an acquisition and cross-servicing agreement; increasing interoperability in defense systems by including more cooperative development in C^3I (command, control, communications, and intelligence) and other areas; and sustaining host nation support (HNS).

The report also calls for acquiring theater missile defenses (TMD), but suggests that Japan should have an independent national capability for defending against ballistic missile attack. Although this holds the potential for an important initiative to redefine the security alliance, there is, in practice, a growing "TMD gap." Whereas the United States is already well into the development phase of THAAD (Theater High Altitude Area Defense) and the Navy Aegis TMD systems, as well as having launched a joint development project with the European Union (EU) for lower-tier TMD, Japan is still in the midst of conducting a . . . study of such systems. Thus the reality is that Japan may be forced to either buy new systems off the shelf or develop its own. There is a widespread assumption in the Japanese bureaucracy that Tokyo will be able to coproduce U.S. missile defense systems, although that may be highly controversial in the U.S. Congress. In any case, along with TMD, all these issues involv[e] upgrading the mechanics of the alliance. . . .

A MATURE ALLIANCE

In redefining the security alliance, a key element is, within the bounds of Japan's constitutional and political limits, making it a more equal partnership. Article 6 of the security treaty, for example, calls for allowing the United States to use various "facilities and areas" (e.g., bases) in Japan "for the purpose of contributing to the security of Japan and the maintenance of international peace and security in the Far East." This mandate, in the unfolding security environment in Northeast Asia, hints at the urgency of an acquisition and cross-servicing agreement (which the United States has with NATO countries) to facilitate, for instance, U.S. military activity in the event of a crisis in Korea. In this regard, enhanced joint planning and joint training also assume importance, as does interoperability, particularly of C^3I.

Although in military-to-military terms such progress in deepening the workings of the alliance is crucial, in terms of public support burden sharing in the form of HNS will loom larger, particularly after Korea is reunified, in determining the support of the U.S. public for the alliance. In Japan's tight budget environment, sustaining HNS will require difficult choices and tradeoffs, because it already consumes more than 10 percent of the total defense allocation.

Enhancing a two-way flow of technology is potentially even more important in terms of U.S. public perceptions of the alliance. Whether it has been because of liberal practices in the U.S. private sector or the willingness of the U.S. government to permit Japan to obtain increased defense production capabilities under license over the past four decades, there is a widespread view, magnified by revisionist conceptions of Japan, that cooperation has been essentially a one-way street. Initiatives such as the Technology-for-Technology (TFT) program, aimed at fostering a flow of dual-use technology to the United States, can help build support to the degree that they allow Washington to demonstrate that they are a two-way street. The impact of such technology cooperation on U.S perceptions of Japan as a friend and ally goes well beyond views of the security relationship. Japanese contributions to TMD development would also clearly reinforce the overall relationship.

But a disturbing Japanese attitude on technology transfer is evident in . . . discussions with working- and senior-level Japanese officials. Despite the fact that some 80 percent of their military hardware is produced in Japan, much via licensing or coproduction, Japanese officials openly display a very niggardly attitude toward the transfer of dual-use technology to the United States. It is almost as if the experience of the past four decades had never occurred, and they are starting from a zero, "what have you done for me lately" position. Generally absent is any view that technology cooperation might provide an opportunity to offset the one-way commitment of the security treaty.

It is too soon to pass judgment on technology-sharing issues but it is also difficult to be optimistic. After the political controversy, much of it ill-founded, over the codevelopment of the FSX fighter, public suspicion of a predatory Japan renders future projects, in which complementary U.S. and Japanese technologies might combine, extremely problematic.

SUMMING UP WHERE INTERESTS LIE

. . . A large array of convergent interests suggest that the security alliance makes sense for both parties. For Japan, the history of the past century has been that it has been prosperous and peaceful when in an alliance with a leading maritime power: Britain in the first quarter of the century, the United States in the second half. Disaster has struck when Tokyo has been strategically independent. Moreover, in a very volatile Northeast Asia, Japan has few alternatives. There is no apparent replacement for the United States as a security partner, and if Japan were to end the alliance and pursue an independent course it would lead to deep suspicion throughout the Pacific and a destabilizing arms race (both conventional and nuclear) with Korea and China. Remarks in early June 1995 by former foreign minister Michio Watanabe describing Japan's invasion and colonization of Korea as a "peaceful merger,"

and the Murayama government's failure to pass a fiftieth anniversary resolution apologizing for past behavior reinforce suspicion and a sense of illegitimacy in the region.

... Japan's $42.1 billion defense budget is deceptive. But its development
of a high-tech defense capability ... and its launching of the H-2 rocket [in
1994], giving it both a ballistic missile and independent reconnaissance
potential, mean that Japan is closely watched in the region.

For the United States, a forward presence in Japan, particularly the home-
porting of a carrier in Yokosuka, is key to responding to regional contingencies all the way to the Indian Ocean and the Persian Gulf, guarding the sea
lines of communication, and more broadly providing a strategic equilibrium
and sustaining U.S. credibility as a Pacific power. Few in Asia would look forward to discovering what the security environment would look like absent
the U.S.–Japan security alliance.

THE IMPACT OF JAPAN'S ROLE ON THE ALLIANCE

Any discussion of the impact of Japan's role on the U.S.–Japan alliance gets to
the larger issue of whether Japan will develop more of a sense of stewardship
in the international system. Apart from a finely honed skill at writing checks
with the dual purpose of providing "protection money" and lubricating markets as part of the world's largest bilateral Official Development Assistance
program, Japan is rarely accused of demonstrating leadership.

Whether it is Japan's stance on the Uruguay Round, during which Tokyo
hid under the table as the United States and Europe fought it out; on the Gulf
war, when it took inordinate efforts before Japan belatedly became gener-
ously involved; or even initially on the conference on extension of the Nuclear
Non-Proliferation Treaty, Japan has yet to grow into assuming the responsibilities necessary for the sort of prestige and respect it seeks. Even in its desire
for a permanent UN Security Council seat, its principal argument has been
financial. . . .

The renewal of the security alliance certainly depends on Japan's willingness to expand its military cooperation in the areas discussed above. That is
necessary, but not sufficient. For over time, it is this larger sense that Japan is
sharing the burdens of forging and maintaining a viable international system
in the areas of trade, finance, and the environment that is likely to best sustain
the alliance. . . .

Whether the alliance will be sustained, or whether there will be a looser
form of partnership, will depend on how it meets the series of challenges outlined above. Developments in Korea or China could strengthen the alliance
or could become new *shokku* [shocks] that alter the relationship. One idea
that may be worth pondering is whether there is some new, high-profile
U.S.–Japan initiative that could capture the imagination of the respective
publics in both countries. I would suggest two candidates. Particularly if the
U.S. space station is canceled, one such initiative would be a joint moon

base/manned mission to Mars project. The space programs in both countries suffer from a lack of clear goals and new directions. Such an initiative could rationalize both, supersede the space station, which in its currently reduced form has less scientific value, develop defense-related spinoffs, and offer expansion into a multilateral enterprise to include Russia, and perhaps at some point the EU. Apart from the great TV visuals it would provide, such a project could offer a new sense of mission to the respective space programs as well as a wider sense of partnership.

A potential initiative more directly related to security involves Japan's nuclear program and nonproliferation. This could be a U.S.–Japan joint venture with both a global and regional payoff. It would involve a Japanese decision to indefinitely postpone its commercial breeder reactor program. If Japan abandoned this program—for which, if market forces are considered, there is little economic basis now or over at least the next 50 years—it could open the way for U.S.–Japan regional and global initiatives. Globally, such a Japanese move would permit the Clinton administration to move beyond the limited fissile-material-for-weapons cutoff it is pursuing and call for a ban on commercial use of plutonium, thus reinforcing the nonproliferation regime. Regionally it could give impetus to an Asian counterpart to the European Atomic Energy Community, an ASIATOM, that would build a framework for nuclear cooperation in Northeast Asia between the four major powers (the United States, Japan, China, and Russia) and the two Koreas. . . .

A dramatic shift in Japan's plutonium policy would have a substantial impact on regional security dynamics. If Japan were to surrender fissile material to IAEA control, fears of a nuclear Japan would have no conceivable basis. It would help to deprive China of a rationale for a nuclear buildup while the major nuclear powers are rapidly building down—there will be a 90 percent reduction in U.S. and Russian nuclear warheads from the height of the Cold War at the end of the implementation of the second Strategic Arms Reduction Treaty. Moreover, any Korean enthusiasm for reprocessing would also lose its momentum and much of its rationale.

If proliferation is in reality a high-priority security issue, then given the enormous costs being borne by the United States to get rid of the baggage from the Cold War, the goal of moving away from the use of plutonium and establishing international management of the substance should be viewed as a form of burden sharing. There is now a window of opportunity to launch a U.S.–Japan plutonium initiative.

CONCLUSION

Regardless of whether ideas make sense when translated into practical action, there is a discernible deficit of political imagination and political leadership in Japan and the United States that may be one of the largest impediments to renewing the alliance. . . . But given the large degrees of economic and technological interdependence, and the shared stakes in managing the trade and financial systems as well forging a regional and global structure of peace, it is difficult to see any alternative to a relationship of enhanced cooperation between the United States and Japan, whether as formal allies or looser partners. If such cooperation does not take place, it is difficult to envision a viable, durable international system.

16.   CHINA: WHY OUR HARD-LINERS ARE WRONG

Robert S. Ross

Critics of U.S. China policy have been enjoying unprecedented attention lately. Between those who want to get tough with China and those who want to be more accommodating, the Clinton administration's second-term project to consolidate and expand cooperative Sino–U.S. relations has been vastly complicated. Advocates of nearly every stripe have had a hand in distorting China's impact on American interests and Washington's policy record since the late 1980s, which, despite its bad press, has had important successes. Character assassination has been so rampant and policy critiques so politicized that the normal rules of evidence used to evaluate a serious, complicated set of policy choices have been among the first casualties. Lost, too, in many cases, has been any sense of the geopolitics of the problem—that cool-headed assessment of capabilities and motives that ought to be our first task, not an emotionally exhausted afterthought.

Particularly egregious have been many of the claims of those neo–cold warriors in their efforts to persuade Americans to abandon engagement and follow a policy of "containing" the "China threat." As an example of the hostile hyperbole that has become quite common, consider this statement of June 9 [1997] from the Washington-based William J. Casey Institute of the Center for Security Policy: "The nature of the threat posed by China is in key respects of a greater magnitude and vastly greater complexity than that mounted by the Soviet Union at the height of the Cold War." It is a rousing statement, to be sure, but by no reasonable or objective measure is it even remotely true.

If we step back and evaluate the issues fairly, two truths come clear: China is not a "rogue state," and U.S. policy has made important gains in affecting

Note: Notes have been deleted.

Chinese behavior over a wide range of issues bearing on important American interests. Both points may be demonstrated by looking at military and economic dimensions of the bilateral relationship, as well as at the heated debate over China's human rights practices.

SECURITY CONFLICTS AND ACCOMMODATIONS

The most serious Chinese challenge to the United States is its potential military power. The Chinese economy is growing and Beijing's ability to increase defense spending is growing with it. But advocates of containing China vastly overestimate Chinese power and underestimate our own.

A larger Chinese economy will not necessarily lead to greater military power. China can import weaponry, but sustained improvement in military capabilities will require indigenous defense modernization. China still cannot manufacture a reliable 1970s-generation fighter plane, much less anything like a U.S. F-16. The need of the People's Liberation Army to import Russian equipment is telling. Buying from Russia is a quick and relatively inexpensive way for China to equip its forces with materiel far superior to indigenous products. But this should not be particularly upsetting to U.S. planners, whose forte is the destruction of Soviet equipment with remarkable speed and skill. Moreover, China lacks the basic ability to maintain Russian equipment. It now requires extensive Russian assistance to repair many of its recently acquired SU-27s and its Kilo submarines.

China has developed a limited number of more modern destroyers, but it is decades away from being able to manufacture and deploy a first-generation, limited capability aircraft carrier. The PLA [People's Liberation Army] lacks the ability to conduct sustained military operations more than 100 miles from the Chinese shoreline. China is a formidable land power, but in maritime Southeast Asia, where U.S. interests are most at stake, China is militarily inferior even to such countries as Singapore and Malaysia.

In the end, China may succeed in modernizing its military. But it may fail, too—economic and technological modernization is a precarious enterprise. As an export processing zone for the advanced industrial countries, China has succeeded in raising living standards and its GNP, but this is a far cry from developing the economic and technological capabilities to field a twenty-first century military force.

U.S. military supremacy is so overwhelming that Washington has the luxury of being able to observe Chinese technology development and weapons production before adopting countervailing policies. . . . Not only is the U.S. defense budget greater than the combined defense budgets of the next six largest competitors, but U.S. technology and weapons modernization are advancing so rapidly that, in all probability, with each passing day and despite its strenuous efforts, China's technological and military capabilities are losing ground rather than catching up with those of the United States.

Politically, too, the American alliance system in Asia is superior to anything the Chinese can hope to have. Logistically, the U.S. alliance with Japan and its access to basing facilities throughout the region give the United States an enormous advantage. Diplomatically, China is increasingly viewed in the region as a problem to be managed, while the United States is seen as a relatively disinterested power-broker whose aims are compatible with regional peace and prosperity for all. A potential Chinese alliance with Burma can hardly offset the U.S. relationship with Japan, South Korea, Australia, and the maritime states of Southeast Asia (including, still, the Philippines). With such logistical and diplomatic superiority to bring to bear, current U.S. defense spending and weapons acquisitions are already more than sufficient to hedge against China's potential development of advanced military capabilities.

It is true, nevertheless, that despite China's limited military capabilities the PLA can use force effectively and is not shy to do so. The PLA has been part of every major crisis in East Asia since 1949. It has the ability to disrupt regional stability and inflict considerable costs on U.S. interests. Clearly, the most serious security conflict in U.S.–China relations remains the Taiwan issue, and it is in principle unresolvable. Beijing wants unification under PRC [People's Republic of China] rule and reserves the right to use force to bring it about. The United States insists on Taiwan's right to make its choices free from military pressure.

Even if the Taiwan issue is intractable in principle, it can be managed so that U.S.–China conflicts of interest do not disrupt cooperative relations; this has clearly been the U.S. experience from the early 1970s to the early 1990s. U.S. policy has guaranteed Taiwan's security and, as important, has provided an environment in which Taiwan developed a prosperous economy and a flourishing democracy. These successes form the bedrock of Taiwan's diplomatic autonomy, and the only concession Washington had to make to help Taiwan achieve them was to refrain from actions that could be interpreted as support for formal Taiwanese independence.

Equally important, Washington's multifaceted assistance to Taiwan did not make improved relations with China impossible. Diplomatically, what seemed a zero-sum game between Taiwan and the mainland turned out not to be zero-sum at all for American policy. The main reason for this was China's strong desire to cooperate with the United States against the Soviet Union, but it was not the only reason. Mutually beneficial economic relations and cooperation in maintaining regional stability on a wide range of issues were also important, and they remain so despite the fact that the Soviet Union is no longer there as a common enemy. Indeed, a good deal less has changed than is often assumed. China today no less than before wants to avoid heightened U.S.–China adversarial relations, much less a literal fight with the United States over Taiwan. That being so, Washington can continue to protect Taiwan's most vital interests—security from mainland power and continued economic and political development—and avoid great power conflict and escalation of regional tension by employing more or less the same Taiwan policy that has worked well over the past twenty-five years. The United States can fulfill its moral obligations to Taiwan and assure its "realist" objectives toward both Taiwan and the mainland without having to do either more against the mainland or less in favor of Taiwan.

Chinese weapons exports have drawn much attention from critics of U.S. China policy. . . . It is true that Chinese commercial enterprises have exported chemical weapons materiel. But it is also true that its weapons proliferation policy is in substantive compliance with all international arms control agreements.

Since the end of the Cold War, and with the partial exception of its strategic relationship with Pakistan, China has not exported a single missile, transferred any nuclear technology, or engaged in proliferation of chemical weapons raw materials in violation of any international arms control regime. Contrary to several reports, China has not exported the M-9 missile to Syria. Its missile exports to the Middle East have consisted solely of short-range missiles that are not covered by the Missile Technology Control Regime (MTCR). Its cooperation with Algeria in nuclear energy, which dates back to the mid-1980s, has been under the continuous inspection of the International Atomic Energy Agency. In 1995 Beijing canceled its nuclear energy project with Iran. Its 1996 ring magnet transfer to Pakistan did not violate the Nuclear Non-Proliferation Treaty (NPT). China's policy on chemical weapons proliferation has been equally compliant. Although in May 1997 Congress imposed sanctions on Chinese firms for exporting chemical weapons materiel to Iran, these exports did not violate the Chemical Weapons Convention.

China's most serious proliferation activities have been its nuclear assistance to Pakistan in the 1980s and its missile transfers to Pakistan in the 1990s. But just as post–Cold War U.S. weapons and technology transfers to Britain and Japan reveal that Washington engages in nuclear and missile proliferation when it suits its interests, Chinese transfers to Pakistan reflect its security interests. In some respects China's Pakistan policy may fairly be compared to American indulgence toward Israel's nuclear weapons. While the United States was never the principal supplier of Israeli nuclear technology or know-how, Washington and Beijing both prefer that their respective allies be able to deter attacks from more powerful adversaries on their own. It is safer that way, and avoids complicating their own relations with other countries. Just as Washington does not want its support for Israel needlessly to jeopardize its relations with Arab countries, Beijing does not want its support for Pakistan to derail its efforts to improve relations with India.

This is not to equate Pakistan with Israel, Japan, and Britain, which have well deserved reputations for prudence. No moral equivalency is intended or required. But the United States should avoid the conceit that a given mode of behavior can be wrong for every country in the world but still right for the United States because of the purity of its motives. Obviously, when other countries develop similar policies to pursue similar objectives, interest rather than morality is the appropriate standard of judgment. Washington does not turn an occasional deaf ear toward proliferation because it believes that proliferation is morally good, but because there are occasions when it is a necessary and a lesser evil. There is no reason to assume that China's motives in its relations with Pakistan turn on a different sort of reasoning—and every reason to think, by the way, that had the United States acted as a truer ally to Pakistan, much of what China provides that country would have been rendered unnecessary.

Overall, Chinese policy has supported the development of the global non-proliferation order. China has progressively joined international arms control agreements. In 1992 it formally joined the NPT. In 1996, despite the implications for its unreliable nuclear deterrent and grumbling from the PLA, Beijing signed the Comprehensive Test Ban Treaty. Over PLA objections, it has also signed and ratified the Chemical Weapons Convention, and agreed to the Land Mine Protocol to the Convention on Inhumane Weaponry. Recently, Chinese leaders have expressed interest in joining the Zangger Group, the export control arm of the NPT. Chinese participation in these regimes reflects American success at pressuring Beijing to accept global responsibility for controlling proliferation, even at a cost to China's own interests.

There are important arms control regimes from which China is shut out, including the MTCR and the Wassenaar Group, which oversees conventional weapons exports. It is America that has blocked Chinese participation. Chinese absence from the MTCR is most troubling. Washington can have but limited confidence that Beijing will refrain from missile proliferation when it was party neither to the original negotiations nor to subsequent adjustments to the MTCR. Even in these circumstances, Chinese exports to Pakistan stand as its only violation of the MTCR, and these—particularly the 1992 transfer of M-11 missiles—were only made in direct retaliation for the U.S. sale of 150 F-16s to Taiwan, itself an unambiguous violation of the August 1982 U.S.–China communiqué. As in any bilateral relationship, contemporary or historical, China is inclined to retaliate when American violations of U.S.–China agreements undermine its interests. This is not roguish but realist.

In the non-nuclear realm, the United States does not oppose proliferation of missiles because they are "weapons of mass destruction," but because they are the only delivery system against which the United States has no defense. But for most countries, U.S. F-16s, which Washington sells freely, are more threatening and more destructive than a Chinese M-11 missile. It is not at all clear that U.S. arms exports are any less "destabilizing" than Chinese exports.

Obviously, Chinese exports of weapons not covered by arms control regimes could undermine U.S. interests. But thus far the impact has been minimal. Exports of low-technology short-range cruise missiles and chemical weapons precursors to Iran do not enhance Iran's ability to contend with the U.S. Navy or Air Force as much as they undermine American diplomatic efforts to enforce dual containment. But here China's record is not much different from that of many other countries, including several U.S. allies. The most flagrant challenge to Washington's dual containment policy with respect to Iraq comes not from China but from France, Turkey, and Russia, all of whom have strained to lighten the sanctions regime for financial reasons.

Meanwhile, Japan and the members of the European Union trade with Iran as they do with any other country, and greatly resent U.S. efforts to stop them from doing so. German dual-use technology exports to Iran continue unchecked. This commerce is more important to Tehran than anything that China provides.

China's record is far from perfect when it comes to arms dealing, but it is not the flagrant violator it is often represented as being. Its more controversial exports reflect legitimate security interests rather than predatory political or opportunistic commercial interests. Moreover, some Chinese violations reflect not central government policy but rather Beijing's limited control over economic enterprises and its inability to establish an effective export control regime. . . .

With specific reference to the Middle East, the most sensitive area in which Chinese behavior has been criticized, China has for the most part respected U.S. interests, and it has not done so without cost to itself. China has no inherent reason to refrain from proliferation to regions outside East Asia; since such countries cannot harm China directly, it might simply have allowed economic interests to drive its export policy. Instead, China has accommodated U.S. policy because both the Bush and Clinton administrations . . . effectively combined coercive threats with constructive diplomacy. Since China's first missile exports to the Middle East in 1988, the systematic application of limited and well-targeted sanctions has persuaded Chinese leaders that Washington pays close attention to these PRC exports, and that exports that violate international regimes or harm U.S. interests risk disrupting U.S.–China cooperation. At the same time, the continuation of engagement in other areas has worked to convince Chinese leaders that cooperation with the United States is still feasible and worthwhile. The net result is that U.S. policy has compelled Beijing to comply with international arms control regimes and cooperate with U.S. interests more generally than might have been expected.

ECONOMIC CONFLICTS AND COSTS

The most important economic conflicts between the United States and China concern Chinese piracy of intellectual property rights (IPR), the large and growing U.S. trade deficit with China, the terms for Chinese admission to the World Trade Organization (WTO), and prison-labor exports. But as is the case concerning security conflicts, the attention given to Chinese economic policy is disproportionate to its impact on U.S. interests. Similarly, criticism of U.S. trade policy fails to acknowledge American success in bringing China's behavior into greater compliance with those interests.

Chinese IPR piracy has been the focus of periodic U.S.–China tensions. Seeking Chinese cooperation in reducing financial losses to U.S. entertainment and software industries, Washington has threatened economic sanctions if China does not change its domestic policies. But while Chinese piracy of

IPR is certainly a problem, the extent of losses both in absolute and comparative terms is much exaggerated. The widely used figure of $2 billion is an industry estimate premised on an inelastic demand curve. That is, estimates of losses are calculated on the basis of the profits that would have been earned if the hypothetical quantity of licensed sales were to equal actual pirated sales. Obviously, this is very unrealistic; no one expects fully above-board retailers to sell the same number of products at seven or ten times the black market price. The actual profits from licensed sales would have been but a small fraction of $2 billion. U.S. financial losses are not irrelevant, and it is true that a matter of principle is involved, but these losses are negligible given the scale on which Hollywood and the American computer software industry operate.

Equally important, critics fail to apply a comparative perspective on Chinese IPR piracy. Piracy is a worldwide phenomenon and no country is fully effective at stopping it. Indeed, industry groups have targeted not China but Greece, Paraguay, and Russia as priority countries for U.S. IPR policy. Nor is China among the eleven countries that these groups have recommended be placed on the special 301 "priority watch list." According to industry estimates, losses to U.S. firms from piracy in Japan are nearly double those from piracy in China. In absolute terms, the greatest losses to American industries occur in the United States itself. Further, if industry estimates used assumptions based on more realistic elastic demand curves, then estimates of relative losses to Chinese IPR piracy would be even smaller.

Moreover, in contrast to losses from other markets, Chinese enforcement abilities are relatively weak; indeed, IPR piracy in China affects domestic manufacturers on a wide range of name-brand consumer goods, including computer software products, more than it affects U.S. industries. It also harms the legitimacy of the Chinese government. Its inability to prevent the manufacture and sale of inferior imitations of popular name-brand consumer goods has earned it a reputation among its own people for ineffective protection of consumer interests. To a large extent, lax PRC enforcement of intellectual property rights is not by design, but reflects the government's general inability to develop effective regulatory and legal systems.

But despite the chaos in Chinese society, American policy has succeeded in encouraging reforms that meet the interests of U.S. manufacturers. Beijing has fundamentally fulfilled its 1992 agreement with the United States to enact domestic legislation protecting the intellectual property rights of foreign companies. The 1995 U.S.–China agreement on the implementation of Chinese domestic legislation has also scored important successes. Between May 1996 and March 1997, due in part to Chinese government offers of rewards for information, Beijing shut down thirty-seven illegal compact disc factories, and Chinese courts have begun to sentence IPR violators to significant prison terms.

The American trade deficit with China is large and growing, but the relevant policy issue is the impact of the deficit on the U.S. domestic economy. It is, in fact, very small, largely because Chinese exports to the United States primarily consist of goods that American workers no longer make, such as low-cost textiles, shoes, toys, and inexpensive low-technology electronic goods. The United States stopped making such things over twenty years ago when Japanese products captured the American market. Subsequently, as Japanese labor costs increased, products from Taiwan, South Korea, and Hong Kong dominated the U.S. market. Now, as labor costs in Taiwan, South Korea, and Hong Kong have increased, Chinese consumer goods are in turn taking their places. Chinese export success has primarily affected the overall trade deficits and labor conditions of Taiwan, South Korea, and Hong Kong, not those of the United States. The proof is in the data: The cumulative U.S. trade deficit with China, Hong Kong, Taiwan, South Korea, and Japan *has not appreciably grown since 1988;* only the distribution of the U.S. deficit among these markets has changed.

America's response to a trade imbalance should reflect the extent to which that imbalance is the result of a trading partner's conscious policy choices as opposed to other factors. In the case of Japan, Washington confronted this issue in the 1980s and the lesson of that experience should be clear: the U.S. deficit with Japan declined not in response to changing Japanese trade policy, but in response to changes in exchange rates and in the Japanese economy itself. The trade deficit with China also reflects economic conditions. China's national savings rate is far higher than that of the United States, and the Chinese are much poorer per capita than Americans. Thus, the United States can readily import inexpensive Chinese consumer goods, while there is a limited market in China for America's expensive high-technology goods. Contrasting economic conditions guarantee that the United States will have a large trade deficit with China regardless of how much pressure the United States applies and how much Chinese trade policy changes. . . .

Regardless of the economic causes of trade deficits, it is generally in the American interest to minimize the obstacles to doing business in China, so long as doing so does not obviously prejudice American strategic interests. But American businesses widely agree that despite the corruption that exists there and the fact that its laws and regulations are largely unenforceable, it is already far easier to do business in China than in Japan or South Korea. Thus, in sectors in which the United States has a global comparative advantage—including civilian aircraft, grain export, computers, high-technology electronic goods such as cellular telephones, and industrial machinery—it does well in the Chinese market. As in the case of IPR piracy, American attention to the trade deficit is disproportionate to the impact of that deficit on U.S. interests and to the role that U.S. and Chinese government policies can play in affecting it.

Nevertheless, U.S. trade policy has achieved some important successes in improving access to China's market. In response to the threat of punitive tariffs advanced by the Bush administration in 1992, Beijing agreed to make transparent its trade regulations. By 1995 Beijing had substantively complied with this agreement, making it easier for foreign businesses to operate in China. In response to pressure from the Clinton administration, Beijing agreed [in 1997] for the first time to liberalize foreign access to its textile market. While these developments will not fundamentally affect the trade balance, they do promote America's objective in expanding market access and promoting fairer U.S.–China trade. They also show that, contrary to established opinion on American op-ed pages, the Chinese are not intrinsically duplicitous; they will implement negotiated agreements to maintain U.S.–China cooperation.

Another important issue concerns China's admission to the WTO. This problem is frequently portrayed as having been made difficult by China's refusal to accept the norms of the international liberal trade order. The Chinese have indeed resisted U.S. proposals, but the conflict is one of interest, not principle. Admission to the WTO is based on individually negotiated agreements reflecting the economic interests of both the applicant and the existing WTO membership. As was the case with Japan, South Korea, Hong Kong, and Singapore at earlier stages of their development, China's leaders seek an agreement that will protect its infant industries from international competition. This is Hamiltonian in character, not Stalinist. But the size of China's market and its potential economic influence require Washington to adopt a more demanding posture toward Chinese protectionism than that which it had earlier adopted toward the protectionism of the smaller Asian economies.

The solution to this conflict is not Chinese isolation from the WTO. At present, China protects its domestic industries and still enjoys many WTO benefits indirectly from the MFN status it receives from the advanced industrial economies. Without U.S. concessions to Chinese interests, China will remain outside the WTO, its protectionist policies will continue to influence the global economy, and it will bear no obligation whatsoever to liberalize those policies. It is in the U.S. interest to create Chinese obligations to liberalize its trade by bringing China into the WTO. This may require a prolonged liberalization schedule as well as granting the PRC permanent MFN status. Such concessions would be politically controversial, but they promote our interests. Not only would they commit China to eventual trade liberalization, but Chinese membership in the WTO would replace often counterproductive unilateral American pressure with more politically acceptable multilateral pressure that could, additionally, reinforce the efforts of pro-reform Chinese politicians. . . .

The final trade issue concerns Chinese export of goods made by so-called slave labor in Chinese prisons. On this issue, American hypocrisy and obfuscation frame the debate. The issue is not whether there are political prisoners in China. Of course there are. Nor is the issue whether the Chinese government compels its prisoners to work and then exports the goods to gain an unfair trade advantage. It does. But so does the United States. American prisoners are frequently compelled to work, making license plates or clothing, or in chain-gangs doing road construction, and there is no American law prohibiting export of prison-made goods. By U.S. standards, too, the conditions in Chinese prisons are horrendous, but they have to be if Beijing is not to make prisons more comfortable than villages in the impoverished Chinese countryside. Finally, there is no evidence that China has exported to the United States goods made by human rights prisoners.

HUMAN RIGHTS: NOT WHETHER BUT HOW

China's human rights violations are numerous and grave. The United States has a moral imperative and a mandate from its people to include human rights diplomacy in its China policy. The issue is not whether to try to change China for the better, but how most effectively to go about it.

The focus of American debate these days is over the wisdom of having normal trade relations with China and conducting regular high level U.S.–China diplomatic exchanges while Chinese leaders imprison political dissidents. Congressional pressure on the White House has tried to hold U.S.–China cooperation hostage to the fate of Chinese dissidents and has thus turned these dissidents into bargaining chips. Chinese leaders care little if a dissident remains in jail or is released to the constant supervision of a hoard of security police. Our making clear to China that the release of dissidents is the quid pro quo for improved U.S.–China relations gives Beijing a vested interest in keeping dissidents in jail until it can secure a payoff for releasing them. . . .

It is difficult to see how punishing Beijing's imprisonment of dissidents by downgrading political and economic relations will promote political liberalization in China. Should the United States stigmatize China by sanctioning its human rights violations, it will most likely encourage the Chinese leadership to adopt more repressive domestic policies; hostile U.S.–China relations, after all, can only intensify Beijing's concern with subversion and domestic instability. Overt American diplomatic pressure has not encouraged China to loosen its restraints on political speech; and sanctions, while they may make their American sponsors feel better, will only make the situation in China worse.

The harsh criticism of U.S. human rights policies by congressional critics and human rights groups fails—or refuses—to recognize American successes. Part of the problem is one of definition. By limiting the definition of human rights to the freedom of public dissent, human rights activists obscure a wide range of activity that should also be free from government interference. A broader, and better, benchmark is the extent to which people can live their lives free from government harassment and intimidation. By this standard, China has made considerable and rapid progress, for which the United States and its democratic allies can rightly claim significant credit.

As is the case with all one-party authoritarian systems, the Chinese government monitors a wide range of public activity. Within the constraints of one-party rule, however, the Chinese people increasingly enjoy unprecedented access to Western entertainment programs on television, in cinemas, and on stage. The Chinese consumer market is flourishing, with production determined by consumer demand for Western-style clothing, make-up, entertainment magazines, and fast food. The most popular movies are produced in Hollywood, and the most popular pop music comes from Hong Kong, Taiwan, and the United States. American basketball players are superstars in China, too.

These developments are not trivial. Through them Chinese society has developed values antithetical to those of its leadership. Increasing interaction has meant that Western cultures are penetrating China's society and have started to create the conditions for political cleavages between government and society, and ultimately for political change. . . .

Chinese leaders continue to direct abhorrent human rights abuses, including torture of Tibetan independence activists and imprisonment of leaders of unapproved religious activities. But compared to many countries in the Middle East and Southwest Asia—in which the sale and lifetime servitude of child brides is commonplace, religious tolerance is nearly nonexistent, women suffer intolerable abuse, and Western popular culture is barred—and to the one-party dictatorships of sub-Saharan Africa, where even slavery is tolerated and degrading and harmful tribal customs brook no challenge, China's performance, and particularly its recent record of positive change, does not cry out for special censure. South Asian countries, even including democratic India, tolerate slavery, and the horrid abuse of women in India is especially disturbing. The point is not that China's human rights record is good, but that abhorrent violations occur throughout the Third World and that, as in both security and economic issues, U.S. attention to China's human rights situation is disproportionate to China's violations when viewed comparatively and in the context of its improving situation. . . .

Both the Western success at contributing to change in China through broad-based personal ties, and the Western failure to change appreciably the lot of Chinese dissidents by threatening to limit those ties, underscore the importance of resisting demands that the United States reduce its level of engagement with China. Some of the most successful foreign activities in China, including programs in legal training and for the promotion of democracy, have been funded by the U.S. government and American philanthropic organizations. The record of Western interaction with post-Mao China is overwhelmingly positive. It suggests that we should put an end to the detrimental politicization of human rights policy, and expand U.S.–China cooperation wherever practicable.

There are no unmanageable U.S.–China conflicts. The Taiwan problem raises the most sensitive and dangerous issues, yet even here Beijing and Washington have established a way to satisfy their respective interests without undermining cooperative relations. In both economic and security relations, conflicting interests are amenable to negotiation and mutually satisfactory outcomes. As in any negotiation between great powers, solutions will require mutual compromise. But through negotiations with China, the United States can further a wide range of bilateral and regional interests and maintain regional and global stability, while simultaneously promoting change in China that reflects American values. . . .

The United States and the Global South

17. THE GULF BOTTLENECK: MIDDLE EAST STABILITY AND WORLD OIL SUPPLY

Richard N. Cooper

Since the disturbances caused by the Iraqi invasion of Kuwait . . . , the international flow of oil has gone uninterrupted and unimpeded, but that tense summer of 1990 rekindled memories of the volatile oil prices of previous decades. In 1973, 1979, 1980, and 1990, major disruptions in the flow of Middle Eastern oil caused world oil prices to surge, and in 1986, the practical collapse of the Organization of Petroleum Exporting Countries (OPEC) led to a 50 percent drop in prices. The Middle East remains the key to the stability of global energy markets. With the world's dependence on the region poised to increase dramatically, what are the prospects for continued calm in Middle Eastern oil markets?

Middle Eastern oil implies reserves located in the Persian Gulf because other oil sources in the Middle East are far less important: Algeria and Libya are relatively inelastic suppliers, Egypt consumes most of the oil it produces, and Sudan is inhospitable to foreign investors. This leaves the Arabian peninsula oil producers—Saudi Arabia, the United Arab Emirates (UAE), Kuwait, Oman, Qatar, and Yemen, in order of oil exports—and Iraq and Iran as the primary international suppliers of oil in the Middle East.

FUELING GLOBAL GROWTH

The world economy is in relatively good balance at present and can look forward to reasonable growth over the next decade or two. Economic performance in Japan and Europe has been lackluster recently but will likely improve early in the next century. Growth is robust in the Far East, South Asia, and Latin America, while the United States is growing at or near its potential. Growth in the former Soviet Union will pick up from the no-growth adjustments of the past few years, and even Africa may turn in a better performance, although that continent is economically too small to affect the world economy.

Modern economies are still based heavily on energy, though the efficiency with which it is used is improving steadily and is vastly greater than it was 25 years ago. Developing countries, in particular, are relying increasingly on hydrocarbon fuels as they move from subsistence to manufacturing economies. Oil is still the unmatched fuel for transportation, and with modernization, the demand for transportation has increased substantially. Synthetic oil can be made from coal and from natural gas, but it remains uncompetitive in cost relative to petroleum.

Taking these and various other factors into account, the U.S. Department of Energy projects world demand for oil to grow by 30.4 million barrels per day (mmbd) between 1995 and 2015, or by 44 percent (rather less than the projected 49 percent growth in total energy demand). Of this increase in demand, only 7.5 mmbd are projected to come from today's developed countries of Europe, Japan, and North America. The remaining 22.8 mmbd increase in demand will be generated by today's relatively poor countries, including 14.1 mmbd from Asia (excluding Japan). China alone will increase its demand for oil—and thus its oil imports—by five mmbd.

Perhaps surprisingly, the world will not have difficulty supplying these increased quantities of oil. Technological developments have greatly improved the prospects for, and reduced the costs of, identifying and developing new oil reserves, both on land and under water. But the most economical oil remains in the Persian Gulf region, and if the countries of that region are willing to undertake the necessary investments in exploration and development, this great increase in demand can be satisfied at only modest increases in price. The U.S. Department of Energy projects that the price of oil in 2015 will be U.S.$25.43 a barrel (in 1994 dollars); other forecasters assume an even lower price.

Based on these price and investment assumptions, oil production outside of OPEC will grow by less than three mmbd between 1995 and 2015, leaving a 28 mmbd increase to come from OPEC countries. Of the OPEC countries, Venezuela can be expected to be the only significant contributor from outside the Persian Gulf. This leaves over 25 mmbd of additional production—equal to total OPEC oil production in 1994 (18 mmbd of which came from the Persian Gulf)—to come incrementally from the Gulf. If these projections are realized, the share of world oil production coming from the Persian Gulf will rise from 29 percent in 1994 to over 46 percent in 2015.

We know from the experiences of 1973–74 and 1979–80 that a several-fold rise in oil prices, generated by an actual or an anticipated shortage of oil (actual oil production did not fall in 1979, but the anticipation of shortage led to extensive buildup of stocks), can wreak havoc on the economies of countries around the world. Fluctuations in oil prices, after all, were largely responsible for the stagflation—deep recession combined with inflation—of the 1970s and the developing-country debt crisis of the 1980s. The economic damage from oil price shocks can be severe. How high is the risk of another such disruption?

THE EDGE OF INSTABILITY

It is usually suggested that the Persian Gulf is a turbulent and politically unstable part of the world. In fact, there has been remarkable political stability in the region, at least as measured by the longevity of its leaders and key decision-makers. King Hussein of Jordan came to the throne 45 years ago in 1952. President Hafez al-Assad of Syria has been in power since 1971, and the leaders of Libya, Oman, and the UAE have each been in power for over 25 years. Saddam Hussein has been president of Iraq since 1979 and was a key government figure even before he assumed that role. Hosni Mubarak became president of Egypt after Anwar Sadat's assassination in 1981, and King Fahd of Saudi Arabia rose to power in 1982. As Crown Prince, Fahd had been the Saudi decision-maker for seven years before his coronation. Even the Iranian revolution and its clerical regime are now [nearly 20] years old.

Compared with many other parts of the world, this is a picture of durability and stability to outsiders and residents alike. In South America, for instance, most countries changed not only leaders but governmental regimes during the 1980s and also introduced extensive changes in both economic and human rights policies. African nations typically face periodic coups, punctuated by civil or tribal wars. Even democratic Turkey had military coups in 1970 and 1980, although in both cases the military leaders returned the country to democracy after a few years.

What then makes the Middle East seem turbulent and politically unsettled? There are at least three reasons. First, there has been continued, although diminishing, official hostility toward Israel from most Arab states in the region and from revolutionary Iran since 1979. Syria, for example, is still formally at war with Israel. Much public resentment toward Israel persists among Arab populations, fed by Israel's occasional intransigence toward Palestinians, even while governments one by one slowly come to terms with Israel's existence.

Second, many states in the region have designs on their neighbors. In fact, only Jordan has settled borders. In addition to Palestinian territorial ambitions toward Israel and its occupied territories and Syrian concern over the Israeli-occupied Golan Heights, Iran and Iraq have ambitions of their own. Iran has sought to destabilize the regimes of several other countries and has occupied several islands in the Persian Gulf claimed by the UAE. Iraq has long coveted Kuwait, formally recognizing its borders with Kuwait in November 1994, but only after a test of wills with the United States in which Iraq provoked a preemptive U.S. military deployment by moving tanks, artillery, and other forces toward the Kuwaiti border. After the resumption of limited Iraqi oil exports in early 1997 under UN Resolution 986 relieved domestic economic pressure on

Saddam Hussein, he threatened to raise oil prices to Jordan if that country did not crack down on Iraqi opposition groups there. There is every reason to suspect that Hussein, subdued but unreconstructed, would move against Kuwait again if he thought he could do so with impunity. To complicate matters further, several countries are actively trying to develop weapons of mass destruction and the means to deliver them. As a result, many Middle Eastern governments feel threatened by their neighbors.

Third, some governments face strong and even violent dissent from their own citizens. All Middle Eastern governments except Israel's are in many respects authoritarian, with Syria and Iraq ruled by especially cruel and brutal dictators. Effective political opposition is not undertaken mainly by potential democrats and civil libertarians, but rather by religiously or ethnically motivated enemies of the existing regime. The rulers of Syria and Iraq are drawn from minorities of the population and have not hesitated to suppress opposition from other groups violently. Moreover, Islam as a religion and as a creed for political organization holds political rulers accountable to the rule of law as well as to specific religious injunctions on behavior. Rulers that deviate from acceptable behavior, therefore, risk religious wrath, and authoritarian regimes provide no peaceful outlet for this dissatisfaction, although Jordan's parliament is beginning to address this problem. The clerical regime in Iran faces the age-old tension between Islamic severity and Persian indulgence, as well as tensions with Iranians who wish to be part of the modernizing world.

During the next decade, several Middle Eastern countries will face acute problems of succession. Since today's rulers have often successfully avoided cultivating potential political rivals, they have few capable potential successors. Assad of Syria . . . , Mubarak of Egypt, Muammar al-Qaddafi of Libya, and Hussein of Iraq all lack designated or competent successors. As these regimes come to an end, serious, perhaps violent, struggles for power will occur in these countries. In contrast, democratic Israel, clerical Iran, and most of the kingdoms have regular and accepted processes for succession, with royal succession perhaps being the smoothest and least disruptive.

It is important to recognize that tensions within the region will not disappear even with a complete and amicable settlement of the Arab-Israeli disputes and a formal conclusion of the peace process. Paradoxically, disagreements with Israel provided some common cause for Arab states and permitted them to submerge other fundamental differences among them. But territorial disputes and societal discontent will not disappear with a peace agreement, and Arab-Israeli discussions will probably make only fitful progress over the next two decades, so that the issue will also continue to nag at the region.

It is also worth noting that the Persian Gulf is embedded in a larger region of tension and potential for violent conflict. Mutual suspicion between Greece and Turkey periodically threatens to break into open hostility, with Cyprus as a focal point. So far, this has been prevented by their joint membership in the

North Atlantic Treaty Organization (NATO) and ties with the United States. Further to the East, the Kashmiri problem entered its fiftieth year in 1997, with no hint of a process that could lead to its resolution. While neither India nor Pakistan wants war, their mutual suspicions could result in a fatal miscalculation. Afghanistan remains embroiled in civil war, as does Tajikistan of the former Soviet Union. Conflicts in the neighborhood could embroil countries in the oil-exporting Persian Gulf, at least indirectly, if oil exporters are tempted or expected to provide financial support to one of the antagonists. While this remains a risk, the distances involved are substantial—Kuwait is about as far from Karachi and from Istanbul as Boston is from Miami—and disruption to oil flow is possible but unlikely.

INCENTIVES AND INTERDEPENDENCY

Despite the potential for instability, oil producers have little incentive to disrupt production and will likely try to limit any interruption to oil flows. Oil accounts for over 85 percent of the export earnings of most of the Gulf countries, except for Qatar, where oil accounts for 75 percent of export earnings. More significantly, oil sales account for three-quarters or more of government revenues since the oil is owned by the state in all these countries. Imports, especially food imports, are critical to maintaining the living standards of the populations. The governments of these countries are therefore vitally dependent on their oil exports for the well-being of their citizens and for their own survival. To a high degree, the interests of oil-exporting countries and those of oil-importing countries converge: the latter badly need oil, and the former badly need the revenue from its sale. The two groups have a common interest in maintaining a steady flow of oil into world markets. When Iraq invaded Kuwait in 1990, its primary objective was to seize the revenues from Kuwait's oil production (and perhaps Kuwait's large overseas assets as well), not to throttle the production of Kuwaiti oil. If successful, however, Iraq probably would have intimidated Saudi Arabia into cutting back production enough to raise the world price from the then-prevailing U.S.$18 a barrel to, perhaps, U.S.$25 a barrel.

The interests of oil producers and consumers, however, are not perfectly aligned concerning oil prices. Here there is some divergence of interest between importers and exporters, but, more importantly, among oil exporters themselves. Saudi Arabia, Kuwait, and the UAE have very large proven and probable oil reserves, 90 to 150 times their current annual production. Iraq and Iran have somewhat smaller oil reserves relative to normal production, although Iran has very large reserves of natural gas.

The consequence of these divergent reserve-to-production ratios is that Iraq and, especially, Iran have a greater interest in higher oil prices than do other, larger-scale producers. Of course, all producers can gain through higher prices in the short run, and these countries' financially-strapped ministries of finance welcomed the price increase of late 1996. Given the heavy world dependence on Persian Gulf oil expected in the next two decades, Persian Gulf producers could raise prices in the short run if they all acted together to cut back on production. However, cooperation among these states has proven difficult since each wants the others to bear the burden of restricted output.

Furthermore, the lesson of the 1973 OPEC decision, led by the Shah of Iran, to triple oil prices has not been lost on those with large oil reserves: while the revenue gains were large in the first few years, this price increase not only generated a world recession but also induced extensive energy conservation, which is still proceeding over 20 years later. Technologies stimulated by the high oil prices of the seventies are still being installed as old equipment and buildings are gradually replaced by newer, more energy-efficient variants. Countries with large oil reserves fear a decline in the value of those reserves if effective substitutes for oil are found and therefore desire relatively stable but remunerative prices, low enough to inhibit the development of higher-cost, alternative sources of oil supply as well as energy-saving innovations. However, these processes of induced innovation and replacement of existing capital take a long time; countries with relatively low reserves have everything to gain by high prices in the short run, provided that other countries restrain production to achieve them.

To increase oil production by 18 mmbd over the next two decades will require a great deal of investment by Persian Gulf countries in oil well development and infrastructure for collection and shipment. Will those countries undertake the requisite investment in time? All these countries are experiencing rapid population growth with few opportunities for productive employment. At 3.6 percent a year, Iraq and Saudi Arabia have among the highest population growth rates in the world. Oil revenue is desperately needed to provide for increased housing, education, fresh water and sanitary facilities, as well as for employment. This will encourage these countries to invest in increased production capacity if they believe that doing so will allow them to sell more oil. As long as political stability seems likely, these states can borrow the necessary funds in world capital markets against future oil revenues.

For these reasons, Persian Gulf governments are unlikely to disrupt the flow of oil deliberately. There is one possible exception: as suggested above, Iran would welcome much higher oil prices if they could be brought about without restricting Iranian oil production—that is, by restricting production in Saudi Arabia, Kuwait, the UAE, or Iraq instead. To achieve this, Iran could perhaps harness Shi'i oil workers in eastern Saudi Arabia. This minority in a predominately and emphatically Sunni country could be encouraged to strike or riot on either religious or political grounds. The much higher percentage of foreign oil workers in Kuwait and the UAE make successful agitation in those countries less likely. Such a possibility is of concern to the Saudi Arabian government and has led it to adopt stringent security measures against possible Iranian subversion as well as political and religious policies aimed at minimizing potential dissidence among Shi'i Arabs.

THE WRENCH IN THE PIPELINE

Although most governments are unlikely to disrupt the flow of oil, non-state actors or governments that perceive that they have nothing to lose can significantly interfere with the flow of oil from the Persian Gulf. There are two sources of exit for Persian Gulf oil. One is through pipelines to loading terminals in the Gulf and then to tankers which exit through the Strait of Hormuz. The other is through pipelines to loading terminals on the Red Sea in Saudi Arabia or the Mediterranean Sea in Turkey. Before reaching the loading terminals, the oil must be gathered from disparate oil fields and separated from gas and other unwanted materials. There are four potential bottlenecks at which oil flow could be disrupted: gas-oil separators (large, expensive pieces of equipment), pipelines to terminals, large loading terminals (which are relatively few in number), and the Strait of Hormuz. For oil pumped to the Red Sea, the Suez Canal might seem to be a significant bottleneck. Ironically, the closure of the Suez Canal for the 15 years following 1967 encouraged the use of supertankers, which are too large to use the Suez Canal but offer cost-effective transportation. Since these vessels do not use the Suez Canal, blockage of the Suez Canal would have only limited impact on oil markets. Furthermore, the most rapidly growing markets for oil will be in Asia, and tankers destined for ports there can exit the Red Sea to the south without using the Suez Canal.

Gas-oil separators are highly specialized and expensive machines with long procurement lead times. A loss could be significant but can be avoided by installing excess capacity and pre-ordering spare machines, as Saudi Arabia has allegedly done. Pipelines are long and vulnerable and can be cut without too much difficulty. But they are just as easy to repair. Loading terminals are robust and relatively easy to protect physically against major raids, except raids by a well-armed foreign power. Of course, successful protective, preventive, and remedial measures require that a government is effectively in charge. As noted, governments have a strong interest in maintaining the flow of revenue from oil. By the same token, however, well-organized dissident groups may wish to deny revenue to the government. Civil war or even major and persistent guerrilla actions could be highly disruptive, but they are also highly unlikely during the coming decade. As long as the region remains politically stable, major disruptions will be difficult to effect. Should that stability erode, gas-oil separators, pipelines, and loading facilities become significantly more vulnerable.

Interfering with the flow of oil through the Strait of Hormuz would require significant effort. Despite its constrictive appearance on a map of the world, it is not a small body of water. The Strait is about 35 miles wide at its narrowest point (twice the width of the English Channel) and exceeds 45 meters in depth through most of its width, sloping gradually from the Iranian side to over 200 meters deep off the coast of Oman. The two traffic channels—one for incoming vessels, the other for outgoing, separated by two miles and each two miles wide—lie wholly within the territorial waters of

Oman at the narrowest point of the Strait. In the mid–1990s, traffic averaged around 60 ships a day, roughly one-quarter of which were tankers. While this is heavy traffic, it is only one-third of the traffic which passes through the slightly narrower Strait of Malacca, and somewhat lighter than the traffic through the much narrower Bosporus.

The Strait of Hormuz is thus much too large and too deep to be physically blocked, as the Suez Canal was in 1967. Shipping could, however, be attacked by military forces, and the Strait could be mined by a national power of some means. Iran is establishing the means by which to do both. In addition to a formidable air force, Iran has acquired two Kilo-class submarines from Russia and has two more on order. It has also acquired land-based silkworm missiles from China and has located them near the Strait. Iran mined the Persian Gulf during the 1980–88 Iran-Iraq war, especially after Iraqi planes attacked its off-shore oil-loading terminals, and presumably maintains a large inventory of mines.

Such actions in the Strait of Hormuz—in the territorial waters of Oman—would be an act of war. Conceivably, Iran could deny responsibility for mine explosions that damaged one or several ships. It could even feign participation in mine searches. The presence of mines would inhibit commercial shipping, and insurance rates on Gulf-bound vessels would rise substantially, perhaps prohibitively. Some disruption could be caused, although, short of war, the disruption would be strictly temporary. Even in the event of war, the Strait could be made safe for navigation in a few weeks if U.S. forces were engaged to do so. Furthermore, it must be kept in mind that Iran has no immediate interest in preventing oil from being shipped out of the Persian Gulf—or merchant goods from being shipped into the Gulf—since it is highly dependent on both the oil revenues and the imported goods. An attempt by Iran to block the Strait of Hormuz would be an act of desperation, induced only by extreme provocation, such as an attempted embargo or blockade.

APPROACH, ASSIST, AND DIVERSIFY

What can the rest of the world, and the United States in particular, do to reduce its vulnerability to disruptions in the supply of Persian Gulf oil, on which the world will become increasingly dependent over the next few decades? First, it can avoid isolating Iran to the point where mining the Strait of Hormuz would become tempting to Iran. Second, it can help Saudi Arabia to secure its physical facilities, encourage the installation of some excess capacity, and perhaps even share some of that cost. Third, it can continue to diversify sources of energy, through a vigorous program of research to improve energy efficiency and to develop economic alternatives to oil as a fuel for motive transportation.

Fourth, the United States can continue to develop sources of oil other than the Persian Gulf. This is partly a question of developing new technologies to open up hitherto inaccessible areas, such as deep-water continental shelves, and to improve extraction rates from existing wells. It is also a question of political and economic steps to open up known economic sources of oil, of which the Caspian Sea region is the most promising. Caspian oil and gas deposits are extensive, and might be possible to extract them economically, but they are far from major markets and even export through pipelines will be expensive.

Ironically, the most economic route for a pipeline might be through Iran to the Persian Gulf. That obviously would not reduce dependence on the Gulf region. Alternatives involve pipelines through Russia or Georgia to the Black Sea, increasing congestion in the narrow Bosporus, or through Armenia or Iran and Turkey to the Mediterranean. Russian domestic and international politics provide the major near-term obstacle to finding an acceptable route, but that problem will presumably be solved in the next several years. Ultimately the Caspian region—Turkmenistan, Kazakhstan, and Azerbaijan— could produce as much as 6 mmbd of oil, contributing considerably to the growing world demand for oil.

Fifth, the International Energy Agency should maintain its emergency oil sharing plans, which *inter alia* involve the requirement that members (basically Europe, North America, and Japan) maintain oil stocks equal to at least 90 days of imports. A major component of this is the U.S. Strategic Petroleum Reserve (SPR), which at the end of 1996 stood at 564 million barrels, down 28 million barrels from the previous year. It would be a mistake to sell off more SPR oil for transitory budgetary gains just as the world is once again entering a period of tight oil markets and rapidly growing demand for oil.

The interests of oil producers in the Middle East and oil-consuming nations are fundamentally aligned. There is no incentive for the governments of the region to constrict supply or interfere with global energy markets. Furthermore, the Middle East is far more stable than is commonly assumed. Despite these compelling reasons for calm with respect to the stability of Middle Eastern energy supplies, Middle Eastern oil production facilities, pipelines, and shipping channels are quite vulnerable both to non-state actors and to regional powers, should they choose to interfere. As the world becomes increasingly dependent on Middle Eastern oil, it is critical that importing nations begin laying the groundwork for future stability by working to improve relations with supplying countries, protecting oil facilities in the region, and developing other energy resources.

18. U.S.–MEXICO: OPEN MARKETS, CLOSED BORDER

Peter Andreas

*F*ree market reform and economic integration are celebrated themes across the Americas. But while the hemisphere is embracing a common vision of an unregulated free trade zone, two of Latin America's leading exports remain those most strictly regulated by the United States: illegal drugs and migrant workers. Indeed, U.S. import restrictions on these goods (or "bads," depending on one's perspective) are increasing in the form of more policing. Despite the advice of otherwise influential free market proponents, . . . the political logic of criminalization continues to trump the economic logic of liberalization.

However, the awkward and often overlooked predicament facing U.S. policymakers is that their promotion of borderless economies based on free market principles in many ways contradicts and undermines their efforts to keep borders closed to the clandestine movement of drugs and migrant labor. The unleashing of market forces—the loosening of government controls over the flow of goods, services, information, and capital—has unintentionally encouraged and facilitated not only legal economic activity but illegal activity as well. As all forms of cross-border exchange have become more extensive and intensive in recent years, so too have U.S. law enforcement efforts to weed out the illicit from the licit. Thus, even as free market reforms push for shrinking the regulatory state, market prohibitions push for expanding the policing dimensions of the state.

This trend is most striking along the 1,951-mile U.S.–Mexican border, where the United States is moving both to open the border to the legal flow of goods and to close the border to the illegal flow of drugs and migrant labor. On the one hand the border is being liberalized, but on the other hand it is being fortified—not to deter invading armies (the traditional function of border fortifications) but to deter a perceived invasion of "undesirables." . . . "After years of neglect, this administration has taken a strong stand to stiffen the protection of our borders," declared President Bill Clinton in his 1996 State of the Union address, adding, "We are increasing border controls by 50 percent." Thus, even as old barriers between the United States and Mexico are torn down and the two nations are drawn closer together, new barriers are rapidly being built up to keep them apart.

The simultaneous opening and closing of the southwest border is part of a larger transformation of inter-American relations in the post–Cold War era. Much of U.S. policy toward its southern neighbors can be characterized as driven by two agendas: promoting free market reforms and enforcing market prohibitions. In practice, this means tightening controls over prohibited cross-border economic flows even while trying to create a borderless free trade area. Jonathan Winer, the deputy assistant secretary of state for law enforcement and crime, has advocated such increased regulation: "Every country must develop tough new policies aimed at restoring its borders so that they are again meaningful protection against criminals, drugs, weapons, and illegal immigration."

U.S. drug and immigration control strategies focus primarily on curbing the foreign supply and secondarily on targeting the sources of demand: consumers of drugs and employers of migrant workers. In other words, confronting the demand side of the problem—America's dependence on both psychoactive substances and cheap labor—takes a back seat to supply-side law enforcement initiatives.

Rising alarm over the clandestine influx of drugs and people is promoting a fusion between U.S. national security and law enforcement missions. The Defense Department has taken on important policing tasks (particularly drug interdiction), the National Security Council now oversees efforts to deter alien smuggling, and the intelligence agencies are elevating drug trafficking and other forms of transnational crime to the top of their agendas. Perhaps as a symbolic sign of the times, President Clinton . . . even appointed a retired military general as the nation's new "drug czar."

Heightened concern over illegal cross-border activity is, of course, partly driven by the scramble by various U.S. agencies for new missions in the post–Cold War security environment. Between the early 1980s and the early 1990s, the Pentagon underwent a metamorphosis, transforming itself from a reluctant ally on the sidelines of the U.S. antidrug campaign to a frontline participant. Similarly, the CIA has begun to overcome its traditional inhibitions toward engaging in law enforcement–related work. Facing sharp budget cuts, the State Department is trumpeting its leadership role in an expanding global law enforcement campaign.

But these changes are not merely a product of bureaucratic opportunism. They are also an attempt to pacify rising domestic anxieties. Foreign policy priorities have clearly shifted in the public's mind. In a Gallup poll commissioned by the Chicago Council on Foreign Relations in late 1994, respondents were asked to rank 16 foreign policy goals by their order of importance. Curbing the flow of illegal drugs into the United States was the first priority of 89 percent of those polled. This was followed by protecting the jobs of U.S. workers (83 percent), preventing the spread of nuclear weapons (82 percent), and curbing illegal immigration (72 percent).

While drug trafficking and illegal immigration have long been U.S. policy concerns, it is only in recent years that they have arguably become the defining source of tension for U.S.–Latin American relations. During the Cold War, controlling the spread of communist insurgents preoccupied U.S. leaders. In post–Cold War relations, however, the degree of conflict or harmony depends to an important extent on how clandestine drug and migration flows are managed politically. Just as politicians in earlier years did not want to appear "soft on communism," in today's political climate they do not want to appear "soft on drugs" or "soft on illegal immigrants." Consequently, relations between the United States and many countries in the region are "narcotized," as foreign aid and diplomatic favor are tied to compliance with U.S. drug control objectives. Similarly, fears of uncontrollable waves of immigrants play an increasingly pivotal role in U.S. foreign policy toward its southern neighbors.

At the same time, illegal drugs and migrant labor are key exports for many countries in the region. During a period when the value of traditional exports is fluctuating, illegal drugs and migrant labor are a vital source of revenue for many debt-burdened economies. Moreover, labor migration and the drug trade help cushion the unemployment crisis across the region, providing an underground exit option for millions of impoverished workers.

Even as the United States pushes to expand the role of market forces and the private sector throughout the hemisphere, the sobering reality is that the drug export industry is a leading market force and an integral component of the private sector in many countries. Indeed, the drug trade is in many ways the quintessential expression of the kind of rugged, high-risk entrepreneurialism advocated by U.S. free market proponents. In a number of countries, the drug export sector is fully integrated into the national economy, and it is this sector that is most dynamic and responsive to global market demands.

The export of both drugs and migrant labor are profoundly affected by the market-based reforms that are sweeping the region. This can be partly explained by simple economic logic: Opening economies through market liberalization reduces the ability of governments to withstand external market pressures, and the enormous demand for illegal drugs and migrant labor in the United States is no exception. After all, countries that follow the tenets of neoclassical economic theory should specialize in those exports in which they have a comparative advantage. This means that the market niche of some countries is the exportation of illegal drugs and migrant labor. This is strikingly evident in the case of Mexico.

THE CLANDESTINE SIDE OF INTEGRATION

The illegal flow of drugs and migrant labor is a significant part of the cross-border economic relationship between the United States and Mexico. While rarely discussed in official policy debates, free market reforms and economic integration have fueled both legal and *illegal* economic flows. This is not to suggest that market reform and integration are somehow the underlying cause of these flows. However, they do in some ways unintentionally facilitate and encourage such clandestine forms of exchange.

The Drug Trade

While Mexico has long been enmeshed in the drug trade, the nature and scope of its involvement have undergone a transformation in the last decade. Most significant is Mexico's emergence as the primary shipping point for Colombian cocaine into the United States. The State Department estimates that the percentage of the cocaine bound for the U.S. market entering through Mexico was negligible during the mid-1980s but had increased to as much as 70 percent by 1995. According to a March 1996 State Department report, Mexico also supplies about 20 to 30 percent of the heroin consumed in the United States and up to 80 percent of the imported marijuana. In addition, the Drug Enforcement Administration (DEA) claims that Mexican traffickers have virtually taken over the expanding U.S. market for methamphetamines. The DEA estimates that Mexico earns more than $7 billion a year from the illegal drug trade. Some Mexican estimates place the figure much higher. The prosecutor general's office estimates that drug traffickers operating in Mexico accumulated revenues of approximately $30 billion in 1994.

Mexico's growing role in the drug trade has significantly increased the power and wealth of Mexico's trafficking organizations, which in turn has acutely exacerbated already well-entrenched problems of political corruption. Corrupt officials sell an essential service to drug traffickers: the nonenforcement of the law. Not surprisingly, as Mexico's role in the illicit drug trade has grown, so too has the buying off of law enforcement—not only within Mexico, but on the U.S. side as well. Not coincidentally, Mexico's expanding role in the drug trade parallels the opening of the Mexican economy and the deepening of U.S.–Mexican economic integration. The drug export sector, it seems, is an unintended beneficiary of these economic changes.

Colombian cocaine traffickers began turning to Mexico as a major entry point to the U.S. market in the early 1980s after the United States cracked down on cocaine shipping through the Caribbean. A strategic alliance has developed between Colombian and Mexican trafficking groups. The Colombians process the cocaine and ship it to Mexico, and the Mexicans specialize in smuggling it into the United States. In addition to Mexico's geographical advantage, increasing economic ties between Mexico and Colombia and between Mexico and the United States make the country an ideal transshipment point. Mexican imports of legal goods from Colombia increased from $17 million in 1980 to $121 million in 1985 (at the same time, Mexican imports from the rest of Latin America decreased from $768 million to $630 million). According to political scientist Richard Friman, expanding trade between Mexico and Colombia helped establish broad economic linkages within which illegal trade could be hidden. The U.S. cocaine market, in turn, became even easier to penetrate as economic ties between the United States and Mexico expanded. Legal exports from Mexico to the United States doubled between 1986 and 1993. Hiding drug shipments within the growing volume of goods exported from Mexico to the United States has become an increasingly favored method of smuggling cocaine.

These trends thrive under the North American Free Trade Agreement (NAFTA). A report written by an intelligence officer at the U.S. embassy in Mexico City claims that cocaine traffickers have established factories, warehouses, and trucking companies as fronts in Mexico in anticipation of the boom in cross-border commerce under NAFTA. As Assistant U.S. Attorney Glenn MacTaggart said, "If NAFTA provides opportunity for legitimate businesses, it may clearly provide opportunities for illegitimate businessmen."

Trucking provides the most concrete illustration of this trend. According to one senior customs official, to inspect every truck coming across the border would create a traffic jam all the way to Mexico City. To avoid hampering commerce, only a small percentage of trucks are fully inspected. Under the NAFTA agreement, trucking into the United States from Mexico is increasing rapidly. In 1994, 2.8 million trucks crossed over from Mexico. In 1993, on the eve of NAFTA, the number was 1.9 million. The U.S. Southwest Border Capital Improvement Program will improve the road network so that it will be able to handle more than double today's traffic level—as many as 8.4 million trucks annually.

Mexican truckers will soon be allowed to operate throughout the border states of Arizona, California, New Mexico, and Texas, and they will eventually be able to travel anywhere in the United States and Canada. Trucks can carry illegal goods as easily as legal goods. . . . Most regulations on trucking in Mexico have been lifted since 1989, allowing licensed trucks to move without inspection throughout the country. . . .

Concerns about drug control were not discussed during the negotiations over NAFTA. "This was in the 'too hot to handle' category," notes Gary Hufbauer, an economist at the Institute for International Economics in Washington, D.C. Reportedly, U.S. customs and drug enforcement personnel openly call NAFTA the "North American Drug Trade Agreement."

While trade liberalization and economic integration help Mexico's traffickers penetrate the U.S. market, the privatization of state-owned enterprises and the deregulation of the Mexican banking system facilitate the laundering of their drug profits. As the *Economist Intelligence Unit* notes, "Liberalization of the Mexican financial services sector and capital markets in recent years has provided opportunities for money-laundering and the investment of the illicit gains from the drugs trade." According to James Moody of the FBI, many of the state-owned companies privatized under the Salinas administration were bought by drug traffickers. The purchase of state-owned enterprises not only facilitates the laundering of drug profits but also provides an influx of dollars for the cash-hungry banking system.

Meanwhile, the liberalization of agriculture and the cutting of government subsidies in rural areas are increasing the incentive for peasant farmers to produce illegal crops such as marijuana. As one group of researchers concluded in their study, *Crossing the Line,* "social disruption and economic pressure from free-market reforms have intensified in rural areas, fueling the tendency to grow illicit crops as a household survival strategy." . . .

Illegal Labor Migration

Roughly 1.6 million Mexicans reside illegally in the United States. While 1 to 3 million Mexicans enter the United States illegally each year, only about 100,000 are believed to stay permanently. Most come for temporary employment. Mass labor migration from Mexico is a long-established pattern, arising from a variety of push-and-pull factors that date back to the nineteenth century. More recently, however, the pattern of labor migration has been reinforced by the opening of the Mexican economy and growing U.S.–Mexican economic integration.

U.S. officials have long maintained that increased economic linkages between the United States and Mexico help curb migration. Yet these linkages have often had the opposite effect. The border industrialization program that began in the 1960s led to a proliferation of export assembly plants in Mexico. Rather than deterring migration as U.S. officials had promised, the program has encouraged migration from the interior of Mexico to the border, which in turn has led to increased migration to the United States. Many illegal immigrants who enter the United States from Mexico are essentially unintended imports from this duty-free export-processing zone. The border export-processing industry has experienced particularly rapid growth in recent years. For example, the number of factories along the California-Mexico border (called *maquiladoras*) has quadrupled in the last decade. The end result, as migration specialist Saskia Sassen points out, is that "the *maquila* program has consolidated a transnational border economy, within which trade, investment, and people move rather freely."

NAFTA is not a major departure from the past, but instead reinforces and institutionalizes these already well-established cross-border economic ties. The border region in particular is expected to experience significant economic expansion in coming years. If previous experience is any indication, this should encourage more migration from Mexico's interior to the border, which in turn will serve as a springboard into the United States.

Concerns over labor migration were deliberately excluded from the NAFTA negotiations. In the campaign to sell the trade agreement domestically, U.S. officials argued that NAFTA would promote U.S. immigration-control objectives.

Attorney General [Janet] Reno even warned that if NAFTA was not passed, "effective immigration control [would] become impossible."

Yet even those migration specialists who argue that the trade pact will likely help curb illegal immigration in the long term, due to NAFTA-induced economic development in Mexico, concede that NAFTA will probably stimulate more migration in the short and medium term. . . . Numerous studies suggest that the combination of NAFTA and Mexico's own domestic free market reforms will add, at least through the end of the decade, as many as several hundred thousand to the number of Mexicans who migrate to the United States annually. This, in turn, will strengthen the already extensive cross-border migration networks that are so crucial as a social base and bridge for new arrivals. In other words, migration is a cumulative process: Future migrants will build on the settlement networks and job contacts established before them. Consequently, even the anticipated long-term reduction of migration due to NAFTA-created jobs remains questionable.

The liberalization of Mexican agriculture is a particularly important stimulus for increased migration. A study by migration specialists Raúl Hinojosa Ojeda and Sherman Robinson suggests that NAFTA will lead to the uprooting of about 1.4 million Mexicans from the countryside. This rural exodus is due to Mexican agricultural reforms and the liberalization of trade. Between 30 and 50 percent of all Mexican workdays in agriculture are devoted to corn and bean cultivation. Since the United States produces both crops more cheaply, the phased-in liberalization of agriculture under NAFTA will lead to a growing influx of U.S. imports (agricultural exports to Mexico increased 38 percent in NAFTA's first year). Of those peasant farmers expected to be displaced, Hinojosa Ojeda and Robinson calculate that 800,000 will remain in Mexico and 600,000 will migrate illegally to the United States over a 5- to 10-year period.

These trends are exacerbated by the fact that, since the late 1980s, Mexico has been reducing electricity, fertilizer, water, and credit subsidies to peasant farmers. Price supports for crops, which have traditionally helped to inhibit rural migration, have also been cut. Moreover, restrictions on the sale of communal farm lands—about 70 percent of Mexico's cropland and one-half of its irrigated land—have been lifted. While the government initiated a 15-year direct income-subsidy program in late 1993 for producers of corn and other basic crops, this has primarily served as a limited form of welfare rather than providing the kind of public investment (affordable credit, crop insurance, and infrastructural improvements such as irrigation and drainage) necessary to modernize Mexican agriculture and make small-scale farmers more productive and competitive.

These sweeping changes in the countryside typically uproot peasants from traditional modes of existence and can stimulate a mass exodus from the land. Nearly 30 percent of the country's 93 million inhabitants make their living in agriculture. Luis Tellez, the former undersecretary for planning in Mexico's Ministry of Agriculture and Hydraulic Resources, estimates that 1 million peasants are likely to leave the land every year and that as many as 15 million peasants will leave agriculture in the next decade or two. While it is impossible to know exactly how many will end up crossing the northern border, this will understandably be a logical option for some. This is especially likely given that U.S. labor projections for the next decade show some of the fastest growth sectors will likely add the same low-skill, low-paying jobs that have attracted migrant workers.

Not only does economic liberalization end up fueling migration, but exporting part of the country's growing unemployment burden provides an important cushion for the Mexican government as it carries out its economic reform program and struggles to recover from the devastating economic crisis sparked by the collapse of the peso. The Mexican economy shrank 6 percent and lost 1 million jobs in 1995. Some estimate that one-fifth of the total Mexican workforce is employed in the United States. Remittances from Mexican migrants total an estimated $3 billion annually, making them one of the country's leading sources of revenue.

BARRICADING THE BORDER

As economic integration—both legal and illegal—between the United States and Mexico has deepened and spread, so too has U.S. border policing. Between 1990 and 1996, there has been a 65 percent increase in the number of agents and an 89 percent increase in the number of support staff for the Border Patrol along the southwest border. . . .

The U.S. Customs Service is also reasserting its presence along the border. For example, it reportedly spent $350 million to improve and update facilities on the southwest border and sent almost 1,000 additional inspectors there between 1989 and 1993. And in February 1995, customs announced as much as a 20 percent increase in resources devoted to inspecting cross-border traffic as part of an initiative along the U.S.–Mexican border called Operation Hard Line. "We intend to blitz this border with Operation Hard Line," said Commissioner of the U.S. Customs Service George Weise, adding, "This is a war."

To help filter out illegal cross-border activity, border control strategists are developing an elaborate net of state-of-the-art electronic surveillance technology. Alan Bersin, the U.S. attorney for the Southern District of California, explains that the border has two purposes: "On the one hand, it is intended to facilitate trade in order to bring our nation the significant benefits of international commerce and industry. At the same time, it is geared to constrain and regulate the free movement of people and goods in order to block the entry of illegal migrants and unlawful merchandise." According to Bersin, "the key to resolving these apparently contradictory purposes lies in the strategic application of modem technology. We can and must have a border that is both secure and business-friendly." . . .

U.S. border control strategists are increasingly turning to technologies and equipment designed initially for military purposes. Magnetic footfall detectors and infrared body sensors, originally used in Southeast Asia, are scattered along the more remote stretches of the border. Along the border south of San Diego, Army reservists have constructed a 10-foot-high steel wall made up of 180,000 metal sheets originally designed to create temporary landing fields in the desert during the Persian Gulf war. Mexicans call it the "iron curtain." Graffiti on the steel barricade reads "Welcome to the New Berlin Wall."

Experimental technologies developed for the Army and the CIA are now being tested for border enforcement. For example, the Border Patrol is evaluating a photo-identification system developed by Hughes Aircraft. . . . Other devices include an electric current that stops a fleeing car, a camera that can see into vehicles for hidden passengers, an ion scanner designed to detect hidden drugs, and a computer that checks commuters by voiceprint. . . .

The tightening of border controls also involves growing links between the military and law enforcement. Strict rules against the use of the military for law enforcement functions have gradually been loosened since the early 1980s.

Military personnel on the border are used for support activities, such as surveillance and intelligence, communications, cargo inspection, road repair, fence construction, and training. . . . Military equipment, such as helicopters and interceptor and radar planes (including AWACS), has also been provided for the border interdiction campaign. In some cases, the drug war is aided by Cold War leftovers. For example, the North American Aerospace Defense Command, which was originally created to track incoming Soviet missiles and bombers, has redirected some of its activities toward targeting drug smugglers.

Yet despite the rapid buildup of border policing, many clandestine border-crossers are adapting rather than being deterred. As border controls are tightened, migrants increasingly rely on professional people-smugglers, or "coyotes," who take them across the border for a fee. Forcing migrants to depend on smugglers is creating a highly profitable and increasingly sophisticated binational underground business in "human trafficking." As one Border Patrol agent puts it, "The more difficult the crossing, the better the business for the smugglers." Tactics by the border-enforcers—such as higher and more impenetrable fencing and more extensive and sophisticated surveillance technology—are countered with new tactics by the smugglers (entry through more remote points along the border, increased use of fraudulent border-crossing documents, and more payoffs to corrupt officials).

The interplay between law enforcement and law evasion thus fuels its own dynamic of escalation. For example, as a sign of U.S. resolve, in September 1993 the Border Patrol in El Paso, Texas, initiated "Operation Blockade" (later renamed "Operation Hold the Line"), in which 450 agents working overtime covered a 20-mile area of the border. Illegal border crossings there plummeted. The limits of such a Maginot-line strategy soon became clear: Suppressing the flow in one area simply redirected it elsewhere. . . . And so the game of cat-and-mouse continues, feeding the escalation of law enforcement.

Escalation is also driven by political logic: High-profile policing operations have powerful symbolic appeal and help appease domestic pressure to "do something." At the same time, they help sustain government programs struggling to preserve their funding in a period of austerity and slashed budgets. Law enforcement agencies, especially those charged with the missions of immigration and drug control, have been largely insulated from the current movement to roll back government and cut spending. The budget of the INS, for example, . . . increased by 72 percent between 1993 and 1996. Despite the otherwise tarnished image of "big government," there is broad political support for a highly interventionist state when it comes to controlling drugs and immigration.

COPING WITH U.S.–MEXICAN INTEGRATION

The enormous economic and political investment by both the United States and Mexico in the regional integration process suggests that their futures are inextricably intertwined. The question, therefore, is not whether U.S.–Mexican integration will deepen and expand but exactly how the process is regulated and managed. How harmonious or conflict-ridden this integration process will be depends to an important degree on how the issues of labor migration and drug trafficking are handled. Coping with these clandestine cross-border flows requires recognizing the unintended side-effects of free market reforms and economic integration.

This reality cannot be denied or defied simply by walling off the American Southwest. The building of new Berlin Walls may be politically popular, but it has a poisonous impact on the U.S.–Mexican relationship and may ultimately undermine many of the promised gains of economic integration. Consequently, even though conservative isolationists may claim otherwise, barricading the border and delinking the U.S. and Mexican economies are neither viable nor desirable policies. A fully militarized border would have an unacceptable impact on human rights and legitimate commerce. It would also be highly destabilizing to Mexico.

Dealing with Drugs

Our faith in law enforcement solutions perpetuates the myth that the problem is primarily one of stopping the foreign drug supply. Such faith also draws attention away from potentially more sensible alternatives. For example, in the case of curbing the demand for drugs, despite studies that show treatment to be more cost-effective—not to mention more humane—than international and border law enforcement, treatment remains severely underfunded. . . . Largely ignoring the social and economic conditions that lead so many Americans to abuse drugs, the U.S. approach to curbing the demand for drugs is primarily based on punitive measures: Large numbers of drug users are being locked up on drug possession charges, only to find that drugs are easily available and widely abused within the nation's prison system.

Changing course in drug policy requires redefining the problem as fundamentally a public health rather than a law enforcement and national security concern. . . .

Efforts to cut the foreign drug supply have a long history of failure. And the likelihood of success diminishes further as market liberalization and economic integration propel ever more extensive cross-border exchange. As the experience along the U.S.–Mexican border illustrates, trying to close the border to the flow of drugs while trying to open it to the flow of virtually everything else is a formula for frustration. . . .

Unfortunately, these realities tend to be overlooked and obscured in the official policy debate. Evaluations of free market reform are largely divorced and insulated from evaluations of drug market prohibition. Thus, congressional committees and government agencies endlessly debate how to attack the drug supply and gain greater cooperation from Mexico and other Latin American countries. State Department reports and congressional hearings continually track the amount of drugs interdicted and the number of traffickers arrested. Meanwhile, those concerned with the implementation of market-based reforms carefully monitor the debt service record, export earnings, inflation levels, and the pace of privatization in Mexico and other nations throughout the region. The reports they publish rarely even mention the drug trade, let alone discuss its ties to the formal economy and its contribution to foreign exchange reserves. It is as if drug trafficking were not an economic matter at all. But while such institutionalized denial may be politically convenient, it perpetuates both a fundamental misreading of the problem and unworkable strategies for dealing with it.

Managing Migration

Even as policymakers scramble to beef up border controls, little is being done to tame the powerful economic forces that drive so many Mexicans to illegally enter the United States. It is not that border enforcement is irrelevant; the Border Patrol is no doubt making life much harder for illegal border-crossers. But the underlying push-pull factors that motivate illegal labor migration remain stronger than ever. On the pull side, important sectors of the U.S. economy, such as agriculture and the garment industry, remain heavily dependent on illegal workers. While these workers live in increasing fear of law enforcement, the government crackdown is noticeably less focused on the employers who hire them. Employer sanctions are weak, poorly designed, and minimally enforced.

The first priority should be to raise and enforce labor standards. Genuine enforcement of existing workplace rules (for example, minimum wages, overtime, and environmental, health, and safety regulations) would make it more difficult for employers to engage in the extreme exploitation of workers, thus undermining their most important incentive to hire illegal labor. These efforts should especially target sweatshop employers, who are most notorious for their abuse of workers and disregard of labor standards. However modest the impact may be, an emphasis on raising labor standards by tightening work-place controls would go much further toward addressing the root of the problem than simply tightening border controls.

Domestic efforts on the pull side must be combined with initiatives to address the conditions in Mexico that push labor migration. Mexico, for example, could be encouraged to increase the minimum wage in an attempt (however modest) to begin narrowing the enormous wage gap between the two countries. This, of course, would require reversing the Mexican government's long history of suppressing wages and attempts at labor organization. The United States and Mexico could also work together to slow down the growth of the border region, since this area has traditionally served as a magnet for northward migration. Another possibility is for the United States to urge Mexico to more slowly carry out its agricultural reforms, which add millions of people to the potential migration flow. At the same time, through tax incentives and financial and technical assistance, the United States could help Mexico develop programs that promote the growth of small- and medium-scale labor-intensive industries in rural regions, where most job displacement is occurring. Such measures require active state intervention in managing the economic transition in the countryside rather than the current laissez-faire approach. So far, the Mexican government appears to have no plan for handling the millions of workers who are being displaced as a result of market reforms. The United States has an obvious interest in working closely with Mexico to devise and promote development strategies and safety nets that minimize the incentive for workers to move to "El Norte."

Multilateral institutions can also assist these efforts by incorporating migration concerns more centrally into their programs. There is little indication that the most influential of these organizations, the IMF and the World Bank, seriously consider migration issues in their policy decisions. Indeed, many of the market-based reforms they support end up fueling migration, at least in the short and medium term. The hope, of course, is that economic development will reduce migration pressures in the long term. But given the current state of the Mexican economy, the long term may be far into the next century. In the meantime, therefore, the difficult process of economic restructuring should be carefully managed to minimize and cope with the mass displacement of Mexican labor. This requires active government involvement rather than blind faith in market solutions—especially since the market solution tends to be to simply export much of the labor surplus to the United States.

These measures for coping with the less-celebrated and often overlooked side of U.S.–Mexican integration do not provide a definitive, quick-fix solution. They do, however, suggest some of the ways in which we can more effectively and humanely manage these cross-border problems. Real progress in this direction is impossible, however, as long as Washington's primary policy response continues to be escalation rather than reevaluation.

19. BACK TO BASICS: REASSESSING U.S. POLICY IN LATIN AMERICA

Howard J. Wiarda

*E*very once in a while, in foreign policy as well as in other policy and scholarly issues, it becomes necessary to go back to first principles, to reexamine
assumptions that have long been taken for granted. It is now time to do that
with regard to the assumptions underlying the so-called "Washington Consensus" on U.S. policy toward Latin America, which holds that the United
States should promote democracy, open markets, free trade, and counter-
narcotics activities in the region.

The issue is complicated by the fact that few of us disagree with these policy goals per se. To be opposed to democracy, open markets, free trade, and
counter-narcotics would be akin to being against God, motherhood, and
apple pie—assuming we still believe in these latter items. The issues are thus
mainly of shadings, nuance, meanings, as well as the ever-present traps posed
by the ingrained Wilsonian missionary urge to bring the blessings of American civilization to "less-fortunate" peoples. The issue relates also to the
deeper difficulty the United States has in understanding and empathizing with
other countries.

Roughly twenty years—from the end of the Alliance for Progress in the
late 1960s to Bush's Enterprise of the Americas initiative in the early 1990s—
have been expended in arriving at the now-accepted consensus, and although
it is difficult to rethink policy assumptions, especially after so much bureaucratic effort and time have been invested, it must be done to avoid even more
difficult problems later on. Such exercises have a certain history; in time policymakers reexamined President Kennedy's fabled Alliance for Progress initiative and abandoned it after concluding that the assumptions on which it was
based may have been wrong in the first place. Policymakers must reexamine
U.S. policy toward Latin America, and they must do so very carefully,

because the assumptions upon which the policies has been based go to the core of our beliefs as scholars and citizens and to the heart of what the United States stands for as a nation.

THE DEMOCRACY INITIATIVE

It is often noted that 19 of the 20 Latin American countries (all except Cuba) are now democratic. In policy circles that is often as far as the discussion goes, the presumption being that we are all agreed on what democracy means and that there is a worldwide and unilinear progression to a U.S.–style system of government. This is a happy and optimistic scenario, but it leaves a lot of questions unanswered.

Do Latin Americans want democracy, and, if so, how badly? Do they want democracy as badly as we want it for them and, if not, isn't that a problem? Twenty years ago, when the enthusiasm for Latin America's newly established democracies was at its height, 85–90 percent of the population saw democracy as the only legitimate form of government. Now, since democracy has failed to deliver the expected goods and services, disillusionment has set in, and in key countries like Venezuela support for democracy is down to a dangerously low 60 percent.

Another question that arises is this: do Latin Americans mean the same thing by democracy as we do? At some levels yes, at others no. Everyone agrees that the human rights situation in Latin America is much better now than it was under military dictatorships, and even the Latin American left tends to think that "mere" formal democracy is better than authoritarianism. But the same public opinion surveys mentioned above indicate that Latin Americans have little support for liberal pluralism, with only about 25–30 percent supporting parties (any party) and only 15–20 percent supporting labor unions (any union). Democracy in these surveys means "strong government" (60–65 percent), patronage (in Brazil), or welfare (in Uruguay). Latin American majorities opt for elected but strong, nationalistic, statist, organic, corporatist regimes. None of these figures or definitions augurs well for liberal, Lockean, pluralist democracies in the American world.

Indeed, this meaning of democracy is closer to the historical Latin American and Rousseauian tradition of centralized, organic, top-down, corporatist democracy than it is to American-style pluralism with its checks and balances. And the presidents who almost personify these values—Rafael Caldera in Venezuela, Alberto Fujimori in Peru, former president Joaquín Balaguer in the Dominican Republic—are precisely the ones under criticism in the United States for *not* following the U.S. political and/or economic model. Not only do we in the United States have different conceptions of democracy, but this difference is leading to policy conflicts as well.

The growing disillusionment with democracy and the sense that democracy in Latin America is not working as well as it should force us to rethink earlier policy assumptions. Not unexpectedly, the region is now back in a situation of democracy with adjectives: guided democracy, limited democracy, tutelary democracy, delegated democracy. Hence U.S. policymakers need to think not of some either-or, unilinear, and inevitable progression toward U.S.–style democracy but of a *continuum* of regimes strung out between authoritarianism and democracy, with *multiple* starting points, multiple routes to get there, and a variety of democratic endpoints. It is unclear whether or not U.S. policymakers have either the intellectual categories or the policy sophistication to deal with these complexities.

Much the same could be said for the U.S. policy focus on developing civil society. Of course, as good Tocquevillians, Americans all favor such moderating intermediaries between the state and the governed. But how do U.S. leaders know that happy, liberal, Madisonian pluralism will emerge from these Agency for International Development (AID)–sponsored programs and not just an updated version of Latin American corporatism with its state—or elite—controlled group structure? In fact, there is abundant evidence in AID's own files that corporatism is the result of its "civil society" programs at least as often as they create genuinely independent interest groups and pluralism.

Both these trends—toward limited democracy in the political sphere and toward corporatism in the interest groups or state-society arena—were not unforeseen by scholars, but so far they have left policymakers in a quandary. To date, these policymakers have been unable to come to grips with the powerful, and perhaps disturbing, policy implications of these developments.

OPEN MARKETS

The open markets component of the "Washington Consensus" is also far shakier than it was a few years ago. Again, the fault lies with the basic assumptions underlying the program.

To begin with, U.S. policy has again been based on the hypothesis that "all good things go together." Policymakers assume that democracy in the political sphere is *and ought to be* closely related to open markets in the economic sphere. In the long run this correlation may be valid, but in the short run, economic growth and its accompanying social changes are often disruptive of both stability and democracy.

As a practical matter, open markets mean state downsizing and privatization. But that often means fewer jobs available in the public sector for politicians—even democratic ones—to reward their friends, cronies, and clienteles, and to buy off their enemies, by putting them on the public payroll.

Two logics are at work here, an economic one and a political one. In the economic sphere, everyone understands that some degree of market opening is necessary to stimulate investment, growth, jobs, and prosperity. Politically, however, privatization and state downsizing mean fewer patronage opportunities, which may result in the destabilization of the regimes that the United States is seeking to help. Privatization on a "crash" basis cannot work in

Latin America—especially in a democratic Latin America—because too many jobs and sinecures are involved. Why should U.S. analysts expect Latin American politicians to commit political suicide ("political will," economists call it) with any greater eagerness than their North American colleagues when faced with the necessity of cutting Social Security or Medicare?

Related is the fear many Latin American politicians have of "letting go." Much of Latin America is still underorganized, lacking in institutions and infrastructure, with weak and inefficient industry, and lacking a strong entrepreneurial tradition or class capable of competing with the world's economic superpowers. Latin Americans fear that deregulation, privatization, and state downsizing may produce not a burst of new prosperity but rather chaos and national disintegration. Understandably, they are reluctant to reduce the state's size until they are certain that the private sector is sufficiently strong to fill the void and that economic decline and breakdown will not result. So far, few of them have been willing to take that risk—and when a radical neoliberal reform agenda was followed as in Mexico, it nearly produced economic collapse.

Another related issue is corruption. Recently the Washington policy community has latched onto the cause of eradicating corruption as the latest panacea to solve Latin America's problems; the usual study groups, nongovernmental organizations, and interagency task forces have mobilized. But nowhere in these groups' outpouring of lamentations can we find a good, working definition of corruption, nor can Washington distinguish between the patronage necessary to oil the wheels of government and sheer bribery that goes beyond the pale. Can one imagine U.S. policymakers or AID realistically accepting such a distinction or acknowledging pragmatically that the really tough cases lie in the gray area in between? The issue cries out for a realistic, nonmoralistic treatment that emphasizes gray and in-between areas and a gradation in the degrees of corruption, but it is hard to imagine the U.S. government taking such an approach.

These issues of open markets, privatization, and state downsizing have now been enormously complicated by the Mexican peso crisis of 1994. It needs to be emphasized that Mexico's crisis was not brought on by the North American Free Trade Agreement (NAFTA) or the neoliberal reform agenda. Rather it came as a result of a political decision not to devalue the peso before the 1994 presidential election and thus to preserve continuity and stability by keeping the long-dominant Institutional Revolutionary Party in power. But in Mexico as well as some other countries of Latin America, job losses, a banking crisis, the devastation of the middle and working classes, food riots, general lawlessness, and sharp reductions in the national economy ensued. Because of Mexico's experience, no politician, especially not a democratic one, can afford at this stage to campaign on an open-market or neoliberal platform. The open market reform program has not been halted entirely in most countries, but because of the events in Mexico it has certainly been slowed or postponed.

This is, of course, what many politicians in Latin America have wanted. Observers tend to forget that the neoliberal triumph was never complete; indeed, a host of out-of-office central bankers and former cabinet members eager to discredit an open market strategy and return to the protectionist import-substituting industrialization of the past have been lurking "in exile" in the international lending agencies. Now with the Mexican crisis and the growing reluctance to go any further with open markets in other countries, these advocates of a closed, quasi-mercantilist policy are poised for a come-back.

IS HEMISPHERIC FREE TRADE REALLY DESIRABLE?

The third leg of the Washington Consensus is free trade. U.S. policymakers have presented a vision of a free trade area stretching from the Arctic Circle to Tierra del Fuego. Free trade enthusiasts suggest that the economies of North and Latin America would benefit from such an arrangement, but poli-cymakers would do well to remember that regional free trade agreements can present many challenges and impose many hardships even as they open up new avenues of opportunity.

It needs to be recalled that from the beginning, hemispheric free trade was seen as a second-best solution. It only emerged as an option after global trade liberalization was stalled in the early 1980s. Furthermore, regional trading blocs have inherent problems. They do not necessarily do their members a great service; Mexico and other Latin American countries could find them-selves harmed rather than helped by agreeing to trade freely with the United States if it means that their products will be kept out of Asia or Europe.

It also needs to be remembered that NAFTA—which is often seen as a starting point for a hemispheric free trade zone—was originally more of a strategic plan than an economic one. In the wake of Mexico's belly-up debt crisis of 1982 and an increasingly shaky political system, Presidents Reagan and Bush pushed NAFTA as a way of stabilizing Mexico. The debate over NAFTA in the United States has mainly been along economic lines, but the original (and largely forgotten) purpose was mainly strategic, and the eco-nomic program was only one part of a larger design.

The passage of NAFTA may have been President Clinton's finest legislative hour, but there were also political costs involved. For example, as the adminis-tration began to look forward to the 1996 election, it was unwilling to take positions on free trade that would cost it votes among important constituen-cies, and therefore it refused to implement further, let alone expand, the agree-ment. It publicly put NAFTA on hold, while allowing lower-level "framework agreements" to go forward.

U.S. inaction served to spur Mercosur's expansion as a South American trade bloc, including the 1995 accession of Chile (once scheduled to be next in line for NAFTA) as an associate member. The almost inevitable result has been the growth of the perception that Mercosur is a rival NAFTA, not a complement to it. Moreover, in the aftermath of Mexico's continuing financial crisis, Mercosur is viewed as the trade bloc that "works" while NAFTA is seen as problematic.

Recently, these regional trade blocs have been subjected to even harsher criticisms on ·hard economic grounds. A World Bank study warns that, because of NAFTA, Mexico might well take away fully one-third of the exports previously sent to the United States by the nations of the Caribbean. The implementation of Mercosur agreements has also brought about negative economic results. Brazil's currency may be overvalued by as much as 50 percent, producing a situation in which sky-high prices place many goods and services way beyond the reach of most Brazilians—all for the sake of maintaining parity with Argentina in Mercosur itself. The trade agreement that "works" has not only taken away trade from other South American countries outside its umbrella but also serves to protect inefficient firms that are within the bloc from more efficient producers outside it.

Meanwhile, NAFTA has produced fewer jobs than expected in both the United States and Mexico, providing long-time critics of the program with new reasons to attack it and discouraging policymakers from implementing it fully or expanding it to new countries. The crises of the Mexican political system and of its economy, which are widely but wrongly blamed on NAFTA, nevertheless make it difficult for politicians on either side of the border to expand the program. In reexamining the assumptions underlying U.S. policy on hemispheric free trade, officials should consider very carefully the costs of regional free trade agreements and the difficulties that have attended the growth of NAFTA and Mercosur.

DRUG WARS

The international drug trade is a relatively new and very complicated issue in U.S. foreign policy. It is complicated in part because it involves both domestic and foreign policy considerations. And unlike the issues of democracy, open markets, and free trade, there is on this topic barely even a semblance of agreement between the United States and Latin America.

Drugs are. both big business and a big problem. The amount of money involved is huge. At the same time, drug trafficking is associated with violence, crime, and high-level corruption. It is ruining a generation of young people, devastating inner cities, and poisoning society. It is also undermining the judicial systems, police, militaries, and political systems of several Latin American countries. The strategy for dealing with the drug issue in the early Reagan administration was to focus on the domestic or consumption side: disrupting supplies and networks, arresting users as well as sellers, and implementing widespread drug testing. But these strategies met with little success, and some aspects of this approach to combating drug abuse ran afoul of interest groups (teachers, pilots, and unions) as well as the American Civil Liberties Union, which argued that indiscriminate testing violated the rights of U.S. citizens.

Unable to deal effectively with the problem on the domestic side, during the 1980s the United States turned to the international side, naively thinking that it would be easier. U.S. leaders quickly discovered that it was no less difficult to solve the drug problem on the supply end than it was on the demand end. First, since drugs in Latin America are often involved in cultural and religious expression, attitudes toward drugs are different, and their use does not carry the same stigma that it does in the United States. Second, since Latin American farmers could earn ten to 20 times more by producing drugs than by growing traditional crops, incentives favored drugs, and the United States could not provide sufficient subsidies to encourage alternative crops. Moreover, drugs bolstered Latin American economies, helped the balance of payments, provided jobs, and paid for social programs.

Most Latin Americans saw drugs as a U.S. problem that the United States should solve; all they were doing, in accord with the new free market economy, was filling a demand. Moreover, since many government and military officials used money from drug trafficking to supplement meager salaries, clamping down meant putting high officials in jeopardy—obviously a sensitive issue if it involved cabinet and armed forces chiefs or even, as in Colombia, the president of the country. The State Department, which usually sought to have good relations with these countries, came in conflict with the Drug Enforcement Agency and the Federal Bureau of Investigation (FBI) which wanted to put even high-ranking officials in jail. In one instance, the FBI threatened an American ambassador with obstruction of justice charges unless he went along with a hair-brained scheme to publicize all the names of persons in the country the agency wanted to "talk to."

Efforts to cut off drug supplies at their source were further complicated by the fact that drug "factories" in Latin America employed such low-level technology and were so easy to move that it was almost impossible to find or eliminate them. Also, the sprays used to kill marijuana cause cancer—hardly condonable especially by newly democratic governments. It quickly became clear that resolving the drug issue at the source or production point was at least as problematic as on the consumption side. Nor did the U.S. public support any of the libertarian plans that would decriminalize drug use.

The result was a handful of new, multifaceted plans that sought to combat drugs on both the domestic (consumption) and international (production) sides, meanwhile reviving the educational and rehabilitational campaigns that earlier had offered promise. But just as those strategies were implemented, new data showed that drug use among teenagers was on the rise again in the suburbs as well as the inner cities.

In addition, because of the drug issue, relations with countries like Colombia that are important to the United States on a variety of issues besides drugs became so poisoned that they verged on rupture. Clearly on the drug issue even more than on the others discussed, a rethinking of policy assumptions is overdue.

FORGING A NEW CONSENSUS

Much of the policy discussion relating to Latin America these days in Washington involves the need to revive policies that have been ignored in recent months or years. . . . The mantra is now familiar: democracy, open markets, free trade, counter-narcotics. The agenda has become formulaic, recited from memory without further thought.

The argument presented here is not with any of these principles as principles. The United States should encourage democracy, open markets, free trade, and effective anti-drug measures; indeed it is hard to conceive the United States could stand for anything other than these principles.

Rather, the problems with U.S. policy are the absence of nuance; the lack of any sense of how to get from here to there; the "true believer," missionary, and tunnel vision mentalities that accompany these orthodoxies; and the ethnocentrism involved. The United States lacks an understanding that Latin America and other developing areas often mean something different by democracy and human rights than North Americans do, and the lack of appreciation for the many transitional, overlapping, crazy-quilt patterns and "halfway houses" that exist.

It may be that the set of policies represented by the "Washington Consensus," rather like the Alliance of Progress of thirty years ago, is about the best that the United States can do as a policy for Latin America. After all, we in the United States almost never pay attention to Latin America, let alone read about it.

If U.S. policymakers can do no better than the "Washington Consensus," it is a sad commentary on the ability of the United States to understand other cultures and countries on their own terms rather than through its own rose-colored glasses. The United States needs to do more than simply dust off some old and by now rather stale policies; it also needs to rethink fundamentally the assumptions undergirding the policy. Anything short of that is likely to turn Samuel Huntington's vaunted predictions of a "clash of civilizations" into reality—not just in Latin America but in other areas as well.

20. PIVOTAL STATES AND U.S. STRATEGY

Robert S. Chase, Emily B. Hill, and Paul Kennedy

THE NEW DOMINOES

[Long] after the collapse of the Soviet Union, American policymakers and intellectuals are still seeking new principles on which to base national strategy. The current debate over the future of the international order—including predictions of the "end of history," a "clash of civilizations," a "coming anarchy," or a "borderless world"—has failed to generate agreement on what shape U.S. policy should take. However, a single overarching framework may be inappropriate for understanding today's disorderly and decentralized world. America's security no longer hangs on the success or failure of containing communism. The challenges are more diffuse and numerous. As a priority, the United States must manage its delicate relationships with Europe, Japan, Russia, and China, the other major players in world affairs. However, America's national interest also requires stability in important parts of the developing world. Despite congressional pressure to reduce or eliminate overseas assistance, it is vital that America focus its efforts on a small number of countries whose fate is uncertain and whose future will profoundly affect their surrounding regions. These are the pivotal states.

The idea of a pivotal state—a hot spot that could not only determine the fate of its region but also affect international stability—has a distinguished pedigree reaching back to the British geographer Sir Halford Mackinder in the 1900s and earlier. The classic example of a pivotal state throughout the nineteenth century was Turkey, the epicenter of the so-called Eastern Question; because of Turkey's strategic position, the disintegration of the Ottoman Empire posed a perennial problem for British and Russian policymakers.

Twentieth-century American policymakers employed their own version of a pivotal-states theory. Statesmen from Eisenhower and Acheson to Nixon and Kissinger continually referred to a country succumbing to communism as a potential "rotten apple in a barrel" or a "falling domino." Although the domino theory was never sufficiently discriminative—it worsened America's strategic overextension—its core was about supporting pivotal states to prevent their fall to communism and the consequent fall of neighboring states.

Because the U.S. obsession with faltering dominoes led to questionable policies from Vietnam to El Salvador, the theory now has a bad reputation. But the idea itself—that of identifying specific countries as more important than others, for both regional stability and American interests—is sensible. The United States should adopt a discriminative policy toward the developing world, concentrating its energies on pivotal states rather than spreading its attention and resources over the globe.

Indeed, the domino theory may now fit U.S. strategic needs better than it did during the Cold War. The new dominoes, or pivotal states, no longer need assistance against an external threat from a hostile political system; rather, the danger is that they will fall prey to internal disorder. A decade ago, when the main threat to American interests in the developing world was the possibility that nations would align with the Soviets, the United States faced a clear-cut enemy. This enemy captured the American imagination in a way that impending disorder does not. Yet chaos and instability may prove a greater and more insidious threat to American interests than communism ever was. With its migratory outflows, increasing conflict due to the breakdown of political structures, and disruptions in trade patterns, chaos undoubtedly affects bordering states. Reacting with interventionist measures only after a crisis in one state threatens an important region is simply too late. Further, Congress and the American public would likely not accept such actions, grave though the consequences might be to U.S. interests. Preventive assistance to pivotal states to reduce the chance of collapse would better serve American interests.

A strategy of rigorously discriminate assistance to the developing world would benefit American foreign policy in a number of ways. First, as the world's richest nation, with vast overseas holdings and the most to lose from global instability, the United States needs a conservative strategy. Like the British Empire in the nineteenth and early twentieth centuries, the interests of the United States lie in the status quo. Such a strategy places the highest importance on relations with the other great powers: decisions about the expansion of NATO or preserving amicable relations with Russia, China, Japan, and the major European powers must remain primary. The United States must also safeguard several special allies, such as Saudi Arabia, Kuwait, South Korea, and Israel, for strategic and domestic political reasons.

Second, a pivotal-states policy would help U.S. policymakers deal with what Sir Michael Howard, in another context, nicely described as "the heavy and ominous breathing of a parsimonious and pacific electorate." American policymakers, themselves less and less willing to contemplate foreign obligations, are acutely aware that the public is extremely cautious about and even hostile toward overseas engagements. While the American public may not reject all such commitments, it does resist intervention in areas that appear peripheral to U.S. interests. A majority also believes, without knowing the relatively small percentages involved, that foreign aid is a major drain on the federal budget and often wasted through fraud, duplication, and high operating costs. Few U.S. politicians are willing to risk unpopularity by contesting such opinions, and many Republican critics have played to this mood by attacking government policies that imply commitments abroad. Statesmen responsible for outlining U.S. foreign policy might have a better chance of persuading a majority of Congress and the American public that a policy of selective engagement is both necessary and feasible.

Finally, a pivotal states strategy might help bridge the conceptual and political divide in the national debate between "old" and "new" security issues. The mainstream in policy circles still considers new security issues peripheral; conversely, those who focus on migration, overpopulation, or environmental degradation resist the realist emphasis on power and on military and on political security.

In truth, neither the old nor the new approach will suffice. The traditional realist stress on military and political security is simply inadequate—it does not pay sufficient attention to the new threats to American national interests. The threats to the pivotal states are not communism or aggression but rather overpopulation, migration, environmental degradation, ethnic conflict, and economic instability, all phenomena that traditional security forces find hard to address. The "dirty" industrialization of the developing world, unchecked population growth and attendant migratory pressures, the rise of powerful drug cartels, the flow of illegal arms, the eruption of ethnic conflict, the flourishing of terrorist groups, the spread of deadly new viruses, and turbulence in emerging markets—a laundry list of newer problems—must also concern Americans, if only because their spillover effects can hurt U.S. interests.

Yet the new interpretation of security, with its emphasis on holistic and global issues, is also inadequate. Those who point to such new threats to international stability often place secondary importance (if that) on U.S interests; indeed, they are usually opposed to invoking the national interest to further their cause. For example, those who criticized the Clinton administration in the summer of 1994 for not becoming more engaged in the Rwandan crisis paid little attention to the relative insignificance of Rwanda's stability for American interests The universal approach common to many advocates of global environmental protection or human rights, commendable in principle, does not discriminate between human rights abuses in Haiti, where proximity and internal instability made intervention possible and even necessary, and similar abuses in Somalia, where the United States had few concrete interests.

Furthermore, the new security approach cannot make a compelling case to the American public for an internationalist foreign policy. The public does not sense the danger in environmental and demographic pressures that erode stability over an extended period, even if current policies, or lack thereof, make this erosion inexorable and at some point irreversible. Finally, the global nature of the new security threats makes it tempting to downplay national governments as a means to achieving solutions.

A pivotal-states strategy, in contrast, would encourage integration of new security issues into a traditional, state-centered framework and lend greater clarity to the making of foreign policy. This integration may make some long-term consequences of the new security threats more tangible and manageable. And it would confirm the importance of working chiefly through state governments to ensure stability while addressing the new security issues that make these states pivotal.

HOW TO IDENTIFY A PIVOT

According to which criteria should the pivotal states be selected? A large population and an important geographical location are two requirements. Economic potential is also critical, as recognized by the U.S. Commerce Department's . . . identification of the "big emerging markets" that offer the most promise to American business. Physical size is a necessary but not sufficient condition: Zaire [now the Congo] comprises an extensive tract, but its fate is not vital to the United States.

What really defines a pivotal state is its capacity to affect regional and international stability. A pivotal state is so important regionally that its collapse would spell transboundary mayhem: migration, communal violence, pollution, disease, and so on. A pivotal state's steady economic progress and stability, on the other hand, would bolster its region's economic vitality and political soundness and benefit American trade and investment.

For the present, the following should be considered pivotal states: Mexico and Brazil; Algeria, Egypt, and South Africa; Turkey; India and Pakistan; and Indonesia. These states' prospects vary widely. India's potential for success, for example, is considerably greater than Algeria's; Egypt's potential for chaos is greater than Brazil's. But all face a precarious future, and their success or failure will powerfully influence the future of the surrounding areas and affect American interests. This theory of pivotal states must not become a mantra, as the domino theory did, and the list of states could change. But the concept itself can provide a necessary and useful framework for devising American strategy toward the developing world.

A WORLD TURNING ON PIVOTS

To understand this idea in concrete terms, consider the [1995] Mexican crisis. . . . Mexico's modernization has created strains between the central and local governments and difficulties with the unions and the poorest groups in the countryside, and it has damaged the environment. Like the other pivotal states, Mexico is delicately balanced between progress and turmoil.

Given the publicity and political debate surrounding the Clinton administration's rescue plan for Mexico, most Americans probably understood that their southern neighbor is special, even if they were disturbed by the means employed to rescue it. A collapse of the peso and the consequent ruin of the Mexican economy would have weakened the U.S. dollar, hurt exports, and caused convulsions throughout Latin America's Southern Cone Common Market and other emerging markets. Dramatically illustrating the potency of new security threats to the United States, economic devastation in Mexico would have increased the northward flow of illegal immigrants and further strained the United States' overstretched educational and social services. Violent social chaos in Mexico could spill over into this country. As many bankers remarked during the peso crisis, Mexico's troubles demonstrated the impossibility of separating "there" from "here."

Because of Mexico's proximity and its increasing links with the United States, American policymakers clearly needed to give it special attention. As evidenced by the North American Free Trade Agreement, they have. But other select states also require close American attention.

EGYPT

Egypt's location has historically made its stability and political alignment critical to both regional development and relationships between the great powers. In recent decades, its proximity to important oil regions and its involvement in the Arab-Israeli peace process, which is important for the prosperity of many industrialized countries, has enhanced its contribution to stability in the Middle East and North Africa. Furthermore, the government of President Muhammad Hosni Mubarak has provided a bulwark against perhaps the most significant long-term threat in the region—radical Islamic fundamentalism.

The collapse of the current Egyptian regime might damage American interests more than the Iranian revolution did. The Arab-Israeli peace process, the key plank of U.S. foreign policy in this region for the past 20 years, would suffer serious, perhaps irreparable, harm. An unstable Egypt would undermine the American diplomatic plan of isolating fundamentalist "rogue" states in the region and encourage extremist opposition to governments everywhere from Algeria to Turkey. The fall of the Mubarak government could well lead Saudi Arabia to reevaluate its pro-Western stance. Under such conditions, any replay of Operation Desert Storm or similar military intervention in the Middle East on behalf of friendly countries such as Kuwait or Jordan would be extremely difficult, if not impossible. Finally, the effect on oil and financial markets worldwide could be enormous.

Egypt's future is not only vital, but very uncertain. While some signs point to increasing prosperity and stability . . . the preponderance of evidence paints a dimmer picture. Jealously guarding its power base and wary that further privatization would produce large numbers of resentful former state employees, the government fears losing control over the economy. Growth rates lurch fitfully upward, and although reform has improved most basic economic indicators, it has also widened the gap between rich and poor. Roughly one-third of the population now lives in poverty, up from 20–25 percent in 1990.

A harsh crackdown on fundamentalism has reduced the most serious short-term threat to the Mubarak regime, but a long-term solution may prove more elusive. The government's brutal attack on the fundamentalist movement may ultimately fuel Islam's cause by alienating the professional middle class; such a policy has already greatly strengthened the more moderate Muslim Brotherhood and radicalized the extremist fringe.

Environmental and population problems are growing. Despite the gradually decreasing birthrate, the population is increasing by about one million every nine months, straining the country's natural resources, and is forecast to reach about 94 million by 2025.

Recognizing Egypt's significance and fragility, successive U.S. administrations have made special provisions to maintain its stability. In 1995 Egypt received $2.4 billion from the U.S. government, making it the second-largest recipient of American assistance, after Israel. That allocation is primarily the result of the Camp David accords and confirms Egypt's continuing importance in U.S. Middle East policy. Current attempts by American isolationists to cut these funds should be strongly resisted. On the other hand, the U.S. government and Congress should seriously consider redirecting American aid . . . to improve infrastructure, education, and the social fabric, [which] would ease the country's troubles.

INDONESIA

While Egypt's prospects for stability are tenuous, Indonesia's future appears brighter. By exercising considerable control over the population and the economy for the last several decades, Indonesia's authoritarian regime has engineered dramatic economic growth. . . . Poverty rates have dropped drastically, and a solid middle class has emerged. At first glance, Indonesia's development has been a startling success. However, the government now confronts strains generated by its own efforts.

Along with incomes, education levels, and health status, Indonesia's population is increasing dramatically. With the fourth-largest population in the world and an extra three million people added each year, the country is projected to reach 260 million inhabitants by 2025. The main island of Java, one of the most densely populated places on earth, can scarcely accommodate the new bodies. In response, the government is forcing many citizens to migrate to other islands. This resettlement program is the focal point for a host of other tensions concerning human rights and the treatment of minorities. The government's brutal handling of the separatist movement in East Timor continues to hinder its efforts to gain international respect. President Suharto's regime has made a point of cooperating with Chinese entrepreneurs to boost economic expansion, but ethnic differences remain entrenched. Finally, the government's favoring of specific businesses has produced deep-rooted corruption.

Because of the government's tight control, it can maintain stability even while pursuing these questionable approaches to handling its people. However, as a more sophisticated middle class emerges, Indonesians are less willing to accept the existing concentration of economic and political power. . . .

A reasonable scenario for Indonesia would be the election of a government that shares power more broadly, with greater respect for human rights and press freedoms. The new regime would maintain Indonesia's openness to foreign trade and investment, and it would end favoritism toward certain companies. Better educated, better paid, and urbanized for a generation, Indonesians would have fewer children per family. Indonesia would continue its leadership role in the Association of Southeast Asian Nations (ASEAN) and the Asia-Pacific Economic Cooperation forum (APEC), helping foster regional growth and stability.

The possibility remains, however, that the transfer of power in Jakarta could trigger political and economic instability, as it did in 1965 at the end of President Sukarno's rule. A new regime might find it more difficult to overawe the people while privately profiting from the economy. Elements of the electorate could lash out in frustration. Riots would then jeopardize Indonesia's growth and regional leadership, and by that stage the United States could do nothing more than attempt to rescue its citizens from the chaos.

Instability in Indonesia would affect peace and prosperity across Southeast Asia. Its archipelago stretches across key shipping lanes, its oil and other businesses attract Japanese and U.S. investment, and its stable economic conditions and open trade policies set an example for ASEAN, APEC, and the region as a whole. If Indonesia, as Southeast Asia's fulcrum, falls into chaos, it is hard to envisage the region prospering. It is equally hard to imagine general distress if Indonesia booms economically and maintains political stability.

Despite the difficulty, the United States must have a strategy for encouraging Indonesia's stability. Part of this will involve close cooperation with Japan, which is by far the largest donor to Indonesian development. A more sensitive aspect of the strategy will be encouraging the regime to respect human rights and ethnic differences. The strategy also calls for calibrated pressure on Indonesia to decrease its widespread corruption, which in any case is required to achieve the country's full integration into the international business world.

BRAZIL

Brazil borders every country in South America except Ecuador and Chile, and its physical size, complex society, and huge population of 155 million people are more than enough to qualify it as a pivotal state.

Brazil's economy appears to be recovering from its 1980s crisis, although the indicators for the future are inconsistent. . . . Many basic social and economic indexes point to a generally improving quality of life, including the highest industrial growth since the 1970s (6.4 percent in 1994), declining birth and death rates, increasing life expectancy, and an expanding urban infrastructure. In the longer term, however, Brazil must address extreme economic inequality, poor educational standards, and extensive malnutrition. . . .

Were Brazil to founder, the consequences from both an environmental and an economic point of view would be grave. The Amazon basin contains the largest tropical rain forest in the world, boasting unequaled biodiversity. Apart from aesthetic regrets about its destruction, the practical consequences are serious. The array of plants and trees in the Amazon is an important source of natural pharmaceuticals; deforestation may also spread diseases as the natural hosts of viruses and bacteria are displaced to other regions.

A social and political collapse would directly affect significant U.S. economic interests and American investors. Brazil's fate is inextricably linked to that of the entire South American region, a region that before its debt and inflation crises in the 1970s bought large amounts of U.S. goods and is now potentially the fastest-growing market for American business over the decades to come. In sum, were Brazil to succeed in stabilizing over the long term, reducing the massive gap between its rich and poor, further opening its markets, and privatizing often inefficient state-run industries, it could be a powerful engine for the regional economy and a stimulus to U.S. prosperity. Were it to fail, Americans would feel the consequences.

SOUTH AFRICA

Apartheid's end makes South Africa's transition particularly dramatic. So far, President Nelson Mandela's reconciliation government has set an inspiring example of respect for ethnic differences, good governance, and prudent nurturing of the country's economic potential. . . .

There are indications, however, that South Africa could succumb to political instability, ethnic strife, and economic stagnation. Power-sharing at the cabinet level belies deep ethnic divisions. . . . As Mandela's government struggles to improve black living standards and soothe ethnic tensions, the legacy of apartheid creates a peculiar dilemma. It will be hard to meet understandable black expectations of equity in wages, education, and health, given the country's budget deficits and unstable tax base. As racial inequalities persist, blacks are likely to grow impatient. Yet if whites feel they are paying a disproportionate share for improved services for blacks, they might flee the country, taking with them the prospects for increased foreign direct investment.

While the primary threats to South Africa's stability are internal, its effectiveness in containing them will have repercussions beyond its borders. Even before apartheid ended, South Africa had enormous influence over the region's political and economic development, from supporting insurgencies throughout the "front-line states" to providing mining jobs for migrant workers from those same countries. If South Africa achieves the economic and political potential within its grasp, it will be a wellspring of regional political stability and economic growth. If it prospers, it can demonstrate to other ethnically tortured regions a path to stability through democratization, reconciliation, and steadily increasing living standards. Alternatively, if it fails to handle its many challenges, it will suck its neighbors into a whirlpool of self-defeating conflict.

Although controlling the sea-lanes around the Cape of Good Hope would be important, especially if widespread trouble were to erupt in the Middle East, American strategic interests are not otherwise endangered in southern Africa. Yet because South Africa is the United States' largest trading partner in Africa and possesses vast economic potential, its fate would affect American trading and financial interests that have invested there. It would also destabilize key commodity prices, especially in the gold, diamond, and ore markets. More generally, instability in South Africa, as in Brazil and Indonesia, would cast a large shadow over confidence in emerging markets. American policy toward South Africa should reflect its importance as a pivotal state. . . .

ALGERIA AND TURKEY

Algeria's geographical position makes its political future of great concern to American allies in Europe, especially France and Spain. . . . The replacement of the present regime by extremists would affect the security of the Mediterranean sea-lanes, international oil and gas markets, and, as in the case of Egypt, the struggle between moderate and radical elements in the Islamic world. All the familiar pressures of rapid population growth and drift to the coastal cities, environmental damage, increasing dependence on food imports, and extremely high youth unemployment are evident. Levels of violence remain high as Algerian government forces struggle to crush the Islamist guerrilla movement.

While a moderate Islamist government might prove less disturbing than the West fears, a bloody civil war or the accession of a radical, anti-Western regime would be very serious. Spain, Italy, and France depend heavily on Algerian oil and gas and would sorely miss their investments, and the resulting turbulence in the energy markets would certainly affect American consumers. The flood of middle-class, secular Algerians attempting to escape the bloodshed and enter France or other parts of southern Europe would further test immigration policies of the European Union (EU). The effects on Algeria's neighbors, Morocco and Tunisia, would be even more severe and encourage radical Islamic elements everywhere. Could Egypt survive if Algeria, Morocco, Tunisia, and Muammar al-Qaddafi's Libya collaborated to achieve fundamentalist goals? Rumors of an Algerian atomic bomb are probably premature, but the collapse of the existing regime would undoubtedly reduce security in the entire western Mediterranean. . . .

Although Turkey is not as politically or economically fragile as Algeria, its strategic importance may be even greater. At a multifold crossroads between East and West, North and South, Christendom and Islam, Turkey has the potential to influence countries thousands of miles from the Bosporus. The southeast keystone of NATO during the Cold War and an early (if repeatedly postponed) applicant to enlarged EU membership, Turkey enjoys solid economic growth and middle-class prosperity. However, it also shows many of the difficulties that worry other pivotal states: population and environmental pressures, severe ethnic minority challenges, and the revival of radical Islamic fundamentalism, all of which test the country's young democratic institutions and assumptions. There are also a slew of external problems, ranging from bitter rivalries with Greece over Cyprus, various nearby islands' territorial boundaries, and Macedonia; to the developing quarrel with Syria and Iraq over control of the Euphrates water supply; to delicate relationships with the Muslim-dominated states of Central Asia. A prosperous, democratic, tolerant Turkey is a beacon for the entire region; a Turkey engulfed by civil wars and racial and religious hatreds, or nursing ambitions to interfere abroad, would hurt American interests in innumerable ways and concern everyone from pro-NATO strategists to friends of Israel.

INDIA AND PAKISTAN

Considered separately, the challenges facing the two great states of South Asia are daunting enough. Each confronts a population surge that is forecast to take Pakistan's total (123 million in 1990) to 276 million by 2025, and India's (853 million in 1990) to a staggering 1.45 billion, thus equaling China's projected population. While such growth taxes rural environments by causing the farming of marginal lands, deforestation, and depletion of water resources, the urban population explosion is even more worrisome. With 46 percent of Pakistan's and 35 percent of India's population under 15 years old, according to 1990 census figures, tens of millions of young people enter the job market each year; the inadequate opportunities for them further strain the social fabric. All this forms an ominous backdrop to rising tensions, as militant Hindus and Muslims, together a full fifth of the population, challenge India's democratic traditions, and Islamic forces stoke nationalist passions across Pakistan.

The shared borders and deep-rooted rivalry of India and Pakistan place these pivotal states in a more precarious position than, for example, Brazil or South Africa. With three wars between them since each gained independence, each continues to arm against the other and quarrel fiercely over Kashmir, Pakistan's potential nuclear capabilities and missile programs, and other issues. This jostling fuels their mutual ethnic-cum-religious fears and could produce another bloody conflict that neither government could control. What effect a full-scale war would have on the Pakistan-China entente is hard to predict, but the impact of such a contest would likely spread from Kashmir into Afghanistan and farther afield, and Pakistan could find support in the Muslim world. For many reasons, and perhaps especially the nuclear weapons stakes, the United States has a vital interest in encouraging South Asia's internal stability and external peace.

Could this short list of important states in the developing and emerging-markets regions of the globe include others? Possibly. This selection of pivotal states is not carved in stone, and new candidates could emerge over the next decades. Having an exact list is less important than initiating a debate over why, from the standpoint of U.S. national interests, some states in the developing world are more important than others.

BETTER WISE THAN WIDE

The United States needs a policy toward the developing world that does not spread American energies, attention, and resources too thinly across the globe, but rejects isolationist calls to write it off. This is a realistic policy, both strategically and politically. Strategically, it would permit the United States, as the country that can make the greatest contribution to world security, to focus on supporting pivotal states. Politically, given the jaundiced view of Americans and their representatives toward overseas engagements, a strategy of discrimination is the strongest argument against an even greater withdrawal from the developing world than is now threatened.

As the above case studies suggest, each pivotal state grapples with an intricate set of interrelated problems. In such an environment, the United States has few clear-cut ways to help pivotal states succeed. Therefore, it must develop a subtle, comprehensive strategy, encompassing all aspects of American interaction with each one. Those strategies should include appropriate focusing of . . . development assistance, promoting trade and investment, strengthening relationships with the country's leaders, bolstering country-specific intelligence capabilities and foreign service expertise, and coordinating the actions of government agencies that can influence foreign policy. In short, the United States must use all the resources at its disposal to buttress the stability of key states around the globe, working to prevent calamity rather than react to it. Apart from avoiding a great-power war, nothing in foreign policy could be more important. . . .

21. DON'T NEGLECT THE IMPOVERISHED SOUTH

Robin Broad and John Cavanagh

*F*or four and a half decades, the Cold War offered Americans a prism through which to view the three-quarters of humanity who live in the impoverished countries of Latin America, Africa, and Asia. The United States fought or funded wars and covert operations in dozens of these countries—including Cuba, the Dominican Republic, Guatemala, Iran, Korea, Nicaragua, and Vietnam—with the stated goal of preventing the spread of Soviet-backed communism. Shaped to meet this goal, U.S. economic and military policies toward the so-called Third World, or South, were relatively simple and straightforward.

Today, . . . the Third World still erupts into the forefront of U.S. foreign policy with alarming regularity. The [Clinton] administration and media tend to categorize these episodes into one of three oversimplified images. The first and dominant one can be termed "the Rwanda image," and includes countries where, the media tells us, everything is falling apart, and people kill one another in large numbers. Bosnia in 1995, Haiti in 1994, or Somalia in 1993 fit the bill. A second image, promoted by beleaguered defense contractors and Pentagon hawks, paints certain volatile Third World nations and the former Soviet Union as emerging security threats equal to that posed by Moscow at the height of the Cold War. Here, North Korea and Iraq stand out, each with leaders easily caricatured by the media as Hollywood villains. Finally, there is the . . . newer image of a financially tattered Mexico and the fear that other nations may plunge rapidly into similar crises; tens of billions of dollars of short-term speculative capital race around the globe, abandoning yesterday's favorite "emerging market" for promises of quick returns elsewhere.

Content to respond to crises in these three categories, the Clinton administration has yet to forge an overarching policy framework that addresses the deep and changing problems of the South, which comprises approximately 150 countries. In fact, aside from attention to some crisis spots, the administration forfeited its chance to craft a new North-South policy agenda, preferring instead one that places in the foreground only a handful of these countries, . . . which [are the] 10 promising "big emerging markets" for U.S. exports and investments.

When pressed to articulate themes or values that underlie U.S. policy toward these countries and the rest of the South, Clinton administration officials unite around the rhetoric of markets and democracy: Freer markets, through such pacts as the North American Free Trade Agreement (NAFTA), will, they claim, bring both growth and greater democracy. Remarkably, the positions of most Republican leaders in Congress differ only slightly in substance from this agenda. They support the free-trade agenda and the notion that U.S. foreign policy should support U.S. business. A vocal minority who are more protectionist includes the powerful chairman of the Senate Foreign Relations Committee, Jesse Helms (R–NC). Despite his dramatic overstatements and misstatements that seek to distance him from the Democrats, Helms's attack on Clinton's North-South agenda has concentrated on one issue: cutting U.S. aid drastically (much of which, he likes to say, is "going down foreign rat-holes").

Thus, Washington is poised to continue neglecting the South, except in response to crisis-based chaos or through free-trade agreements and business promotion aimed at a few Third World countries. This lack of a broader North-South economic agenda, however, may well turn out to be one of the great blunders of the Clinton administration. The danger of neglect lies beneath the facile surface images of the Third World reality: a deteriorating living standard for the poorest 2.5 billion people in the world, widening inequalities in almost every nation on earth, and employment and environmental crises that beg global initiatives. . . .

What is required . . . is a deeper understanding of the new dynamics between North and South and a more comprehensive policy agenda. Unfortunately, Clinton's narrow policies are based on three deeply flawed assumptions (also shared by most Republican leaders) about the nature of the changes in the global economy.

The first incorrect assumption is that free trade and the promotion of U.S. business interests overseas are good for U.S. workers and communities. . . . As the former deputy director of policy planning at the State Department, John Stremlau, wrote in the Winter 1994–95 issue of *Foreign Policy*, the administration's big-emerging-markets program "should create millions of new and better-paying jobs for Americans, spur domestic productivity, ease adjustment to technological change, restrain inflation, [and] reduce trade and fiscal deficits."

The second flawed assumption of U.S. policy is that free trade and increased U.S. engagement in the 10 biggest emerging markets will not only help these economies but will also enhance growth in other Southern countries. Jumping on the big-emerging-markets bandwagon, American CEOs echo administration claims that U.S. policies are leading to the growth of huge middle classes—in such countries as China, India, and Indonesia—that will drive the world economy in the twenty-first century.

A third assumption is that the economic gap between rich and poor countries is now narrowing—a trend that the administration claims is aided by free trade and attention to the 10 Third World countries with big emerging markets. Indeed, there is a widespread perception among U.S. policymakers that the Third World debt crisis that widened the gap during the 1980s has ended, that new capital is flowing into the Third World, and that the gap is beginning to close. These perceptions are reinforced by World Bank projections that over the next decade Third World countries will actually grow faster than richer countries, thus catching up.

A careful analysis of social and economic data from the United Nations, the World Bank, the IMF [International Monetary Fund], and other sources, offers a shockingly different picture of trends in the global economy and the gap between rich and poor countries. There are two ways to measure what is happening economically between North and South. The first is to measure which is growing faster, and therefore whether the gap between them is growing or shrinking. The second is to measure financial resource flows between the two.

On the first issue the picture is clear: The North-South gap widened dramatically in the decade after 1982 as the Third World debt crisis drained financial resources from poor countries to rich banks. Between 1985 and 1992, Southern nations paid some $280 billion more in debt service to Northern creditors than they received in new private loans and government aid. Gross national product (GNP) per capita rose an average of only 1 percent in the South in the 1980s (in sub-Saharan Africa, it fell 1.2 percent), while it rose 2.3 percent in the North.

Situating the "lost decade" of the 1980s within a longer time period reveals no drastic change: In 1960, per capita gross domestic product (GDP) in the South stood at 18 percent of the average of Northern nations; by 1990, it had fallen only slightly to 17 percent. In other words, the North-South gap remained fairly constant.

However, such aggregate figures camouflage a complex reality: For a small group of countries, primarily such Asian big emerging markets as China, Hong Kong, Singapore, South Korea, and Taiwan, the gap with the North has been closing. But—and here is the rub—for most of the rest, the gap has been slowly *widening*. In sub-Saharan Africa the picture is even worse. Not only has the gap expanded significantly, but for many of these countries, per capita GNP has continued to fall.

Likewise, a look at various resource flows between North and South reveals a reality out of sync with prevailing assumptions. Despite the perception of an easing of the debt crisis, the overall Third World debt stock continues to swell by almost $100 billion each year (it reached $1.9 trillion in 1994). Southern debt service still exceeds new lending, and the net outflow remains particularly crushing in Africa. While it is true that a series of debt reschedulings and the accumulation of arrears by many debtors have reduced the net negative financial transfer from South to North over the last few years, the flows remain negative.

Part of the reason some analysts argue that the debt crisis is no longer a problem is that since the early 1990s these outflows of debt repayments have been matched by increased inflows of foreign capital. Here too, however, a deeper look at disaggregated figures reinforces the disconcerting reality. According to World Bank figures, roughly half of the new foreign direct investment by global corporations in the South in 1992 quickly left those countries as profits. In addition, investment flows primarily to only 10 to 12 Third World countries that are viewed as new profit centers by Northern corporations and investors. More than 70 percent of investment flows in 1991 and 1992 went to just 10 of the so-called emerging markets: Mexico, followed by China, Malaysia, Argentina, Thailand, Brazil, Indonesia, Venezuela, South Korea, and Turkey.

There is another problem with these capital flows. Several of these countries (Brazil, India, Mexico, South Korea, and Taiwan) have attracted substantial short-term flows by opening their stock markets to foreigners and by issuing billions of dollars in bonds. Between 1991 and 1993 alone, foreign direct investment as a share of all private capital flows into poor countries fell from 65 to 44 percent as these more speculative flows increased. . . . Events in Mexico provide an indication of the fickleness of these new investment flows: During the last week of 1994, an estimated $10 billion in short-term funds fled the country.

In addition, Third World countries have been hurt by the declining buying power of their exports vis-à-vis their imports. Southern nations have long pointed out the general tendency of the prices of their primary product exports to rise more slowly than the prices of manufactured goods imports. This "terms of trade" decline was particularly sharp between 1985 and 1993 when the real prices of primary commodities fell 30 percent. This translates into billions of dollars: The 3.5 percent decline in the purchasing power of Africa's 1993 exports, for example, cost the continent some $3 billion.

The inescapable conclusion is that the North-South economic gap is narrowing for about a dozen countries but continues to widen for well over 100 others. Hence, without a major shift in policy, the world of the twenty-first century will be one of economic apartheid. There will be two dozen richer nations, a dozen or so poorer nations that have begun to close the gap with the rich, and approximately 140 poor nations slipping further behind.

GLOBALIZATION OF NORTH AND SOUTH

What about the administration's assumption that policies promoting U.S. business are good for overseas as well as domestic markets—that free markets and globalization raise standards of living across the board in both North and South? Here, too, the Clinton administration has missed a fundamental new reality of the global economy. As U.S. firms have shifted from local to national and now global markets over the past half century, a new division of winners and losers has emerged in all countries. A recent book, *Global Dreams: Imperial Corporations and the New World Order,* written by one of the authors and Institute for Policy Studies co-founder Richard Barnet, chronicles how powerful U.S. firms and their counterparts from England, France, Germany, and Japan are integrating only about one-third of humanity (most of those in the rich countries plus the elite of poor countries) into complex chains of production, shopping, culture, and finance.

While there are enclaves in every country that are linked to these global economic webs, others are left out. Wal-Mart is spreading its superstores throughout the Western Hemisphere; millions in Latin America, though, are too poor to enjoy anything but glimpses of luxury. Citibank customers can access automated-teller machines throughout the world; the vast majority of people nevertheless borrow from the loan shark down the road. Ford Motor Company pieces together its new "global car" in Kansas City from parts made all over the globe, while executives in Detroit worry about who will be able to afford it.

Thus, while on one level the North-South gap is becoming more pronounced for the vast majority of Third World countries, on another level these global chains blur distinctions between geographical North and South. These processes create another North-South divide between the roughly one-third of humanity who comprise a "global North" of beneficiaries in every country and the two-thirds of humanity from the slums of New York to the favelas of Rio who are not hooked into the new global menu of producing, consuming, and borrowing opportunities in the "global South."

In contrast with the Pollyanna-ish assumptions of the Clinton administration, globalization, accelerated by the administration's new free trade and investment agreements, has deepened three intractable problems that now plague almost every nation on earth including the United States: income inequalities, job losses, and environmental damage.

Income Inequalities

The major adverse consequence of quickening global economic integration has been widening income disparity within almost all nations as the wealthier strata cash in on the opportunities of globalization, while millions of other citizens are hurt, marginalized, or left behind. Years ago, economist Simon Kuznets hypothesized that as economies develop there is initially a growth-equity trade-off, i.e., income inequalities rise as nations enter the early stages of economic growth and fall in more mature economies. Today, however, the inequalities are growing everywhere—to such an extent that in late 1994 the *Economist* acknowledged that "it is no coincidence that the biggest increases in income inequalities have occurred in economies . . . where free-market economic policies have been pursued most zealously" and that "it is a combination of lightly regulated labour markets and global economic forces that has done much more . . . to favour the rich over the poor."

One sees this in the perverse widening of the gap between rich and poor within nations and across the globe. Thirty years ago, the income of the richest fifth of the world's population combined was 30 times greater than that of the poorest fifth. Today, the income gap is more than 60 times greater. Over this period the income of the richest 20 percent grew from 70 to 85 percent of the total world income, while the global share of the poorest 20 percent fell from 2.3 to 1.4 percent.

The number of billionaires grew dramatically over the past seven years, coinciding with the spread of free-market policies around the world. Between 1987 and 1994, the number more than doubled from 145 to 358. According to our calculations, those 358 billionaires are collectively worth some $762 billion, which is about the combined income of the world's poorest 2.5 billion people. . . . At the bottom, 2.5 billion people—approximately 45 percent of the world's population—eke out an existence using just under 4 percent of the world's GNP. At the top, 358 individuals own the same percent.

Job Losses

With the exception of a few East Asian economies, every nation—North and South—is grappling with high or rising unemployment, and many, including the United States, are suffering from deteriorating working conditions for a sizable share of the workforce. [Unemployment rates in the United States have fallen since this article was first published in 1995.—Eds.] Worldwide, more than 800 million people are unemployed or seriously underemployed, with tens of millions more falling into this situation each year. Technology has combined with globalization in a devastating manner to spawn this crisis of work. Unlike previous industrial revolutions, the two most important technological innovations in recent decades—information/computers and biotechnology—destroy more jobs than they create. At the same time, rapid strides in transportation and communications technologies allow increasing numbers of jobs to be sent to countries other than the United States. Whereas a generation ago, firms shifted only apparel and consumer electronics jobs overseas, today they can move virtually the entire range of manufacturing and agricultural tasks (and a number of service jobs as well) to China, Mexico, or a range of other countries.

As corporations and governments alike strive to compete globally by cutting costs, the move to slash jobs accelerates. *Fortune* 500 firms have cut approximately 400,000 jobs a year for the past 15 years. As many as one-third of U.S. workers are swimming in a global labor pool; their jobs can be moved elsewhere, and this fact confers on their global corporate employers' enhanced power to bargain down wages and working conditions.

U.S. car companies, for example, can attain roughly equivalent levels of productivity and quality at their Mexican plants today as in their U.S. plants.

The denial of basic worker rights in Mexico, however, severely hampers Mexican workers' efforts to negotiate improvements in their working conditions, and their wages remain a fraction of those of U.S. autoworkers. The credible threat of moving more production to Mexico gives the U.S. companies bargaining chips against their U.S. workers when wages and benefits are set. Overall Mexican productivity climbed by at least 24 percent during the boom years from 1987 to 1992, while wages rose only 13 percent. . . . Likewise, according to the U.S. International Trade Commission, Brazilian workers were 59 percent as productive in 1986 as U.S. workers but earned 17 percent of the average U.S. wage. Even in Bangladesh, shirtmakers are about 60 percent as productive as their American counterparts but earn only 3 to 5 percent of a U.S. salary.

In the South, roughly 38 million people enter stagnating job markets each year. Markets for Third World products are expanding quite slowly in the rich countries, and biotechnology innovations that create synthetic substitutes for everything from vanilla to cocoa and coffee threaten to eliminate the livelihood of millions of Third World agricultural workers. As in the United States, real wages have fallen in most of Latin America and parts of Asia since the early 1980s—a shock that hits women particularly hard since they earn 30 to 40 percent less than men doing the same jobs.

As job pressures grow across the South, many people leave for Europe and North America, where job markets are also tight. Violent acts of xenophobia and racism in the North are some of the ugliest manifestations of this current era of inequality and joblessness.

Environmental Damage

Just as jobs and working conditions become bargaining chips for firms in a deregulated global economy, so too do environmental standards. If the Mexican government can attract foreign firms by ignoring violations of environmental laws, it will do so, and, arguably, it must do so or lose investment. The same logic fuels the Republican party's crusade to eliminate a wide range of environmental and other regulations in the United States.

Another pressure on the environment in the South is the constant admonition by the World Bank and the IMF to increase exports. Since most of the world's minerals, timber, fish, and land are in the South, exports tend to be natural-resource intensive. The depletion of these resources hurts yields for millions of small farmers and fishers. The frenzy to ship more goods overseas accelerates environmental degradation and thus diminishes the real, long-term wealth of Southern nations.

On the other hand, as Southern countries have rightly pointed out, most of the world's consumption, greenhouse gas emissions, ozone-depleting chemical emissions, and industrial pollution occur in the North. The heaviest burden for global environmental action rests there. But the creation of a "global North" in the South through the big-emerging-markets strategy also spreads environmental havoc. Following annual economic growth rates averaging 10 percent since 1978, China's commercial sector consumes more than 1 billion tons of coal annually; thus China produces nearly 11 percent of the world's carbon dioxide emissions. If this rate of climb continues, the impact on global warming will be catastrophic. In India, increased consumption will exacerbate a situation where scale already exceeds carrying capacity: 16 percent of the world's population is degrading just 2.3 percent of the world's land resources and 1.7 percent of its forest stock. And to compensate for falling oil revenues, Indonesia is tearing down the world's second-largest tropical rainforest, becoming the world's largest exporter of processed wood products.

COMPARATIVE DISADVANTAGE

The North-South reality of the mid-1990s hardly matches the soothing scenario suggested by the Clinton administration. Rather, we find the ominous combination of a growing gap between the majority of the Southern and Northern countries as well as the existence of a privileged minority in a "global North" and a marginalized majority in a "global South." Indeed, our analysis suggests three sets of problems that demand attention:

- Most of the "global South"—some 45 percent of humanity who reside mainly in the 140 poorest countries of the Third World—is locked in poverty and left behind as the richer strata grow.
- Roughly 20 percent of the world's population—who are at the upper end of the two-thirds in the "global South," mainly in the big emerging markets—is beginning to enter the global consuming class in a fashion that threatens the environment and exacerbates social tensions.
- An increasing number of workers among the top one-third, or "global North," of the world is experiencing falling incomes and an erosion of worker rights and standards.

Thus far, U.S. policy has largely ignored the bottom 45 percent, concentrated on the middle 20 percent in the big emerging markets, and exacerbated the tensions within the top third. The challenge for U.S. policymakers is to focus on this new global picture with a two-tiered set of policies—one aimed at the forsaken 45 percent primarily in Southern countries and the other focused on the growing inequalities and the job and environmental crises mainly in the big emerging markets and the richer countries of the North. . . .

The Bottom 45 Percent

The main U.S. policy arena addressing the problems of the world's poor is the debate over aid. Helms is achieving deep cuts in aid but wrongly asserts that most poor countries are "foreign rat-holes" and are, hence, undeserving of assistance. Virtually all countries in the world now pursue the same basic package of market-opening, privatizing, government-trimming, export-driven policies. While it is true that there is more corruption and inefficiency in some countries than in others, this is as true for favored countries that are at the center of U.S. policy (e.g., Mexico) as for the 140 neglected countries (e.g., [the Congo]).

At the same time, anyone who has studied development projects and policies on the ground cannot help but acknowledge the truth in some of Helms's criticisms: Much U.S., World Bank, and other aid either fails to ease poverty or is conditioned on the recipient nation adopting policies that deepen social and environmental pain. More of the same aid is not the way to close the gap. The key is to make less aid more effective. . . . A growing number of aid experiments throughout the world . . . channel small amounts of funds directly to entities run by local citizen groups with guidelines that stress sustainability, participation, and equity.

While it would be a good step to redirect more aid in this manner, a great deal more needs to be done outside the realm of aid to stop the hemorrhage of resource flows from the bottom 140 countries to the North. The most fruitful avenue is to try to close the gap by taking less money out of the South rather than by getting more money in. Here the focus needs to shift back to debt. The place to begin is with the roughly 17 percent of Third World debt owed to the World Bank and the IMF—with far higher percentages owed by the poorest African nations. The World Bank and the IMF could readily use their reserves . . . to cancel much of the outstanding debt owed to them by the poorest countries. The World Bank could likewise write off loans to other countries for projects and programs that have failed by its own economic criteria and/or have had severe adverse effects on local populations and the environment. . . .

As governments debate World Bank restructuring, it is important to note that there are alternatives to the World Bank's formula of excessive dependence on exports and capital inflows. If the goal is to prevent nations from falling into debt again, then debt reduction can be conditioned on policies that encourage productive investment, provide assistance to small entrepreneurs and farmers, and encourage less indebted economies. . . .

Economic reformers . . . also push for effective systems of fair taxation, while acknowledging how difficult that goal is since most tax systems are poorly enforced. Most critics of the World Bank model acknowledge the need to maintain smaller export sectors to finance vital imports of capital goods but place greater emphasis on production for the domestic market, as was done in South Korea and Taiwan in their early years of industrialization.

The World Bank and the Agency for International Development should also be restrained from pressing dozens of countries into simultaneous export binges on everything from cut flowers to coffee; the impact of so many countries exporting the same products will inevitably be to depress world prices. And these institutions should nurture the small but growing movement that is stimulating trade in goods produced under conditions that respect worker rights and the environment and recognize the deep discrimination that frequently exists against female producers. . . .

Not surprisingly, the agenda suggested for the bottom 45 percent draws from a more traditional set of remedies on how to shrink the North-South gap. However, attacking the trio of problems outlined for the global North and South—the inequities, joblessness, and environmental degradation—demands that these be implemented in conjunction with a newer set of policy instruments.

The Big Emerging Markets and Anxiety at the Top

Rather than quickening the pace to compete in an increasingly deregulated global economy, the United States can lead in calling for new rules to temper economic integration's socially and environmentally destructive effect upon unequal nations. It is important to recall that the United States rose to this same challenge on a national level in the 1930s when large firms were integrating the U.S. national economy and, in the process, playing rich unionized states off poor nonunion states. A strong trade-union movement created the momentum for Franklin Roosevelt's administration to set new national rules for minimum wages, maximum hours of work, and decent health and safety standards.

In the 1990s, this same dynamic now occurs on a global stage, where global corporations play workers and environmental standards against one another to bargain richer countries down to the standards of the poorer ones. Free-trade agreements that accelerate integration without explicitly safeguarding labor and environmental rights and standards are only deepening global job and environmental crises. Therefore, internationally recognized standards on worker rights (including freedom of association, the right to collective bargaining, and a ban on discrimination based on gender or race) and the environment, which have been hammered out by member governments of the International Labor Organization (ILO) and various international environmental treaties, need to be grafted onto new trade agreements so that firms benefiting from lower tariffs would be obligated to respect those rights and standards.

The first steps in this direction have already been taken. Since 1984, U.S. trade law has conditioned the granting of "trade preferences" to a developing country's respect for internationally recognized worker rights. Threats by the U.S. government to withdraw trade preferences have led to important reforms in a number of countries. . . .

In addition to social clauses on trade agreements, global corporations should be held to codes of conduct that require compliance with these rights and standards. A number of U.S. firms, including Levi Strauss and Sears, have taken a step toward comprehensive corporate codes by agreeing to voluntary codes for the firms with which they subcontract in the Third World.

New corporate codes and socially responsible trade and investment agreements would not solve all the world's job, environmental, and inequality problems, but they could be implemented in the short term and would help reverse the negative dynamic we now face. In the long term, such policies would be more effective if supplemented with strong national policies to address the job and environmental problems jointly.

Even with the best codes of conduct and social clauses on trade agreements, increased trade is likely to continue to be based on the unsustainable exploitation of natural resources. This creates two challenges: first, to raise standards of living in the big emerging markets and other Southern nations without exceeding the Earth's environmental limits and, second, to get Northern societies to acknowledge the costs to the environment of their already high standards of living. Across the board, nations—and individuals—need to acknowledge the environmental costs of economic decisions.

One way to reduce trade in natural resources (such as virgin timber) and the use of resource-intensive products (such as cars) is for governments to adopt accounting systems that factor in the real costs of natural-resource depletion and environmental degradation. In fact, technical work on "environmental accounting" is already quite advanced, as seen in the World Resources Institute's work in Costa Rica, Indonesia, and other developing countries. Even the U.S. Commerce Department has begun recalculations for a "green GDP." In this regard, the World Bank and the GDP should be required to adopt a system of "shadow pricing" that accounts for environmental costs in their projects and programs. This would be an important step in the direction of seeing "green GDPs" become the conceptual framework across the globe.

ENLIGHTENED SELF-INTEREST

. . . There is an impetus for a shift in policy regarding the poorer majority of the world. In the tough debate over NAFTA, citizens' groups—trade unions, environmental groups, organizations of small farmers, consumer activists, religious groups, women's groups, and others—emerged in Canada, Mexico, and the United States to press for safeguards on labor, the environment, and agriculture. While only small gains were realized in the final agreement, the democratization of the debate over international economic policy continued during the [Uruguay Round of General Agreement on Tariffs and Trade (GATT) deliberations] and is likely to characterize the next debates over integration in the Americas and Asia. Similar citizen coalitions throughout the world have likewise gathered momentum for reform of the World Bank and the IMF.

In other words, segments of civil society seem ahead of U.S. policymakers in comprehending that the widening inequalities within nations and between North and South pose crucial challenges that are in our enlightened self-interest to meet. Working conditions in a number of Third World countries have an increasing impact on working conditions in the United States. Growing inequalities in the South are increasing the flow of people, drugs, and environmental problems into the North. The rapid rise of the rich and the emergence of a middle class in the big emerging markets increase instability and tension vis-à-vis the vast numbers of people left behind—witness the growing labor unrest in China, Indonesia, and Mexico, as well as the continuing rebellion in Mexico's Chiapas state.

. . . The attendant problems of the post–Cold War global economy will inevitably become clearer as an increasing number of people in the North and South are hurt. There is no way to get around the need for a fundamental rethinking of the North-South agenda. The question is simply whether the United States will take the lead in resolving these problems or will instead wait and be led.

Part III: CAPABILITIES

In 1949 the Soviet Union successfully tested an atomic bomb. The event had a profound impact on the Truman administration's thinking about how best to pursue the containment of the Soviet Union, which by this time had become the avowed goal of American foreign policy. A government-wide reevaluation of then-current policy and policy instruments followed. In April 1950, Truman's National Security Council (NSC) issued its now-famous, top-secret memorandum 68, which concluded that it was within the power of the United States to not only contain the Soviet Union, but also to destroy it. It thus proposed a massive buildup of American military power and called for a nonmilitary counteroffensive against the Soviet Union, which included covert economic, political, and psychological warfare designed to foment unrest and revolt in Soviet bloc countries. The prescriptions of NSC-68 comprised the basic parameters of containment as it was practiced until the very breakup of Soviet power following nearly half a century of Cold War competition with the United States.

In the new post–Cold War era, American policymakers find themselves confronted with new challenges and circumstances but without the guideposts that for decades shaped grand strategy, defined bureaucratic objectives, and justified high levels of defense and foreign affairs expenditures. Instead, officials in Washington now believe they must direct their attention to a range of security threats that were overshadowed by decades of superpower confrontation. As R. James Woosley was fond of repeating during his tenure early in the Clinton administration as director of the Central Intelligence Agency, "We have slain a large dragon. But we live in a jungle filled with a variety of poisonous snakes."

The preceding chapters show that not all analysts agree on the salience of the security challenges now facing the United States or on the best means of dealing with them. Nonetheless, officialdom remains committed to the view that the United States must hone its capabilities in ways that will promote and protect American interests in a changed and changing world. The 1997 Quadrennial Defense Review, the third in a series mandated by Congress as a vehicle designed to set U.S. military policy for the next century, is illustrative.

The 1997 review identified five dangers the Pentagon concluded it must now guard against: (1) regional dangers, including attacks on friendly nations, ethnic conflict, religious wars, and state-sponsored terrorism; (2) weapons of mass destruction, including Russian nuclear arms and the global proliferation of biological, chemical, and nuclear weapons; (3) transnational dangers, such terrorism, the drug trade, organized crime, and uncontrolled migration; (4) asymmetric attacks, including terrorism, information warfare, the use of unconventional weapons, and environmental sabotage; and (5) "wild card" scenarios, such as a new technological threat or the takeover of a friendly state by anti-American factions.[1]

Similarly, U.S. diplomacy has directed attention to a more diverse set of challenges than characteristically defined its Cold War agenda. Since 1993, the Department of State has officially committed itself to "building democracy; promoting and maintaining peace; promoting economic growth and sustainable development; addressing global problems; and providing humanitarian assistance."[2] Meanwhile, the intelligence community, despite widespread concern that it lacks purpose in the post–Cold War environment, continues to be funded at levels commensurate with the last decade of the Cold War (e.g., $26.6 billion in fiscal year 1997).

Although intelligence spending has remained relatively constant, the diplomatic community and defense planners have confronted a harsh reality: although targeting a more diverse set of foreign and national security priorities, they have fewer economic resources available today to sustain America's military and diplomatic capabilities. For instance, defense spending as a proportion of the overall federal budget declined to 15 percent in 1997 from a Cold War peak of 28 percent.[3] Of particular concern to defense planners is the decline in procurement funding, which, as of 1996, had fallen more than 70 percent in inflation-adjusted dollars since 1985.[4] Because much of the nation's military equipment was acquired during the 1980s defense buildup, the Pentagon worries that it will be impossible to upgrade or replace weapons systems that are becoming outdated.

American diplomatic resources have suffered a similar fate. Not only does the United States continue to devote less than 1 percent of its national wealth to foreign aid, ranking it below twenty industrialized nations, but all foreign policy spending has shrunk dramatically. Before leaving his post in 1997, Secretary of State Warren Christopher reported that the overall international affairs budget had fallen by 50 percent since 1985 (in constant dollars). This change takes on added significance when we realize that—contrary to popular belief—foreign policy spending constitutes a minute portion of the federal budget, about 1.2 percent. Dwindling funds have forced the State Department to cut employees, close embassies and consulates, and devote only modest resources to post–Cold War initiatives. It has also prompted a sharp reduction in various forms of foreign assistance. These are among the circumstances that led some State Department officials to complain that the United States is endangering its international interests by conducting "foreign policy on the cheap."[5]

The decline in foreign affairs spending is a reflection of the panoply of domestic and international changes the United States has experienced in recent years: the absence of compelling new security threats as Cold War antagonisms dissipated; continued U.S. military superiority relative to all potential competitors; greater political sensitivity to domestic priorities, including a concerted effort to eliminate persistent federal budget deficits; diminished public interest in international affairs; and the unwillingness of the American people to tolerate higher taxes, cuts in entitlement programs[6]— or bloody foreign encounters.

How, then, should we view the shrinkage of the foreign and national security resource base? For those who subscribe to the view that American primacy in a one-superpower world must be maintained, the narrowed resource base jeopardizes American security, with probable adverse long-term consequences. For those who believe America should "come home," the recent decline in expenditures accurately reflects the need to reorient priorities in the new era, including a greater focus on domestic needs. Indeed, for some the decline in defense spending made possible by the end of the Cold War is truly a "peace dividend," without which politicians' long-promised commitment to balance the federal budget would not likely have been realized.[7] But from either perspective, the overarching imperative is to balance commitments with resources.

How to accomplish that is a long-standing concern, not something peculiar to the post–Cold War era. More than half a century ago, during World War II, the eminent journalist Walter Lippmann warned that a "gap" would likely emerge between the nation's commitments and its ability to live up to them. Anticipating the arguments that the "declinists" would advance four decades later, Lippmann urged that "foreign policy consists of bringing into balance . . . the nation's commitments and the nation's power."[8] Failure to do so, he warned, would court disaster. He also worried about the absence of a domestic consensus for dealing with the impending peace once the war raging in Europe and Asia ended: "Our failure now to form a national policy will, though we defeat our enemies, leave us dangerously exposed to deadly conflicts at home and to unimaginable perils from abroad. . . . Rent by domestic controversy, for want of a settled foreign policy, we shall act not upon reflection and choice but under the impulse of accidents and the impact of force."[9] Lippmann's concerns appear apt not only to the Cold War on the horizon in the 1940s, when the second great war of the twentieth century which he witnessed would end, but also to the domestic concerns that now animate American foreign policy at the dawn of the millennium. Commitments and resources must still be matched.

THE DIPLOMATIC DIMENSION

Over the course of American history, diplomacy has been a key national power resource and a means of ensuring numerous foreign policy successes, including wartime alliances, peace settlements, trade pacts, and arms control treaties. Not only will diplomacy continue its salience in the new era, it will likely play an even greater role. Instead of an antagonistic world divided by political ideology and military alliances, the United States now faces an international environment in which the globalization of the world economy has accompanied the spread of democratic political systems and market economies. Globalization in turn demands that maintenance of America's preeminent position within the international system depends on co-opting, rather than provoking, the major states that have the potential to frustrate the exercise of U.S. hegemony. Thus the United States will be compelled to rely on its soft power, its ability to persuade and to set the agenda in diplomatic negotiations, not on its coercive power as measured by its military resources, if it is to promote and protect its interests effectively.

Diplomacy will also be critical in responding to a host of transnational challenges and nontraditional foreign affairs concerns, including terrorism, drug trafficking, global migration, and environmental degradation. These problems cannot be remedied by unilateral action; all require international cooperation for which diplomacy is essential. Relatedly, diplomacy will be crucial in fostering and maintaining the collective action necessary to address future regional and ethnic conflicts. Diplomats will also be called on to assist U.S. companies wishing to expand their trade opportunities. Although the trade orientation is partially a product of the Clinton administration's foreign policy and the State Department's new focus in the post–Cold War world, it is also tied to the fact that diplomacy allows the United States to tackle new challenges in a relatively affordable and flexible manner.

In the first reading in Part III, "Tin Cup Diplomacy," Hans Binnendijk offers a guarded assessment of the nation's diplomatic capabilities in the new era. Noting the dramatic decline in the international affairs budget, he praises the "innovative U.S. approaches [that] have masked the impact of reductions, especially in vital areas of the world." These efforts have included a growing reliance on domestic agencies, the military, foreign countries, and intergovernmental organizations to supplement the State Department's meager personnel and budgetary resources. Yet Binnendijk warns that there are limits to how long the United States can depend on ad hoc and "tin cup" solutions before its international influence erodes. The personnel, agencies, and programs that have traditionally managed U.S. foreign policy are so badly strained and poorly funded that "we now run the risk of developing diplomatic Alzheimer's disease." For Binnendijk, America's global leadership in the new era will be determined by whether the executive and legislative branches can find and sustain arenas of cooperation through which to stem the decline in foreign affairs funding.

THE MILITARY DIMENSION

A preference for military might and a penchant for overt and covert intervention in the affairs of others have been hallmarks of American foreign policy since World War II, and especially since NSC-68 was promulgated. The ability of the United States to pursue its goals through such means has depended on policymakers' capacity to draw on a broad array of economic, intelligence, and military strategic and tactical assets. Public diplomacy abroad (and sometimes at home) and foreign economic and military aid and sales are exemplary. Militarily, nuclear weapons have figured prominently among the nation's assets, as the United States historically depended heavily on the deterrent threat of nuclear weapons to preserve its own physical security and that of its allies against a potential Soviet military attack. Conventional weapons contributed to the U.S. posture of "extended deterrence," as in Europe where the United States committed itself to defend its North Atlantic Treaty Organization (NATO) allies from a Warsaw Pact attack at whatever level it might occur.

Conventional military forces also provided the means with which to seek influence over political events in other countries. By dispatching an aircraft carrier from one theater to another, conducting military exercises near the border of an adversary, sending military aircraft over its capital city at supersonic speeds, or engaging in other shows of force, the United States repeatedly used its vast military might to shape political outcomes abroad without resorting to the actual use of force. But on seven conspicuous occasions, overt military force was used: in Korea (1950–1953), Lebanon (1958), Vietnam (1962–1973), the Dominican Republic (1965), Grenada (1983), Panama (1989), and, most recently, Iraq and Kuwait (1991). A common characteristic of these interventionist episodes is that all occurred in the Global South. Except for Panama and the Iraq-Kuwaiti conflict, a second characteristic is that all were motivated by fear of communism and Soviet expansionism.

Clearly the reasons for the symbolic or actual use of American military force will be different in the new era. Varying types of limited military involvement in Bosnia, Haiti, Somalia, Northern Iraq, and Rwanda are early indications of this emerging reality. What is still unclear, however, is whether the United States will be compelled as well as prepared to engage in larger-scale conflicts such as those resembling the scope of the Persian Gulf War or North Korea's invasion of South Korea. The confusion over this issue is reflected in the inconsistencies surrounding American military capabilities. As noted, the overall defense budget, including weapons procurement funding, has declined dramatically since the end of the Cold War. Not surprisingly, these changes have been accompanied by a shrinking force structure. Before the fall of the Soviet Union, there were 18 active Army divisions, 15 aircraft carrier groups, 540 ships, and 24 active Air Force fighter wings. By fiscal year 1997, active duty divisions stood at 10, aircraft carrier groups declined to 12, Navy ships fell to 128, and active Air Force wings had been cut to 11. In addition, there has been a corresponding reduction in the Defense Department's employment base. By fiscal year 1997 the number of active duty personnel had dropped to 1.45 million from 2.1 million, members of the National Guard and Reserves to 900,000 from 1.7 million, and civilian employees to 800,000 from 1.1 million.[10]

Despite the downward trend in defense resources, there has been comparatively little change in defense planning or strategy. Before 1989, the American military was positioned to fight two and one-half wars. As the Cold War faded, the Bush administration altered the strategy marginally, to a two-war doctrine which anticipated that the United States should be prepared to fight concurrently two major regional wars, presumably in the Middle East and Asia. The underlying logic was to deter any potential adversary from initiating a conflict while the United States was engaged in another major war. At the beginning of the Clinton administration, there were indications that this strategy would be revised to reflect the new president's planned defense cuts. One proposal, for instance, embraced a "win-hold-win strategy," where the United States would seek to win a major regional war, hold the line in another (largely with air power), and then fight the second war to win. Yet the Pentagon's 1993 "Bottom-Up Review" and the 1997 Quadrennial Defense Review ultimately retained the two-war strategy, hardly a significant departure from the Cold War approach.

This state of affairs has pleased few defense analysts. One group maintains the current strategy is prudent, but that prevailing budget and force levels are inadequate to sustain it. Another contends the two-war strategy is hopelessly outdated and requires reformulation. The latter viewpoint was embraced by the National Defense Panel, a committee of civilian experts and retired military officers charged by Congress to evaluate how military strategy and forces should be configured in the future. The panel concluded in 1997 that the two-war strategy, instead of corresponding to America's real security environment, is obsolete and little more than "a means of justifying the current force structure—especially for those searching for the certainties of the Cold War era."[11]

This view is echoed by the author of the first of the four chapters on U.S. military capabilities in *The Future of American Foreign Policy*. In "A New Millennium and a Strategic Breathing Space," Russell E. Travers argues the United States is approaching a point in time where for at least the next decade or two it "will be confronted with less risk of large-scale conflict than has been the case since the end of World War I." This assessment is based on an evaluation of the relative capabilities of other actors within the international system. Global trends in such areas as defense expenditures, military readiness, and weapons development indicate that others are incapable of matching the size and sophistication of America's armed forces. In fact, Travers directly challenges the wisdom of the present two-war strategy, concluding that "no regional threats will . . . pose a substantial problem for the U.S. military well into the next century." Still, he stresses that this is not a time for retrenchment. The world remains a dangerous place where "U.S. adversaries will increasingly turn to asymmetric responses"—such as terrorism and information warfare—to counter American military superiority. Thus the United States must remain engaged and well prepared militarily but reorient its capabilities to meet "a host of transnational and low-intensity threats" as it seeks to extend its "strategic breathing space" indefinitely.

The changing nature of America's security environment and defense policy extends to the use of nuclear weapons. In November 1997, President Clinton issued a directive designed to update the nation's nuclear policy for the first time since 1981. Reflecting positive developments in U.S.–Russian relations and the administration's earlier Quadrennial Defense Review, the revised guidelines sought to relate the nation's still-formidable nuclear capabilities to the security challenges the United States faces in the post–Cold War era. Instead of preparing for a protracted, all-out nuclear war with Russia, American nuclear capability now will be oriented toward contingencies involving China, "rogue" states, and those posing threats with nonnuclear weapons of mass destruction.

In certain respects, the revised nuclear posture incorporates the views expressed in the second reading on U.S. military capabilities, which is drawn from the Henry L. Stimson Center's Project on Eliminating Weapons of Mass Destruction, chaired by General Andrew J. Goodpaster (retired). In "U.S. Nuclear Posture: A Case for Change," the Goodpaster committee expresses clear agreement with the Clinton administration's policy about the continuing importance of both a survivable nuclear deterrent and the appropriateness of a smaller strategic arsenal (e.g., 2,000–2,500 warheads). Such a force size would be consistent with the levels proposed for a third Strategic Arms Reduction Treaty (START) with Russia. Yet the Goodpaster report diverges from current policy when it concludes that "a declaratory role for U.S. nuclear weapons to deter chemical or biological weapons . . . would be of marginal military utility and any potential gain would be outweighed by the negative effects on U.S. proliferation efforts." This position relates to the report's wider theme that nuclear capability has lost much of its political and military utility in the new era. Instead of being critical to the nation's global position, nuclear weapons actually create more disadvantages than advantages for the United States. Consequently, "national security would be best served by a policy of phased reductions in all states' nuclear forces and gradual movement toward the objective of eliminating all weapons of mass destruction from all countries."

Even as the threat of nuclear war recedes, chemical and biological weapons of mass destruction (WMD) are a growing concern, especially since these are weapons the weak can use against the strong with comparative ease. Defense Secretary William Cohen dramatized the dangers on national television during a showdown with Iraq in the fall of 1997. Cohen displayed a five-pound bag of sugar and proclaimed that if the sugar were anthrax, a deadly biological agent, it could kill half the population in Washington, D.C. Not long after that he warned that the United Nations believed Iraq may have produced as much as two hundred tons of a deadly nerve gas, "theoretically enough to kill every man, woman, and child on the face of the earth." Meanwhile, the Pentagon initiated a program designed to inoculate all U.S. military personnel against certain biological agents.

In the next chapter, "The New Threat of Mass Destruction," Richard K. Betts addresses the growing threat posed by chemical and biological weapons. Recognizing that the draw-down of nuclear inventories has reduced the danger of "complete annihilation," Betts worries that there is "more danger of mass destruction," as "the probability that some smaller number of WMD will be used is growing." Despite this, new thinking on how to cope with the dangers posed has not yet developed, and traditional concepts of deterrence, drawn from nuclear deterrence theory developed during the Cold War, are of little relevance.

Surprisingly, Betts urges revival of an active civil defense program, something not seriously thought about since the early phases of the Cold War. He notes that even comparatively minor actions, like stockpiling protective masks and developing standby programs for mass vaccinations against biological agents, could reduce widespread death and destruction caused by WMD. He also argues that "civil defenses are especially worthwhile considering that they are extraordinarily cheap compared with regular military programs or active defense systems."

Betts also goes beyond civil defense to ask whether a withdrawal from global involvement might not be the best means to protect against the possibility that an angry group might resort to the use of WMD against the United States itself. "Because the United States is now the only superpower and weapons of mass destruction have become more accessible, American intervention in troubled areas is not so much a way to fend off such threats as it is what stirs them up."

Even as the capacity of potential adversaries to inflict damage on the United States increases, U.S. conventional weapons and forces are undergoing rapid changes which may make U.S. military capabilities stronger despite diminished resources. Such a development would be a direct consequence of advances in information technologies in the civilian sector, which may propel a Revolution in Military Affairs (RMA), a subject to which defense analysts have devoted considerable attention ever since the United States swiftly defeated Iraq in the Persian Gulf War.

In "Racing toward the Future: The Revolution in Military Affairs," Steven Metz explains that "an RMA is a rapid and radical increase in the effectiveness of military units that alters the nature of warfare and changes the strategic environment." Today the conventional wisdom is that the U.S. military will undergo such a transformation in the next century where continued advances in weapon, computer, and information technology will afford it "increased stealth, mobility, and dispersion, and a higher tempo of operations, all under the shield of information superiority." The Department of Defense, Metz explains, has been particularly receptive to this perspective because it views the RMA concept as a way to cope with fewer resources and reduce the number of lives lost in future wars. Metz believes these goals are attainable but warns the vigor with which the United States is now pursuing the RMA may not be prudent in the long term. Instead, it "may generate unintended political and diplomatic side effects and lead to a more dangerous world . . . by provoking asymmetric responses and arms races" on the part of America's enemies.

THE ECONOMIC DIMENSION

When the United States emerged from World War II, it was the world's unrivaled hegemonic power; little seemed beyond its reach. The German and Japanese challenges to the existing global order had been turned back as both were decisively beaten in war, and even America's victorious allies in Western Europe and the Eurasian landmass lay exhausted and in ruins. In the years immediately following the war, the United States achieved a level of economic and military power unparalleled in history. In 1947 it accounted for 50 percent of the combined gross world product. It was also the world's preeminent manufacturing center and its leading exporter, and its monopoly of the atomic bomb gave it military superiority. Thus the United States did indeed seem poised on the threshold of an American century.

Today, little more than a decade after many observers were predicting the nation's decline, it appears the United States is at the dawn of another American century. U.S. military superiority contributes to this emerging reality. As we noted in the introduction to this book, optimism about the state of its economy is another contributing factor. Surging domestic productivity, declining unemployment, and expanding exports have enabled the United States to eclipse the economic performance of other major industrialized states, which have been mired in various economic shortcomings.

Against this background, the economic challenge the United States faces at the dawn of the millennium is whether it can sustain its economic robustness into the future. Noteworthy in this respect is that while the U.S. economy is preeminent in the world, its share of gross world product has declined steadily since War World II, dropping by more than half, from 50 percent to about 22 percent, between the late 1940s and the late 1980s. Furthermore, the World Bank projects a further decline in the next century, to 17 percent by 2020.[12] The final four chapters in Part III offer different perspectives on the issue of how best to position the U.S. economy for the twenty-first century, with particular attention given to the role that government should play in facilitating the nation's economic competitiveness.

For Peter Morici in "Export Our Way to Prosperity," the issue of whether the United States can sustain and improve upon currently favorable economic conditions rests largely with its capacity to open foreign markets. As globalization transforms international economics, such a strategy is prudent because "U.S. competitiveness is improving, and the economy increasingly relies on exports to sustain growth and create good jobs." Morici stresses that "an effective U.S. policy for opening foreign markets does not require unequivocal reliance on multilateral institutions" like the World Trade Organization

(WTO). Instead, other methods such as regional pacts, bilateral agreements, and transatlantic cooperation may be more appropriate as long as "they produce results consistent with the central WTO goal of fostering market-responsive trade." In fact, Morici contends that forging a stronger economic relationship with Europe is particularly critical, because it "would offer broader markets to firms in both continents and create benefits for nations in Latin America, Asia, and Africa." It would also "place significant additional pressure on Japan to open its markets."

In contrast with Morici, Clyde V. Prestowitz, Jr. and Saul Goldstein in "Trade Policy for a New Era" advocate a trade policy that borders on neomercantilism, arguing that "we don't want to simply engage in laissez-faire trade." Instead of following the free trade orthodoxy that has governed economic policy since World War II, they maintain that the United States must go further and "integrate coherent technology, trade, and industrial policies with the rest of [its] macroeconomic tools." Such an approach is necessary, because at a time of rapid globalization, "displacement of key U.S. industries by foreign competitors has important impacts on U.S. productivity, technology development, and national security. Hence, trade . . . policy should be focused on industry-by-industry trade dynamics and less on overall deficits and surpluses." Put more simply, it matters what America makes and trades with others. Prestowitz and Goldstein believe this issue is so important that it warrants "close cooperation between government and business." They also support an industrial policy that acknowledges that "being a leader in critical industries is important and that the United States must respond to the industrial policies of other nations in an appropriate fashion."

Advocates of managed trade and other forms of neomercantilism often cite, as justifications for their policy prescriptions, the fact that the income of American wage earners (measured in constant dollars) has generally remained stagnant for more than two decades. At the same time, the differences between the nation's richest and poorest citizens has widened markedly. To many Americans, the causes underlying these disturbing facts are found in the world political economy. In particular, the rapid globalization of the world economy coupled with the perception that U.S. trade partners engage in neomercantilist practices fuels the belief of many Americans that they have been victimized by an international economic system in which capital and production are highly mobile, but labor is not. Thus workers cannot compete with "cheap foreign labor" in countries that otherwise engage in unfair trade practices. To compensate, critics of the free trade orthodoxy support efforts by the U.S. government to "right" a playing field that they believe is "tilted" against American businesses, which inhibits their ability to compete with foreign producers.

Paul Krugman, a prominent trade theorist, criticizes this prescription in the next selection, "Competitiveness: A Dangerous Obsession." Taking issue with the neomercantilist claim that U.S. income growth is largely tied to international competitiveness, Krugman writes: "It is simply not the case that the world's leading nations are to any important degree in economic competition with each other, or that any of their major economic problems can be attributed to failures to compete on world markets." Rather, evidence concerning a decline in American living standards after 1973 indicates U.S. income growth is related overwhelmingly to domestic productivity. Thus while it may be interesting to compare states as though they were engaged in a zero-sum struggle over international market shares, such a view is neither an accurate description of reality nor a useful guide for action. For American policymakers, Krugman warns, "thinking and speaking in terms of competitiveness poses three real dangers. First, it could result in the wasteful spending of government money supposedly to enhance U.S. competitiveness. Second, it could lead to protectionism and trade wars. Finally, and most important, it could result in bad public policy on a spectrum of important issues."

Part III concludes with a discussion of the European Union (EU)'s plan for a single currency and the profound impact this development will likely have on the nation's foreign policy, transatlantic relations, and international standing. The topic may seem arcane, but it is profoundly important. As Helmut Schmidt, former chancellor of West Germany, observed, "Americans do not yet understand the significance of the euro, but when they do, it could set up a potential conflict. The arrival of the euro will imply the overriding importance of the dollar will be reduced in the world. And it will change the whole world situation so that the United States can no longer call all the shots."[13]

C. Randall Henning expresses a similar view in his essay, "Europe's Monetary Union and the United States." He writes that "the United States [will] confront a larger, more cohesive, and more self-confident and powerful partner in the monetary union than it faced in the past." These circumstances, however, do not imply the United States can or should impede this probable outcome. Rather, Henning argues that "the EU's efforts toward monetary integration . . . deserve American political support."

Henning carefully examines the three factors—convergence criteria, German reticence, and the multispeed approach—most often cited as reasons for the monetary union's implausibility, and concludes a single European currency is a very likely event. Thus "the United States must become more proactive" on this issue. Such a posture is warranted, Henning believes, given the "far-reaching consequences for the United States and international economic cooperation." On one hand, monetary union "would create benefits for the rest of the world as well as for Europe." Chief among these advantages would be the European Union's ability to behave as a more efficient and flexible bargaining unit during international negotiations. On the other hand, establishment of a single currency would reduce America's global influence on monetary matters and challenge the rationale behind EU member states holding individual seats in international financial institutions. "Rather than ignoring these issues until the final stage of the integration process," Henning instructs, "governments on both sides of the Atlantic should confront them before they become serious problems."

NOTES

1. William S. Cohen, Report of the Quadrennial Defense Review (Washington, D.C.: U.S. Department of Defense, May 1997), Section II.

2. U.S. Department of States, "FY 1994 International Affairs Budget: Promoting Peace, Prosperity, and Democracy," *U.S. Department of State Dispatch Supplement 4* (April 1993), p. 2.

3. Cohen, Secretary's Message.

4. Pat Towell, "Perry Cites Readiness as Top Priority . . . and Modernization as Long-Term Goal," *Congressional Quarterly Weekly Report* 54 (March 1996), p. 628.

5. Craig Johnstone, "Foreign Policy on the Cheap: You Get What You Pay For," *U.S. Department of State Dispatch* 7 (March 1996), p. 146, and Warren Christopher, "Foreign Affairs Budget: Our Foreign Policy Cannot Be Supported on the Cheap," *U.S. Department of State Dispatch* 6 (April 1996), pp. 285–291.

6. Joshua Muravchik, "Affording Foreign Policy," *Foreign Affairs* 75 (March/April 1996), pp. 8–10.

7. *Newsweek*'s economics columnist Robert J. Samuelson argues that neither Bill Clinton nor congressional Republicans should "get the most credit for erasing budget deficits." Instead, Mikhail Gorbachev should. The reason is simple: without the savings from reduced defense spending, massive deficits would persist. Samuelson explains it this way:

> Federal spending comprises four major categories: defense, domestic discretionary (a catcall stretching from FBI to NASA to health research to education and housing), entitlements (programs for which people automatically qualify, from Social Security to Medicare to food stamps) and interest on the federal debt. Aside from defense, none has declined in the past decade as a share of GDP or in inflation-adjusted dollars. Between 1988 and 1998, entitlement spending went from 10.2 percent of GDP to an estimated 11.3 percent. In the same period, domestic discretionary spending has risen from 3.2 to 3.4 percent of GDP. (Robert J. Samuelson, "The Peace Dividend," *Newsweek*, January 26, 1998, p. 49)

8. Walter Lippmann, *U.S. Foreign Policy: Shield of the Republic* (Boston: Little, Brown, 1943), p. 9.

9. Lippmann, p. 5.

10. Cohen, Section V.

11. Quoted in Tim Weiner, "Two-War Strategy Is Obsolete, Panel of Experts Says," *New York Times*, December 2, 1997, p. A16. Retired General William E. Odom is among those who share a critical view of the current strategic posture, arguing that "America's defense does not require a larger budget, but rather a major reallocation to meet the challenges of the post–Cold War world." William E. Odom, "Transforming the Military," *Foreign Affairs* 76 (July/August 1997), p. 54.

12. "World Bank Report Sees Era of Emerging Economies," *New York Times*, September 10, 1997, p. D7.

13. Quoted in William Drozdiak, "Down with Yankee Dominance," *Washington Post National Weekly Edition*, November 24, 1997, p. 15.

The Diplomatic Dimension

22. TIN CUP DIPLOMACY
Hans Binnendijk

*F*ifty years ago the United States entered a new international system armed with resources to meet the new challenge of communism. At the height of the Marshall Plan, for example, some 16 percent of the U.S. federal budget was dedicated to supporting Europe alone. Today we are again in the early stages of a new international system, but without a unifying challenge to raise foreign affairs resources much above 1 percent of the federal budget. Remarkably, with tin cup diplomacy and some triage, the United States has been able to deal fairly successfully with post–Cold War complexity. Our capabilities are now fraying, however, and international leadership cannot be sustained unless the resource slide is reversed.

Reductions in the international affairs budget have been deep, with constant dollar cuts of about 34 percent over the past decade, including a 14 percent cut in just the last two years. Defense expenditures have also fallen 34 percent since 1986. Expressed as a percentage of GNP, defense and international affairs spending together has dropped from 6.9 percent to 3.7 percent during this period. International affairs cuts have also been targeted at specific accounts. For example, the drop in international security assistance has been 74 percent over the decade, so deep that if aid to Israel, Egypt, and Turkey is excluded, the United States has basically given up security assistance as an instrument of foreign policy. Other areas particularly hard hit are the United Nations, information and exchange programs, and multilateral development aid.

Note: Notes have been deleted.

Analysts disagree about the impact of the international affairs cuts. The Georgetown University Institute for the Study of Diplomacy concluded [in 1996] that resource problems are already harming the capacity of the United States to lead and that the national security capital built up during the Cold War is being depleted. The Heritage Foundation, on the other hand, has argued that some key accounts have increased and that no real harm has been done.

There is some truth to both sides of these apparently contradictory conclusions. Innovative U.S. approaches have masked the impact of reductions, especially in vital areas of the world. Passing the tin cup and designing ad hoc solutions have worked so far. In Central Europe, for example, the Partnership for Peace is a bargain at $100 million, while the United States intends to pay for less than 10 percent of the NATO enlargement bill. In Korea, U.S. creation of the Korean Peninsula Energy Development Organization helped halt North Korea's nuclear program, and Japan and South Korea are picking up more than 90 percent of the tab for it. In the former Soviet Union, Western disbursements of more than $20 billion since 1991 have been made primarily by international financial institutions. In the case of Mexico, the United States found an obscure account—the Exchange Stabilization Fund—to provide $20 billion in financing to deal with the 1994 financial crisis there. In the Zaire crisis, the United States promised to help the new leadership retrieve billions of Mobutu's stolen dollars as an incentive to stop the massacres—a skillful use of someone else's money. Only in the Middle East has the United States continued to pour aid funds in at pre-1990 levels. But when it came to Operations Desert Storm and Vigilant Warrior in the Persian Gulf, the United States again successfully turned to its allies to pay most of the bills.

According to a new book [edited by Mary Locke and Casimin Yost] entitled *Who Needs Embassies?*, U.S. embassies in strategically significant countries have also managed, at least until now, to pursue critical U.S. interests successfully despite fraying caused by cutbacks. The book examines recent U.S. operations in five key countries—Germany, South Korea, South Africa, Israel, and Guatemala—and concludes that despite policy successes, demands on these embassies are increasing dramatically even as they are being pinched financially. In addition, the State Department reports that thirty-one new missions or embassies have been created since 1991, mostly in countries formerly part of the Soviet Union or Yugoslavia. And the National Defense University's *Strategic Assessment 1996* shows that the number of U.S. personnel stationed in our embassies has actually increased from 15,000 to 19,000 during the past ten years.

But all this is misleading. What has been happening is that other U.S. agencies have stepped in overseas to help the often beleaguered State Department. Most of the increase in U.S. embassy personnel, for example, is from the military or from U.S. law enforcement agencies. In Mexico City, over thirty U.S. agencies are represented at the embassy, and seventeen work on counterdrug efforts. A Defense Department publication entitled "Foreign Military Interaction: Strategic Rationale" lists thirteen different defense engagement programs overseas, most of which have diplomatic purposes. The National

Guard works closely with "sister states" in Central Europe, where it helps to implement the Partnership for Peace. And three new U.S.–run regional military education centers have been established for Europe, Asia, and Latin America.

Allied nations and other organizations are also filling some of the gaps left by the United States. In Bosnia, private voluntary organizations provide vital services that thirty years ago would have been performed by the U.S. government. In Haiti, Canadians and Pakistanis perform international policing functions that the United States left to them last summer [1997]. In North Korea, the International Atomic Energy Agency provides continuous on-site monitoring of nuclear material, and its teams include a substantial number of specialists from the U.S. Department of Energy. During the Cold War, of course, all treaty verification obligations were carried out directly by the United States, either through remote technical means, or, where agreed, treaty-specified U.S. on-site inspections. In El Salvador, our stabilizing influence has been partially replaced by the United Nations.

If tin cup diplomacy is working, why then the concern about budget cuts? Because while these activities may be useful, they cannot compensate fully and indefinitely for the shortfall in the core foreign affairs budget. In order to save key programs, State has had to sacrifice others. For example, *Who Needs Embassies?* notes that in order to support democratic transitions in countries such as Guatemala and South Africa, resources for other embassies in those regions have been sucked dry. To open the thirty-one new missions of the kind mentioned above, State had to close thirty-five other embassies and consulates. Some of the less important embassies that have stayed open suffer like our poorly constructed embassy in Guinea-Bissau. In what should become a classic cable, sent to Washington in February [1997], the embassy sought guidance on pesticides to kill both the hundreds of rats that eat documents and the thousands of locusts that penetrate into the deepest security areas of the post, At the Agency for International Development (AID), planners will cut the number of overseas AID missions by more than half in order to save critical programs. And the U.S. Information Agency (USIA) is closing libraries by the dozen, giving rise to the concern that our friends see American librarians and development officers leaving just as Drug Enforcement Agency personnel arrive.

Behind the façade of success, then, our basic foreign affairs infrastructure is eroding. The State Department has cut two thousand employees and USIA has cut 25 percent of its workforce . . ., many of them experienced regional experts that are needed to deal with today's complex world. Half of State's computers and three-quarters of its phone systems are obsolete. The archaic State Department Wang computer system cannot read e-mail documents prepared in a Windows program. Some of our embassies, such as those I visited recently in China and South Korea, are apparent firetraps. Departing overseas personnel routinely leave their posts three to four months before their replacements arrive, in order to save money but at the expense of continuity. In other embassies, biographic files on key local figures are no longer kept up to date, so valuable information is sacrificed. There are not enough funds to enable political officers to travel often outside the capital city, and consequently reporting suffers. We now run the risk of developing diplomatic Alzheimer's disease.

International affairs budget cuts are also beginning to affect our ability to influence events and to practice preventive diplomacy. It is only because an unrivaled military stands behind the diplomatic tin cup that the United States retains any influence at all. Our Economic Support Fund, designed in 1977 to provide influence-generating economic aid, is now focused almost exclusively on Israel and Egypt. In the multilateral banks, we are losing our ability to block loans of which we do not approve and direct other loans to projects we support. In Panama, we may lose access to military bases critical to the counter-narcotics fight because we cannot afford security assistance. In Africa, declining foreign aid resources coincide with a marked increase in civil conflict in failed states.

The negative impact of these budget cuts has reached the point where constructive actions are now being taken in the administration, on Capitol Hill, and in the private sector to regenerate our capabilities. Negative budget trends may have bottomed out. The [Clinton] administration has agreed with Congress to undertake an ambitious merger of the State Department, the Arms Control and Disarmament Agency (ACDA), USIA, and AID. ACDA and USIA would become one with State, while AID would remain separate but would report to the secretary of state rather than the president. This would eventually result in greater efficiency and possibly some savings, but more importantly it has created a smoother relationship between the two branches of government on the question of foreign affairs resources. That cooperation is also evident in the deal made with Senator Jesse Helms to repay over three years $819 million owed in arrears to the United Nations. In exchange for authorizing the funds, Senator Helms extracted various useful UN reforms, and he intends to shave future American contributions to UN operations from 25 to 20 percent of the total bill, in order to bring U.S. dues in line with new international realities.

Secretary of State Madeleine Albright has also given higher priority to fixing the resources problem. She has initiated a much needed effort to explain to the American people the benefits of engagement overseas. . . . Albright's State Department has created a new strategic planning system that for the first time sets out specific budget-driven policy goals, designs a strategy to implement them, and establishes indicators to judge progress. Ambassador Max Kampelman took the lead in stimulating private sector initiatives such as the "Advocacy of U.S. Interests Abroad" project, which, under the guidance of the Stimson Center, seeks to create a clearer national consensus on foreign policy goals and means.

Both efforts attest to the recognition that the pendulum has swung too far and that the foreign affairs budget has been cut too deep. Now is the time to sustain the new cooperation between the administration and Congress so that the United States can indeed lead the world into the twenty-first century.

The Military Dimension

23. A NEW MILLENNIUM AND A STRATEGIC BREATHING SPACE

Russell E. Travers

*T*he world is a dangerous place; so U.S. national security officials must assume. But how dangerous? What threats will confront the United States as it enters the twenty-first century? What does America's future risk equation look like? Few questions demand as much thoughtful attention from Washington as these; unless and until they are answered, the basis for a reasoned debate on the legitimate defense needs of the country—relative to a wide array of competing priorities—will not exist.

Unfortunately, a number of factors have obscured the distinction between actual threats, potential risks, and unadulterated bogeymen. First, no consensus exists over the U.S. role in the world, on the scope of U.S. vital national interests, or indeed on what a security "interest" is in the first place; as such it is difficult to define threats to those interests. Second, transitional periods, like this post–Cold War era, are inherently challenging to strategists; uncertainty levels are high and no one can say with confidence what the world will look like in a decade or two. And third, the subject of "threats" is complicated; the United States has an abundance of avowed global strategists, but few go beyond platitudes ("Iran is a threat to the Persian Gulf," for example) when talking about the military and technical nature of threats.

By themselves these factors could lead toward "worst case" threat analysis—throwing up one's hands and assuming that all potential threats can and will become real. And when this tendency joins with a host of domestic political considerations, the result is that pundits of varying credibility tout a

Note: The views expressed in this chapter are those of the author and do not necessarily reflect the official policy of the Defense Intelligence Agency, the Department of Defense, or the U.S. Government.

dizzying array of alleged threats. This excessively robust threat portrayal leads to an overly conservative risk equation, which in turn skews U.S. resource decisions. And the U.S. public, which generally lacks interest in foreign affairs, ends up confused and deferring to the "experts." In the end, the country is not well served.

This [chapter] will suggest that the United States needs to reevaluate the threats it faces today and over the next decade. Yes, the world is dangerous, and Americans will be at risk around the globe. As a result of terrorist attacks, Americans, at a personal level, may even feel less safe than they did during the Cold War. But, generally speaking, a growing gap exists between many avowed threats and reality of the U.S. security posture. . . .

The [chapter] concludes that the United States is on the threshold of a protracted military breathing space. During this period, U.S. leaders will be confronted with less risk of large-scale conflict than has been the case since the end of World War I. With the luxury of a very favorable risk equation, U.S. leaders can accelerate the pace of adapting to the post–Cold War era. . . .

THE SUM OF ALL OUR FEARS

The general parameters of what might be called the "sum of all our fears" model of defense planning are well known. Over the next decade, it argues, the United States will face the possibility of attacks by rogue states, with Iraq and North Korea generally considered the most likely candidates. In addition, the United States needs to guard against a resurgent Russia that could again threaten Europe. Iran will be a major threat in and around the Persian Gulf. And China's economic potential could be rapidly channeled into the military and threaten U.S. interests. Ethnic, religious, and sectarian violence will also provide a never-ending series of Somalias, Haitis, and Yugoslavias.

Technologically, according to this view, the United States could lose its superiority in advanced weapon systems. For one thing, the proliferation of weapons of mass destruction and delivery systems will continue and the United States could be threatened by pariah states with intercontinental ballistic missiles (ICBMs) early in the next century. Even more broadly, a wide array of advanced conventional systems could be fielded and made available to any countries willing to pay. And in the somewhat more distant future, U.S. defense planners could confront a "revolution in military affairs" achieved in the defense establishments of a few potential adversaries—a combination of technological advance and new operational concepts that could render U.S. systems obsolete and inflict battlefield defeat on U.S. forces.

This rendition of possible future threats is indeed daunting, and would pose quite a challenge if all or even most of it were to come to pass. Fortunately, it will not. In actuality, the United States is on the threshold of a strategic breathing space that could easily extend a decade or two. During this period, myriad challenges will continue to claim U.S. attention—but operations against an enemy capable of large-scale sustained combat will not be one of them.

TOWARD A MORE REASONED VIEW OF THE FUTURE

Despite the significant uncertainty that exists regarding the nature of future threats to U.S. interests, a number of facts can provide insights into the future security environment. Together they suggest that the "sum of all our fears" model of threat analysis is exaggerated.

First, among the world's major defense spenders, national security concepts are changing; the historic discontinuity occasioned by the demise of the Soviet Union is having worldwide repercussions in the military sphere. Worldwide military expenditures are down some 40 percent from the late 1980s. Perhaps 50 percent of global defense spending from this period was attributable to the Cold War, and the Cold War's end is gradually wringing those resources out of the system; the implications for future military capabilities are immense. Moreover, reflecting a decline in threat perceptions and a change in the security calculus occurring in much of the world, the share of the world's gross domestic product directed to defense has dropped precipitously. Although still important, the military component of national security policy is neither as useful nor as central in advancing interests as it once was. Simply put, the defense industrial powers are growing up, focusing more on economic and cultural avenues to power and less on military ones.

Second, with the change occurring in many countries' risk equation, long-term defense planning is a mess. Countries are uncertain of their enemies, of how they should shape their militaries, and even of the missions for which their militaries should prepare. Most countries have published post–Cold War doctrines or white papers, but defense cuts often make the documents outdated even before they are issued; consequently, they are of little use for helping with force development, weapons acquisition, or conducting trade-off analysis. The worldwide trend is to defer hard decisions on weapons systems.

And third, as the world adjusts to the end of the U.S.–Soviet rivalry, militaries are caught in the middle. Rapid downsizing has caught defense establishments unprepared. Increasingly, "two-tiered" militaries have become the norm: Except for select "upper tier" units, readiness—judged by factors such as flying hours, ground forces training, and equipment availability—has declined. Although developing countries are buying some modern equipment, most are having problems with training and maintenance—and the gap between technological potential and demonstrated performance is growing. Finally, as a result of diminished defense budgets, weapons development has slowed substantially around the world.

If these trends continue, it may be that no country other than the United States will ever again demonstrate the capabilities that we displayed during the Persian Gulf War. Nonetheless, defense planners legitimately point to a number of concerns: the "uncertainties" inherent in this period of transition; the existence of "rogue" states; the availability of nuclear, biological, and chemical (NBC) weapons technology and sophisticated conventional weaponry; and a very messy state of affairs in the developing world. To examine these factors in more detail, I will now look closer at the various countries and technological developments of concern.

REGIONAL SNAPSHOTS

Regionally, looking forward 10–15 years, what potentially hostile countries might be able to execute large-scale conventional offensive operations that could threaten U.S. interests? In the current vernacular, what major regional contingencies (MRCs) are likely to emerge early in the next century? The short answer could well be *none*.

Korea

North Korea probably poses the most complex security situation in the world: the potential for either explosion or implosion, with neither offering the prospect of much warning. Despite the problems confronting the North, the United States cannot rule out the possibility of explosion—an armed attack on South Korea. With the bulk of North Korea's million-man military located within 100 kilometers of the 38th Parallel, careful attention will be directed at the thousands of tanks and artillery pieces poised opposite South Korea. Clearly this military has serious problems in training, logistics, and readiness (including malnutrition in the ranks); explosion may indeed be occasioned less by a deliberate attack in hopes of unifying the peninsula, than by a last-ditch lashing out. This dangerous situation could continue for several years, and should deterrence fail, an extraordinarily devastating war could occur.

But assuming deterrence succeeds, how much longer can North Korea continue as an over-militarized, closed society? Having been largely cut off from the largess of its Chinese and Russian benefactors, and finding itself with almost nothing anyone in the world values to sell (apart from a few missiles), how long can such a system carry on devoting an inordinate share of its limited wealth to a nonproductive military sector? . . .

The North Korean regime is moving toward an inevitable demise; the only questions are how and when it will fall. Either explosion, an attack South, or implosion, a civil war or revolution within the North, would pose significant challenges. But the window is rapidly closing for any possibility for a large-scale attack by the North; within a few years and perhaps sooner, its military and society will simply have decayed beyond a point at which it can mount large-scale military operations.

Iraq

The other country used most often to illustrate a major regional contingency is Iraq, potentially threatening the Saudi oil fields. Coming out of Desert Storm, Saddam Hussein sought to retain offensive military capabilities, and

Iraq will warrant close scrutiny while he remains in power. On the other hand, U.S. planners need to keep the size and scope of this threat in perspective. . . . Iraq's military remains less than 40 percent the size of the force that invaded Kuwait. Moreover, the military mirrors an Iraqi civil society that has been virtually crushed; it is rife with problems. Desertions, purges in the officer corps, training shortfalls, and severe readiness and logistics problems all undercut the military's capabilities. And although these problems mainly affect the regular military (roughly three-fourths of the overall force), even the Republican Guard has had similar problems. Few militaries in the world have demonstrated the capability to rapidly prosecute large-scale armor operations across hundreds of miles; with the Iraqi force in its current state of decay, disrepair, and continued vulnerability to air strikes, it simply does not have the capacity to conduct such operations deep into Saudi Arabia (as opposed to conducting much shallower attacks against the Kurds or into Kuwait). Moreover, still psychologically devastated from its disaster in the Gulf war, the Iraqi military has no stomach to fight the United States.

Under certain assumptions, this situation might eventually change. But the assumptions are pretty heroic: that Saddam remains in power; that he controls Iraq's insurgency problems, the Sunni tribes, and military coup plotting; and that he gets past international economic sanctions, somehow reconstructing civil society and channeling oil proceeds to the military. Under such circumstances, Iraq could perhaps once again pose a conventional threat to Saudi Arabia, but the combination seems unlikely. And if the assumptions do not hold, the Iraqi military will continue a downward spiral toward a protracted inability to pose a large-scale threat to Gulf oil supplies.

Iran

Beyond North Korea and Iraq, the United States must also contend with a potential military threat from Iran. Sitting astride the Strait of Hormuz, participating in state-sponsored terrorism, and advocating radical Islamic fundamentalism, Iran will continue to be of concern. But U.S. planners must be sophisticated in considering the threats posed by Iran. It is primarily Iran's use of the opposite extremes of the conflict spectrum—from terrorism to weapons of mass destruction, including NBC weapons—that is now and will remain a concern.

In contrast, Iran's conventional military capabilities do not constitute a major threat to the region. It is slowly improving capabilities to execute operations around the Strait in such areas as mining and cruise missiles, but the last thing Tehran wants today and in the foreseeable future is a military confrontation with the United States. Like its Iraqi counterpart, the Iranian military has serious problems. Iran's effort to maintain two separate militaries (regular and Revolutionary Guard) weakens command and control. Cut off from U.S. arms and spare parts, the Iranians now maintain aircraft from four countries (Russia, China, France, and the United States); their logistics system is a nightmare. Similarly, the pilot cadre, trained by the United States, is aging, and Iran's indigenous pilot training has been extremely poor. Other training—such as the crews of the much-vaunted, Soviet-built Kilo submarines, for example—is also suspect. And Iran's air defense system has long been porous; even with China's help, Iran's *future* air defenses may only approximate the limited Iraqi capabilities shown in the Gulf war.

Moreover, Iran's potential to improve its military capabilities is limited by a daunting list of social and economic problems. Iran's population could balloon from 65 million people today to 100 million by the year 2010, and the country's stagnant economy is ill-equipped to absorb such population growth. A lack of economic reform, debt restructuring that will require hard currency to meet future interest payments (thereby limiting arms purchases), and a decrepit oil and gas infrastructure will bedevil Iran for decades. Ample reasons exist to be concerned about Iran—its use of terrorism, for example, and its pursuit of NBC weapons—but its ability to conduct sustained conventional operations is not one of them.

Russia

Russia's political volatility, coupled with its very large military, lead some to be concerned that it could reemerge as a major conventional threat to Europe. Those concerns are misplaced. Absent some action by the West that serves to galvanize a Russian population and substantially to increase threat perceptions, Russian conventional forces will be limited to small-scale operations for well over a decade. The problems confronting the Russian military are so deep and so all-encompassing that it could be decades before it could again be considered healthy; Chechnya bears witness to the serious shortcomings of the Russian Army. By virtually every standard that is used to measure military capabilities, Russia's military is in deep trouble. The personnel system is in virtual crisis: the conscript pool is avoiding service; contract service is too expensive; the better young officers are leaving; and too many senior officers remain in the ranks. Training is abysmal: Fighter pilots fly 30 hours a year— well below most developing-world standards and only 15 percent as much as U.S. standards; ground forces rarely train above the company or battalion level; and the navy is relegated to a few ships and submarines putting to sea. Readiness has been adversely affected by a lack of housing, lack of pay, disease, malnutrition, corruption, and crime. Block obsolescence of major combat systems like aircraft, ships, and battle tanks looms unless Russia begins to increase its procurement of new equipment.

These problems stem from a precipitous decline in defense expenditures, which are down 80 percent from Soviet levels. Inadequate funding has led the military leadership to talk about bankruptcy, brink of collapse, irreversible decline, and a fight for survival; and trying to retain a force 40 percent the size of Soviet levels on a budget only 20 percent that of the Soviet era is a recipe for a hollow military. Although the defense budget is probably at or near its bottoming-out point, no substantial increase will accrue to the military over the next decade. The future for the Russian general-purpose forces will continue to be bleak well into the next century.

China

Finally, many view China as a country of concern, not because of what it once was, but because of what it might become. China's military is benefiting from impressive economic growth, but many Western observers have an exaggerated view of how rapidly it is developing because of inadequate appreciation of the very low starting point of the People's Liberation Army (PLA). Overall, this military is too big and too old to pose a threat to the U.S. military any time soon; in its training and doctrine, it is decades behind its Western counterparts. Other than its potential to play missile diplomacy against its neighbors, the PLA has very limited ability to project force very far from its shores. Nor is China improving this force at a breakneck pace: high-profile purchases of SA-10 surface-to-air missiles, SU-27 fighters, and Kilo submarines from Russia have given a misleading sense of the overall modernization rate of the Chinese military. Assuming China proves able to assimilate technology fully (a 30 percent to 40 percent failure rate in the high-profile space launch vehicle program is noteworthy), modernization will pick up after the turn of the century. But consider the quality of this equipment: the Chinese Air Force will only begin fielding an indigenously-built fighter-attack aircraft equivalent to the 1970s-vintage U.S. F-16 sometime after the year 2000; its ground forces are striving to build a battle tank that is the equal of the former Soviet Union's T-72 of the 1970s; and the Chinese Navy may have a single aircraft carrier by 2010.

Generally speaking, China will enter the twenty-first century with small elements of its force having advanced just to the use of 1980s vintage equipment—a substantial improvement by Chinese standards, but modest compared to the world's leading militaries. And equipment is only part of the challenge; with the vast majority of its conscript force not having graduated high school, the PLA will have to prove that it can integrate this equipment into complex, joint operations. China is undoubtedly an improving regional military power, but even if it avoids any political, economic, or social setbacks, it is still decades away from being able to project sufficient power to constitute a significant challenge to the U.S. military.

TECHNICAL SNAPSHOTS

No regional threats will therefore pose a substantial problem for the U.S. military well into the next century. Either the countries at issue have substantial political, social, economic, and military problems, or they are not at a sufficiently advanced state militarily to be of substantial concern; all of them are experiencing difficulties simply manning, training, and equipping their forces.

The issue of future technical threats, on the other hand, is more complex, because U.S. planners must be concerned about foreign systems that may not be fielded for a decade or more. Yet here, too, much of the hype about future foreign weapons systems is overdone. They generally date to the Cold War and many are either undergoing reevaluation or running up against budget constraints. The gap between countries' desires for new weapons and their ability to pay for them—the disparity between what has been sought for in research and development (R&D) and what will actually be procured—is growing. As it does so, the menu of threats to U.S. forces in the coming decades is shrinking.

Russia is the clearest case in point. Moscow's defense industrialists have acknowledged ongoing R&D on weapons systems in most war-fighting mission areas—strategic missiles, tanks, planes, submarines, helicopters, and tactical missiles. And because the Russians, like the Soviets before them, were among the world leaders in technological sophistication of weapons, these systems, if fielded in meaningful numbers, would constitute the leading-edge technological threats facing the U.S. military.

The key, of course, is *whether* these systems will be deployed. In fact, a large percentage either will not be—at least not without substantial delay—or will be procured only in small numbers. Russian defense expenditures have been in freefall, and in percentage terms procurement has fallen more than the overall budget. The logical question becomes, if Russia is so badly off economically, how can it even afford to continue research on so many systems? Life-cycle cost analysis provides the answer: R&D may account for 10 percent of the cost of a fighter aircraft, procurement 30 percent, and operations and maintenance (O&M) 60 percent. The Russian R&D picture may be relatively robust, but procurement has been decimated and O&M is dismal. The Russians are gambling that the budgetary picture will improve substantially in the future—but there is no reason to believe it will do so over the next decade.

Given the disarray in Russia's defense industrial base, therefore, one should be leery of Western hand-wringing about Russian systems that will allegedly constitute a threat to the U.S. military. Come 2005, many Western analysts might look back sheepishly at all the systems the Russians did *not* procure in militarily significant numbers.

U.S. allies also face a mismatch between military desires and procurement budgets. They are working on an array of advanced systems, but procurement budgets have taken large hits over the last few years; even France is facing procurement cuts that could reach 35 percent. Virtually all major defense industrial powers face a "bow wave" over the next decade—that is, they have insufficient money programmed for desired procurement. Like the Russians, America's allies indicate they see exports as a critical way of supporting their systems, but the arms market is too soft. Without sufficient domestic or foreign markets, many systems currently in development are going to die.

In sum, any suggestion that the United States is at risk of losing technological superiority as friends, allies, and adversaries alike push ahead rapidly with R&D on new and exotic weapons does not hold up. . . .

One corollary to this overall slowdown in weapons development relates to the revolution in military affairs (RMA). Although RMA proponents tend to avoid precisely defining the concept, generally speaking, RMA has its roots in the writings of Soviet Marshal Nikolai Ogarkov. In the early 1980s, he envisioned a military technical revolution (MTR) that would include a vast array of high tech weapons; since he wrote, the concept of MTR has been broadened to an RMA that would also include new organizational and operational concepts. The entire concept has a bit of a surreal quality. Yes, technological change is occurring at a dizzying pace. But given the state of disarray within many militaries, the rather traditional things they are trying to buy, the continued budget limitations they face, and the uninspired nature of foreign military theoretical literature, the RMA may be just one more casualty of the end of the Cold War.

THREATS REMAIN

. . . Without modern militaries capable of meeting U.S. forces on the battlefield, U.S. adversaries will increasingly turn to asymmetric responses to U.S. operations. This could involve weapons of mass destruction, as suggested above. It could also comprise technological "trumps" to U.S. systems—information warfare used to attack the electronic networks on which U.S. military operations now depend—though as far as deployed U.S. forces are concerned, this will probably prove to be a minor irritant. Of greater concern will be attempts to attack U.S. "will," such as taking peacekeepers hostage or imposing early casualties on U.S. forces; and almost certainly the asymmetric attack on U.S. will and staying power of greatest concern will be terrorism. The Japanese subway attack and Chechen use of radiation weapons in Moscow demonstrate that readily available technology can be lethal. The single most important question for U.S. "defense" policy in the years ahead may be how the United States will maintain capabilities to deter and, if necessary, attack terrorism sponsored from abroad.

As the 1990s have shown, portions of the lesser-developed world are coming to resemble virtual "states of nature" in their level of violence and institutional collapse, and wars such as those in Bosnia, Rwanda, and Somalia will confront the world with immense challenges over the next decade. The pressures of population growth, urbanization, religious extremism, ethnic hatreds, disease, lack of arable land, and water shortages are guaranteed sources of conflict. These will prove to be the mainstay of conflicts that will bedevil the United States; combat will be neither organized nor high tech, but it will be brutal. In most cases these conflicts will not immediately affect U.S. strategic interests, at least not in any traditional sense, thus proving a potent argument against risking American lives; but at what future cost does the United States ignore current problems?

Beyond the immediate humanitarian costs of these conflicts, some will eventually implicate U.S. interests. As they do so, they will raise a host of vexing questions for defense planners. How can the United States help to alleviate these pressures and treat causes rather than symptoms? If those efforts are unsuccessful, can the U.S. military be used in a preventive diplomacy role? And if the military is engaged in conflict, what kind of force is best matched to a mission requiring neither heavy nor high tech forces? How the United States answers these questions will say a great deal about whether it plays a constructive role in large parts of the developing world over the next 10 to 20 years.

A ROADMAP FOR OPERATING IN THE BREATHING SPACE

How, then, can the United States avoid a focus on yesterday's threats and take advantage of its opportunity to shape tomorrow's reality? . . . What follows is a package of general policy prescriptions . . . that constitute a roadmap for the use of a strategic breathing space. . . .

1. *Stay engaged.* The biggest U.S. mistake of the interwar period was its return to isolationist tendencies. Today, the private sector, concerned about trade and globalization, will try to ensure that *economic* retrenchment on regional and global free trade pacts does not occur, but U.S. political leaders will need to make a forceful case with the American public, on both deterrent and stability grounds, for overseas commitment of U.S. forces. . . .

2. *Be a worthy world leader.* . . . The United States should remain the world's leading advocate of international law and fight any impulse to set it aside for narrow political or economic purposes; doing otherwise demeans the United States as a country. . . . [But] Washington must not become giddy with idealism; when the United States must stand up to a tyrant or use military force, it should hit hard and leave no possibility that our resolve could be misunderstood.

3. *Minimize future threats.* Throughout this period the United States should address future vulnerabilities. Arms control can help: Russia, for example, is unlikely to maintain START II levels of nuclear weapons and will seek to negotiate lower totals. The United States will be able to pursue a minimum nuclear deterrent force of our design, saving substantial money and perhaps eliminating an entire leg of the triad of strategic forces carried on ICBMs, SLBMs (submarine-launched ballistic missiles), and bombers. And although R&D for a national missile defense should continue, as much-delayed rogue-state missile threats pass further into the future, national missile defense (as opposed to theater defenses) will prove an unwise use of resources. Beyond military issues, the United States should also address its long-term vulnerability to oil.

4. *Be patient.* America's national fetish with instant gratification will not serve it well during this period. When dealing with Russia's transition to freedom, U.S. relations with China, or the Mideast peace process, progress is going to be a series of two steps forward and one back. Long-term, focused attention will be required, and setbacks will be many—particularly in the developing world. Most often, . . . expensive peacekeeping operations . . .

treat symptoms rather than causes. Rather, U.S. policy needs to be focused on things like infrastructure and education—the kinds of long-term developmental assistance that may not pay off for years. Beyond advancing governmental and multilateral assistance, we should continue promoting (subsidizing, if necessary) direct private investment overseas.

5. *Don't fight the last war.* As the United States prepares its military for the twenty-first century, it needs to consider whether Desert Storm–like wars are what it needs to be concerned about. It is neither self evident, nor even likely, that large-scale, combined-arms–sustained combat is the threat of the future. This doesn't mean that the United States should cut force structure; if the United States is going to remain engaged worldwide, it requires a large military to cover the range of missions, deployments, rotations, and other tasks associated with that responsibility. But it may mean that the U.S. military should alter its force composition in favor of lighter and more combat-support forces: the demand for heavy forces and state-of-the-art weapons will diminish as the United States focuses primarily on the low end of the conflict spectrum. And if the American people do not want their troops doing peace-keeping missions, perhaps U.S. and allied governments ought to rethink the issue of a UN standby force to perform that mission.

6. *Prepare for . . . what?* A host of transnational and low-intensity threats pose a series of unique challenges to U.S. military planners: international organized crime; trafficking in nuclear materials; asymmetric warfare, including terrorism, weapons of mass destruction, and, potentially, information warfare; and so on. Designed to exploit U.S. vulnerabilities and avoid U.S. strengths, these challenges will rarely lend themselves to traditional military solutions. To meet these threats, the United States will need a robust intelligence community capable of analyzing the world and giving early warning of these extraordinarily complex problems. As such fundamental concepts as war, crime, and terrorism converge, and as traditionally distinct domestic and international issues blur together, U.S. planners will need to rethink the national security structure and interagency process. They are not well suited for today's world.

7. *Think longer-term, but don't get locked in.* The fiscal tension between maintaining force structure and modernization is real. Throughout the period of this breathing space, advanced weapons platforms will have limited utility in dealing with low-intensity problems; they will be manpower intensive, but not high-tech weapons intensive. Clearly, the United States needs to continue R&D on a host of advanced military systems in the face of future uncertainty. Yet, U.S. defense planners should push irrevocable decisions into the future; if current trends continue, many of the foreign systems in development are going to die from lack of procurement funds. The United States should stretch out programs and be prepared to cut back future buys; although it must maintain technological superiority, the military may increasingly modernize along the F-117 model: a few versions of the most advanced technologies that serve as force-multipliers for a military whose equipment mostly consists of upgraded older models. Small force packages of the highest-end U.S. technology, backed

up by 1980s- and 1990s-vintage weapons, will easily counter all developing threats.

8. *Be bold.* Whether through a new strategic relationship with Russia, arms export restraints, new confidence-building measures, elimination of entire classes of weapons systems, or some other action, the United States has a historic opportunity to shape the environment. One example of the kind of bold thinking demanded today emerges from the simple fact that the world is eventually going to have to deal with the phenomenon of failed states. Despite the obvious reluctance of all advanced industrial nations to become involved in "nation building," sooner or later governments, international institutions, nongovernmental organizations, and the affected local populations must face up to the protracted process of "state building." Convincing Americans of the need for the United States to assist in such long-term commitments will be no small task. . . .

9. *Attend to the home front.* As the United States goes about trying both to mold the outside world and to guard against it, the greatest threats to future U.S. national security may well prove to be internal. As the American public's lack of interest in foreign affairs demonstrates, the body politic intuitively senses the existence of a strategic breathing space abroad. Nevertheless, a wide range of domestic problems are eating away at the U.S. national will and psyche. If the United States is in the process of creating a permanent underclass increasingly disaffected from civil society, and it is seeing the rise of other groups that essentially reject the authority of its federal structures, then it may be confronted with significantly greater domestic threats than any foreign tyrant with a few tank divisions.

Finally, recall that this [chapter] proposes the existence of a "breathing space," not "peace in our time." . . . The United States must keep shaping the security environment to prevent a sudden reversal of the trends toward declining threats summarized above. . . . That will require a full range of peacetime engagements. Moreover, it is conceivable that a large-scale threat could reappear on the more distant horizon; the United States should therefore retain sufficient flexibility that it could recalibrate, should U.S. planners detect evidence that a substantial military challenge is emerging. . . .

. . . The United States will almost certainly enter the new millennium in an extraordinarily favorable strategic position. Militarily, the United States is on the verge of a breathing space that could easily extend one to two decades. Of course, the country must hedge against long-term uncertainty, and threats and risks clearly do remain; but scope and scale are critical. It is entirely possible that no regional power will prove capable of conducting large-scale conventional operations against U.S. forces or allies for more than a decade; and the pace of foreign weapons development has slowed substantially. The United States has not seen such a favorable strategic position since the end of World War I; it will possess a very favorable risk equation and the luxury of a tremendous degree of flexibility to shape the world, as well as to guard against it. The key is to avoid the danger of wasting such a historic opportunity shadow boxing with an array of nonexistent threats.

24. U.S. NUCLEAR POSTURE: A CASE FOR CHANGE

Steering Committee of the Project on Eliminating Weapons of Mass Destruction, Henry L. Stimpson Center, General Andrew J. Goodpaster (retired), Chair

*T*he Cold War's end and the dangers of nuclear proliferation demand a fundamental reappraisal of the role of nuclear weapons in U.S. policy and in global politics. In the changing strategic environment, nuclear weapons are of declining value in securing U.S. interests, but pose growing risks to the security of the United States and other nations. The only military role of nuclear weapons in this new era—the deterrence of other *nuclear* threats—could be met with far fewer nuclear weapons. U.S. national security would be best served by a policy of phased reductions in all states' nuclear forces and gradual movement toward the objective of eliminating all weapons of mass destruction from all countries. . . .

THE DECLINING UTILITY OF NUCLEAR WEAPONS IN THE POST–COLD WAR WORLD

For over forty years, nuclear weapons have played a central role in U.S. foreign and defense policies. Throughout the Cold War, the United States relied on nuclear weapons to deter conventional and nuclear attacks by the Soviet Union and China on American territory, certain friendly states, and U.S. forces abroad. The extension of U.S. nuclear security assurances also

Note: Some notes have been deleted; others have been renumbered.

dampened pressures for proliferation in Germany, Japan, South Korea, and other nations that otherwise might have chosen to seek to preserve their security through the independent possession of nuclear weapons.

But the possession of nuclear weapons and reliance on nuclear deterrence also entailed significant costs and risks:

Economic Costs. The development and maintenance of large nuclear arsenals absorbed tremendous resources in the United States and the Soviet Union, and the final price tag for nuclear activities—especially environmental and safety costs—continues to rise. It is estimated that the U.S. will spend between $200 and $500 billion on environmental cleanup related to nuclear weapons facilities. The costs of cleaning up the monumentally worse contamination in the former Soviet Union is beyond calculation. During a time of intense competition for budgetary resources, moreover, maintenance of the nuclear weapons infrastructure and currently planned force levels could divert scarce funds from other military programs of greater utility to U.S. national security.

Political Costs. Throughout the Cold War, the central role of nuclear weapons in U.S. and Soviet policies put the two states at odds with many non-nuclear states over non-proliferation policy and exposed them to increased dangers, particularly in crisis situations. If international support for non-proliferation continues to grow stronger, the United States' reliance on nuclear weapons is likely to be a source of renewed tension in relations with many non-nuclear states.

Nuclear Accidents and Incidents. Although the two nuclear superpowers devoted significant resources to the development of elaborate security and safety systems, both countries suffered a number of near-accidents and false alarms on several occasions. These incidents never resulted in catastrophic consequences and were relatively few in number compared to the total number of nuclear operations. Yet, even an advanced industrial power such as the United States with redundant safety and security arrangements was unable to eliminate these risks entirely. The risk of accident will persist so long as nuclear weapons exist. If an accident ever occurred, the human, environmental, and economic costs would be catastrophic.

Risk of Nuclear Use. Most importantly, the very existence of nuclear weapons entails a risk that these weapons will be used one day, with devastating consequences for the United States and other nations. The manipulation of nuclear risk in U.S.–Soviet relations, as during the Cuban Missile Crisis and the 1973 Middle Eastern crisis, by its nature implied a danger that a crisis could escalate and end in a cataclysmic nuclear exchange. In the multipolar structure of international relations that characterizes the post–Cold War period, the risks of nuclear use could increase with every new nuclear power.

During the Cold War, the contributions of nuclear weapons to U.S. national security and international stability were believed to outweigh the dangers associated with their integration in foreign and defense policies and, indeed, their very existence. There was no feasible alternative to reliance on nuclear deterrence, in any event. As long as the U.S. faced a nuclear-armed and implacable foe in Moscow, there was little reason to reconsider the desirability of reliance on nuclear deterrence.

The strategic context that undergirded the Cold War calculus of nuclear risks and benefits has changed fundamentally, however. The dawn of the nuclear age forced policy makers and military strategists to reexamine traditional assumptions about the uses and purposes of military force in interstate relations. In a similar vein, the new strategic situation demands a fundamental reassessment of the assumptions and theories that have guided U.S. nuclear policy for four decades. What is the political and military utility of nuclear weapons in the post–Cold War era? Alternately, what costs and dangers does continued reliance on nuclear deterrence imply? In particular, what implications, if any, does the U.S. nuclear posture have for international efforts to stem the spread of weapons of mass destruction? These are the key questions that need to be addressed.

. . . U.S. nuclear weapons are of declining military and political utility in both addressing the residual threats of the Cold War and in countering emerging threats to the security of the United States. There is no need for the United States to use nuclear weapons against a non-nuclear opponent; sufficient U.S. conventional forces can and should be maintained to counter non-nuclear threats. In our view, the only military role of nuclear weapons should be to deter nuclear threats to the population and territory of the United States, to U.S. forces abroad, and to certain friendly states. Although the United States must be concerned about the proliferation of all weapons of mass destruction, a combination of defensive measures and strong conventional forces could neutralize the need for a nuclear retaliatory threat to deter chemical and biological attacks. Moreover, the nuclear deterrent function, the one necessary function in our view, can be preserved at much lower force levels, as long as other states move in tandem with the United States toward smaller nuclear forces. There is no military justification to maintain U.S. and Russian strategic nuclear stockpiles at their current or even planned START II levels.

Current rationales for nuclear weapons are primarily political. Perceptions of the political and military utility of nuclear weapons, while changing, have been slow to catch up with the new strategic realities. Given the uncertainties surrounding the Russian reform movement, a certain reluctance to abandon traditional ways of thinking about nuclear weapons is understandable, and will necessarily constrain rapid movement to lower-force levels.[1] However, the assumed military and political value of nuclear weapons should be weighed against the dangers of continuing nuclear reliance. . . .

In the long-term, only a policy aimed at steadily curbing global reliance on nuclear weapons—including our own—is likely to progressively eliminate nuclear dangers. Under existing political conditions, the elimination of nuclear weapons is infeasible. But . . . much can be done in the current climate to reduce nuclear risks, while working progressively to narrow the roles that nuclear weapons play in U.S. policy and in interstate relations.

ELIMINATING NUCLEAR RISKS:
AN EVOLUTIONARY U.S. NUCLEAR POSTURE

An evolutionary nuclear posture would establish a clear long-term objective—eliminating all nuclear weapons from all states—but enable the United States to undertake changes in the size and operational status of its nuclear forces in a gradual manner. The path toward the objective would be achieved in phases, with progress toward each successive phase influenced by key developments in domestic and world politics. Each phase would correspond to a different strategic environment and would involve changes in nuclear roles, in the operational status and size of nuclear forces, and in arms control arrangements. All elements would move in concert through the phases, an approach that would allow the United States to ensure that each successive step enhanced U.S. security.

Initial steps could be undertaken in the current environment; subsequent phases would require further progress toward diminishing the salience of nuclear weapons in national policies and in interstate relations. The most far-reaching steps presume the resolution of regional conflicts and the establishment of stringent non-proliferation regimes for nuclear, chemical, and biological weapons. Progress toward elimination does *not* imply the creation of a world government. But it does presume that, over time, states will become less reliant on military force, and will not rely on nuclear weapons at all, to settle their differences and secure their interests.[2] Essential prerequisites for progress toward this objective are increased openness and access to information regarding the activities, facilities, and materials related to national defense postures and weapons of mass destruction, and arms control regimes that would make reductions in nuclear weapons and in weapons materials irreversible. Without enhanced transparency, the military capabilities and intentions of states will continue to be shrouded in uncertainty and national decisionmakers will be reluctant to place trust in existing or new constraints on arms. In the long term, effective regional and collective security regimes are likely to be necessary if states are to be persuaded to forego acquisition of all weapons of mass destruction.

The path [toward eliminating nuclear risks] entails four broad phases[3]:

- *Phase I:* During the first and current phase, the United States and Russia would work to shift the foundation of their relationship away from mutual assured destruction toward pragmatic cooperation, and would reduce their nuclear arsenals to roughly 2,000 warheads each. [In 1998 India and Pakistan joined the ranks of declared nuclear powers when each conducted a series of nuclear weapons tests.—Eds.]

- *Phase II:* During the second phase, nuclear deterrence would become far less central to maintain stable and friendly relations among the declared nuclear powers, which would allow the five nuclear states to reduce their arsenals to hundreds of nuclear weapons each.
- *Phase III:* During the third phase, nuclear weapons would be further marginalized in national policies and interstate relations through the establishment of reliable cooperative security and verification regimes, and all remaining nuclear powers would reduce their arsenals to tens of weapons. At this point, the international community would evaluate the relative costs and benefits of eliminating all nuclear weapons from all nations.
- *Phase IV:* During the final phase, an international community of sovereign states would have effective and reliable security alternatives to the threat of mass violence and sufficiently stringent verification and safeguard regimes to allow for the complete elimination of nuclear weapons from all countries.

These phases are not intended to predict future trends, nor to prescribe a precise vision of how the world should evolve. Many developments in the international system are unforeseeable. Moreover, the United States alone certainly cannot impose order on the international community. But as the most powerful state in the international system, U.S. policies and actions can make a difference in determining the direction, rate, and content of change in the international system. The four phases depicted above suggest one set of guidelines for U.S. policy that might allow it to create the conditions necessary to eliminate nuclear risks.

Nuclear weapons would continue to play an essential role in U.S. security and foreign policy throughout Phase I. The military role of nuclear weapons would be to provide deterrence against *nuclear* threats to the territory and population of the United States, to U.S. forces abroad, and to certain friendly nations.[4] This essential function could be accomplished at lower force levels, so long as the United States and Russia take care to preserve rough symmetry in numbers and operational practices.

Nuclear weapons already have become less salient in U.S.–Russian relations, as evidenced by the two START accords, the detargeting agreements, and bilateral cooperation on nuclear safety and security issues. In the current strategic environment, the massive employment of nuclear weapons against Russia is increasingly implausible. As long as Russia and other states possess nuclear forces, however, the United States must retain a survivable nuclear capability.

. . . Nuclear weapons also will remain essential to deter nuclear threats against those states to whom security assurance have been extended, and against U.S. forces deployed overseas. The European and Asian security environments are fraught with uncertainties; new nuclear threats to U.S. interests and friendly nations may emerge in several regions. The European Union's plans to create a European Security and Defense Identity, separable but not separate from NATO, are unlikely to be realized in the foreseeable future, and NATO will remain essential to the continued security and stability of Europe. In Asia, Russia has retrenched, but retains formidable nuclear capabilities, and concerns about the future domestic and foreign policies of China persist, while the situation on the Korean peninsula could easily deteriorate. During this [current] period of transition, the U.S. nuclear deterrent can provide valuable reassurance and protection to allied nations.

As in the past, U.S. nuclear weapons [continue] to dampen pressures for proliferation in particular regions. Although friendly nations such as Germany, Japan, and South Korea have chosen not to acquire nuclear weapons for a variety of reasons, American security assurances have certainly contributed to these decisions and have provided a powerful political constraint on any groups that might otherwise advocate pursuit of an independent nuclear capability. For the foreseeable future, U.S. security assurances will remain essential to preserve the non-proliferation regime.

Although new nuclear, chemical, or biological threats could emerge [in the near term], the United States should eschew commitments to any roles for nuclear weapons *other than the deterrence of nuclear threats.*

The risks posed by the potential proliferation of biological and chemical weapons are real. A number of states have already acquired, or seek to acquire, quantities of chemical or biological weapons. Under certain circumstances, these weapons might be used against, or threaten, U.S. allies or U.S. armed forces seeking to protect other countries. During the Persian Gulf War, for example, Iraq apparently had filled bombs, artillery shells, and missiles with biological agents, and was conducting research on mycotoxin, plant pathogens, and bacteria that could attack crops and wreak damage against U.S. forces and its allies. According to U.S. intelligence sources, a number of additional countries hostile to U.S. interests, including North Korea, Iran, and Libya, are believed to be seeking actively to acquire chemical or biological capabilities.

U.S. policy must address these new threats. However, a declaratory role for U.S. nuclear weapons to deter chemical or biological attacks, as some have suggested, would be of marginal military utility and any potential gain would be outweighed by the negative effects on U.S. non-proliferation efforts. We take this position for four reasons:

- *First,* despite claims to the contrary, the deterrent effect of nuclear weapons against chemical or biological threats has neither been proven nor refuted by firm evidence. Many have already concluded that Iraq was deterred from using biological or chemical weapons during the Persian Gulf War because of an ambiguous nuclear threat from then President George Bush. No one knows this for certain, however.
- *Second,* where a biological or chemical threat is present, the United States may benefit from the deterrent effects of nuclear weapons even without a declaratory commitment to the nuclear option. This is not to suggest that the U.S. should shift to a policy of implicit—but not explicit—reliance on the first use of nuclear weapons as a response to a

chemical or biological attack. Such a policy would win few concessions from potential proliferators and might create dangerous misunderstandings with U.S. friends and allies. But as long as the United States retains nuclear weapons, in fact, it will have the capability to respond to an unconventional attack with unconventional means. Any potential user of unconventional weapons will recognize this possibility, regardless of U.S. statements. In the Persian Gulf War, for example, whether a nuclear threat was made explicit or not, the fact that the United States possessed nuclear weapons meant that Iraqi decision-makers had to take into account the possibility of a nuclear response.

- *Third,* reliance on nuclear weapons to deter, or to respond to a chemical or biological attack, could further legitimate nuclear weapons and increase the apparent desirability of their possession in the eyes of other nations' decision-makers. Such an elevation of nuclear weapons in U.S. policy would send the wrong signal to would-be proliferators and could fracture the growing international consensus against the spread of weapons of mass destruction.

- *Fourth,* there are better ways to respond to biological or chemical attacks. Passive defense measures, for example, could drastically reduce the number of potential casualties from a biological attack. The United States' conventional deterrent could be strengthened as well. Retaining conventional superiority is essential, of course. In addition, U.S. leaders and citizens might have to be willing to support particular objectives for the employment of military forces, objectives from which the U.S. has shrunk in the past. Aggressive leaders may not be deterred by the prospect of devastating damage to their populations; a pledge to destroy threatening regimes themselves might be necessary to be effective.

While the military role of nuclear weapons [today can] be met with far fewer weapons than are now planned, attitudes about the role of nuclear weapons in relations among states have been slower to change, and could preclude movement to even lower levels in the near term. . . . The United States should encourage new thinking about the role of nuclear weapons in U.S.–Russian relations and in international relations more generally, doing all in its power to reduce the currency of nuclear weapons further and to undercut any prestige attributed to their possession. While nuclear weapons today may enhance the perceived power of the United States, they are no longer central to this country's international rank. The continued security and well-being of the United States depend primarily on its economic and political standing relative to other states, and on its overwhelming conventional superiority. . . .

A RENEWED COMMITMENT TO ELIMINATION

Under current political conditions, the elimination of nuclear weapons is infeasible. The objective will only be achieved—if it can be achieved at all—

after far-reaching changes occur in the principles that guide state policies and actions. The evolutionary posture described in this [chapter] suggests one possible path by which that objective might be achieved. The phases depicted are not intended to be predictive, nor to provide a precise blueprint for U.S. policy and actions. Our intent is only to underscore the important linkages between the international strategic environment, the roles that nuclear weapons fulfill in U.S. defense and foreign policy, and the size and operational status of U.S. nuclear forces, and to suggest that it is in the interest of the United States now to embrace seriously far-reaching goals for an evolutionary nuclear posture. . . .

As the leading military and political power in the world, the United States bears a special responsibility to spearhead the movement to gradually decrease and, if possible, eliminate the dangers associated with nuclear weapons. Adoption of an evolutionary nuclear posture, and a revitalized commitment to the long-term objective of eliminating all nuclear weapons, could bring important national security benefits to the United States while entailing minimal risks. . . .

The prospects for a nuclear-free world may be decades over the horizon. . . . Regardless of the amount of time required, it is virtually certain that the world will never be rid of nuclear risks without a serious political commitment to the objective of progressively eliminating weapons of mass destruction from all countries.

NOTES

1. Robert S. McNamara does not believe "uncertainties surrounding the Russian reform movement" should "necessarily constrain" balanced movement to lower-force levels.

2. Robert S. McNamara and Will Marshall do not agree that the achievement of elimination requires the resolution of regional conflicts and wide-ranging renunciation of the use of force. They argue that if it is accepted that it is inconceivable that the United States would use nuclear weapons against a non-nuclear opponent, it is not necessary to presume either the "resolution of regional conflicts" or that states will find other means to settle their differences and secure their interests.

3. Because the report repeatedly states that the only military utility of nuclear weapons is to deter one's opponent from their use, Robert S. McNamara and Will Marshall believe the balanced reductions proposed in each of the four phases can be achieved without the establishment of cooperative security regimes, as desirable as these are in and of themselves.

4. Victor Utgoff believes that moving in Phase I to restrict the role of U.S. nuclear weapons only to deterrence of nuclear attacks would constitute a fundamental change in U.S. deterrence policy, a change for which some of the political transformations postulated for later phases are prerequisites. He believes that a key value of U.S. nuclear security assurances is the hedge they provide to allies against overwhelming conventional attack by stronger neighbors. By providing assurance against both nuclear attack and unexpected conventional defeat, he argues, U.S. nuclear deterrence undermines to the greatest possible extent the incentives of allies to seek nuclear weapons of their own.

25. THE NEW THREAT OF MASS DESTRUCTION

Richard K. Betts

During the Cold War, weapons of mass destruction were the centerpiece of foreign policy. Nuclear arms hovered in the background of every major issue in East-West competition and alliance relations. The highest priorities of U.S. policy could almost all be linked in some way to the danger of World War III and the fear of millions of casualties in the American homeland.

Since the Cold War, other matters have displaced strategic concerns on the foreign policy agenda, and that agenda itself is now barely on the public's radar screen. Apart from defense policy professionals, few Americans still lose sleep over weapons of mass destruction (WMD). After all, what do normal people feel is the main relief provided by the end of the Cold War? It is that the danger of nuclear war is off their backs.

Yet today, WMD present more and different things to worry about than during the Cold War. For one, nuclear arms are no longer the only concern, as chemical and biological weapons have come to the fore. For another, there is less danger of complete annihilation, but more danger of mass destruction. Since the Cold War is over and American and Russian nuclear inventories are much smaller, there is less chance of an apocalyptic exchange of many thousands of weapons. But the probability that some smaller number of WMD will be used is growing. Many of the standard strategies and ideas for coping with WMD threats are no longer as relevant as they were when Moscow was the main adversary. But new thinking has not yet congealed in as clear a form as the Cold War concepts of nuclear deterrence theory.

The new dangers have not been ignored inside the Beltway. "Counterproliferation" has become a cottage industry in the Pentagon and the intelligence

Note: Notes have been deleted.

community, and many worthwhile initiatives to cope with threats are under way. Some of the most important implications of the new era, however, have not yet registered on the public agenda. This in turn limits the inclination of politicians to push some appropriate programs. Even the defense establishment has directed its attention mainly toward countering threats WMD pose to U.S. military forces operating abroad rather than to the more worrisome danger that mass destruction will occur in the United States, killing large numbers of civilians.

The points to keep in mind about the new world of mass destruction are the following. First, the roles such weapons play in international conflict are changing. They no longer represent the technological frontier of warfare. Increasingly, they will be weapons of the weak—states or groups that militarily are at best second-class. The importance of the different types among them has also shifted. Biological weapons should now be the most serious concern, with nuclear weapons second and chemicals a distant third.

Second, the mainstays of Cold War security policy—deterrence and arms control—are not what they used to be. Some new threats may not be deterrable, and the role of arms control in dealing with WMD has been marginalized. In a few instances, continuing devotion to deterrence and arms control may have side effects that offset the benefits.

Third, some of the responses most likely to cope with the threats in novel ways will not find a warm welcome. The response that should now be the highest priority is one long ignored, opposed, or ridiculed: a serious civil defense program to blunt the effects of WMD if they are unleashed within the United States. Some of the most effective measures to prevent attacks within the United States may also challenge traditional civil liberties if pursued to the maximum. And the most troubling conclusion for foreign policy as a whole is that reducing the odds of attacks in the United States might require pulling back from involvement in some foreign conflicts. American activism to guarantee international stability is, paradoxically, the prime source of American vulnerability.

This was partly true in the Cold War, when the main danger that nuclear weapons might detonate on U.S. soil sprang from strategic engagement in Europe, Asia, and the Middle East to deter attacks on U.S. allies. But engagement then assumed a direct link between regional stability and U.S. survival. The connection is less evident today, when there is no globally threatening superpower or transnational ideology to be contained—only an array of serious but entirely local disruptions. Today, as the only nation acting to police areas outside its own region, the United States makes itself a target for states or groups whose aspirations are frustrated by U.S. power.

FROM MODERN TO PRIMITIVE

When nuclear weapons were born, they represented the most advanced military applications of science, technology, and engineering. None but the great powers could hope to obtain them. By now, however, nuclear arms have been around for more than half a century, and chemical and biological weapons even longer. They are not just getting old. In the strategic terms most relevant to American security, they have become primitive. Once the military cutting edge of the strong, they have become the only hope for so-called rogue states or terrorists who want to contest American power. Why? Because the United States has developed overwhelming superiority in conventional military force—something it never thought it had against the Soviet Union.

The Persian Gulf War of 1991 demonstrated the American advantage in a manner that stunned many abroad. Although the U.S. defense budget has plunged, other countries are not closing the gap. U.S. military spending remains more than triple that of any potentially hostile power and higher than the combined defense budgets of Russia, China, Iran, Iraq, North Korea, and Cuba.

More to the point, there is no evidence that those countries' level of military professionalism is rising at a rate that would make them competitive even if they were to spend far more on their forces. Rolling along in what some see as a revolution in military affairs, American forces continue to make unmatched use of state-of-the-art weapons, surveillance and information systems, and the organizational and doctrinal flexibility for managing the integration of these complex innovations into "systems of systems" that is the key to modern military effectiveness. More than ever in military history, brains are brawn. Even if hostile countries somehow catch up in an arms race, their military organizations and cultures are unlikely to catch up in the competence race for management, technology assimilation, and combat command skills.

If it is infeasible for hostile states to counter the United States in conventional combat, it is even more daunting for smaller groups such as terrorists. If the United States is lucky, the various violent groups with grievances against the American government and society will continue to think up schemes using conventional explosives. Few terrorist groups have shown an interest in inflicting true mass destruction. Bombings or hostage seizures have generally threatened no more than a few hundred lives. Let us hope that this limitation has been due to a powerful underlying reason, rather than a simple lack of capability, and that the few exceptions do not become more typical. . . . If terrorists decide that they want to stun American policymakers by inflicting enormous damage, WMD become more attractive at the same time that they are becoming more accessible.

Finally, unchallenged military superiority has shifted the attention of the U.S. military establishment away from WMD. During the Cold War, nuclear weapons were the bedrock of American war capabilities. They were the linchpin of defense debate, procurement programs, and arms control because the United States faced another superpower—one that conventional wisdom feared could best it in conventional warfare. Today, no one cares about the MX missile or B-1 bomber, and hardly anyone really cares about the Strategic Arms Reduction Treaty. In a manner that could only have seemed ludicrous during the Cold War, proponents now rationalize the $2 billion B-2 as a weapon for conventional war. Hardly anyone in the Pentagon is still interested in how the United States could use WMD for its own strategic purposes.

What military planners are interested in is how to keep adversaries from using WMD as an "asymmetric" means to counter U.S. conventional power, and how to protect U.S. ground and naval forces abroad from WMD attacks. This concern is all well and good, but it abets a drift of attention away from the main danger. The primary risk is not that enemies might lob some nuclear or chemical weapons at U.S. armored battalions or ships, awful as that would be. Rather, it is that they might attempt to punish the United States by triggering catastrophes in American cities.

CHOOSE YOUR WEAPONS WELL

Until the past decade, the issue was nuclear arms, period. Chemical weapons received some attention from specialists, but never made the priority list of presidents and cabinets. Biological weapons were almost forgotten after they were banned by the 1972 Biological Weapons Convention. Chemical and biological arms have received more attention in the 1990s. The issues posed by the trio lumped under the umbrella of mass destruction differ, however. Most significantly, biological weapons have received less attention than the others but probably represent the greatest danger.

Chemical weapons have been noticed more in the past decade, especially since they were used by Iraq against Iranian troops in the 1980–88 Iran-Iraq War and against Kurdish civilians in 1988. Chemicals are far more widely available than nuclear weapons because the technology required to produce them is far simpler, and large numbers of countries have undertaken chemical weapons programs. But chemical weapons are not really in the same class as other weapons of mass destruction, in the sense of ability to inflict a huge number of civilian casualties in a single strike. For the tens of thousands of fatalities as in, say, the biggest strategic bombing raids of World War II, it would be very difficult logistically and operationally to deliver chemical weapons in necessary quantities over wide areas.

Nevertheless, much attention and effort have been lavished on a campaign to eradicate chemical weapons. This may be a good thing, but the side effects are not entirely benign. For one, banning chemicals means that for deterrence, nuclear weapons become even more important than they used to be. That is because a treaty cannot assuredly prevent hostile nations from deploying chemical weapons, while the United States has forsworn the option to retaliate in kind.

In the past, the United States had a no-first-use policy for chemical weapons but reserved the right to strike back with them if an enemy used them first. The 1993 Chemical Weapons Convention (CWC), which entered into force last April [1997], requires the United States to destroy its stockpile, thus ending this option. The United States did the same with biological arms long ago, during the Nixon administration. Eliminating its own chemical and biological weapons practically precludes a no-first-use policy for nuclear weapons, since they become the only WMD available for retaliation.

Would the United States follow through and use nuclear weapons against a country or group that had killed several thousand Americans with deadly chemicals? It is hard to imagine breaking the post-Nagasaki taboo in that situation. But schemes for conventional military retaliation would not suffice without detracting from the force of American deterrent threats. There would be a risk for the United States in setting a precedent that someone could use WMD against Americans without suffering similar destruction in return. Limiting the range of deterrent alternatives available to U.S. strategy will not necessarily cause deterrence to fail, but it will certainly not strengthen it.

The ostensible benefit of the CWC is that it will make chemical arms harder to acquire and every bit as illegal and stigmatized as biological weapons have been for a quarter-century. If it has that benefit, what effect will the ban have on the choices of countries or groups who want some kind of WMD in any case, whether for purposes of deterrence, aggression, or revenge? At the margin, the ban will reduce the disincentives to acquiring biological weapons, since they will be no less illegal, no harder to obtain or conceal, and far more damaging than chemical weapons. If major reductions in the chemical threat produce even minor increases in the biological threat, it will be a bad trade.

One simple fact should worry Americans more about biological than about nuclear or chemical arms: unlike either of the other two, biological weapons combine maximum destructiveness and easy availability. Nuclear arms have great killing capacity but are hard to get; chemical weapons are easy to get but lack such killing capacity; biological agents have both qualities. A 1993 study by the Office of Technology Assessment concluded that a single airplane delivering 100 kilograms of anthrax spores—a dormant phase of a bacillus that multiplies rapidly in the body, producing toxins and rapid hemorrhaging—by aerosol on a clear, calm night over the Washington, D.C., area could kill between one million and three million people, 300 times as many fatalities as if the plane had delivered sarin gas in amounts ten times larger.

Like chemical weapons but unlike nuclear weapons, biologicals are relatively easy to make. Innovations in biotechnology have obviated many of the old problems in handling and preserving biological agents, and many have been freely available for scientific research. Nuclear weapons are not likely to be the WMD of choice for non-state terrorist groups. They require huge investments and targetable infrastructure, and are subject to credible threats by the United States. An aggrieved group that decides it wants to kill huge numbers of Americans will find the mission easier to accomplish with anthrax than with a nuclear explosion.

Inside the Pentagon, concern about biological weapons has picked up tremendously in the past couple of years, but there is little serious attention to the problem elsewhere. This could be a good thing if nothing much can be done, since publicity might only give enemies ideas. But it is a bad thing if it impedes efforts to take steps—such as civil defense—that could blunt nuclear, chemical, or biological attacks.

DETERRENCE AND ARMS CONTROL IN DECLINE

An old vocabulary still dominates policy discussion of WMD. Rhetoric in the defense establishment falls back on the all-purpose strategic buzzword of the Cold War: deterrence. But deterrence now covers fewer of the threats the United States faces than it did during the Cold War.

The logic of deterrence is clearest when the issue is preventing unprovoked and unambiguous aggression, when the aggressor recognizes that it is the aggressor rather than the defender. Deterrence is less reliable when both sides in a conflict see each other as the aggressor. When the United States intervenes in messy Third World conflicts, the latter is often true. In such cases, the side that the United States wants to deter may see itself as trying to deter the United States. Such situations are ripe for miscalculation.

For the country that used to be the object of U.S. deterrence—Russia—the strategic burden has been reversed. Based on assumptions of Soviet conventional military superiority, U.S. strategy used to rely on the threat to escalate—to be the first to use nuclear weapons during a war—to deter attack by Soviet armored divisions. Today the tables have turned. There is no Warsaw Pact, Russia has half or less of the military potential of the Soviet Union, and its current conventional forces are in disarray, while NATO is expanding eastward. It is now Moscow that has the incentive to compensate for conventional weakness by placing heavier reliance on nuclear capabilities. The Russians adopted a nuclear no-first-use policy in the early 1980s, but renounced it after their precipitous post–Cold War decline.

Today Russia needs to be reassured, not deterred. The main danger from Russian WMD is leakage from vast stockpiles to anti-American groups elsewhere—the "loose nukes" problem. So long as the United States has no intention of attacking the Russians, their greater reliance on nuclear forces is not a problem. If the United States has an interest in reducing nuclear stockpiles, however, it is. The traditional American approach—thinking in terms of its own deterrence strategies—provides no guidance. Indeed, noises some Americans still make about deterring the Russians compound the problem by reinforcing Moscow's alarm.

Similarly, U.S. conventional military superiority gives China an incentive to consider more reliance on an escalation strategy. The Chinese have a longstanding no-first-use policy but adopted it when their strategic doctrine was that of "people's war," which relied on mass mobilization and low-tech weaponry. Faith in that doctrine was severely shaken by the American performance in the Persian Gulf War. Again, the United States might assume that there is no problem as long as Beijing only wants to deter and the United States does not want to attack. But how do these assumptions relate to the prospect of a war over Taiwan? That is a conflict that no one wants but that can hardly be ruled out in light of evolving tensions. If the United States decides openly to deter Beijing from attacking Taiwan, the old lore from the Cold War may be relevant. But if Washington continues to leave policy ambiguous, who will know who is deterring whom? Ambiguity is a recipe for confusion and miscalculation in a time of crisis. For all the upsurge of attention in the national security establishment to the prospect of conflict with China, there has been remarkably little discussion of the role of nuclear weapons in a Sino-American collision.

The main problem for deterrence, however, is that it still relies on the corpus of theory that undergirded Cold War policy, dominated by reliance on the threat of second-strike retaliation. But retaliation requires knowledge of who has launched an attack and the address at which they reside. These requirements are not a problem when the threat comes from a government, but they are if the enemy is anonymous. Today some groups may wish to punish the United States without taking credit for the action—a mass killing equivalent to the 1988 bombing of Pan Am Flight 103 over Lockerbie, Scotland. Moreover, the options the defense establishment favors have shifted over entirely from deterrence to preemption. The majority of those who dealt with nuclear weapons policy during the Cold War adamantly opposed developing first-strike options. Today, scarcely anyone looks to that old logic when thinking about rogues or terrorists, and most hope to be able to mount a disarming action against any group with WMD.

Finally, eliminating chemical weapons trims some options for deterrence. Arms control restrictions on the instruments that can be used for deterrent threats are not necessarily the wrong policy, but they do work against maximizing deterrence. Overall, however, the problem with arms control is not that it does too much but that it now does relatively little.

From the Limited Test Ban negotiations in the 1960s through the Strategic Arms Limitation Talks, Strategic Arms Reduction Talks, and Intermediate-range Nuclear Forces negotiations in the 1970s and 1980s, arms control treaties were central to managing WMD threats. Debates about whether particular agreements with Moscow were in the United States' interest were bitter because everyone believed that the results mattered. Today there is no consensus that treaties regulating armaments matter much. Among national security experts, the corps that pays close attention to START and Conventional Forces in Europe negotiations has shrunk. With the exception of the Chemical Weapons Convention, efforts to control WMD by treaty have become small potatoes. The biggest recent news in arms control has not been any negotiation to regulate WMD, but a campaign to ban land mines. . . .

CIVIL DEFENSE

Despite all the new limitations, deterrence remains an important aspect of strategy. There is not much the United States needs to do to keep up its deterrence capability, however, given the thousands of nuclear weapons and the conventional military superiority it has. Where capabilities are grossly underdeveloped, however, is the area of responses for coping should deterrence fail.

Enthusiasts for defensive capability, mostly proponents of the Strategic Defense Initiative from the Reagan years, remain fixated on the least relevant form of it: high-tech active defenses to intercept ballistic missiles. There is still scant interest in what should now be the first priority: civil defense preparations to cope with uses of WMD within the United States. Active defenses against missiles would be expensive investments that might or might not work against a threat the United States probably will not face for years, but would do nothing against the threat it already faces. Civil defense measures are extremely cheap and could prove far more effective than they would have against a large-scale Soviet attack. . . .

By the later phases of the Cold War it was hard to get people interested in civil defense against an all-out Soviet attack that could detonate thousands of high-yield nuclear weapons in U.S. population centers. To many, the lives that would have been saved seemed less salient than the many millions that would still have been lost. It should be easier to see the value of civil defense, however, in the context of more limited attacks, perhaps with only a few low-yield weapons. A host of minor measures can increase protection or recovery from biological, nuclear, or chemical effects. Examples are stockpiling or distribution of protective masks; equipment and training for decontamination; standby programs for mass vaccinations and emergency treatment with antibiotics; wider and deeper planning of emergency response procedures; and public education about hasty sheltering and emergency actions to reduce individual vulnerability.

Such programs would not make absorbing a WMD attack tolerable. But inadequacy is no excuse for neglecting actions that could reduce death and suffering, even if the difference in casualties is small. Civil defenses are especially worthwhile considering that they are extraordinarily cheap compared with regular military programs or active defense systems. Yet until recently, only half a billion dollars—less than two-tenths of one percent of the defense budget and less than $2 a head for every American—went to chemical and biological defense, while nearly $4 billion was spent annually on ballistic missile defense. Why haven't policymakers attended to first things first—cheap programs that can cushion the effects of a disaster—before undertaking expensive programs that provide no assurance they will be able to prevent it?

One problem is conceptual inertia. The Cold War accustomed strategists to worrying about an enemy with thousands of WMD, rather than foes with a handful. For decades the question of strategic defense was also posed as a debate between those who saw no alternative to relying on deterrence and those who hoped that an astrodome over the United States could replace deterrence with invulnerability. None of these hoary fixations address the most probable WMD threats in the post–Cold War world.

Opposition to Cold War civil defense programs underlies psychological aversion to them now. Opponents used to argue that civil defense was a dangerous illusion because it could do nothing significant to reduce the horror of an attack that would obliterate hundreds of cities, because it would promote a false sense of security, and because it could even be destabilizing and provoke attack in a crisis. Whether or not such arguments were valid then, they are not now. But both then and now, there has been a powerful reason that civil defense efforts have been unpopular: they alarm people. They remind them that their vulnerability to mass destruction is not a bad dream, not something that strategic schemes for deterrence, preemption, or interception are sure to solve.

Civil defense can limit damage but not minimize it. For example, some opponents may be able to develop biological agents that circumvent available vaccines and antibiotics. . . . Which is worse—the limitations of defenses, or having to answer for failure to try? The moment that WMD are used somewhere in a manner that produces tens of thousands of fatalities, there will be hysterical outbursts of all sorts. One of them will surely be, "Why didn't the government prepare us for this?" It is not in the long-term interest of political leaders to indulge popular aversion. If public resistance under current circumstances prevents widespread distribution, stockpiling, and instruction in the use of defensive equipment or medical services, the least that should be done is to optimize plans and preparations to rapidly implement such activities when the first crisis ignites demand.

As threats of terrorism using WMD are taken more seriously, interest will grow in preemptive defense measures—the most obvious of which is intensified intelligence collection. Where this involves targeting groups within the United States that might seem to be potential breeding grounds for terrorists (for example, supporters of Palestinian militants, home-grown militias or cults, or radicals with ties to Iran, Iraq, or Libya), controversies will arise over constitutional limits on invasion of privacy or search and seizure. So long as the WMD danger remains hypothetical, such controversies will not be easily resolved. They have not come to the fore so far because U.S. law enforcement has been unbelievably lucky in apprehending terrorists. The group arrested in 1993 for planning to bomb the Lincoln Tunnel happened to be infiltrated by an informer, and Timothy McVeigh happened to be picked up in 1995 for driving without a license plate. Those who fear compromising civil liberties with permissive standards for government snooping should consider what is likely to happen once such luck runs out and it proves impossible to identify perpetrators. Suppose a secretive radical Islamic group launches a biological attack, kills 100,000 people, and announces that it will do the same thing again if its terms are not met. (The probability of such a scenario may not be high, but it can no longer be consigned to science fiction.) In that case, it is hardly unthinkable that a panicked legal system would roll over and treat Arab-Americans as it did the Japanese-Americans who were herded into concentration camps after Pearl Harbor. Stretching limits on domestic surveillance to reduce the chances of facing such choices could be the lesser evil.

IS RETREAT THE BEST DEFENSE?

No programs aimed at controlling adversaries' capabilities can eliminate the dangers. One risk is that in the more fluid politics of the post–Cold War world, the United States could stumble into an unanticipated crisis with Russia or

China. There are no well-established rules of the game to brake a spiraling conflict over the Baltic states or Taiwan, as there were in the superpower competition after the Cuban missile crisis. The second danger is that some angry group that blames the United States for its problems may decide to coerce Americans, or simply exact vengeance, by inflicting devastation on them where they live.

If steps to deal with the problem in terms of capabilities are limited, can anything be done to address intentions—the incentives of any foreign power or group to lash out at the United States? There are few answers to this question that do not compromise the fundamental strategic activism and internationalist thrust of U.S. foreign policy over the past half-century. That is because the best way to keep people from believing that the United States is responsible for their problems is to avoid involvement in their conflicts.

Ever since the Munich agreement and Pearl Harbor, with only a brief interruption during the decade after the Tet offensive, there has been a consensus that if Americans did not draw their defense perimeter far forward and confront foreign troubles in their early stages, those troubles would come to them at home. But because the United States is now the only superpower and weapons of mass destruction have become more accessible, American intervention in troubled areas is not so much a way to fend off such threats as it is what stirs them up. . . .

26. RACING TOWARD THE FUTURE: THE REVOLUTION IN MILITARY AFFAIRS

Steven Metz

*T*he Persian Gulf War may have signaled a historic change in the nature of armed conflict. By most indicators the Iraqi military that occupied Kuwait was proficient and well equipped with modern weaponry, especially tanks, artillery, and air defense systems. Battle-tested in a long war with Iran, it should have been a fearsome enemy for the United States–led coalition. Pundits and political leaders expected a bloody struggle. But once the war began, Saddam Hussein's forces were brushed aside with stunning suddenness and minimal human cost to the United States and its allies, leaving the world to ponder the war's meaning.

Initially, American military leaders saw Desert Storm as the payoff for years of accumulated improvement in training, personnel quality, doctrine, leadership, and equipment. Some analysts unearthed deeper lessons. Rather than attributing the outcome to evolutionary advancements in the United States military, they saw Desert Storm as the prologue to a fundamental transformation in the nature of warfare—a "revolution in military affairs," or RMA. This idea had such immense strategic and political implications that American military leaders, defense policymakers, and strategic analysts soon adopted it, changing the RMA concept from a theoretical construct to a blueprint for the armed forces of the twenty-first century.

Today the RMA has become the basis of most long-term thinking in the Defense Department and, increasingly, for the militaries of other advanced states. But the full implication of this is not yet clear; many dimensions of the RMA await analysis. For example, little thought has been given to how the RMA might affect arms races and weapons proliferation—a serious oversight. If armed conflict is undergoing historic and significant change, "traditional" arms races will persist into the next century even as new and very different ones take shape. The more these new problems are anticipated, the easier they will be to deal with. To assess the proliferation and arms control issues that will challenge world leaders 10 years from now requires tracing the evolution of thinking on the RMA and its effect on military strategy in the United States and around the world.

THE EVOLUTION OF AN IDEA

The concept of military revolutions grew from Soviet writing of the 1970s and 1980s, particularly a series of papers by Marshal Nikolai Ogarkov. When American defense analysts initially considered this idea, they focused on the technological dimension. One of the first major study groups in the United States labeled its final report *The Military Technical Revolution*.[1] But it quickly became clear that this was an overly narrow approach that understated the importance of concepts and organizations. The idea of a "military-technical revolution" soon evolved into the more holistic concept of a revolution in military affairs.

There is now a loose consensus among scholars, policymakers, and military strategists on the most salient aspects of RMAs. In simple terms, an RMA is a rapid and radical increase in the effectiveness of military units that alters the nature of warfare and changes the strategic environment. RMAs result from mutually supportive changes in technology, concepts, and organizations; technological advancement alone does not make an RMA. Analysts also agree that RMAs are, by definition, strategically significant. States that understand and exploit them accrue geopolitical benefits; those that do not slide into military weakness.

Even given this simple conceptual base, writers differ on when RMAs have occurred in the past. Ironically, there is greater agreement on the nature of the current RMA. Scholars, military strategists, and defense policymakers acknowledge that what drives it is a vast improvement in the quality and quantity of information made available to military commanders by improvements in computers and other devices for collecting, analyzing, storing, and transmitting data. The United States Army, for instance, talks of "digitized" battle in which a commander would use an array of sensors and data-fusion technologies to obtain a near-perfect picture of the battlefield that would provide the location and status of all friendly and most enemy units, thus dispersing what has been called the "fog of war." Such a development would certainly represent a sea change in the nature of armed conflict. The presence (or absence) of accurate information has long shaped the conduct of warfare. If the RMA does lift the "fog of war," the results will be stunning, giving those armed forces that master the changes immense advantages.

The increasing quality and quantity of military information will have a number of corollary effects. One is an alteration of the traditional relationship between operational complexity and effective control. Accurate, real-time information and advanced, computer-based training and simulation models will allow more complex military operations than in the past. Simultaneous operations across one or more military theaters might soon be possible. At the same time, the relationship between accuracy and distance in the application of military force might change as extremely precise, standoff strikes become the method preferred by advanced militaries. The RMA could relegate the close-quarters clash of troops to history.

The RMA might change military strategy as well. Futurists Alvin and Heidi Toffler have argued that information is becoming the basis of economic strength, especially in what they call "Third Wave" states. During the "First Wave" of human development, production was primarily agricultural, so military strategies were designed to seize and hold territory or steal portable wealth. During the "Second Wave" industrial production dominated, which meant that war was often a struggle of attrition where belligerents wore down their enemies' capacity to feed, clothe, and equip armies. Following this logic, "Third Wave" warfare will seek to erode or destroy the enemy's means of collecting, processing, storing, and disseminating information.[2] Instead of using explosives to kill and destroy, the warrior of the future might fight with a laptop computer from a motel room, attacking digital targets with strikes launched through fiber-optic webs in order to damage or alter enemy information infrastructure and data resources. The opening words of the next global war might be "Log-on successful" rather than "Tora, Tora, Tora." From the perspective of arms control, it is a chilling thought that something as uncontrollable as a few thousand lines of computer code could become a dangerous weapon.

THE AMERICAN ORTHODOXY

No organization undertakes a revolution without a pressing incentive. This certainly holds for the United States military. The Defense Department is pursuing the RMA in response to two important post–cold war strategic trends. One is a decline in the American military force structure and budget without a concomitant decline in responsibilities and missions, which has generated a growing mismatch between means and ends. The other is what military and civilian leaders see as the American public's limited tolerance for the human toll of armed conflict. These two issues form the core dilemma of current United States national security strategy and drive the quest for the RMA.

During the wide-ranging reassessment of national security strategy in the early 1990s, people like Andrew Marshall, director of the Defense Department's Office of Net Assessment, and Admiral William A. Owens, former vice chairman of the Joint Chiefs of Staff, concluded that an American military built along the principles of the RMA could be smaller yet more powerful than the present one. To use jargon that has become a mantra within the military, the goal was to "leverage technology" to solve strategic dilemmas. By the mid-1990s the RMA had moved from the realm of theorists and military historians to the world of force structure planning and programming.

The RMA quickly entered the mainstream thinking of the American armed forces. Courses appeared at war colleges and staff schools, RMA-related articles became common in military journals, and military think tanks began to produce studies, reports, exercises, and war games. Institutions designed to develop, test, and refine RMA-related concepts emerged throughout the Department of Defense. Government labs explored technologies to make the RMA possible, especially in areas such as information gathering, assessment, and dissemination, nonlethal weapons, robotics, unmanned military systems, new materials, and new energy sources.

Other nations quickly joined the bandwagon. The Australian military hosted one of the first major RMA conferences outside the United States in Canberra, Australia, in February 1996. At the National Institute for Defense Studies in Tokyo, a series of RMA seminars attracted the attention of senior policymakers. The French have also begun exploration of the RMA.

Still, the United States military is clearly the leader in RMA thinking and continues to define the "orthodoxy." In 1996 this was codified in Chairman of the Joint Chiefs of Staff General John Shalikashvili's Joint Vision 2010, which is the best distillation of official United States thinking on the RMA and the future security environment. Joint Vision 2010 projects no revolutionary change in the global strategic environment over the next decade. The primary task of American armed forces, Shalikashvili [contended], will continue to be to deter conflict and, if that fails, to fight and win the nation's wars. Power projection enabled by an overseas presence will remain the fundamental strategic concept, and the military forces of other nations still the primary foe.

Joint Vision 2010 does, however, anticipate great strides in the adoption of new technology, concepts, and organizations. It predicts that technology will allow even more emphasis on long-range precision strikes. New weapons based on directed energy will appear. Advances in low observable ("stealth") technologies will augment the ability to mask friendly forces from enemies. And improvements in information and systems integration technologies will provide decision makers with fast and accurate information. In combination, these technologies will allow increased stealth, mobility, and dispersion, and a higher tempo of operations, all under the shield of information superiority.

Four operational concepts form the heart of Joint Vision 2010. The first, *dominant maneuver,* would allow overwhelming force against an opponent by conducting synchronized operations from dispersed locations rather than from a few large bases or camps. The second key concept is *precision engagement.* This would be based on a "system of systems" that would allow United States forces to locate a target, attack it with great accuracy, assess the effectiveness of the attack, and strike again when necessary. In many cases, the strike systems themselves would be "stealthy." The third operational concept, *full-dimension protection,* entails protecting friendly forces from enemy information warfare, missile attacks, and other threats. The final concept is *focused logistics,* which fuses information, logistics, and transportation technology to deliver tailored logistics packages at all levels of military operations. If attained, these four concepts would give American forces full spectrum dominance over anticipated enemies in the first two decades of the twenty-first century, assuming such enemies cannot develop effective responses to American advances.

While largely excluded from Joint Vision 2010, there is one other important component of current American thinking on the RMA: a desire to use technology to make warfare "cleaner" by reducing the casualties and collateral damage normally associated with combat operations. To a great extent, this is a response to the global communications explosion that has expanded the audience for armed conflict beyond the participants. To be politically acceptable, military operations must minimize casualties. Precision conventional strikes are part of this, but even more radical change may be possible through explicitly nonlethal weapons such as acoustic, laser and high-power microwaves; nonnuclear electromagnetic pulses; high-power jamming; obscurants, foams, glues, and slicks; supercaustics that erode enemy equipment; magnetohydrodynamics; information warfare; and soldier protection. The American military's interest in nonlethality has increased dramatically, but the full implications—especially for human rights and ethical limits on the use of force—await exploration.

STOKING A NEW ARMS RACE?

The military described in Joint Vision 2010 will be able to counter a traditional enemy relying on massed, armor-heavy formations in relatively open terrain. But, since Desert Storm showed the futility of pitting an old-fashioned military against a cutting-edge one in maneuver warfare, future opponents are unlikely to repeat Iraq's mistakes. Indeed, the world is unlikely to cede permanent military superiority to the United States. A few advanced nations may emulate the American version of the RMA, but those with the technological capacity to do so do not have the political incentive.

Most potential enemies will not have the scientific and technological resources to emulate the United States military and will instead seek asymmetric counterweights. Like guerrilla warfare in Vietnam, these may not give American enemies the ability to win battlefield victories, but they will allow them to raise the cost of the conflict, possibly to the point of paralyzing American policymakers. One example is the "Somali strategy," in which small groups of warriors armed with relatively low-cost weapons operate among civilians in an urban environment. The United States military envisioned in Joint Vision 2010 would have more trouble with such an opponent than with an Iraq- or North Korea-style enemy. Even more ominously, potential enemies may turn to terrorism against "soft" targets in the United States, perhaps using weapons of mass destruction, in order to deter American military action. Even though terrorism may not be the preferred method of fighting, enemies of the United States may feel that its military power leaves them no alternative.

Finally, information warfare is likely to stoke an arms race of its own. Even today there is sharp competition between computer hackers and virus-writers and businesses, networks, and law-abiding individuals. As armed forces become more information- and computer-dependent, this competition may shift to the military realm. Hacking, virus-writing, and crashing data information systems—as well as defending against enemy hackers and virus writers—may become core military skills, as important as the ability to shoot. In this particular arena, the American armed services are less clearly superior to potential enemies than in traditional military functions, so the spiral of response and counter-response is likely to be intense.

MARCHING TOWARD THE FRINGE

The RMA described in Joint Vision 2010 does not represent a fundamental transformation of armed conflict; it is more "hyper-evolutionary" than revolutionary. But it is possible to use existing trends to speculate on the direction armed combat may take beyond 2010 and imagine the problems that could emerge. For example, future armed conflict may involve little or no direct human contact. Advances in robotics and nanotechnology—the ability to manipulate and manufacture individual molecules—may soon allow the construction of tiny but "brilliant" military machines capable of complex decision making. This could turn warfare into a machine-on-machine struggle, with humans on the sidelines. Machines may become self-repairing, self-replicating, even self-improving. At some point, cyborgs—complex machines with some attributes of living organisms—may become feasible and the proliferation of militarily relevant genetic material a key issue for arms control.

Even more ominously, technology to manipulate human thoughts, perceptions, attitudes, and beliefs using electronic or chemical means might become feasible. This could entail direct "mind control," holograms, and "morphing" an individual by creating, manipulating, and transmitting a computer-generated image indistinguishable from a real one. It is easy to imagine the horror of such developments, but it is equally easy to understand how a beleaguered leader might decide that the immorality of psychotechnology is justified by a serious security threat (especially if the public has already become accustomed to such techniques through the entertainment and advertising industries). If one nation opens this Pandora's box and demonstrates substantial progress in psychotechnology, others will surely follow, unleashing another kind of arms race.

Finally, future warfare may also see changes in who fights, with the "privatization" of warfare made possible, perhaps even likely. If the current RMA allows the development of small but effective armed forces, powerful transnational mercenary corporations may arise. The same factors that led to the proliferation of mercenaries in the past—the expense of training and sustaining a military force, the sporadic need for one, and a moral disdain for the profession of arms—show signs of rebirth. In coming decades, high-tech, transnational mercenary corporations or the private armies of other transnational corporations may be able to challenge or defeat the armed forces of less advanced states.

DISTANT RUMBLINGS

Only the historians of the future will know whether a full-scale RMA was under way in the 1990s. But for those living through these times—especially policymakers who must deal with arms control and proliferation—there is little doubt that there is at least a revolution in weaponry. This can be seen in the shifting valuation of weapons systems. In the past, valuation was based on the ratio of cost to destructiveness. Now what might be called "discernment"— accuracy and, increasingly, decision-making capacity—is equally important. To some extent, availability and usability will still structure the arms races of the early twenty-first century, but the technology-driven global dispersion of information, the advent of "brilliant" systems requiring less training, the development of highly realistic computer-based training systems, and the declining distinction between weaponry and other types of information technology will encourage proliferation and arms races. At the same time, information-based weapons systems will erode the concept of national arms industries, again complicating traditional state-centric arms control regimes.

Decisions made in Washington in the coming years will determine whether the RMA stokes future arms races and proliferation problems. Other nations are interested in the RMA, but only the United States has the money, technological prowess, and strategic incentive to embrace it. So far the American approach, while a logical response to vexing strategic problems, has not been shaped by concern for long-term political implications. Pursuit of an RMA is not the wrong policy, but pursuit of the RMA described in Joint Vision 2010 may generate unintended political and diplomatic side effects and lead to a more dangerous world rather than a more stable one.

In part, this problem is structural. Within the United States government, responsibility for military strategy and arms control policy is split. . . . The architects of American military strategy are not oblivious to political and diplomatic concerns, but they must respond primarily to the nation's strategic dilemma. Their attention to the diplomatic and political impact of military strategy is minimal. . . .

Still, the American approach to the RMA could be recast so that long-term political and diplomatic considerations would receive greater emphasis. This would require redirecting the RMA from simply improving power projection. Seeking a radical improvement in the American military while the United States faces no powerful enemy raises suspicions. To many other states, the only logical reason for the United States to augment its military power in the current security environment is to pursue hegemony. So long as United States military strategy seeks power projection, other states will develop countermeasures to American military prowess, thus sparking arms races, whether symmetric or asymmetric. While this may be an acceptable risk, American policymakers and military strategists should at least explore the possibility of a less provocative variant of the RMA.

In addition, the United States should develop a coherent strategy to defend national information assets. Information systems are daily becoming more central to national life (and thus national security), but no government agency has clear responsibility for coordinating efforts to protect them. Enemies will recognize this vulnerability and attempt to use it to counter the American military, unleashing a spiral of escalation. The United States should also publicly eschew and condemn the development of any technology designed to manipulate human thoughts, beliefs, or perceptions. However alluring this "nonlethal" technology might appear at first glance, its danger is immense. Finally, the United States should expand the time horizons of its efforts to control arms races and proliferation. This would entail crafting regimes to control forms of military technology that, although technologically feasible, are not yet fielded. It is much easier to manage the development of a new form of technology than to control one that has matured to the point that powerful organizations have a vested interest in it.

The political difficulties of altering the current trajectory of the RMA should not be underestimated. In the short term, the RMA will benefit the United States by easing or alleviating some key strategic problems. The United States military of 2010 will be smaller than the current military, but it will also be more effective. In the long term, however, the RMA will create new problems for the United States by provoking asymmetric responses and fueling arms races. The record of the United States at forgoing short-term benefits for long-term gains offers little ground for optimism.

NOTES

1. Michael J. Mazarr, et al., *The Military Technical Revolution: A Structural Framework* (Washington, DC: Center for Strategic and International Studies, March 1993).

2. Alvin and Heidi Toffler, *War and Anti-War: Survival at the Dawn of the 21st Century* (Boston: Little, Brown, 1993).

The Economic Dimension

27. EXPORT OUR WAY TO PROSPERITY

Peter Morici

*I*n 1934, the United States abandoned more than a century of protectionism with the enactment of the Reciprocal Trade Agreements Act. The bilateral agreements that followed rolled back the Smoot-Hawley tariffs and signaled the emergence of U.S. leadership across a whole range of global issues. After World War II, the United States did not retreat into isolationism. Instead, it sought to ensure durable democracies in West Germany and Japan, guarantee joint security, and create a commonweal of prosperity to unite friend and foe.

The General Agreement on Tariffs and Trade (GATT), the International Monetary Fund, and the World Bank were established to promote trade and investment responsive to market forces, convertible currencies, and aid for developing nations. The United States supported the creation of what is now the European Union (EU). These institutions established a multilateral system that ignited a virtuous cycle of international commerce and growth for nations choosing outward-looking, market-oriented development strategies.

Ultimately, the economic success of the West, as much as its commitments to defense, won the Cold War and instigated the transformations now under way in Eastern Europe, Russia, and China. The success of export-oriented development strategies in Japan and the Asian tigers (Hong Kong, Singapore, South Korea, and Taiwan) revealed the folly of state-directed, import-substitution strategies. The spread of economic reforms throughout the Second and Third Worlds testifies to the growing appeal of the notion that markets, not ministries, should guide commerce and the development strategies of national economies.

Today, Americans navigate a world much of their own design, yet they are uneasy and ambivalent. Isolationists on the Right and Left point to declining real wages and hemorrhaging trade deficits as evidence that liberal trade policies now threaten American prosperity and could instigate economic decline.

Such charges ignore technological and social forces that are radically altering American society and the opportunities global commerce offers to turn these changes to U.S. advantage. This said, an effective U.S. policy for opening foreign markets does not require unequivocal reliance on multilateral institutions. Although the new World Trade Organization (WTO) provides the foundation for an effective global commercial regime, it does not offer sufficient means for dismantling all important barriers to trade.

GLOBALIZATION AND AMERICAN SOCIETY

The Eisenhower years may be characterized as the quiet before the storm. Owing in large part to immigration rules implemented after World War I, the contribution of new arrivals to net population growth averaged less than 5 percent during the 1930s, 1940s, and 1950s, as compared with more than 30 percent during the first 20 years of the century. Country quotas were heavily biased toward easily assimilated northern Europeans. These developments, along with the unifying cultural influences of national mobilization, the nearly universal conscription for two world wars, and a pervasive mass media, made Americans perhaps more homogenous than at any time since the founding of the republic.

During the 1950s, exports and imports of goods and services accounted for only about 9 percent of gross domestic product (GDP), and the devastation of World War II left American industries in unusually strong, globally competitive positions. Americans, in the largest numbers ever, found good jobs plentiful, enjoyed rising incomes, lived in single breadwinner households, sent their children to public schools that reinforced Anglo-Saxon culture and values, and had little to fear from international competition. Workers straight from high school could take factory jobs and achieve lifestyles rivaling those of college graduates a generation earlier or a generation later.

In the 1970s and 1980s, several forces gathered momentum to alter this reality. Owing in large measure to immigration law reform, the failures of statist development strategies and authoritarian governments in Latin America, and U.S. involvement in Asia, U.S. immigration became decidedly less European and swelled to 38 percent of net population growth in the 1980s.

More immigrants, maturing baby boomers, the increased aspirations of women, and the impact of the civil rights movement on opportunities for minorities combined to accelerate labor-force growth and increase the proportion of the adult population competing for more-satisfying, better-paying jobs. More non-Europeans and newly empowered African American, Latino, and Asian communities turned the melting pot into a collage, as the United States became the world's most multicultural society.

Meanwhile, both the Kennedy and Tokyo Round tariff cuts decidedly opened the American market to foreign competition, and trade rose from 11 percent of GDP in 1970 to 21 percent by 1980. Japan, followed by the Asian tigers and then China, flooded U.S. markets with toys, textiles, steel, and automobiles. Many good-paying jobs in manufacturing—both on the factory floor and in professional suites—disappeared.

More workers and imports led to depressed wages, and a more diverse population and workforce required unsettling adjustments in public institutions and the workplace. The children of the families that prospered after World War II discovered that good jobs were scarce, endured falling wages, required two paychecks to live reasonably, sent their children to schools emphasizing multicultural values, and faced employers who pushed for diversity for pragmatic as well as legal reasons.

Other factors certainly contributed to the scarcity of good-paying jobs. At first, the American competitive dominance of the 1950s and 1960s contributed to a complacency that resulted in a drop in productivity growth and a loss of competitiveness and market shares in the 1970s and 1980s. When American businesses finally got the message, it took time to catch up; when they did, breakthroughs in computers, telecommunications, and management methods radically altered work processes, instigated corporate downsizing, and continued the squeeze on the availability of good jobs.

Among American workers, an unfortunate division has emerged. As most Americans saw their prospects decline, a significant minority of mostly college-educated and younger workers actually saw their status and circumstances improve. These men and women are more comfortable with new technology, modern gender roles, and diversity in ways vital for managing the new American labor force and undertaking global business activities. They are [former] Labor Secretary Robert Reich's "glass-tower people." They have found comfortable professional and managerial niches in business and government. Often, they live privatized lives, sending their children to exclusive schools, abandoning the moribund post office for Federal Express, jetting here and there, and communicating on the Internet and by fax and cellular phone.

Although imports and immigration account for only a small portion of the erosion of average American incomes, the ubiquity of Hondas and Toyotas on American highways, the struggle of cash-strapped local governments to meet the needs of new immigrants, and the success of many of these immigrants and their children unfortunately impart to many Americans a sense that something is awry. It is especially unsettling for workers hardest hit by the change—the nearly 50 percent of the workforce with no post-secondary education and older, middle-class workers either caught by corporate downsizing or fearful about the prospects for their children. Working-class decline and middle-class anxiety help the Ross Perots and Patrick Buchanans of the Right play on fears and incite xenophobia. California's Proposition 187, which [denies] most public services to illegal immigrants, proposals for draconian cuts in immigration, and opposition to the North American Free Trade Agreement (NAFTA) and the WTO are all, in part, manifestations of this phenomenon. These realities are also cousin to some of the intemperate criticisms of affirmative action.

Meanwhile, a significant opposition to free trade has emerged among some scholars and policy analysts. In the 1970s, trade liberalization was largely opposed by parties with clear self-interests in limiting import competition—most notably a few basic industries and organized labor—and by some economists and other intellectuals on the radical Left. By the time of the NAFTA and Uruguay Round debates, the ground had shifted. Although most mainstream economists continued to vocally support free trade, a small group of economists applying mainstream tools of analysis, as well as some political scientists and others lacking a direct personal stake in stifling imports, joined the opponents of free trade. Environmentalists and activists began viewing the rules and dispute-settlement provisions of international trade agreements as threatening U.S. regulatory sovereignty, and think tanks emerged in Washington that supported their views and strengthened their voice. Although their analyses are often based on severe assumptions, they have achieved influence through the media and in the Congress. The result is a liberal trade policy besieged from the Right and the Left. . . .

EXPORTS AND GROWTH

Given all of these trends, why should [Washington] continue to place so much emphasis on new trade agreements to open foreign markets? The reason is that U.S. competitiveness is improving, and the economy increasingly relies on exports to sustain growth and create good jobs.

. . . Corporate downsizing . . . is not a collapse of U.S. industry in the wake of supercompetitive imports; rather, it mostly reflects the spread of new technologies, especially advances in microelectronics, software and telecommunications, and better management methods. For example, by applying computer-aided design and production and by combining manufacturing and design teams, General Motors is substantially shortening the development cycle for new vehicles—this will permit GM to introduce new models more frequently and to devote 5,000 fewer workers to these activities, including fewer engineers. U.S. manufacturing productivity growth has accelerated to 2.8 percent per year since 1985—up from 1.7 percent for the period from 1973 to 1985; the cost competitiveness of U.S. industry has improved substantially vis-à-vis rivals in Japan, the Asian newly industrialized countries, and Western Europe.

Japanese automobiles notwithstanding, the United States has not lost, but has indeed regained, leadership in many leading-edge technologies. Consider U.S. leadership in personal computers, software, microprocessors, telecommunication, and aerospace and the resurgence of the U.S. semiconductor and chipmaking equipment industries. Together, lower costs and the aggressive application of technology in new and improved products have translated into an impressive export-led expansion.

From 1985 to 1994, exports surged 112 percent as U.S. GDP increased 25 percent. Exports generated one-third of the economic growth and about

5 million new jobs in the private sector. Manufactured exports led the way, increasing 129 percent, and these now account for 60 percent of U.S. sales of goods and services abroad. The exports are heavily concentrated in machinery, transportation and scientific equipment, drugs, and other high-technology goods. Export industries pay higher wages, and technology-intensive activities pay the highest wages—almost one-fifth higher than those of other manufacturing industries. Manufacturing jobs supported by exports increased from about 2.4 to 4 million from 1985 to 1994, yet overall manufacturing employment fell from 19.1 to 18.7 million. Why? Quite simply, many U.S. firms making highly competitive durable goods and providing sophisticated business services have trimmed their payrolls, because productivity improvements—in offices, on the factory floor, in design studios, and among the sales force—are outpacing domestic and foreign market growth. . . .

Innovations in microelectronics and software are [also] altering service activities that are normally more resistant to productivity improvements, such as customer service in the utilities and retail activities in the financial sectors. . . . Further, the "glass-tower people" are at the vanguard of the emerging American workforce, as more young people are now preparing to work in technologically demanding environments. . . . In a world of globalized production and markets, a culturally diverse corps of managers and professionals could prove to be a decisive competitive advantage.

Overall, with productivity growth likely to remain strong and the proportion of the labor force with advanced education expanding, the basic constraint on the creation of enough good jobs will remain the limited scope of the American market and limited access to foreign markets. If U.S. trade negotiators can unlock new markets in Europe, Asia, and Latin America, the United States will enjoy an export-led boom, and the American dream will be resurrected and redefined in a prosperous, multicultural society.

However, effective trade policy must be complemented by equally sound domestic policies. A well-educated labor force is a necessary, but not a sufficient, condition for competitive success in high-technology activities. . . . As products and industries mature, jobs that were once esoteric and exotic become more routine, and employment disperses geographically. . . . The key is to stay on the leading edge of technology and to keep American workers engaged in the core functions of defining innovation and managing global enterprises. . . .

Receding into protectionism would increase the demand for workers adversely affected by structural change and lessen somewhat the wage gap between workers with no post-secondary education and others. However, protection that reduces imports would reduce exports as well by driving up the dollar and encouraging retaliation by our trading partners. It would give false importance to fading industries like apparel, low-end auto parts, and furniture, and stifle the growth of technology-intensive industries like aircraft, computer equipment and software, and financial services. Productivity and wage growth would be constrained, and the employment aspirations of increasingly well-educated, younger workers would be frustrated to placate less-educated, older workers. By reducing the availability of truly attractive jobs, protectionism would exacerbate racial and ethnic divisions and jealousies: It could help make America a poorer, balkanized society.

THE WTO AND REGIONAL AGREEMENTS

Improving export opportunities through the WTO is essential to long-term U.S. trade and foreign policy goals. However, it is important to structure policy on reasonable expectations about what can be achieved in that forum and a clear understanding about the U.S. actions that will be necessary to achieve these expectations. It is equally important to recognize that not all vital U.S. trade interests can be addressed adequately, or in a timely fashion, through the WTO. Other approaches may be appropriate if they produce results consistent with the central WTO goal of fostering market-responsive trade.

The Uruguay Round Agreements (URAs) will increase U.S. imports of labor-intensive manufactures and exports of technology-intensive goods and services. This increase will be accomplished in part by cutting tariffs by about 40 percent, but it will also depend on successful implementation of new and expanded WTO rules governing nontariff barriers (NTBs).

The URAs impose new, stricter disciplines on government practices that directly affect the movement of goods across borders; however, the URAs also reach deeply into activities once considered squarely within the domain of domestic policy. For example, the agreements promise greater transparency in writing product standards and testing procedures and in soliciting bids on government contracts, Western-style intellectual property laws and beefed-up enforcement in developing countries, some discipline on trade-related investment measures, and national treatment and right of establishment for foreign service providers.

Ultimately, real improvements in U.S. market access abroad will strongly depend on foreign governments rewriting and applying laws and regulations to be consistent with the letter and spirit of the URAs. Disagreements over interpretation will inevitably arise. For the WTO to be effective, national governments must honor the decisions of dispute-settlement panels.

Some in Congress may lament the loss of sovereignty to the WTO; however, it is clear that American exports and prosperity are, in some measure, connected to its success. In turn, the WTO can succeed only if the United States is perceived abroad to be playing by the rules, and this will prove delicate because of its pursuit of regional trade agreements and continuing trade problems with Japan.

Full elimination of NTBs would require harmonization and integration of national regulatory practices. Although the URAs provide for greater transparency and nondiscrimination, they do not mandate transnational regimes, and signatory countries insisted on many exceptions for their current practices. The United States and the EU have found that they can effectively supplement multilateral progress through regional arrangements—namely, the Canada–U.S. Free Trade Agreement (CUSFTA), NAFTA, the European

Community's 1992 initiative, and the European Economic Area. In regional discussions, national approaches to business law and regulation share more in common, and with sweeping market access packages at stake, governments seem willing to go further.

These regional arrangements have been generally consistent with the GATT and the WTO. For example, CUSFTA and NAFTA were built on the GATT: They broaden and deepen the three countries' WTO rights and obligations as they apply to intracontinental trade. As the United States seeks to expand NAFTA southward, it encounters governments implementing aggressive economic and political reforms and seeking to modernize their legal and regulatory structures, in part to be attractive to U.S. investors. Many governments may see real advantages in achieving greater harmonization with U.S. and Canadian norms, adhering to NAFTA rules, and accepting WTO disciplines.

In the Asia-Pacific Economic Cooperation forum, however, such WTO-consistent arrangements are not as certain an outcome. Asian countries have quite different commercial institutions from those prevalent in North America—e.g., the Japanese *keiretsu*, the Korean *chaebol*, and the reliance on family businesses and clan relationships in China and Hong Kong. This makes the process of achieving greater conformity among national practices more difficult. Given the impressive success of many of these economies, their governments may be reluctant to refashion domestic regimes to accept U.S. models and prescriptions for domestic business laws and regulations. As with our diverse experience with Japan, broader regional cooperation in commerce could result in genuine liberalization or merely managed trade. A lot will depend on how successive U.S. trade issues with Japan are resolved.

DEALING WITH JAPAN

It is proving extraordinarily difficult to write and exclusively rely on multilateral rules to resolve major bilateral frictions among the principal players in the WTO when they strongly disagree about which government practices distort trade and which private practices undermine the market access promised by WTO rules. The former is well illustrated by U.S. disputes with the EU over subsidies such as aid to Airbus. The latter is perhaps best illustrated by U.S. and EU complaints about the purchasing practices of the Japanese *keiretsu*, which often reflect private consensus about which activities should receive preference in domestic markets. These practices not only limit U.S. and EU exports to Japan but also to the rest of Asia. As the *keiretsu* extends its reach through overseas investments, preferences for Japan's technology-intensive products are set up, locking out other competitors. Japanese success may also encourage emulation by other Asian countries, further limiting U.S. and EU exports. The United States, needing to expand exports to sustain growth, cannot let these situations go unaddressed in either Japan or other Asian markets.

Since the WTO is structured to deal primarily with government actions and may determine that it lacks jurisdiction in critical U.S.–Japanese disputes, the United States is prudent to first try to address these practices in bilateral talks. While Japan does not see these private practices as inherently protectionist and has profited from them, it resists U.S. pressure and seeks to push the United States into WTO disputes. Because the United States lacks an analog to the *keiretsu,* virtually any response it takes to Japanese intransigence, other than formal WTO complaints, will involve actions that could be found to violate the WTO. Therefore, the ability of the United States to prevail will much depend on its ability to convince the other WTO heavyweight—the EU—that Japan is a special case and that its brand of syndicate capitalism is inconsistent with an effective, durable WTO.

Two realities in this economic relationship will prove important. First, although conventional economics tells us that U.S. budget deficits and high Japanese savings are the reason for U.S. trade deficits with Japan, the facts indicate other variables may be at play. From 1985 to 1994, the U.S. current-account deficit with Japan climbed from $47 billion to $65 billion. Even as U.S. fiscal performance improved, the yen appreciated against the dollar some 57 percent, and American product quality and productivity improved. The bilateral deficit remains stubbornly high because the Japanese market is particularly difficult to penetrate in technology-intensive manufactures and sophisticated business services. . . .

Second, the same Japanese policies that encourage high savings, investment, and exports also discourage domestic consumption. Japan is thus dependent on exports to achieve growth; however, Japan is now pushing up against the limits of U.S. and other trading partners' capacities to accept Japanese exports without importing more itself, causing economic stagnation in Japan. When Japan was only a small player in the international economy, it could premise its growth strategy on exports growing more rapidly than imports and use the proceeds to buy foreign enterprises, real estate, and securities. Now, it is too large for these tactics. In Japan, investment has been falling . . . , unemployment is at a record level, and banks are teetering on the edge of insolvency. Mercantilism is slowly choking the Japanese economy to the detriment of global growth. With West European unemployment at more than 10 percent, the EU can ill afford this.

The United States can be expected to continue to press Japan and to practice an implicit policy of *conditional reciprocity* by threatening trade sanctions of appropriate proportion when Japanese practices and customs undermine the benefits expected from WTO commitments. If the president can keep the American people convinced that any inconveniences imposed on them by sanctions are necessary, and if European trade officials offer at least tacit support, the United States may be able to obtain agreements that fundamentally alter Japanese purchasing practices and open markets for products from all nations. In turn, Japanese and global growth would accelerate, setting an example for Korea, China, and other Asian nations.

The Europeans clearly recognize the problems posed by Japanese trade practices; however, they are wary of U.S. unilateralism, especially the use of Section 301 to threaten trade sanctions. If they choose not to support the

United States—either explicitly or quietly in the hallways of the WTO—then the United States may have to settle for less. The result could be managed trade with Japan, which salves American business wounds but does little to open the Japanese market generically and to ensure a strong WTO. This would set the tone for greater reliance on managed commerce throughout Asia. In such an environment, the United States, with much stronger productivity and technology than the EU, is in a better position than the EU to compete for influence and commerce in Asia.

At worst, European indifference, or even criticism, about U.S. efforts to open the Japanese market could contribute to American humiliation in the WTO should a case, such as the . . . dispute between Kodak and Fuji, result in U.S.–imposed trade sanctions and a reprimand of U.S. actions by a dispute-settlement panel. The *keiretsu* would continue to lock out foreign competitors at home and to lock up markets in East and Southeast Asia through its investments. The WTO would come under serious attack in Congress and could ultimately be rendered ineffective by American indifference. Consequently, Japanese mercantilism would emerge as the trade policy of choice throughout much of Asia, and perhaps elsewhere, and competitive protectionism could undermine global prosperity and security. In the face of such a challenge, the United States could be expected to emphasize laissez-faire principles in the Occidental world and to play Japan's managed-trade game in the Orient.

PLAYING THE EUROPE CARD

Worries have emerged in the EU that America's focus on Latin America and Asia could cause the important U.S.–EU trade relationship to drift into disrepair. . . .

After intra-EU trade is factored out, the United States and the EU account for more than 35 percent of global trade, and U.S. and EU positions on trade issues often have a decisive impact on the multilateral agenda. Setting goals for the liberalization of transatlantic commerce in areas such as investment, product standards, procurement, competition policy, and environmental regulations would establish minimum expectations for the next round of WTO-sponsored multilateral trade negotiations and would greatly improve prospects for its success.

. . . A deepened U.S.–European relationship would offer broader markets to firms on both continents and . . . create benefits for nations in Latin America, Asia, and Africa. And, finally, it would place significant additional pressure on Japan to open its markets, while substantially lowering the risk of a train wreck in the WTO. By playing the Europe card boldly, American policymakers could show the kind of private-sector ingenuity that has resurrected U.S. technological and competitive leadership.

28. TRADE POLICY FOR A NEW ERA

Clyde V. Prestowitz, Jr., and Saul Goldstein

*T*he ... Uruguay Round of the General Agreement on Tariffs and Trade (GATT) [concluded in late 1993] probably is the last of the classic Cold War–era multilateral trade talks. In the new post–Cold War era, trade policy will no longer be the handmaiden of geopolitics; nations will pursue a trade policy focused squarely on economic goals.

Since the conclusion of World War II, the United States has championed the cause of free trade and open markets. It has pushed for liberalization of world markets by focusing on the procedures, rules, and processes governing international commerce under GATT.

The overriding concern, however, has been geopolitical issues. As a result, trade always [took] a back seat. Despite the protests of business and commerce, the U.S. State Department consistently ... used trade policy to achieve its foreign-policy objectives of firmly cementing our trading partners into the free-world camp.

During the Kennedy and Johnson administrations, the State Department recommended "firm executive branch resistance of American industry demands for curtailment of Japanese imports." Even as recently as the Gulf War of 1991, U.S. geopolitical objectives took priority over U.S. domestic interests. In exchange for cooperation with United Nations sanctions to isolate Iraq, Turkey received promises from then Secretary of State James Baker to raise U.S. import quotas on Turkish textiles, as well as increased economic aid.

America's post–Cold War national goal is not controversial: We should strive to raise our productivity and, thereby, increase our standard of living. The fundamentals for a healthy and vibrant economy are not debatable;

Note: Some notes have been deleted.

everyone agrees, for example, that current levels of capital formation must be increased to levels at least equivalent to those of other leading industrial nations. Also, a policy of budget-deficit reduction, low inflation, and low interest rates must be pursued.

The greatest trade policy in the world will not work if there is hyper-inflation, if there is inadequate capital to invest, or if the cost of capital is higher than elsewhere in the world. While it is essential to get the macro-economic fundamentals right, it also is necessary to complement these with effective trade policy.

Nations such as Japan, Korea, and Taiwan not only pursue these noncontroversial, growth-oriented fundamentals, but they integrate their technology, industrial, and trade policies with broader macro-economic goals. They recognize that the aggregate economy is made up of pieces, and the health of these pieces is important to the health of the overall economy.

In fact, they view the structure of the economy as an important factor in determining overall economic productivity. Therefore, what their economy produces is important, and, by extension, what they trade is important. Their economic success suggests it is a matter of priority to understand how regulatory, defense, and other economic policies, including trade, are linked and how they affect the structure of the economy. To put it simply, the effects of our trade policy will be felt throughout the economy.

U.S. policymaking often has been negligent because it has been led by people who embrace a notion captured in a quip from a former Bush administration economic adviser: "Potato chips, computer chips, what's the difference? They're all chips."

Implicit in this statement is the belief that what we make does not matter. This theory holds that the natural resource base of each nation will lead that nation to produce what it can produce best. Therefore, the content and structure of our trade is unimportant.

Following this theory, our trade policy focused on obtaining something called "free trade" by addressing processes, rules, and procedures. Moreover, we eschewed a broader industrial policy that would have linked domestic technology policy with trade policy. We were concerned that excessive government interference would result in the government "picking winners and losers" in the civilian sector. We believed that structure did not count—that the mix between high-technology industries and low-technology industries was unimportant.

As a result, we did not respond to the industrial policies of countries targeting the industries of tomorrow. After all, mainstream economists contended that these nations were only hurting themselves by subsidizing Airbus, targeting the supercomputer industry, or dumping products, at below cost, in our market. These acts were simply gifts to consumers. If they wiped out entire U.S. industries, don't worry, because our growing economy was creating new jobs, and people could always find work.

But if you believe that structure does count—that what we make does matter—then we must integrate coherent technology, trade, and industrial policies with the rest of our macro-economic tools.

TRADE PROBLEMS MATTER

Most of the discussion of our trade problem is in terms of the size of the trade deficit, but trade friction arises more from the composition of the trade deficit than from its size. For example, the United States has had a large trade deficit with Saudi Arabia for a long time and virtually no trade friction; it has a trade surplus with Europe, yet lots of trade friction. Theoretically, trade with Japan could be balanced by shipping the Japanese enough logs, scrap aluminum, waste paper, and Alaskan crude oil to balance out the Toyotas, copiers, and VCRs we import. But would that really solve the trade problem?

Trade friction arises when foreign competition chases key U.S. industries out of business. When this happens under conditions that seem inequitable, the friction becomes virulent. Displacement of key U.S. industries by foreign competitors has important impacts on U.S. productivity, technology development, and national security. Hence, trade analysis and policy should be more focused on industry-by-industry trade dynamics and less on overall deficits and surpluses.

However, trade deficits, or more precisely, current-account deficits, become significant at some point because they lead to devaluation and indebtedness. The standard view is that, because trade is multilateral, bilateral deficits are irrelevant; a deficit with Japan supposedly is offset by a surplus with Mexico.

Moreover, because trade is viewed as a function of savings, investment, and government spending, deficits usually are attributed to a lack of domestic savings. The cure is increased savings and a reduction of government spending. Underlying this classic view, however, is the assumption that net exports are the result of savings, investment, and government spending. The well-known accounting equation is: "Savings minus investment plus budget surplus equals trade balance."

The conventional explanation of this identity is that nations with high private savings rates and budget surpluses or small budget deficits likely will run trade surpluses. At the same time, nations with low savings rates and large budget deficits will run trade deficits.

While this is true as far as it goes, it is not the only interpretation of the accounting identity. Because this is an equilibrium equation, it is as possible for action to operate from right to left as from left to right. As Harvard economist and former Undersecretary of State Richard Cooper has written, "This accounting identity says nothing about the dynamics of the impact of policy actions on the economy."[1]

Recent econometric work by Robert Blecker shows that net exports affect savings, investment, government surpluses, and deficits and not simply vice-versa.[2] This cutting-edge work indicates that a significant portion of the U.S. trade deficit is structural in nature and that at least part of the drop in U.S. savings rates is caused by structural barriers and practices contributing to the U.S. trade deficit.

To illustrate the point, suppose that the Japanese government removed all barriers to imports of supercomputers. The result: U.S. net exports would grow as sales by such firms as Cray increased. Cray would realize lower costs and achieve higher profits, turning some of this capital into savings, taxes, and debt reduction.

Thus, the United States should not rely simply on the traditional macro-economic tools to reduce trade deficits. A real structural trade deficit will not readily respond to a currency devaluation, for example. Of course, there is an exchange rate at which imports become prohibitive. If we went to 50 yen to the dollar tomorrow, we wouldn't buy anything from Japan. But by devaluing our currency to overcome a structural trade deficit, we would wind up hurting ourselves and not reducing the trade deficit by much.

Although disentangling the impact of all the factors that contribute to the U.S. trade deficit is difficult, some indicators of the possible size of the U.S. structural trade deficit with Japan exist.

In the latter half of the 1980s, the U.S. trade balance with Europe swung from a deficit of roughly $20 billion to a surplus of the same magnitude following the Plaza Accord devaluation.[3] Although the United States has about the same amount of trade with Japan, halving the value of the dollar only resulted in the U.S. deficit dropping from about $60 billion to about $40 billion. Moreover, the U.S. deficit with Japan is [again much higher], suggesting there is a strong structural element in U.S.–Japanese trade.

A structural trade deficit is one that does not respond readily to exchange-rate changes because it arises not from macro-economic causes, but from such factors as formal trade barriers, varying regulatory regimes, and informally restrictive business practices.

It is not unfair for other countries to have different views of industrial or anti-trust policies. Institutions such as foreign cartels, *keirestu* and *chaebol* in Japan and Korea, and controlled distribution are not necessarily unfair, as current U.S. trade laws characterize them. Yet, these differences often put U.S. manufacturers at a disadvantage because they cannot achieve the same economies of scale as other manufacturers.

International stock markets are another example where structural differences occur. Both the Tokyo Stock Exchange and the New York Stock Exchange are markets where businesses raise capital, but the asymmetries between these two markets give rise to wholly different outcomes. There is nothing wrong with these differences, but they can cause serious competitive disadvantage. If the parameters governing the New York Stock Exchange were somehow altered to mirror those of the Tokyo Stock Exchange, the outcome would change drastically. One of the most obvious effects is that small- and medium-sized firms would be crushed because the Tokyo Stock Exchange favors large firms.

The long-term solution to structural deficits is to harmonize these structural asymmetries. Most people assume this means negotiating specific market shares or forming market cartels, but this is not the case.

For years, the United States has engaged in "managing trade" without negotiating market share. International airline routes, for example, have been decided on a bilateral, reciprocal basis in which issues pertaining to the number of flights and landing rights are negotiated. Market shares, in fact, fluctuate significantly. All of this occurs because we understand that if we simply opened our market to foreign airlines, which often are operated and subsidized by their governments, our carriers would be overrun. Instead, we manage airline travel to achieve equivalent competitive conditions that ensure competition among countries with structural asymmetries.

Structural trade deficits must be resolved with structural means, not macro-economic tools. This is not to say that exchange rates or other macro-economic tools are unimportant. Exchange rates are important, and it is vital to have the right exchange rate. However, we must solve our trade problems with the appropriate measures. This means, in part, weaning ourselves from the tendency to use exchange rates and macro-economic tools to solve problems they cannot solve.

FUTURE TRADE POLICY

An appropriate model for trade policy is the deregulation of the U.S. telecommunication industry. Because of the history and structure of the industry, it was not practical to simply remove regulations and tell AT&T's challengers they could compete. AT&T assuredly would have crushed any newcomer. Certain restrictions, therefore, were put on AT&T to enable MCI, Sprint, and others to develop a significant market share. By managing competition in telecommunications for a time, the government changed the structure of the market and made it more competitive.

In the United Kingdom, the cable television and telecommunications market were deregulated with similar goals of competition in mind. Instead of opening the local market to new competitors, who would have been overrun by British Telecommunications' vast network that was acquired during previous monopolist times, the British Office of Telecommunications (OFTel) shackled the British Telecommunications' giant when it deregulated the market.

The U.S. Baby Bells, led by NYNEX [now Bell Atlantic], are providing local phone service in the United Kingdom via their cable television networks. OFTel has prohibited British Telecommunications (BT) from providing cable television service through its phone network. Thus, the U.S. companies are increasing their share of the phone service market at the expense of BT. . . .

At some point in the not-too-distant future, when the Baby Bells and their combined cable and telephone networks have grown large enough to compete with BT's telephone network, OFTel will remove the current restrictions on British Telecommunications. BT then will be free to provide both telephone and cable services like the U.S. companies.

Another case where trade management could create equivalent competitive conditions is in auto trade between the United States and Japan. In the United States, the same dealer may sell Fords and Nissans or Chevrolets and Toyotas. In Japan, anti-trust law permits manufacturers to exert strong control over auto distribution. For example, to sell cars in Japan, a U.S. company must set up an entirely new dealership network—a costly and time-consuming process. Because markets with such closed dealer systems are more difficult to penetrate than the U.S. market, the American auto industry is at a long-term disadvantage.

Not being able to increase sales in Japan means the American automakers have a lower capacity utilization rate and are less able than their Japanese competitors to capitalize on economies of scale. The result: even if American quality and productivity were far superior, the U.S. auto industry is less able to sell in the world's major markets than its Japanese competitors, who have lower costs.

A theoretical solution would be to negotiate a deal so that either all Japanese dealerships are open or all American dealerships are closed. Or, we could compromise at 50-50 with half the dealerships in each country open and half closed. The objective of U.S. policymakers should be to achieve conditions so U.S. industry is not forced to compete at a disadvantage.

The underlying goal of our trade policy should be to increase trade and help U.S. companies compete in foreign markets. Current trends in technology, combined with the scale of production needed for global market success, guarantee the shrinkage of time and distance. These forces inevitably lead to the integration of world markets under such terms as "globalization," "borderless economy," "mutual interdependence," and "internationalization."

These terms, however, should not be used as excuses to avoid thinking about the consequences of such interdependence. In a world in which what is made and traded matters, the precise terms of interdependence are critical. Typically, we have not worried about trade issues and the terms of market integration because of the belief that all multinational corporations act the same. But they don't.

History teaches that the terms of economic integration are crucial to the relationship between countries and, indeed, the world. India and England were integrated and interdependent, but India was dissatisfied with simply shipping raw materials to England for processing. The United States and Great Britain had similar problems several hundred years ago.

Trade policy is one important tool for achieving favorable terms of economic integration. While we should strive to liberalize trade, we don't want to do this unilaterally. And while we want free trade, we don't want simply to engage in laissez-faire trade.

We must liberalize trade on the basis of equivalent competitive conditions. To do this, we need to use all our tools—macro-economic, such as exchange rates and, where necessary, structural negotiations—to equalize the competitive environment in order to achieve favorable terms of integration.

INDUSTRIAL POLICY

Typically, industrial policy is described as picking winners and losers or as subsidizing industries. What is missed in this caricature is that every country has an industrial policy, conscious or not. All policies affect both the structure of our economy and the health of various sectors of the economy, either negatively or positively.

When the Defense Department spends money on research and development, when agendas for trade negotiations are decided, when capital-gains taxes are introduced, or when tax write-offs on mortgage payments are enacted, industrial policy is at work.

Typically, we have pursued these policies independently without thinking about their effect on the overall productivity of the economy. Lacking any overall guiding criteria, the choices we make are inevitably the result of politics or happenstance.

For example, the breakup of AT&T was an industrial policy; yet, we didn't analyze the breakup from the standpoint of its productivity impact. Instead, it was viewed simply as an anti-trust case.

Why has rice been such an important part of our trade agenda with Japan? Certainly not because analysis shows major economic gains from opening Japan's rice market.

The way we impose environmental or work-rule regulations, the choices we make in trade negotiations, or how we exercise our anti-trust legislation has a huge impact on long-term productivity and should be analyzed from this perspective. That's industrial policy.

Industrial policy is not simply a matter of subsidizing industries. Boeing doesn't need subsidies; it's the world leader in the aircraft industry. What is needed is a response to the attacks on our competitive industrial position by other governments, such as Korea, Japan, or Europe, that have explicit policies aimed at beating Boeing, . . . Cray, and other U.S. companies.

The future health of Cray and our other manufacturers of high-technology goods is integrally related with our trade policies. As the Office of Technology Assessment reported to Congress in 1991, due to the protection of the supercomputer market in Japan, Cray and others lost more than $700 million of sales.

Moreover, large investments in research and development, as well as in plant and equipment, are necessary to produce supercomputers. If Cray and others are able to amortize these investments over only two, instead of all three of the world's major markets, its costs will be higher than necessary, its ability to invest in new research and new plants will be less, and the number of people it can employ fewer and the wages it can afford more meager.

Ensuring the health of these companies means having an active trade policy that achieves measurable results—and is an integral part of an overall economic strategy.

Industrial policy means acknowledging that being a leader in critical industries is important and that the United States must respond to the industrial policies of other nations in an appropriate fashion.

Industrial policy means recognizing that industry swims in a pool and that the temperature and viscosity of the water is determined by the actions of government. To ensure that your Olympic swimmers can go fast, you need close cooperation between government and business. Even the greatest Olympic swimmers in the world won't get far if you put them in wet cement.

NEW ERA

The United States cannot hope to confront the new era of geo-economics successfully if it does not revitalize its domestic economy. U.S. international economic policy must be an extension of and an integral part of that strategy. That policy should focus on stimulating world economic integration, a favorable trade composition, and broad reciprocity in key trading relations. To do this, Americans will have to abandon much of the conventional economic wisdom that has misguided U.S. trade policy for years.

NOTES

1. Robert Blecker, *Beyond the Twin Deficits: A Trade Strategy for the 1990s* (Washington, DC: Economic Policy Institute, 1992), p. 19.
2. Ibid.
3. The Plaza Accord was a meeting where the G-7 nations, the world's leading industrial nations, agreed to seek to devalue the dollar relative to the yen and simultaneously reduce interest rates. Subsequently, the value of the dollar to the yen halved.

29. COMPETITIVENESS: A DANGEROUS OBSESSION

Paul Krugman

THE HYPOTHESIS IS WRONG

In June 1993, Jacques Delors made a special presentation to the leaders of the nations of the European Community [now the European Union], meeting in Copenhagen, on the growing problem of European unemployment. Economists who study the European situation were curious to see what Delors, president of the EC Commission, would say. Most of them share more or less the same diagnosis of the European problem: the taxes and regulations imposed by Europe's elaborate welfare states have made employers reluctant to create new jobs, while the relatively generous level of unemployment benefits . . . made workers unwilling to accept the kinds of low-wage jobs that help keep unemployment comparatively low in the United States. The monetary difficulties associated with preserving the European Monetary System [EMS] in the face of the costs of German reunification . . . reinforced this structural problem.

It is a persuasive diagnosis, but a politically explosive one, and everyone wanted to see how Delors would handle it. Would he dare tell European leaders that their efforts to pursue economic justice have produced unemployment as an unintended by-product? Would he admit that the EMS could be sustained only at the cost of a recession and face the implications of that admission for European monetary union?

Guess what? Delors didn't confront the problems of either the welfare state or the EMS. He explained that the root cause of European unemployment was a lack of competitiveness with the United States and Japan and that the solution was a program of investment in infrastructure and high technology.

Note: Notes have been deleted.

It was a disappointing evasion, but not a surprising one. After all, the rhetoric of competitiveness—the view that, in the words of President Clinton, each nation is "like a big corporation competing in the global marketplace"— has become pervasive among opinion leaders throughout the world. People who believe themselves to be sophisticated about the subject take it for granted that the economic problem facing any modern nation is essentially one of competing on world markets—that the United States and Japan are competitors in the same sense that Coca-Cola competes with Pepsi—and are unaware that anyone might seriously question that proposition. Every few months a new best-seller warns the American public of the dire consequences of losing the "race" for the 21st century. A whole industry of councils on competitiveness, "geo-economists" and managed trade theorists has sprung up in Washington. Many of these people, having diagnosed America's economic problems in much the same terms as Delors did Europe's, are now . . . formulating economic and trade policy for the United States. So Delors was using a language that was not only convenient but comfortable for him and a wide audience on both sides of the Atlantic.

Unfortunately, his diagnosis was deeply misleading as a guide to what ails Europe, and similar diagnoses in the United States are equally misleading. The idea that a country's economic fortunes are largely determined by its success on world markets is a hypothesis, not a necessary truth; and as a practical, empirical matter, that hypothesis is flatly wrong. That is, it is simply not the case that the world's leading nations are to any important degree in economic competition with each other, or that any of their major economic problems can be attributed to failures to compete on world markets. The growing obsession in most advanced nations with international competitiveness should be seen, not as a well-founded concern, but as a view held in the face of overwhelming contrary evidence. . . . Thinking in terms of competitiveness leads, directly and indirectly, to bad economic policies on a wide range of issues, domestic and foreign, whether it be in health care or trade.

MINDLESS COMPETITION

Most people who use the term "competitiveness" do so without a second thought. It seems obvious to them that the analogy between a country and a corporation is reasonable and that to ask whether the United States is competitive in the world market is no different in principle from asking whether General Motors is competitive in the North American minivan market.

In fact, however, trying to define the competitiveness of a nation is much more problematic than defining that of a corporation. The bottom line for a corporation is literally its bottom line: if a corporation cannot afford to pay its workers, suppliers, and bondholders, it will go out of business. So when we say that a corporation is uncompetitive, we mean that its market position is unsustainable—that unless it improves its performance, it will cease to exist. Countries, on the other hand, do not go out of business. They may be happy or unhappy with their economic performance, but they have no well-defined bottom line. As a result, the concept of national competitiveness is elusive.

One might suppose, naively, that the bottom line of a national economy is simply its trade balance, that competitiveness can be measured by the ability of a country to sell more abroad than it buys. But in both theory and practice a trade surplus may be a sign of national weakness, a deficit a sign of strength. For example, Mexico was forced to run huge trade surpluses in the 1980s in order to pay the interest on its foreign debt since international investors refused to lend it any more money; it began to run large trade deficits after 1990 as foreign investors recovered confidence and began to pour in new funds. Would anyone want to describe Mexico as a highly competitive nation during the debt crisis era or describe what has happened since 1990 as a loss in competitiveness?

Most writers who worry about the issue at all have therefore tried to define competitiveness as the combination of favorable trade performance and something else. In particular, the most popular definition of competitiveness nowadays runs along the lines of the one given in [former U.S.] Council of Economic Advisors Chairman Laura D'Andrea Tyson's *Who's Bashing Whom?*: competitiveness is "our ability to produce goods and services that meet the test of international competition while our citizens enjoy a standard of living that is both rising and sustainable." This sounds reasonable. If you think about it, however, and test your thoughts against the facts, you will find out that there is much less to this definition than meets the eye.

Consider, for a moment, what the definition would mean for an economy that conducted very little international trade, like the United States in the 1950s. For such an economy, the ability to balance its trade is mostly a matter of getting the exchange rate right. But because trade is such a small factor in the economy, the level of the exchange rate is a minor influence on the standard of living. So in an economy with very little international trade, the growth in living standards—and thus "competitiveness" according to Tyson's definition—would be determined almost entirely by domestic factors, primarily the rate of productivity growth. That's domestic productivity growth, period—not productivity growth relative to other countries. In other words, for an economy with very little international trade, "competitiveness" would turn out to be a funny way of saying "productivity" and would have nothing to do with international competition.

But surely this changes when trade becomes more important, as indeed it has for all major economies? It certainly could change. Suppose that a country finds that although its productivity is steadily rising, it can succeed in exporting only if it repeatedly devalues its currency, selling its exports ever more cheaply on world markets. Then its standard of living, which depends on its purchasing power over imports as well as domestically produced goods, might actually decline. In the jargon of economists, domestic growth might be outweighed by deteriorating terms of trade. So "competitiveness" could turn out really to be about international competition after all.

There is no reason, however, to leave this as a pure speculation; it can easily be checked against the data. Have deteriorating terms of trade in fact been a major drag on the U.S. standard of living? Or has the rate of growth of U.S. real income continued essentially to equal the rate of domestic productivity growth, even though trade is a larger share of income than it used to be?

To answer this question, one need only look at the national income accounts data the Commerce Department publishes regularly in the *Survey of Current Business*. The standard measure of economic growth in the United States is, of course, real GNP—a measure that divides the value of goods and services produced in the United States by appropriate price indexes to come up with an estimate of real national output. The Commerce Department also, however, publishes something called "command GNP." This is similar to real GNP except that it divides U.S. exports not by the export price index, but by the price index for U.S. imports. That is, exports are valued by what Americans can buy with the money exports bring. Command GNP therefore measures the volume of goods and services the U.S. economy can "command"—the nation's purchasing power—rather than the volume it produces. And as we have just seen, "competitiveness" means something different from "productivity" if and only if purchasing power grows significantly more slowly than output.

Well, here are the numbers. Over the period 1959–73, a period of vigorous growth in U.S. living standards and few concerns about international competition, real GNP per worker-hour grew 1.85 percent annually, while command GNP per hour grew a bit faster, 1.87 percent. From 1973 to 1990, a period of stagnating living standards, command GNP growth per hour slowed to 0.65 percent. Almost all (91 percent) of that slowdown, however, was explained by a decline in domestic productivity growth: real GNP per hour grew only 0.73 percent.

Similar calculations for the European Community and Japan yield similar results. In each case, the growth rate of living standards essentially equals the growth rate of domestic productivity—not productivity relative to competitors, but simply domestic productivity. Even though world trade is larger than ever before, national living standards are overwhelmingly determined by domestic factors rather than by some competition for world markets.

How can this be in our interdependent world? Part of the answer is that the world is not as interdependent as you might think: countries are nothing at all like corporations. Even today, U.S. exports are only 10 percent of the value-added in the economy (which is equal to GNP). That is, the United States is still almost 90 percent an economy that produces goods and services for its own use. By contrast, even the largest corporation sells hardly any of its output to its own workers; the "exports" of General Motors—its sales to people who do not work there—are virtually all of its sales, which are more than 2.5 times the corporation's value-added.

Moreover, countries do not compete with each other the way corporations do. Coke and Pepsi are almost purely rivals: only a negligible fraction of Coca-Cola's sales go to Pepsi workers, only a negligible fraction of the goods Coca-Cola workers buy are Pepsi products. So if Pepsi is successful, it tends to be at Coke's expense. But the major industrial countries, while they sell products that compete with each other, are also each other's main export markets and each other's main suppliers of useful imports. If the European economy does well, it need not be at U.S. expense; indeed, if anything a successful European economy is likely to help the U.S. economy by providing it with larger markets and selling it goods of superior quality at lower prices.

International trade, then, is not a zero-sum game. When productivity rises in Japan, the main result is a rise in Japanese real wages; American or European wages are in principle at least as likely to rise as to fall, and in practice seem to be virtually unaffected.

It would be possible to belabor the point, but the moral is clear: while competitive problems could arise in principle, as a practical, empirical matter the major nations of the world are not to any significant degree in economic competition with each other. Of course, there is always a rivalry for status and power—countries that grow faster will see their political rank rise. So it is always interesting to *compare* countries. But asserting that Japanese growth diminishes U.S. status is very different from saying that it reduces the U.S. standard of living—and it is the latter that the rhetoric of competitiveness asserts. . . .

THE THRILL OF COMPETITION

The competitive metaphor—the image of countries competing with each other in world markets in the same way that corporations do—derives much of its attractiveness from its seeming comprehensibility. Tell a group of businessmen that a country is like a corporation writ large, and you give them the comfort of feeling that they already understand the basics. Try to tell them about economic concepts like comparative advantage, and you are asking them to learn something new. It should not be surprising if many prefer a doctrine that offers the gain of apparent sophistication without the pain of hard thinking. The rhetoric of competitiveness has become so widespread, however, for three deeper reasons.

First, competitive images are exciting, and thrills sell tickets. The subtitle of Lester Thurow's huge best-seller, *Head to Head,* is "The Coming Economic Battle among Japan, Europe, and America"; the jacket proclaims that "the decisive war of the century has begun . . . and America may already have decided to lose." Suppose that the subtitle had described the real situation: "The coming struggle in which each big economy will succeed or fail based on its own efforts, pretty much independently of how well the others do." Would Thurow have sold a tenth as many books?

Second, the idea that U.S. economic difficulties hinge crucially on our failures in international competition somewhat paradoxically makes those difficulties seem easier to solve. The productivity of the average American worker is determined by a complex array of factors, most of them unreachable by any likely government policy. So if you accept the reality that our "competitive" problem is really a domestic productivity problem pure and simple, you are unlikely to be optimistic about any dramatic turnaround. But if you can convince yourself that the problem is really one of failures in international competition—that imports are pushing workers out of high-wage jobs, or subsidized foreign competition is driving the United States out of the high value-added sectors—then the answers to economic malaise may seem to you to involve simple things like subsidizing high technology and being tough on Japan.

Finally, many of the world's leaders have found the competitive metaphor extremely useful as a political device. The rhetoric of competitiveness turns out to provide a good way either to justify hard choices or to avoid them. . . . Many people who know that "competitiveness" is a largely meaningless concept have been willing to indulge competitive rhetoric precisely because they believe they can harness it in the service of good policies. An overblown fear of the Soviet Union was used in the 1950s to justify the building of the interstate highway system and the expansion of math and science education. Cannot the unjustified fears about foreign competition similarly be turned to good, used to justify serious efforts to reduce the budget deficit, rebuild infrastructure, and so on?

A few years ago this was a reasonable hope. At this point, however, the obsession with competitiveness has reached the point where it has already begun dangerously to distort economic policies.

THE DANGERS OF OBSESSION

Thinking and speaking in terms of competitiveness poses three real dangers. First, it could result in the wasteful spending of government money supposedly to enhance U.S. competitiveness. Second, it could lead to protectionism and trade wars. Finally, and most important, it could result in bad public policy on a spectrum of important issues.

During the 1950s, fear of the Soviet Union induced the U.S. government to spend money on useful things like highways and science education. It also, however, led to considerable spending on more doubtful items like bomb shelters. The most obvious if least worrisome danger of the . . . obsession with competitiveness is that it might lead to a similar misallocation of resources. To take an example, recent guidelines for government research funding have stressed the importance of supporting research that can improve U.S. international competitiveness. This exerts at least some bias toward inventions that can help manufacturing firms, which generally compete on international markets, rather than service producers, which generally do not. Yet most of our employment and value-added is now in services, and lagging productivity in services rather than manufactures has been the single most important factor in the stagnation of U.S. living standards.

A much more serious risk is that the obsession with competitiveness will lead to trade conflict, perhaps even to a world trade war. Most of those who have preached the doctrine of competitiveness have not been old-fashioned protectionists. They want their countries to win the global trade game, not drop out. But what if, despite its best efforts, a country does not seem to be winning, or lacks confidence that it can? Then the competitive diagnosis inevitably suggests that to close the borders is better than to risk having foreigners take away high-wage jobs and high-value sectors. At the very least, the focus on the supposedly competitive nature of international economic relations greases the rails for those who want confrontational if not frankly protectionist policies.

We can already see this process at work, in both the United States and Europe. In the United States, it was remarkable how quickly the sophisticated interventionist arguments advanced by Laura Tyson in her published work gave way to the simple-minded claim by U.S. Trade Representative Mickey Kantor that Japan's bilateral trade surplus was costing the United States millions of jobs. And the trade rhetoric of President Clinton, who stresses the supposed creation of high-wage jobs rather than the gains from specialization, left his administration in a weak position when it tried to argue with the claims of NAFTA foes that competition from cheap Mexican labor will destroy the U.S. manufacturing base.

Perhaps the most serious risk from the obsession with competitiveness, however, is its subtle indirect effect on the quality of economic discussion and policymaking. If top government officials are strongly committed to a particular economic doctrine, their commitment inevitably sets the tone for policymaking on all issues, even those which may seem to have nothing to do with that doctrine. And if an economic doctrine is flatly, completely, and demonstrably wrong, the insistence that discussion adhere to that doctrine inevitably blurs the focus and diminishes the quality of policy discussion across a broad range of issues, including some that are very far from trade policy per se. . . .

To make a harsh but not entirely unjustified analogy, a government wedded to the ideology of competitiveness is as unlikely to make good economic policy as a government committed to creationism is to make good science policy, even in areas that have no direct relationship to the theory of evolution.

ADVISERS WITH NO CLOTHES

If the obsession with competitiveness is as misguided and damaging as this [chapter] claims, why aren't more voices saying so? The answer is, a mixture of hope and fear.

On the side of hope, many sensible people have imagined that they can appropriate the rhetoric of competitiveness on behalf of desirable economic policies. Suppose that you believe that the United States needs to raise its savings rate and improve its educational system in order to raise its productivity. Even if you know that the benefits of higher productivity have nothing to do with international competition, why not describe this as a policy to enhance competitiveness if you think that it can widen your audience? It's tempting to pander to popular prejudices on behalf of a good cause . . .

As for fear, it takes either a very courageous or very reckless economist to say publicly that a doctrine that many, perhaps most, of the world's opinion leaders have embraced is flatly wrong. The insult is all the greater when many of those men and women think that by using the rhetoric of competitiveness they are demonstrating their sophistication about economics. . . .

Unfortunately, those economists who have hoped to appropriate the rhetoric of competitiveness for good economic policies have instead had their own credibility appropriated on behalf of bad ideas. And somebody has to point out when the emperor's intellectual wardrobe isn't all he thinks it is.

So let's start telling the truth: competitiveness is a meaningless word when applied to national economies. And the obsession with competitiveness is both wrong and dangerous.

30. EUROPE'S MONETARY UNION AND THE UNITED STATES

C. Randall Henning

*P*rofound skepticism pervades American attitudes toward the European Union's plan to create a monetary union. Thus, the United States has not treated European monetary integration as a serious policy issue. Despite the fact that the prospects for economic and monetary union (EMU) are uncertain, the likelihood that a common currency will be created is much higher than the conventional wisdom suggests. . . . There is a reasonably good chance that at least a "hard core" of European Union (EU) members will achieve sufficient convergence of their economies. The completion of monetary union, in turn, would have far-reaching consequences for the United States and international economic cooperation. Creating the common currency would strengthen Europe's bargaining position vis-à-vis the United States and other countries and would profoundly affect transatlantic relations.

The contrast between the uncertainty over the fulfillment of the formal obligations that the member states have accepted under the EMU plan, which skeptics cite, and the profundity of those obligations, which optimists cite, is stark. . . . The member states have maintained their formal commitment, undertaken in the Treaty on European Union signed at Maastricht in December 1991, to create a monetary union no later than 1999. Shortly after the treaty entered into force in November 1993, the European Monetary Institute (EMI) was created to prepare the groundwork for permanently fixing exchange rates and circulating a common currency. The EMI is the precursor to the European Central Bank (ECB) and is seated, as the ECB will be, in Frankfurt. Furthermore, the EU's Council of Ministers has established formal multilateral surveillance of member states' economic policies. At the European Council meeting in Madrid in December 1995, the heads of government reaffirmed their determination to create the monetary union and agreed on a timetable for decisions leading to it and on a three-and-a-half year transition to the new European currency, which they christened the "euro."

American policymakers have previously underestimated the impetus toward monetary integration in Europe. During the Bush administration, Treasury Secretary Nicholas Brady largely ignored the European negotiations leading to the Maastricht treaty, only to object later to what he perceived to be its constraints on European growth and employment. With other pressing matters on its agenda, the Clinton administration was similarly disengaged during its first three years. During these early phases of European monetary integration, the United States could afford to be passive. However, during the approach to monetary union, the United States must become more proactive.

European integration is very much in the interest of the United States, provided the EU maintains open markets and continues to cooperate with its foreign partners. Monetary union would create benefits for the rest of the world as well as for Europe. The EU's efforts toward monetary integration thus deserve American political support. Nevertheless, EMU would also pose important challenges to the United States that can be anticipated and for which preparations should be made.

EMU IS POSSIBLE

Three reasons are often given for the alleged implausibility of monetary union: the economies of the member states are not sufficiently harmonized and will not meet the convergence criteria of the Maastricht treaty; Germany will not be persuaded to surrender the stable Deutsche mark (D-mark) for a common currency; and countries that would be excluded from early membership by a multi-speed approach will oppose this strategy, thereby blocking monetary union.

Economic Convergence

The Maastricht treaty sets four economic criteria for membership in the monetary union. A country's rate of inflation must be no more than 1.5 percent above "that of, at most, the three best performing Member States," usually interpreted as the average of the three lowest-inflation countries. Long-term interest rates must be held at no more than 2 percent above the average of the long-term interest rates of the three countries with the lowest inflation. Member states must not be found by the Council of Ministers to be running an "excessive" budget deficit, which could be triggered by deficits above 3 percent of gross domestic product (GDP) and ratios of debt-to-GDP above 60 percent. Finally, a government must keep its currency within the "normal" bands of the EMS and not devalue it during the two years prior to entry.

The fact that few countries meet all of these criteria . . . obviously is grounds for skepticism. . . . However, the possibility that a substantial subgroup of countries will . . . qualify for monetary union in 1999 is not at all far-fetched. The chances that monetary union will become a reality at the end of the decade or within a few years thereafter are thus quite good.

There are two main reasons why most of the member states stand at least a fair chance of meeting the convergence requirements in time to qualify for monetary union in 1999. First, the convergence criteria will become easier to meet in most countries as the European economic recovery progresses. Increased growth and reduced unemployment will raise tax revenues and reduce social expenditures (e.g., unemployment compensation), bringing the deficit criterion within reach.

Second, there is wiggle room within the convergence criteria that permits countries that do not quite satisfy them to qualify for monetary union nonetheless. A violation of the fiscal norm that is extraordinary and demonstrably temporary is excusable. For example, a debt-to-GDP ratio that exceeds 60 percent can be excused if the annual deficit is small and the government has demonstrated consistent progress in reducing the ratio. The magic numbers of 3 percent and 60 percent are reference values used to guide the work of the Commission and are not strictly defined criteria in themselves.

If the formation of monetary union were delayed until all EU members qualified, it might never happen. However, it is not necessary for *all* members of the EU to meet these convergence tests at the same time. The treaty provides for the members that meet these tests to proceed before the others, such as Greece, are ready to join. Members not meeting the criteria will take a "derogation," and their status will be reviewed periodically thereafter. If they meet the criteria later, then they can join the monetary union. All of the countries except Britain and Denmark that meet the criteria are, under the terms of the treaty, formally bound to join the monetary union. The interesting question is whether a hard core of countries will qualify in 1998 when the European Council's decision on which member states qualify for monetary union is made. [In May 1998, eleven countries were formally nominated to join the European Monetary Union: Austria, Belgium, Finland, France, Germany, Ireland, Italy, Luxembourg, The Netherlands, Portugal, and Spain.—Eds.]

Recent reports by the European Commission and the EMI suggest that the answer could well be "yes." The Commission and the EMI observe that, with price increases running at about 2 percent or less in most countries, 11 of the 15 member states satisfy the inflation criterion. Long-term interest rates are highly convergent among most countries: Ten member states satisfy the interest-rate criterion. The difficulty, of course, will be with respect to fiscal policy, where most member states fail to meet the deficit and/or debt criteria. Several states that exceed the 3 percent deficit-to-GDP target, however, are within striking distance of that goal. Several countries that exceed the 60 percent debt-to-GDP target are likely to be able to show substantial and consistent progress toward that objective. . . .

The exchange-rate criterion calls for prospective members of the monetary union to maintain their currencies within the "normal" margins for a two-year period. Since July 1993, however, the margins have been wide—15 percent bands rather than the narrow 2.25 percent bands that prevailed until then. If "normal" is interpreted to mean "wide," then this condition is now easily met. For example, with wide bands, it would be easy for Britain and

Italy to rejoin the EMS. . . . It would be possible for the EU to proceed directly to monetary union without first reestablishing the narrow margins.

German Reticence

Germany stands to gain greatly from a strengthening of the EU. A strong EU gives Germany political "cover" for leadership in areas of foreign policy where the government prefers to keep a low profile for historical reasons—all the more important after German unification has revived fears of German power. A strong EU helps Germany to stabilize the countries of Central and Eastern Europe economically and politically. In addition to lowering economic transaction costs, therefore, monetary union would help Germany to both deepen and widen the EU.

Nonetheless, public-opinion polls consistently show that Germans are opposed to giving up the D-mark—a sentiment captured in blaring newspaper headlines days before the Maastricht summit. This opposition is often cited as grounds for believing that Germany will not enter the monetary union even if it satisfies the economic criteria.

However, the German people are primarily concerned about entering into a monetary union with states whose fiscal policies they regard as spendthrift and whose electorate has not developed a monetary culture that supports price stability and central bank independence. In a multispeed monetary union, Germany would join only with those states that had disciplined their budget deficits and established a track record of stability. The German Constitutional Court has reinforced the importance of the convergence criteria when evaluating other countries for membership. Popular German attitudes toward entering a monetary union with a hard core of low-inflation countries like Austria and the Netherlands, but not with countries like Italy, would be much more favorable. . . .

The psychological problem of "giving up the D-mark". . . could be addressed in a couple of ways. First, as has now been agreed, the changeover from national currencies to the single European currency in the third stage will be gradual, lasting three-and-a-half years. During this period, Germans could continue to use D-marks, which by virtue of the monetary union are irrevocably locked to the currencies of the other states participating in the union. Second, when the single European currency is issued, national central banks could issue notes and coins that are customized for each union member. Rather than being uniform in appearance throughout the union, the new currency could be issued with different national symbols and languages in each country. This has been done within other monetary areas, including the United Kingdom and the *Communauté Financière Africaine* franc zone. . . .

To bring Germany into the EMU, Chancellor Helmut Kohl must mount a full-fledged campaign to win over public opinion. The chancellor, though, has a broad arsenal of arguments on which to draw in such an effort. Consistently throughout the negotiations leading to the Maastricht treaty, Germany's partners conceded to German demands on the architecture of monetary union.

German demands were satisfied on the stability orientation of monetary policy, exchange-rate policy, central-bank independence, and the location of the ECB in Frankfurt, the seat of the Bundesbank. When concerns were raised in autumn 1995 about fiscal discipline after the formation of the monetary union, European finance ministers acceded in principle to a fiscal "stability pact" that would tighten the targets and sanctions embodied in the Maastricht treaty. When German finance minister Theo Waigel wanted to rename the single currency the "euro," the European partners acceded to his new choice. Never has a deal been struck within the Union that is so lopsidedly in Germany's favor!

Multispeed Approach

Achieving monetary union in the foreseeable future depends on a multispeed approach—a hard core of low-inflation countries forming the union first, with the others following later. Owing to the opposition within Germany to joining a monetary union with high-inflation, high-deficit countries, a "one-speed" union is not feasible. Fortunately, for the proponents of monetary union, the Maastricht treaty already embodies the multispeed approach through derogations.

Suppose, for example, that the Council of Ministers determines that Italy does not meet the convergence criteria when the Council makes the decision to fix exchange rates irrevocably. In that case, Italy would be given a derogation from its treaty commitment to meet the criteria and would be excluded in the first instance from the monetary union. The Council of Ministers would review Italy's situation at least every two years to determine whether it might be admitted.

There is no technical or legal limit to the number of countries that might receive a derogation. There is no requirement that a majority of countries fulfill the convergence criteria in order for stage three to be established in 1999. Under the terms of the treaty, the countries that are unable to meet the requirements for entry cannot block those that do from forming the monetary union.

The initial exclusion of high-inflation, high-deficit countries, Italy in particular, would nonetheless be a political decision of the highest order for the EU. Although they could not block the formation of the monetary union, excluded countries could conceivably retaliate by blocking European decision making on other issues, such as enlargement. Although the southern-tier countries might threaten such action in order to extract concessions from the northern tier, ultimately it would not be in their interest to block monetary union in this way. A monetary union from which they were temporarily excluded could still form a pivotal group to which they could tie their currencies in whatever EU-wide arrangement replaces the present-day EMS. The existence of the monetary union would provide a powerful incentive to rectify their economic problems in order to be able to join eventually. The multispeed approach would initiate a process by which countries with derogations could later participate; insistence on a one-speed union would thwart the process entirely.

Under a multispeed approach, a number of the economic objections to

EMU are greatly ameliorated. One objection is that the countries of the European Union are subject to asymmetrical shocks that require exchange-rate adjustments. Among the countries of the hard core, though, external shocks have a much more symmetrical effect than among Britain, Germany, Greece, and Portugal, for example. Another objection is that the absence of fiscal transfers between prosperous and depressed regions militates against monetary union. Yet, given the homogeneity of the low-inflation core countries relative to Europe as a whole, large fiscal transfers are less likely to be needed inside the "fast-speed" union.

Meanwhile, the arguments in favor of monetary union endure. Monetary union would complete the internal market by eliminating segmentation of national markets arising from the possibility of exchange-rate change. The members of the union would reap the gains of eliminating the costs of foreign currency transactions. The monetary union would consolidate stability-oriented monetary policies in Europe, many of the sacrifices for which have already been made in a number of countries. Finally, monetary union could lay the basis for further deepening the EU as well as its political integration and expansion toward the East.

STRUCTURAL SHIFT

Economic and monetary union, if it is achieved, will produce a number of consequences for the international community. A European monetary union would be less vulnerable to exchange-rate changes vis-à-vis the U.S. dollar than are the individual European countries currently. There are several reasons for this. First, trade among the EU members continues to grow more rapidly than trade between the EU and the rest of the world. The single-market program has propelled the growth of intra-European trade: A monetary union would tend to increase it further. Thus, the monetary union will become less sensitive to fluctuations of, first, the irrevocably fixed currencies and, then, the euro against the dollar.

Second, the formation of a monetary union would eliminate the tendency of fluctuations in the dollar to drive wedges between the European currencies. Because the D-mark has often played the role of a "counter-pole" to the dollar, a depreciation of the dollar has often placed upward pressure on the D-mark against the other European currencies. This was certainly true, for example, when the dollar fell to record lows against the D-mark shortly before the crisis of September 1992, which drove the pound and lira from the narrow bands. In a monetary union that irrevocably fixes exchange rates, however, the introduction of a common monetary policy would prevent fluctuations of the dollar from exerting different effects on the currencies of the union. And after the introduction of the euro in 2002, of course, no such "wedge effect" would be possible.

Third, with monetary union, the euro will become increasingly important as a vehicle currency for international transactions and as the denominator of international financial instruments. The new European currency will not be introduced immediately upon formation of the monetary union: Under the current conversion plan this step will be delayed for three years. When it is introduced, there will probably be no large, precipitous displacement of the dollar. Nonetheless, much of the increased role of the new European currency can be expected to come at the dollar's expense, and this would reinforce the gradual historical decline in the role of the dollar exhibited over the last several decades.

The combination of these three structural features—the decline of external trade relative to GDP, the elimination of the "wedge effect," and the increased role of the euro—will reduce the vulnerability of EMU members to fluctuations in their currencies with respect to the dollar and other outside currencies.

These structural changes would have two important consequences. First, the monetary union would help to insulate the European economy from the negative effects of exchange-rate volatility and misalignment vis-à-vis non-European currencies. Second, monetary union would enhance the power and influence of Europe in global monetary affairs. Even the smaller hard-core countries would collect within one monetary bloc economic output that is much greater than that of Germany and begins to approach that of the United States. The economies of Austria, the Benelux countries, Denmark, France, Germany, and Ireland are collectively about 65 percent the size of the U.S. economy. Those of the 15 members of the EU are about 20 percent larger than the American economy.

During most of the postwar period, the United States, because of its lessened dependence on trade, has not been as vulnerable to fluctuations in exchange rates as the European countries. When clashing with European governments over macroeconomic policies or the balance of payments, American officials often took advantage of this asymmetry. In several instances, the threat of a precipitous exchange-rate movement pressed European governments to reflate or dampen their economies in accordance with American preferences.

Monetary union in Europe, however, would eliminate this asymmetry. It would help to insulate the economy of the monetary union from fluctuations in the U.S. dollar, to reduce the costs of transatlantic monetary conflict for Europe, and to thereby shield European policymakers from American pressure. As a result, the external monetary policy of the union would very likely favor exchange-rate flexibility at the expense of currency stabilization. The United States would confront a larger, more cohesive, and more self-confident and powerful partner in the monetary union than it has faced in the past.

EXTERNAL POLICYMAKING

The machinery for making external policy in the monetary union will reinforce Europe's evolving preference—stemming from structural shift—for flexible exchange rates vis-à-vis nonunion currencies. The role of the ECB in the making of post–monetary union exchange-rate policy and the voting arrangements within the Council of Ministers are especially important.

The degree of the ECB's legal independence will be extraordinary by international standards. Each one of the national central banks that will be part of the new central banking system will remain independent. The officers of the ECB will be specifically forbidden from soliciting or accepting instructions from governments regarding monetary policy. Price stability within the monetary union will be the legally enshrined priority for the ECB when carrying out its responsibilities. In addition, the ECB's status will be constitutionally enshrined in the European treaties, which can be amended only by unanimous agreement.

In the first few years of the monetary union, the ECB will almost certainly demonstrate its independence in order to establish its credibility in the marketplace. To put to rest any fears that it would compromise internal monetary stability for exchange-rate objectives, the ECB will very likely shun stabilization of the euro vis-à-vis the dollar.

The posture of the ECB will be particularly important in decision making within the monetary union because it is granted the right (and obligation) to participate in exchange-rate policymaking by Article 109 of the Maastricht treaty. The ECB has the right to be consulted on all exchange-rate decisions made by the Council of Ministers. In cases of formal exchange-rate regimes, that consultation should "endeavor to reach a consensus consistent with the objective of price stability."

Subject to these provisos, representatives of the Council of Ministers will hold the authority to establish formal and informal exchange-rate agreements with foreign governments. In formulating "general orientations" for exchange-rate policy, the Council will be able to act on a qualified majority vote. Formal agreements that peg the euro to the dollar or yen, however, will require a unanimous vote within the Council after consulting not only with the ECB but with the European Commission and Parliament as well. This will be an onerous requirement, particularly after the enlargement of the EU.

Superficially, the consolidation of several central banks under one monetary authority might seem to simplify the process of coordinating monetary policy and foreign-exchange intervention among the United States, Europe, and Japan. However, a much larger number of European officials and institutions would be involved in this process *after* European monetary unification than currently. In addition to the member governments sitting on the Council, the Commission and the ECB would participate, as would the European Parliament, in the case of formal arrangements. Under these institutional arrangements, it would be quite unlikely that American or Japanese officials could discreetly negotiate exchange-rate accords such as those struck at the Plaza Hotel or the Louvre in the mid–1980s. Currency agreements are very sensitive; rumors of impending accords spark movements of exchange markets and should be conducted behind closed doors.

RAMIFICATIONS FOR AMERICAN POLICY

The United States and the rest of the world have a strong interest in the creation of a European Union that can form a common position with reasonable efficiency and bargain externally with some degree of flexibility. The EU has an interest in developing greater coherence as an external actor to avoid missing opportunities for international cooperation. The frustration of American negotiators in bargaining with European officials over trade policy during the Uruguay Round shows the importance to the United States of the EU creating streamlined internal decision-making procedures that are conducive to international cooperation. The institutional arrangements described in the previous section, however, are a recipe for a policy of exchange-rate flexibility with respect to currencies outside the European region. The new monetary union, without institutional change, could prove to be a difficult partner for the United States in economic cooperation.

There are two ways in which the United States can now encourage greater international cooperation in support of European monetary union than might otherwise be forthcoming. First, American officials should waste no time in discreetly expressing concern that the machinery of European decision making could impede international monetary cooperation and in asking European officials to explain how Article 109 will be applied in practice. If dissatisfied, the United States could suggest that Article 109 be revised to remove the probable bias against exchange-rate stabilization. . . . Although the Europeans would resist American "meddling," the interests of the rest of the world clearly are affected. Under these circumstances, as in the negotiations prior to Maastricht over the Western European Union and its relationship to NATO, American officials would be justified in representing U.S. interests.

The second constructive response would be to reinvigorate macroeconomic cooperation within the Group of Seven (G-7) meetings of finance ministers and central bankers now—during the transitional and formative years of the prospective European monetary union. By nurturing multilateral cooperation, the United States and the other members of the G-7 could create a benign monetary environment into which EMU could be born. If the governments of the leading market-oriented countries make macroeconomic and exchange-rate decisions in isolation from one another over the next few years—deflecting the responsibility for macroeconomic policy adjustments—then the new European monetary authorities would justifiably take a dim view of G-7 cooperation. But if the benefits of cooperation are instead demonstrated to the people who will govern the ECB and other European institutions, then multilateral cooperation could be grandfathered into the monetary union.

A revived G-7 could address several policy issues that would arise during the transition to monetary union. The first would be the potential problem of excess dollar reserves held by the European central banks. The creation of the ECB and the elimination of foreign-exchange transactions among the member states would obviate the need for much of the international reserves now held in Europe. Estimates vary widely as to the size of the dollar holdings that could become superfluous, but they are sufficiently large that they will likely create exchange-market instability unless the G-7 develops a common strategy for managing the potential "dollar overhang." . . .

The G-7 should also anticipate shifts in investment portfolios and currency instability that are likely to result from the completion of monetary union. The completion of the single market in financial services and the growing demand for financial assets denominated in euros could well produce an unwanted appreciation of the new European currency as the prospects for completing the monetary union become more apparent. The G-7 should designate a set of exchange rates that its members view as appropriate, and it should communicate these rates to the markets. More ambitiously, a formalization of ad hoc cooperation among the members of the G-7 to stabilize the dollar, yen, and D-mark within broad ranges would improve the chances that the ECB and the Council of Ministers would perpetuate this cooperation after the beginning of the third stage, as the euro replaces the D-mark. . . .

Europe has a strong incentive to strengthen G-7 cooperation now, before deciding whether and when to move to the third stage. The September 1992 European currency crisis and the March 1995 devaluations of the Spanish peseta and the Portuguese escudo demonstrated that depreciation of the dollar still drives wedges between the European currencies. This "wedge effect" particularly afflicts the relationship between the D-mark and the high-inflation currencies, but it could also affect the stability of the currencies in the hard-core countries. Global exchange-rate stabilization, therefore, would facilitate the achievement of European monetary union.

When the Common Market was created in the 1950s and 1960s, the existence of the Organization for European Economic Cooperation (which later became the Organization for Economic Cooperation and Development) and the General Agreement on Tariffs and Trade helped to ensure that the Common Market would not succumb to pressures for protectionism and closure. G-7 cooperation could provide a similar context of multilateralism and cooperation for European monetary unification. The prospect of European monetary union, therefore, provides a compelling reason for the governments and central banks of the G-7 to reinvigorate international economic cooperation now, before the window of opportunity closes—perhaps for good.

INTERNATIONAL REPRESENTATION

The completion of monetary union would raise the question of European representation in the international financial institutions and the multilateral development banks. As European integration proceeds, the rationale for individual representation of EU member states weakens and that for consolidating their representation strengthens. The collective quota of the EU members, furthermore, would be substantially less than the sum of their individual quotas. Quotas in the International Monetary Fund (IMF), for example, are allocated on the basis of trade and financial flows, and intra-EU transactions would be excluded when calculating a consolidated quota. The sum of the individual quotas of the members of the hard core is today only slightly smaller than the quota for the United States, which is 18 percent. After consolidation, the quota for a hard-core monetary union would shrink by a large fraction. This recalculation would have important ramifications for the management of the Bretton Woods institutions, because, among other reasons, voting strength within them is proportionate to quotas.

Changes in the relationship of the European countries to the IMF over the past decades bolster the case for consolidating the European quota. Britain, France, and Italy each drew on the IMF during the 1960s and 1970s, and Portugal drew on IMF credit facilities in 1983 before joining the Community. But no member of the EU has borrowed from the IMF in almost 20 years. Instead, EU members have taken advantage of the facilities developed within the Union that provide balance-of payments support. Members of the EMS also have access to the short-term financing facilities available for foreign-exchange intervention. Despite the IMF's mandate to "exercise firm surveillance over the exchange-rate policies of its members," European governments have never subjected their management of the EMS to the purview of the IMF. Although the IMF staff participates in multilateral surveillance within the G-7, it is excluded from multilateral surveillance at the European level. Consequently, as European integration has progressed, the member states of the EU have become progressively less reliant on and less engaged with the IMF.

If monetary integration proceeds, then the United States and the world community should urge the Europeans to consolidate their position for the good of the Bretton Woods institutions, because these organizations have traditionally adjusted country representation and internal governance too slowly to changes in the world economy. As new countries have joined the IMF, fierce struggles have raged over the reapportionment of quotas. The quotas of the fast-growing countries of East Asia, among others, no longer adequately reflect their economic size and their importance to world trade and finance. Consolidation of the European quotas would make room for the enlargement of the quotas of others, contributing to better management of these institutions and international cooperation generally.

European monetary union is sufficiently likely, and its consequences are so profound, that American policymakers should plan now for this contingency and consult with their European counterparts. Economic and monetary union would bring substantial benefits for Europe as well as the rest of the world but would also raise important institutional, policy, and representational questions. Rather than ignoring these issues until the final stage of the integration process, governments on both sides of the Atlantic should confront them before they become serious problems.

Acknowledgments *(continued from the copyright page)*

Eugene Gholz, Daryl G. Press, and Harvey M. Sapolsky, "Come Home, America: The Strategy of Restraint in the Face of Temptation." Abridged from Eugene Gholz, Daryl G. Press, and Harvey M. Sapolsky, "Come Home America: The Strategy of Restraint in the Face of Temptation." *International Security*, 21:4 (Spring 1997), pp. 5–48. Copyright © 1997 by the President and Fellows of Harvard College and the Massachusetts Institute of Technology.

Josef Joffe, "America the Inescapable." Copyright © 1997 by The New York Times Company. Reprinted by permission.

Joseph S. Nye, Jr., "Conflicts after the Cold War: Realism, Idealism, and U.S. Interests." Abridged from Joseph S. Nye, Jr., "Conflicts after the Cold War." The *Washington Quarterly*, 19:1 (Winter 1996), pp. 5–24. Copyright © 1996 by the Center for Strategic and International Studies (CSIS) and the Massachusetts Institute of Technology.

G. John Ikenberry, "The Myth of Post–Cold War Chaos." Reprinted by permission of *Foreign Affairs*, 75 (May/June 1996). Copyright © 1996 by the Council of Foreign Relations, Inc.

Jeffery E. Garten, "Business and Foreign Policy: Time for a Strategic Alliance?" Reprinted by permission of *Foreign Affairs*, 76 (May/June 1997). Copyright © 1997 by the Council on Foreign Relations, Inc.

Richard Rosecrance, "The Rise of the Virtual State: Implications for U.S. Policy." Reprinted by permission of *Foreign Affairs*, 75 (July/August 1996). Copyright © 1996 by the Council on Foreign Relations, Inc.

Ole R. Holsti and James N. Rosenau, "Internationalism: Intact or in Trouble?" This essay was written specifically for this book.

Janet Welsh Brown, "Population, Consumption, and the Path to Sustainability: The U.S. Role." Reprinted with permission from *Current History* magazine, 95 (November 1996). Copyright © 1996, Current History, Inc.

Walter Russell Mead, "No Cold War Two: The United States and the Russian Federation." *World Policy Journal*, XI:2 (Summer 1994). Copyright © 1994, *World Policy Journal*. Reprinted with permission of the World Policy Institute.

Madeleine Albright, "Enlarging NATO: Why Bigger Is Better." The *Economist*, 342 (February 1997). Copyright © 1997, The Economist Newspaper Group, Inc. Reprinted with permission. Further reproduction prohibited.

Werner Weidenfeld, "America and Europe: Is the Break Inevitable?" Abridged from Werner Weidenfeld, "America and Europe: Is the Break Inevitable?" The *Washington Quarterly*, 20:3 (Summer 1997), pp. 37–52. Copyright © 1997 by the Center for Strategic and International Studies (CSIS) and the Massachusetts Institute of Technology.

Robert A. Manning, "Futureshock or Renewed Partnership? The U.S.-Japan Alliance Facing the Millennium." Abridged from Robert A. Manning, "Futureshock or Renewed Partnership? The U.S.-Japan Alliance Facing the Millennium." The *Washington Quarterly*, 18:4 (Autumn 1995), pp. 87–98. Copyright © 1995 by the Center for Strategic and International Studies (CSIS) and the Massachusetts Institute of Technology.

Robert S. Ross, "China: Why Our Hard-Liners Are Wrong." Reprinted with permission. Copyright © The *National Interest*, No. 49 (Fall 1997), Washington, D.C.

Richard N. Cooper, "The Gulf Bottleneck: Middle East Stability and World Oil Supply." Reprinted from the *Harvard International Review*, Summer 1997. Copyright © 1997 by the Harvard International Relations Council.

Peter Andreas, "U.S.-Mexico: Open Markets, Closed Border." Reprinted with permission from *Foreign Policy*, 103 (Summer 1996). Copyright © 1996 by the Carnegie Endowment for International Peace.

Howard J. Wiarda, "Back to Basics: Reassessing U.S. Policy in Latin America." From *Harvard International Review*, 19 (Fall 1997). Copyright © 1997, *Harvard International Review*. Reprinted by Permission.

Robert S. Chase, Emily B. Hill, and Paul Kennedy, "Pivotal States and U.S. Strategy." Reprinted by permission of *Foreign Affairs*, 75 (January/February 1996). Copyright © 1996 by the Council on Foreign Relations, Inc.

Robin Broad and John Cavanagh, "Don't Neglect the Impoverished South." Reprinted with permission from *Foreign Policy* (Winter 1995). Copyright © 1995–96 by the Carnegie Endowment for International Peace.

Hans Binnendijk, "Tin Cup Diplomacy." Reprinted with permission. Copyright © The *National Interest*, No. 49 (Fall 1997), Washington, D.C.

Russell E. Travers, "A New Millennium and a Strategic Breathing Space." Abridged from Russell E. Travers, "A New Millennium and a Strategic Breathing Space." The *Washington Quarterly*, 20:2 (Spring 1997), pp. 97–114. Copyright © 1997 by the Center for Strategic and International Studies (CSIS) and the Massachusetts Institute of Technology.

Steering Committee of the Project on Eliminating Weapons of Mass Destruction, Henry L. Stimson Center, General Andrew J. Goodpaster (retired), Chair, "U.S. Nuclear Posture: A Case for Change." Reprinted with permission from The Henry L. Stimson Center, Washington, D.C.

Richard K. Betts, "The New Threat of Mass Destruction." From *Foreign Affairs*, Vol. 77, No. 1, 1998. Copyright © 1998 by the Council on Foreign Relations, Inc. Reprinted by permission from *Foreign Affairs*.

Steven Metz, "Racing toward the Future: The Revolution in Military Affairs." Reprinted with permission from *Current History* magazine, 96 (April 1997). Copyright © 1997, Current History, Inc.

Peter Morici, "Export Our Way to Prosperity." Reprinted with permission from *Foreign Policy*, 101 (Winter 1995–96). Copyright © by the Carnegie Endowment for International Peace.

Clyde V. Prestowitz, Jr., and Saul Goldstein, "Trade Policy for a New Era." Forum for Applied Research and Public Policy (Winter 1994), pp. 19–24. Copyright © 1994, Forum for Applied Research and Public Policy. Reprinted by permission.

Paul Krugman, "Competitiveness: A Dangerous Obsession." Reprinted by permission of *Foreign Affairs*, 73 (March/April 1994). Copyright © 1994 by the Council on Foreign Relations, Inc.

C. Randall Henning, "Europe's Monetary Union and the United States." Reprinted with permission from *Foreign Policy*, 102 (Spring 1996). Copyright © 1996 by the Carnegie Endowment for International Peace.